ARCHBISHOP

Inside the
Power Structure
of the American
Catholic Church

Thomas J. Reese, S.J.

1817

Harper & Row, Publishers, San Francisco

New York, Cambridge, Philadelphia, St. Louis
London, Singapore, Sydney, Tokyo

FIRST EDITION

Library of Congress Cataloging-in-Publication Data

Reese, Thomas J.
    Archbishop : inside the power structure of the American Catholic Church.

    1. Catholic Church—United States—Bishops. 2. Catholic Church—United States—Government. I. Title.
BX1407.D54R44 1989   262'.12'0973   88-45671
ISBN 0-06-066836-9

89 90 91 92 93 RRD 10 9 8 7 6 5 4 3 2 1

Contents

Introduction

In our western civilization only one formal organization, the Roman Catholic Church, claims a substantial age.

————CHESTER I. BARNARD[1]

Empirical research by psychologists and sociologists on bishops and other
[church] administrators is apparently nonexistent.

————KENNEDY AND HECKLER

American Catholic bishops are front-page news. Their involvement in important national issues is chronicled because they
are influential and sometimes controversial participants in the
political process. Their opposition to abortion and their pastoral
letters on peace and on the U.S. economy have been widely
discussed and debated. A more recent focus of attention has
been the division within the American hierarchy over whether
to include information on condoms in AIDS education programs. Not only the media but also politicians have paid attention to what the bishops are saying. The Reagan White
House attacked an early draft of the peace pastoral. And Ger-
aldine Ferraro could not ignore Cardinal John O'Connor's questions about her stand on abortion.

Despite the media attention given to their positions on public
issues, the bishops actually spend very little of their time on
public policy or writing pastoral letters. Most of their time is
spent on internal church matters in their own dioceses, the
ecclesiastical territories for which they are responsible. But little
is known about what bishops do in their dioceses. What power
do they have? How do they make decisions? How do they
spend their time? When the diocesan work of a bishop does
come to the attention of the press, it tends to be about highly

controversial issues: the closing of a parish or school, a lawsuit dealing with a pedophilic priest, or some other crisis.

Even in his own diocese, the daily work of a bishop is practically unknown. Everyone agrees that bishops are important in the Catholic church, but few people, including Catholics, know much about their local bishop or his work. Most Catholics only meet a bishop once in their lives, when they receive the sacrament of confirmation. Normally the bishop confirms when he visits a parish every year or two. His visit is usually only long enough to talk to the pastor, celebrate the liturgy, and go to the reception for the newly confirmed and their relatives. The people come away with only the briefest impressions of the personality and views of the bishop and with very little understanding of his other work.

The public ignorance about what bishops do is matched by a similar ignorance in the scholarly community. Canon law describes the power and responsibilities of bishops but does not usually examine how that power is actually exercised. Numerous theological books and articles have been written about bishops, but they are primarily abstract, theoretical treatises on the role of bishops in the church. Often these studies say that the bishop is or should be a spiritual leader and pastoral teacher without any concrete explanation of how these roles are carried out.

Some histories and biographies tell about bishops and what they did in the church of the past, but very little describes the bishops of today and what they do in the post-Vatican II church. There are practically no studies of the bishops from a social science perspective, which is surprising since the Catholic church is the oldest surviving complex organization in the world. What was said in the multivolume *The Catholic Priest in the United States* in 1972 is still true: "Empirical research by psychologists and sociologists on bishops and other [church] administrators is apparently nonexistent."[2] This lack of interest on the part of social scientists is shocking considering the long existence of the church and the fact that it has been undergoing major changes in the last thirty years.

Purpose of this Book

This is not a theological or spiritual book. I approached this study as a journalist who is a political scientist and Jesuit priest.[3] It is not an attempt to describe the Spirit working in the church; rather it attempts to describe the people, the processes, and structures through which the Spirit must work. Social scientists cannot measure or evaluate the spiritual nature of the church; they can only describe and analyze its external manifestations in people and organizations.

This book describes what the American archbishops do for a living. It seeks to answer questions such as the following: Who are these men? How do they become archbishops? What do they do besides confirm? How do they spend their time? How do they make decisions? How do they organize and govern their dioceses? What control do they exercise over what is happening in their dioceses?

This study uses social science methodology and theory to gain a greater understanding of church organization and decision making. It examines the decision-making process archbishops use for allocating resources and assigning personnel. It studies how they provide leadership within their archdioceses, how they spend their time, how they get information, how they make decisions, and how they communicate with their priests and people. The role of their chanceries and diocesan consultative bodies in helping them to fulfill their leadership and decision-making roles is also examined.

A major thesis of this book is that archdiocesan governance, like the governance of any organization, is affected by the personality and preferences of the leaders, the environment in which they operate, and the "technologies" employed.[4] "Technologies" are the means, skills, techniques, and knowledge used by an organization to attain its goals. In the church, these technologies (preaching, counseling, education, and so forth) would be organized into ministries. The structures and strategies of an organization, including the church, are determined by its leadership, but they are also rooted in an organization's technology and task environment. An organization's leaders, technology, and task environment do not operate in total independence of one another; each can influence the others.

Church leaders, archbishops, and the people they appoint, can make a difference. Intellectual, interpersonal, organizational, and pastoral talents vary among bishops. This is most frequently noted when comparing a bishop with his predecessor. Cardinal Joseph Bernardin of Chicago relates better with his priests than did his predecessor Cardinal Cody. Cardinal John O'Connor of New York and Cardinal Bernard Law of Boston delegate more to their chancery officials than did cardinals Cooke and Medeiros. Cardinals Bernardin, Law, and O'Connor play larger roles nationally than did their predecessors.

But the same men's influence would be different in a different environment. An archbishop's power is limited (or enhanced) by the canonical, political, financial, demographic, and historical environment in which he must operate. Without resources (money and personnel), without the support of his priests and people, an archbishop is very limited, especially if the environment is hostile or indifferent. Competitors in the environment, such as evangelicals among the Hispanics, can cause concern. Law and tradition encourage stability, but demands and feedback from the environment stimulate adaptations of goals and procedures. These changes are normally incremental. Different archdioceses provide different environments, and even a single archdiocese has a variety of environmental factors that affect governance.

Finally, what an archbishop does is dependent not only on his personality and environment but on the technologies available to accomplish his goals. For some of his goals (construction, financial administration, fund raising, education), he can use technologies that are similar to those used by secular organizations. For his more spiritual goals, ecclesial technologies or ministries (preaching, sacraments, and so forth) that are unique to the church must be employed.

Some technologies or ministries employed by the church are more susceptible to bureaucratic management than others. As a result, various parts of the archdiocese will be governed in different ways. Financial administration, for example, can be highly routinized, even computerized, but pastoral counseling cannot. The more intensive the technology (the more it requires professional skills, imagination, and response to feedback), the less its use can be controlled by regulations and a central office. Nor can ecclesial technologies be easily evaluated. In the face of human freedom and the mystery of grace, ecclesial technologies for "saving souls" or promoting vocations cannot work perfectly. In fact, measuring efficiency and effectiveness of technologies with spiritual goals is by definition impossible, especially where the desire is for quality as well as quantity. This uncertainty and complexity encourages decision makers to limit the number of variables examined (bounded rationality), to seek a satisfactory rather than optimal solution to a problem (satisficing) and to respond with incremental rather than radical changes.

The research for this book was done primarily through interviewing archbishops and their cabinet-level staffs (auxiliary bishops, vicars general, chancellors, secretaries to archbishops, moderators of the curia, and the directors of finances, personnel, pastoral service, social service, and education). Over four hundred people were interviewed.[5] All thirty-one archbishops (including all of the cardinals) agreed to participate in the study and every archdiocese was visited between June 1985 and January 1987. The interviews, almost all of which were taped, provide the factual information for the study and also the opinions and examples that are quoted in the book. In some archdioceses I was also allowed to sit in on meetings of the archbishop's presbyteral and pastoral councils. I was also allowed to attend meetings of some archbishops with their staffs, auxiliary bishops, and cabinets.

Because of the size and complexity of the Roman Catholic church it was necessary to limit the scope of this study. Eastern-rite churches in union with Rome were not examined because their unique structures and traditions would require a separate book. These churches serve only one percent of U.S. Catholics. Nor did I examine the military archdiocese, a nonterritorial archdiocese that ministers to Catholics in the U.S. armed forces.

The study is limited to the thirty-one Latin-rite archbishops and archdioceses. The church in the United States is divided into 175 geographical units called dioceses or archdioceses depending on whether they are headed by a diocesan bishop or an archbishop. These separate and independent sees (a generic term for dioceses and archdioceses) cover every corner of the United States and are grouped into thirty-one provinces each headed by an archbishop who is called the metropolitan of the province. Some of these archbishops and diocesan bishops are assisted by auxiliary bishops.

All together the archbishops, diocesan bishops, and auxiliary bishops add up to almost three hundred Latin-rite bishops working in the United States, plus another eighty or so retired bishops. Interviewing all of them is impractical. Constructing a representative sample of these sees and their bishops (and getting them to agree to participate) is problematic.

As a result, I concentrated on the thirty-one Latin-rite archdioceses: Anchorage, Atlanta, Baltimore, Boston, Chicago, Cincinnati, Denver, Detroit, Dubuque, Hartford, Indianapolis, Kansas City (KS), Louisville, Los Angeles, Miami, Milwaukee, Mobile, Newark, New Orleans, New York, Oklahoma City, Omaha, Philadelphia, Portland (OR), St. Louis, St. Paul, San Francisco, Santa Fe, San Antonio, Seattle, and Washington (DC). These sees are called archdioceses, rather than dioceses, because each is headed by an archbishop rather than a bishop.

As will be explained later, an archbishop's duties and authority are the same as a bishop's except that as metropolitan he has limited supervisory jurisdiction and influence over the bishops in his province who are known as suffragans. Studying archdioceses enabled me to examine a limited number that includes the most important sees in the United States. Their archbishops are also the most well-known Catholic prelates, and include all of the cardinals residing in the United States. As cardinals they elect the pope.

While not a perfectly representative sample, archdioceses are in every part of the country, which guarantees that the study is geographically representative. Archdioceses differ from dioceses primarily in size. Although some archdioceses are very small, they tend to be twice the size of the average diocese. The average U.S. see has 186 diocesan priests and 286,000 Catholics, while the average archdiocese has 395 priests and 695,000 Catholics. Archdioceses also tend to be more Catholic, with 27 percent of their area Catholic as opposed to 22 percent for the nation as a whole.[6] Most dioceses are like the small and medium-sized archdioceses in this study.

Archbishops do the same things as diocesan bishops, plus a few extra things. They tend to be more active than other bishops in the national and international church. Archbishops also tend to be older, better educated, and more experienced at the time of their appointments.[7]

Organization

Archdiocesan governance, like any form of governance, is the result of the interaction of numerous factors. It is primarily affected by the personality and style of the archbishop and the makeup and needs of his archdiocese, which he governs within the boundaries set by canon law. This book therefore begins with a chapter on how bishops are appointed, since who is appointed has a tremendous impact on how an archdiocese is governed. Once he is appointed, the new archbishop must govern his particular archdiocese with the power and constraints of canon law. Chapter 2 describes the canon law governing bishops. It also shows how archdioceses vary greatly in terms of demography, geography, institutions, and history. These social, economic, ethnic, geographic, and cultural factors affect how an archdiocese is governed. Chapter 3 describes the personalities and styles of archbishops and explains what structures archbishops use in governing.

The next three chapters then examine how archbishops deal with important parts of their archdioceses. Chapter 4 describes the relationship between the archbishop and his parishes. For most Catholics, their parish is the church. To reach the people, the archbishop must work through the parish structure. Chapter 5 describes his role in the finances of the archdiocese: how he raises money, how he decides to spend it, and how he controls spending by parishes and other archdiocesan agencies. Chapter 6 studies his relationship to his priests, especially through his appointment of pastors. Without the support of his priests, he can do little. Chapter 7 describes archdiocesan governance of Catholic schools and Catholic social services, two of the biggest ministries of the church.

Chapter 8 examines the role of the archbishop outside his diocese, especially his relations with the bishops of his province, the National Conference of Catholic Bishops (NCCB), and the Vatican. Archbishops can be affected by what happens outside their archdioceses, and they can also have an impact on the national and international church. The Conclusion describes the episcopal decision-making process and summarizes some of the issues archbishops must give attention to.

In all of these chapters, the emphasis is on the role of the archbishop and his top staff: What problems come to them? What decisions do they make? What strategies do they follow? Through extensive quotations from the interviews, they are allowed to tell their own stories.

Finally, it must be remembered that this is not a static system. Archdioceses in the United States are constantly undergoing change. Archbishops retire or die and are replaced by new men. Archbishop Donnellan died after being interviewed. Cardinals Manning and Krol and archbishops Gerety and Power left office after they were interviewed (I also interviewed the new archbishops of Atlanta, Portland, Los Angeles, and Newark). In other archdioceses, cabinet-level staff changed shortly before or after my visit. Even archdioceses with stable leadership were often undergoing reorganization or changes in procedures and policies. As a result, descriptions and examples from individual archdioceses should be considered only snapshots of moving objects.

On the other hand, many of the problems and issues these archbishops face are not going to go away soon. Some archdioceses, like Los Angeles, are just now establishing structures and programs that have been in place for some time in other archdioceses. And as old problems are solved, new ones will arise, and it is likely they will be approached in the ways described here. The church is always changing and always the same.

Since this is the first book of its kind, there will be errors and omissions. It is hoped that more researchers will enter this vast and open field of research to correct and build on what is here.

I wish to thank the American archbishops who allowed me to visit their archdioceses to conduct my interviews: Joseph Bernardin (Chicago), William D. Borders (Baltimore), Thomas A. Donnellan and Eugene Marino (Atlanta), Patrick F. Flores (San Antonio), Peter L. Gerety and Theodore E. McCarrick (Newark), Philip M. Hannan (New Orleans), James A. Hickey (Washington, DC), Raymond G. Hunthausen (Seattle), Francis T. Hurley (Anchorage), Thomas Kelly (Louisville), John Krol (Philadelphia), Daniel Kucera (Dubuque), Bernard F. Law (Boston), Oscar Lipscomb (Mobile), Roger Mahony and Timothy Manning (Los Angeles), John L. May (St. Louis), Edward A. McCarthy (Miami), John J. O'Connor (New York), Edward T. O'Meara (Indianapolis), Daniel E. Pilarczyk (Cincinnati), Cornelius M. Power and William J. Levada (Portland, OR), John

R. Quinn (San Francisco), John R. Roach (St. Paul), Charles A. Salatka (Oklahoma City), Robert F. Sanchez (Santa Fe), Daniel E. Sheehan (Omaha), J. Francis Stafford (Denver), Ignatius J. Strecker (Kansas City, KS), Edmund C. Szoka (Detroit), Rembert Weakland (Milwaukee), and John F. Whealon (Hartford). I am also grateful to their staff members whom I also interviewed. Without their openness and hospitality this book would have been impossible to write. If it helps them in their ministry, it will have been worth the effort.

I am indebted to the Woodstock Theological Center, the Loyola Foundation, the Cambridge Center for Social Studies, *America* magazine, and the California Province of the Society of Jesus for the financial support that made this study possible. Thanks also to my agent, John Breslin, S.J., of Georgetown University. I am also grateful for the hospitality and encouragement of my Jesuit brothers and colleagues, especially those at the Woodstock Theological Center at Georgetown University and *America* magazine in New York City. Other Jesuits welcomed me into their communities as I traveled from archdiocese to archdiocese. Finally, I am especially grateful to those who read the manuscript and gave me both encouragement and many useful suggestions, especially Msgr. John Tracy Ellis, Msgr. George Higgins, Dean Hoge, Rev. James H. Provost (all four of the Catholic University of America), Joseph Fichter, S.J., of Loyola University of New Orleans, Aaron Wildavsky of the University of California, Berkeley, Albert G. McCarthy of the Loyola Foundation, my editors at Harper & Row, and three archbishops who will remain nameless. Although numerous people have helped me while writing this book, I am solely responsible for its content.

1. The Selection of Bishops

We try to find the "saint" who fits the niche.
——ARCHBISHOP LAGHI

God help us all.
——Mother on learning that her son was appointed archbishop

From the time Matthias was chosen by lot to replace Judas as one of the twelve apostles, the process by which bishops, the successors of the apostles, are selected has been an important and often controversial issue in the church.[1] Over the centuries the process has changed.[2] Even the United States has known different methods of selecting bishops.[3] During most of this century, however, the U.S. bishops and archbishops have been appointed by the pope with the aid of his representative in Washington who is called a pro-nuncio.

It is not easy to become one of the thirty-one archbishops in the United States. According to canon law, an archbishop, like any bishop, must be a Catholic single male, at least thirty-five years of age and an ordained priest for at least five years.[4] In fact, the average American archbishop is fifty-three years of age at the time of his appointment. Normally (90 percent of the time) a priest is already a bishop before being made an archbishop. He might have been an auxiliary bishop or a diocesan bishop. An auxiliary bishop helps a diocesan bishop, who heads a diocese, or an archbishop, who heads an archdiocese. An auxiliary bishop is often promoted to diocesan bishop before he becomes an archbishop. Thus an archbishop is usually not only a bishop (90 percent of the time), but also the head of a diocese (61 percent of the time) at the time of his appointment. In only about 10 percent of the cases, a priest who is not a bishop is made an archbishop, as happened in the case of Oscar Lipscomb of Mobile.

What is the system that selects such men to be archbishops?

Bishops and archbishops are appointed by the pope, and they normally stay in office until they die or reach seventy-five years of age. The process leading up to the appointments involves a limited number of participants. It is a complex process shrouded in secrecy with the participants bound by pontifical secret about the names under consideration. "ANY VIOLATION OF THIS SECRET NOT ONLY CONSTITUTES A GRAVE FAULT, BUT IS ALSO A CRIME PUNISHABLE WITH A CORRESPONDING ECCLESIASTICAL PENALTY" warns the pro-nuncio in large bold print when requesting information on a candidate for the office of bishop.[5] Although unwilling to reveal the names and backgrounds of episcopal candidates, key participants were willing to describe to me the process itself, but most did not want to be quoted by name.

In examining the process, it is important to distinguish between this first appointment of a priest as a bishop and his later promotion to a higher position, for example, from auxiliary to diocesan bishop (who heads a diocese—called an ordinary under the old code of canon law) or from bishop to archbishop. The process for selecting an archbishop is fundamentally the same as that for selecting any diocesan bishop. It should be remembered, however, that the pope can make any priest a bishop or archbishop if he wishes.

Province Candidates

For first appointments, the process begins when all the bishops (including auxiliaries) of an ecclesiastical province meet under the chairmanship of their archbishop to consider the names of priests who are possible candidates for the episcopacy.[6] The United States is divided into thirty-one Latin-rite provinces, each headed by an archbishop who is called the metropolitan. The other bishops of the province are called suffragans. The bishops of a province must meet at least once every three years to consider episcopal candidates, although they often meet once a year.

Every bishop in a province has the right to put forward the names of priests he believes would be good bishops. These names are collected by the archbishop and distributed to all of the bishops prior to their meeting. Included with the names is a brief description of each priest's education and his assignments since his ordination.

At the meeting, the bishops share their information and observations on each candidate. They are supposed to indicate whether their information is derived from firsthand knowledge or from what they have heard from others. This is the only stage in the selection process where a group of non-Vatican officials meets to discuss the names of episcopal candidates. Anyone can individually send in names to the pro-nuncio in Washington, DC, but meeting in groups to discuss names is strictly forbidden.

The Vatican "Norms for the Selection of Candidates for the Episcopacy in the Latin Church" is very explicit about the qualities the provincial bishops should look for in a candidate. He must be "a good pastor of souls and teacher of the Faith." They must examine whether the candidates

enjoy a good reputation; whether they are of irreproachable morality; whether they are endowed with right judgment and prudence; whether they are even-tempered and of stable character; whether they firmly hold the orthodox Faith; whether they are devoted to the Apostolic See and faithful to the magisterium of the church; whether they have a thorough knowledge of dogmatic and moral theology and canon law; whether they are outstanding for their piety, their spirit of sacrifice and their pastoral zeal; whether they have an aptitude for governing.[7]

Consideration must also be given to "intellectual qualities, studies completed, social sense, spirit of dialogue and cooperation, openness to the signs of the times, praiseworthy impartiality, family background, health, age and inherited characteristics."[8]

The diocesan bishops are instructed to "take care to obtain all the information needed for carrying out this important and difficult duty."[9] They are encouraged to consult, "although not collectively, priests of the cathedral chapter or diocesan consultors, or members of the council of priests, or other members of the clergy, diocesan or regular, or members of the laity."[10] Although no cathedral chapters exist in the United States, diocesan consultors and priests' councils play an important role in diocesan governance. By specifically mentioning them, the Vatican recognizes that their members would be knowledgeable of the diocese and possible episcopal candidates. Individual members of these consultative organs can be approached for information by their bishop, but group consultations are forbidden.

Vatican officials are very adamant in their opposition to collective or group consultations, because they fear such meetings can be divisive and lead to politicking and pressure group activity. "Nothing resembling group consultations, canvasses or referendums may take place," wrote the pro-nuncio Archbishop Pio Laghi in 1983 to a group of seventy people in Pittsburgh who wanted to be consulted as a group. "This process," explains Thomas P. Doyle, O.P., former secretary to the pro-nuncio, "can never rely on popularity or prevailing opinion of what the church 'ought to be' but on what the church actually is in light of the needs of the local community and the universal church."[11]

"People write on their own, even without being consulted," observed one participant. "They write to the pro-nuncio and to Rome [indicating] whether they want a particular man." When groups ignore canon law and lobby, it is often against a particular candidate rather than for one. But individuals and groups will also push a particular priest they want to become a bishop. "We usually look upon that with a critical eye," said a participant in the process. "If there is any indication of politicking or even the man himself engineering the campaign, it works to his detriment. But sometimes it is very spontaneous;

the priest is loved and respected. The clergy, laity, and religious would like him considered to be their next bishop, and he is, in fact, chosen. Vox populi." This appears to have happened in San Antonio where numerous people and organizations wrote in favor of the appointment of Archbishop Patrick Flores.

One of the first bishops to be aggressive in consulting his priests about episcopal candidates was Bishop Ernest Primeau of Manchester, NH. In 1967 he wrote his presbyterate asking each priest to send him the names of three priests judged by them to be suitable for the episcopacy. The bishop alone saw and tabulated the returns. He then presented the top three names to the provincial meeting of the bishops. This approach became known as the Manchester plan and was promoted by the National Federation of Priests' Councils.[12]

According to a survey by the Canon Law Society of America's Committee on the Selection of Bishops, bishops who consult their dioceses about potential candidates usually do this by letter. They ask priests and sometimes others in the diocese to submit names of priests they think ought to be considered. Rev. James H. Provost reports, however, that the "returns to such mailed requests are reported to be low."[13] One official involved in the process said, "Priests do not appreciate the importance of letters from bishops asking for names. If only 10 percent respond and they are old pastors who want someone who will not threaten them, then that is what they will get."

The candidates nominated by the bishops must be priests who have somehow come to their notice. As a result, normally all of the priests nominated at a province meeting are from the province. The exceptions usually occur when the bishops want a black or Hispanic candidate, and they cannot find a suitable priest within the province. Most candidates are diocesan priests, but the bishops can nominate priests who are members of religious orders. Often the religious appointed bishops in the United States have been black or Hispanic priests.

The candidates put forward by a bishop are usually from his

current diocese or from one where he served as a priest or bishop. These are the priests he knows best. Since many bishops have worked in archdioceses either as priests or auxiliary bishops, it is probable that a larger percentage of the province candidates come from archdioceses than their numbers would call for. The presence of auxiliaries at the meetings also means that the bigger (usually archdiocesan) sees have extra votes at the province meeting. Finally, as chairman of the meeting, the archbishop could also help push forward archdiocesan priests. Since the names of the candidates are secret, this hypothesis cannot be tested. It is clear, however, that while 36 percent of the diocesan priests in the United States are in archdioceses, half the bishops originally came from archdioceses.

"Few bishops know any of the priests from far away dioceses," explains Archbishop Jean Jadot who was Apostolic Delegate to the United States from May 1973 to December 1980. "If the diocese had been divided in two, then they would know, but the link becomes less and less every year." Bishops have difficulties getting information on priests outside of dioceses where they have worked.

Bishops would know priests from other dioceses if they studied with them at an interdiocesan seminary, at the Catholic University of America, or at the North American College in Rome. Bishops who had been professors or administrators in interdiocesan seminaries would also know many priests who had studied there as seminarians.

Finally, priests who hold diocesan or national offices would also become known to bishops. This reinforces the natural tendency of a bishop to nominate priests from his chancery staff or seminary. It is not surprising that chancellors, secretaries to bishops, and seminary rectors have a better chance of getting nominated at province meetings than the pastor of a rural parish. They are better known to the bishops, and as one archbishop said, "They're more gifted and more experienced."

Thus at this very first stage in the selection process, we see some of the forces that help push forward candidates who are from an archdiocese, who have worked in a chancery or a seminary, and who have studied in Rome or at the Catholic University of America.[14] These characteristics will be reinforced as the process goes on.

Province List

After the bishops have discussed the candidates, they vote on them by secret ballot in order to preserve the complete freedom of each one voting. The vote can be "white" (yes) or "black" (no) or neutral. The colors refer to small balls that were used for voting in the past. Often a bishop will abstain from voting (neutral) because he does not know the candidate. A "neutral" bishop is encouraged to learn about the candidate, since all the candidates will be voted on again at the next meeting when names can be added or deleted from the list.

After the votes are taken, the archbishop may ask for more discussion and another vote, if he believes it would be useful. He then is responsible for forwarding the names to the pronuncio in Washington, DC, together with the minutes of the meeting. The report, besides giving the votes, indicates the office (e.g., auxiliary or diocesan bishop) and the type of diocese (large, medium, or small) for which the bishops believe the candidate is suitable.

The form used indicates the candidate's name, diocese, parents' names, schools attended and degrees received, date and place of ordination to the priesthood, foreign languages known (in the United States, Spanish is very important), appointments since ordination, "an appraisal of the candidate in view of qualities necessary for a good pastor of souls and teacher of the faith," and the "names and addresses of associates (clerical, lay, religious) who could give information about the candidate."

The appraisal varies in length from three lines to half a page. To show that a priest would be a "good pastor of souls" the evaluation might indicate that the candidate is pastor of a "large, active parish" that he, "in collegial cooperation with his staff, has made a model of vigorous parish life. . . ." Or a seminary rector might be described as "highly disciplined while at the same time in close contact with the thinking and trends of priestly formation today."

In the evaluation, it is usually important to indicate how the priest is viewed by his peers. If he has been elected president of the priests' council, this would be mentioned. If the priests have been asked to send in names for an auxiliary, the evaluation might note where he ranked in the consultation conducted among the priests. Or the appraisal might indicate that he "played a leadership role among his brother priests. He is highly respected by clergy and laity alike."

Finally, if there is something about the candidate that might raise questions, this would be addressed. For example, if he is elderly, the evaluation would note "he has good health, a vigorous spirit." Or if he is relatively young, "he is very mature, balanced."

The list of candidates is also sent to the National Conference of Catholic Bishops (NCCB), which has a standing Committee on the Selection of Bishops. This committee was formed during Cardinal John Dearden's term as president of the NCCB shortly after the new norms on the selection of bishops were issued by the Vatican in 1972.

Early on, however, "it was found that it could not effectively function," reports Bishop James W. Malone, NCCB president (1983–86). "It still exists, but it does not meet for the purpose in its title." In a conference the size of the United States, most members of the committee do not know the priests who are being considered for the episcopacy. As a result, they have little to contribute. The committee spends most of its time considering the division of dioceses. "The committee never met in my three years as president for the consideration of names of candidates," recalls Archbishop John R. Roach, NCCB president from 1980 to 1983.

The number of names on the list varies depending on the size of the province; it might include anywhere from five to thirty names. The votes on the candidates are not always unanimous. Archbishop Jadot explains: "The voting varies. In a tiny minority, when everyone knows the priest, he gets all positive votes. If he is less known, he gets a number of positive votes and abstentions. And some are contested, half and half. It would be very exceptional to send a name that got a negative vote. This happens when a name, for some reason, is removed from the list."

How important is this list of candidates? Under canon law, the pro-nuncio could nominate for diocesan bishop someone not from this pool of candidates, and the pope could appoint any priest he wanted. In fact, the list appears to be very important. "It would be exceptional," reports Archbishop Jadot, "if a bishop were appointed without being on the list. He might not be on the list of the province where he was appointed, but he would be on some list."

There is some speculation, however, that the lists are not always used. For example, a number of observers doubted that bishops Edward M. Egan and Norbert M. Dorsey were on any province list. These priests were working in Rome when they were appointed auxiliaries in New York (1985) and Miami (1986). A bishop also reported to me that a Hispanic religious from his province became a bishop without being on the list.

Certainly the ten black Catholic bishops consider the province lists important. At a closed-door meeting of the National Conference of Catholic Bishops in 1985, they called for the appointment of more black bishops, including a black archbishop. They said, it was not enough that urban diocesan bishops with large black communities look for black auxiliaries. "It would be better," they said, "if black candidates were proposed and considered regularly at provincial meetings in the same way that other candidates are regularly considered. In that way the names of talented black priests who could serve with distinction in the episcopacy would be submitted to the Nunciature and the Holy See on a regular basis."[15]

Pro-nuncio

The key actor in the next step in the process is the pro-nuncio, the papal representative who resides in the Nunciature, or Vatican embassy, in Washington, DC.[16] Archbishop Jadot, the papal representative from 1973 to 1980, is credited with the appointment of many pastoral bishops in the United States. The current representative, Pio Laghi, was appointed apostolic delegate in December 1980 and became pro-nuncio in 1984. As pro-nuncio, Archbishop Pio Laghi represents the Holy See to both the U.S. government and to the American Catholic hierarchy. Prior to the reestablishment of formal diplomatic relations between the United States and the Holy See in 1984, the pope's representative to the American hierarchy was an apostolic delegate.[17]

After Archbishop Laghi receives the names from the provinces, he places them in a green binder where they are organized in different ways: alphabetically, by province, by ethnic group, etc.

The role of the pro-nuncio in the appointment of bishops is emphasized by all the participants and by all those who have studied the process. He is the one who sends the names of episcopal candidates to Rome together with his evaluation and report. "My role is not just to get information, to just give the facts, but to help the Holy See understand what the facts mean," explained Archbishop Jadot.[18] "The pro-nuncio is very important in the process of choosing bishops," reports the American church historian Msgr. John Tracy Ellis. "Pio Laghi stands very high in Rome."

But the pro-nuncio is not all powerful. His recommendations are influenced by the American bishops and they must be confirmed by Rome if they are to take effect. Archbishop Jadot, for example, who had great influence while Paul VI was pope, lost the confidence of Rome during the reign of John Paul II. On the other hand, Jadot's predecessor, Archbishop Luigi Raimondi, lost the confidence of the American bishops who asked Rome to remove him.

Government Interference

With the establishment of diplomatic relations with the Holy See, some people fear that the American government might attempt to interfere in the appointment of bishops as have many governments through history. The National Association of Laity (NAL) joined Americans United for Separation of Church and State in seeking a court injunction against the establishment of diplomatic relations. In its brief the NAL complained of "the potential for Government intrusion into the internal affairs of the Roman Catholic Church," thus reducing their input into church affairs. The Justice Department responded that such fears are "pure speculation," but that if "the effectiveness of plaintiffs' input were to suffer, that diminution would not be traceable to any act of the United States Government, but to decisions of the church hierarchy."[19]

In other words, the Justice Department said, if the president through his ambassador gets the pope to appoint a certain person the bishop of a diocese, then the NAL should complain to the pope, not the U.S. government. Since the court sided with the government, the Justice Department's brief should make Catholics nervous about how the U.S. ambassador to the Holy See might be used.

President Roosevelt, for example, tried to get Bishop Bernard Sheil appointed as the archbishop of Chicago in 1939. "He is about the only prominent churchman in the country who has even a faint coloration of liberalism," wrote Secretary of the Interior Harold Ickes in his diaries.[20] When that effort failed, President Roosevelt tried to get Sheil appointed the archbishop of Washington, DC. In a memorandum to Myron Taylor, his representative to the Holy See, the president wrote, "it is important that he be a reputable and liberal-minded bishop.

Bishop Bernard J. Sheil, who was understudy to Cardinal Mundelein [of Chicago] would be an agreeable choice."[21] Taylor approached Cardinal Luigi Maglione, the papal secretary of state, but again Roosevelt was unsuccessful. Secretary Ickes complained to his diary, "I do not think that the Vatican would have dared turn him [the president] down if he had made strong representations."[22]

Because of the opposition of the American Catholic bishops to the Reagan administration's economic and nuclear policies, some bishops feared the administration would use its ambassador to the Holy See to attack them in Rome. One archbishop claims that Ambassador William A. Wilson, a California Catholic, gave a list of twenty or thirty troublesome bishops to the Vatican. Ambassador Wilson denies this.

Ambassador Wilson and the State Department say that they avoid discussing the internal affairs of the American Catholic church with Vatican officials.[23] This policy goes back to 1784 when Benjamin Franklin was approached by the papal nuncio at Versailles concerning the appointment of bishops in the United States. The Continental Congress instructed Doctor Franklin to notify the nuncio that the question was outside its jurisdiction. Despite these instructions, Franklin appears to have recommended John Carroll anyway.[24] In 1848 Secretary of State Buchanan instructed the first chargé d'affaires in Rome to "carefully avoid even the appearance of interfering in ecclesiastical questions, whether these relate to the United States or any other portion of the world."[25]

Auxiliaries

After the names of potential candidates have been sent to the pro-nuncio by the archbishops, the next step in the process depends on whether the position to be filled is that of an auxiliary bishop or a diocesan bishop. A diocesan bishop heads a diocese while an auxiliary helps a diocesan bishop. If a diocesan bishop wants an auxiliary, he must first convince the pro-nuncio that there is a need. If his auxiliary has died or been promoted, this will not be difficult. If he wants an auxiliary in a diocese that has never had one or if he requests an additional auxiliary, he will have to make his case.[26]

The size of an archdiocese is the major factor in determining the number of auxiliary bishops it will have. An archdiocese with over 200,000 Catholics will normally have an auxiliary.[27] In 1987, archdioceses with one auxiliary ranged from 206,382 (Omaha) to 537,810 Catholics (Cincinnati). Two auxiliaries were present in archdioceses with 237,560 (Dubuque) to 771,908 Catholics (Hartford). Archdioceses with three auxiliaries ranged from 391,208 (Washington) to 600,469 (St. Paul). Archdioceses with over 1 million Catholics usually have five or six auxiliaries.

Thus, an archbishop might argue that he needs help because of the size of the archdiocese. Sometimes the pro-nuncio responds by saying that if the archdiocese is too large perhaps it should be split. Fear of this response might discourage an archbishop from asking for an auxiliary. But if a large archdiocese cannot be easily split, one or more auxiliaries might be appointed. Two or more auxiliaries are more likely to be appointed in large archdioceses where the archbishop will delegate authority to them over regions of the archdiocese.

Other reasons given for an auxiliary might be that a large ethnic or racial group in the diocese requires special attention. Some archbishops also need help because they must devote time to work outside the diocese. A bishop might also ask for an auxiliary because his health is poor, but in this case the pro-nuncio might suggest that the bishop retire. Although a bishop could petition Rome for an auxiliary without the support of the pro-nuncio, it is highly unlikely that he would be successful.

Finally, even if an auxiliary is clearly needed, there appears to be an unwritten law that if a bishop is less than five years from retirement, then no auxiliary will be appointed, lest he be imposed on the new bishop. Cardinals appear to be exempt from this rule, as can be seen from the two Los Angeles auxiliaries (William J. Levada and Donald Montrose) appointed in

May 1983, a year and a half prior to Cardinal Timothy Manning's seventy-fifth birthday. Within a year of Archbishop Roger M. Mahony's arrival in Los Angeles, both bishops were promoted to their own sees.

Where an auxiliary bishop is needed to help a diocesan bishop, it is the responsibility of the diocesan bishop to draw up a list of three names, a *ternus* or *terna*,[28] and submit it to the pro-nuncio.[29] The process presumes that the diocesan bishop, as head of the diocese, knows who will best help him in his diocese. The pro-nuncio, however, also does his own investigation of the priests and sends the names to Rome with his report and recommendations. When a diocesan bishop is being chosen, it is the pro-nuncio who constructs the ternus which he sends to Rome.

The names proposed in a ternus by a diocesan bishop will normally come from the list of priests who had been proposed by the province bishops. If one of the bishop's candidates is not from this list, the pro-nuncio will want to know why. Sometimes the bishop responds that he was not on the list because the bishop did not want to lose him to another diocese: "I wanted to save him." But if the priest was not proposed at the province level because the other bishops would not support him, then his candidacy as an auxiliary is in trouble. The pro-nuncio or Rome can reject all three names on the ternus.

Archbishop Jadot explains, "Sometimes I would know it was useless to send the names to Rome, and I would say, 'Please put another name forward.' If I turned down a terna, I would inform Rome that I couldn't accept it." Sometimes a name may be rejected because the priest is considered too young. "The ordinary does not always get the auxiliary he wants," explained a participant in the process, "He usually gets one of the three names he proposes but not always the first name." One archbishop said that under Archbishop Jadot, "When I saw three names, I would know who would be appointed. Laghi is more unpredictable than Jadot. More third choices are selected."

Archbishop Jadot reports, "I never saw an auxiliary imposed

on a bishop against his will." Others agree that a ternus for an auxiliary is never sent to Rome without the knowledge and consent of the diocesan bishop. "If there is no agreement between a bishop and Rome," says Jadot, it is "a stalemate—then there is no appointment." This appears to have happened in Chicago under Cardinal Cody, who had only two auxiliaries in their midsixties when he died. Within fifteen months of his appointment as archbishop of Chicago, Cardinal Joseph Bernardin received four new auxiliaries. As the second largest diocese in the country, Chicago needed additional auxiliaries. In addition, Cardinal Bernardin needed auxiliaries so as to be free to devote time to work for the NCCB and the synod of bishops. Cardinal Bernardin says that as archbishop of Cincinnati he got whom he wanted for auxiliary. In Chicago, he was satisfied with the four auxiliaries he received.

Recently, however, some observers have concluded that auxiliaries are being "imposed" on some bishops, but in the cases usually cited, the diocesan bishops consented to the appointments. Especially noteworthy were three appointees who had served as priests in Rome. Cardinal O'Connor, for example, accepted the appointment of Bishop Edward M. Egan as his auxiliary in 1985 because the pope asked him to, despite the fact that the cardinal did not even know Egan. The cardinal, since he was not himself from New York, made it plain to his priests that if he were choosing an auxiliary himself it would be a New York archdiocesan priest.

The same year, Archbishop Raymond G. Hunthausen of Seattle also accepted an auxiliary, Donald W. Wuerl, whom he did not request.[30] Likewise David Foley was sent to Richmond as an auxiliary. These two bishops had special faculties because Rome had lost confidence in the local diocesan bishops. Similarly, in 1986 a coadjutor with special faculties was appointed in Lafayette, LA, after the bishop was sued for negligence in dealing with priests accused of pedophilia. In the past, such special appointments were normally made when the bishop was financially incompetent.

Sometimes an auxiliary from outside is suggested by the pro-nuncio because no one local could clear the hurdles. For example, in Miami it is reported that Archbishop Edward A. McCarthy's ternus was turned down, and he was then offered Norbert M. Dorsey, C.P., whom he accepted in 1986. Defending the appointment, a Vatican official pointed out that there are few native priests in Florida and no native bishops. Most of the Miami priests are from dioceses in the Northeast, Cuba, or Ireland. Miami already had a Cuban auxiliary. The Vatican will rarely consider an Irish-born priest as a candidate for bishop in the United States because preference is given to native clergy. Some people suspect that the Miami priests were so divided that an outsider was considered necessary. As one archbishop explained, "In a couple of dioceses there was difficulty getting auxiliaries because every time a name would surface and the word would go around, the caucus would go to work doing a sack job on the candidate." In fact, after the Miami priests and people got to know Bishop Dorsey, he was very well received.

In another diocese, each ternus the bishop sent in was rejected by Rome. Only later did he discover that the retired bishop of the diocese was using his influence in Rome to kill the recommendations in the hope of getting his own candidate appointed. Finally the bishop put a priest from outside his diocese on the ternus. That priest was appointed although he was not the bishop's first choice.

Frequently in order to get a black or Hispanic auxiliary, the diocesan bishop will accept someone from outside (often a religious) suggested by the pro-nuncio. This appears to have happened in Detroit, Los Angeles, Newark, and Washington. On the other hand, Archbishop Flores of San Antonio reportedly tried to have Rev. Virgil Elizondo, director of the Mexican American Cultural Center, made his auxiliary. Instead a sixty-five-year-old Polish priest, who had spent his life working with Hispanics, was made auxiliary.

Although there has been much criticism of Roman interference in the appointment of auxiliaries, allowing bishops a free hand in choosing their auxiliaries is not without its critics. One official notes:

> I think that a diocesan bishop has entirely too much control over the appointment of auxiliary bishops in his own diocese, which is not very healthy. Oftentimes they are rubber stamps to his own ecclesiology and his own vision of the church, whether that is in one direction or the other. A man should not be appointed just because he would make a good auxiliary without any regard to his potential leadership ability to become an ordinary.

Monsignor Ellis also criticizes diocesan bishops on their choices of auxiliaries: "The church's history reveals many instances where outstanding prelates could not, nonetheless, bring themselves to advance a priest of superior quality lest the latter should outshine them."[31] But some archbishops have chosen auxiliaries who make up for their own weaknesses. For example, Archbishop James Casey of Denver, a quiet introvert, strongly supported his more outgoing auxiliary George R. Evans. Likewise Archbishop John Quinn of San Francisco, who hates administration, delegated a good deal to his auxiliary, Bishop Daniel Walsh.

Diocesan Bishops

Before the ternus is sent to Rome, the pro-nuncio does his own investigation of the candidates and the needs of the diocese. "We try to find the 'saint' who fits the niche," explains Archbishop Laghi. If the appointment is as a diocesan bishop, the pro-nuncio will request from the retiring diocesan bishop (or if he is deceased or moved to another diocese, from the administrator) a report on the condition and needs of the diocese and the qualities desired in the diocesan bishop. Priests, religious, and laity can be consulted both individually and collectively in drawing up this report, as long as individual names are not mentioned.

The Canon Law Society of America (CLSA) recommended a series of questions to help the consultative process:

1. In your opinion, what are the three most important needs of the diocese today?
2. In the light of the needs you have listed, what do you feel are the desirable qualifications of the next bishop of this diocese?
3. Please list three persons you feel would be good choices for the next bishop and explain why.[32]

Bishops, following Roman instructions, have not allowed the use of the last question in public consultations. Public discussion has been limited to the state of the diocese and its needs and the qualifications desired in the bishop.

In St. Louis in 1979, four reports—from the archdiocesan consultors, the pastoral commission, the council of priests, and the council of religious women—were also drawn up and sent to the apostolic delegate. This process was public and involved wide consultation, but there was no public discussion of names.

On the other hand, in Denver after the death of Archbishop Casey in 1986, the administrator says that he was told by Archbishop Laghi to meet with a group of priests to draw up the report and to also submit the names of possible candidates. There clearly was a misunderstanding here since Rome never authorizes group consultation on the names of candidates. In any case, the administrator met with the Denver priests' council, which discussed and voted on a list of names, most of whom were bishops in the region. Bishop J. Francis Stafford of Memphis, who got the appointment, was not on their list. This group consultation does not seem to have had any negative consequences. Some of the Denver priests felt that the pronuncio already knew who was going to be appointed before they were consulted, but others felt that Archbishop Stafford fit the description of the type of person they were looking for although his name did not come up.

In the early 1970s, some priests' senates simply took the initiative and drew up lists of candidates. As elected organizations representing priests, they had a special interest in who was chosen to be their bishop. When Cardinal Lawrence Shehan was approaching retirement in 1972, the Baltimore priests' senate appointed a subcommittee to address the question of his successor. The subcommittee prepared "A Report on the State of the Archdiocese of Baltimore—1972," which was mailed to all the priests and approved by a 225 to 11 vote.[33] In 1973 the subcommittee drew up a list of candidates who were compatible with the priorities expressed in the report. This list was not made public, but information on the qualifications of these candidates was gathered and discussed by the subcommittee. A list of ten men in order of preference was given to the cardinal along with the report on the archdiocese. The cardinal gave the report but not the names to Pope Paul VI and members of the Vatican curia. He later shared both the report and the names with a number of American bishops. Meanwhile the apostolic delegate conducted his own inquiries, and in 1974, William D. Borders was appointed archbishop. He "was one of the candidates recommended highly by the subcommittee."[34]

Also in 1974, on the recommendation of Archbishop James P. Davis, the priests' senate of Santa Fe established an ad hoc committee to gather information and submit recommendations to the apostolic delegate for the appointment of his successor.[35] This committee included lay, religious, and clerical representatives chosen from the priests' senate and the pastoral council. It followed the procedures recommended by the Canon Law Society of America including the soliciting and discussion of names. The committee sent to Archbishop Jadot a report on the needs of the archdiocese and the results of a survey that surfaced sixty-five names. The committee recommended three as the most qualified, including Robert F. Sanchez, who was appointed.

In the Los Angeles archdiocese, on the other hand, there was no public consultation in 1985, nor was there any in Philadelphia in 1987. Rev. Thomas Curry, chairman of the priests' council in Los Angeles, had seen the consultation process in Phoenix and New Mexico and was not impressed.

> I wouldn't want to do it in our diocese. This would be putting people through all kinds of meetings and all kinds of trouble to come up with a picture or a profile of the diocese that I could tell you right out of my head now. Or else to come up with a profile of the kind of man you need. What we need is a combination of Jesus and a few other people. We all know that, but to do that is to raise expectations that you can't fulfill.

Sometimes this consultation process is short-circuited by announcing the appointment of a new bishop at the same time as the resignation of the old bishop. This was done in Portland, OR, and Newark in 1986 where the archbishops retired early and their successors were appointed without any public consultation. Even when a bishop reaches seventy-five, the acceptance of his resignation may not be announced until his successor is appointed, as was the case in Philadelphia. A resignation, though accepted, is not effective until published in the *L'Osservatore Romano*. This *nunc pro tunc* (now for then) policy allows the bishop to remain bishop without becoming the administrator. But it also eliminates any public consultation for drawing up the report.

The report on the diocese is sent by the administrator to the pro-nuncio together with ten to twenty names of people from various age groups and parts of the diocese whom the pro-nuncio can contact to check the accuracy of the report. "Usually the heads of the various administrative bodies and other persons in leadership positions are contacted," explains Thomas P. Doyle, O.P., then of the pro-nuncio's staff.[36] Normally, heads of religious orders in the diocese would be queried as well as lay people who are officers in diocesan lay organizations and members of advisory committees in the diocese. Some people the pro-nuncio may have met personally in his travels, but many names are simply taken by the pro-nuncio from those listed under the name of the diocese in *The Official Catholic Directory*. These people are not only asked about the state of the diocese but are also asked to recommend names of possible candidates to the pro-nuncio.

The condition and makeup of the diocese as described in the report can influence the appointment. Thus Atlanta, a city with a history of good black-white relations, received Eugene A. Marino, the first black U.S. archbishop. Coincidentally, this took place one week after Jesse Jackson won the 1988 Democratic presidential primary in Georgia. Likewise, with large Hispanic populations, the archdioceses of San Antonio and Santa Fe were natural spots for Hispanic archbishops. Los Angeles also needed someone who would be sensitive to Hispanics. Roger Mahony not only knows Spanish but had been very active on behalf of Hispanics in California before he was appointed archbishop of Los Angeles.

When the New York see was vacant, Rev. Fred Voorhes, a staff member of the Congregation for Bishops, noted that "The second language of New York is Spanish, so whether or not a man speaks Spanish is one consideration for that appointment."[37] In fact, John O'Connor could not speak Spanish when he was appointed, but one of the first things he did was to learn it. On another point, Father Voorhes was more accurate in his prediction: "He has to be comfortable with mass media, especially in New York, the communications capital of the nation and perhaps even of the world."

The style of the last bishop can also influence the appointment. Archbishop Jadot recalls:

A bishop is appointed to balance what went before. If the diocese is well managed, but the bishop did not have contact with the people, if he was authoritarian, or a weak administrator [then the opposite would be appointed]. McFarland was sent to Reno in 1974 because it was financially out of hand. Sometimes a bishop might be only concerned with schools and not social programs. There might be diocesan problems hanging around unresolved. The diocese might have to be divided and the bishop has been opposing it or procrastinating—"after my time." Certainly in Chicago the way of operating as bishop was a factor in the choice of Bernardin.

Influence of Bishops

Bishops who have previously served in a diocese would normally be contacted about the needs of the diocese and possible candidates. Cardinal Bernardin of Chicago says he has been consulted on appointments in places where he had served, like South Carolina.

The pro-nuncio must also seek suggestions individually from the bishops and the archbishop in the province to which the vacant diocese belongs.[38] Other bishops and archbishops in the region might also be consulted. If all of these bishops agree on a candidate, his chances of being appointed are high. "It is much easier to get the appointment through," Archbishop Laghi told one archbishop, "when you all sing with one voice."

But one archbishop suspected that there was also a hidden purpose in consulting bishops on other bishops and dioceses. "It is not so much what they want to learn about someone else as they want to have another little insight on you," he says, "what you reveal about yourself when you start talking about the other diocese."

The metropolitan can play an important role in the appointment of bishops in his province. Some archbishops have taken a very active role. One told me,

Since I came as metropolitan, I fought hard to get what I thought was necessary for the vacancies that occurred. In one instance, I feared the appointment of a candidate even weaker than the predecessor. I urged a particular candidate who I knew could do the job, but there were a lot of counter-proposals. Eventually, with the support of the suffragans, excellent men were chosen, the ones I had hoped for. Maybe I shouldn't have been so insistent, but I thought that was the way I was supposed to do it.

Archbishop Borders of Baltimore reports that he always got the men he wanted for suffragans or bishops in his province.

"It wasn't easy a couple of times, but I really did," he says. "The Holy See listens. Sometimes you have to make things rather strong."

"I did not necessarily always get the first person that I suggested for the see," says Cardinal Bernardin. "But I was satisfied that I was consulted and listened to. I was pleased with the people who were ultimately chosen."

Other archbishops have been less successful. Sometimes their suggestions were ignored, and sometimes they were not even consulted about the person who ultimately got the see. One archbishop got involved in two appointments in his province, but the final choice in both cases was someone he was not even asked about. Another archbishop said that the two suffragans appointed in his province were not his choices. A third archbishop said the man appointed was not his first choice but was acceptable. The ignoring of archbishops is not unique to the United States. Cardinal Franz Koenig of Vienna said that he was not consulted on the selection of his successor.[39]

Some archbishops take little interest in the appointments of bishops in their province. Others say they do not know the diocese or the priests well enough to make a recommendation. One claimed not to be of much help even in the appointment of his successor.

I told the delegate, "when it comes right down to it, I don't know a whole heck of a lot about these other bishops to say this is the kind of administrator we should have." I know bishops throughout the country, and I see them at meetings and talk to them, but I don't know what kind of diocese they run. I don't know what the priests or the religious or the laity think of them. I don't know what the financial picture is, not even in my own province.

Role of NCCB

The pro-nuncio also consults with the president and vice-president of the National Conference of Catholic Bishops. This consultation takes place in two stages. Archbishop John Roach, conference president from 1980 to 1983, recalls:

The president receives notification from the pro-nuncio that a see will be opening up or that he is considering the appointment of an auxiliary for a particular diocese. The president is asked to give his impressions of the state of the diocese, the kind of leadership it needs.

Each of the thirteen regions of the United States elects a bishop to be on the committee for the selection of bishops. I would consult with the regional representative. They would not get a list of names, but I would ask what the diocese is like, and he would recount its story. I would forward that to the apostolic delegate.

After the pro-nuncio narrows down the list of candidates to eight or ten names, he sends them to the officers of the NCCB for a second consultation. "The most recent one I got," said Archbishop John May, president of the conference from 1986 to 1989, "had maybe six bishops and then about four or five priests who had been proposed for that particular diocese." This second consultation is a special concession granted by Archbishop Laghi to the U.S. bishops who asked to be consulted about the names that surfaced for a given diocese. Archbishop Jadot avoided this, apart from oral consultation with the president or general secretary.

Because of the size of the United States, often the NCCB officers do not know the priests who are being proposed. "A lot of times I don't know any of the priests," admits Archbishop May of St. Louis. "For instance, Santa Rosa is open. I don't know anybody in Santa Rosa. And really I don't know many priests in that area of California. The few I would know tend to be scholars or people who teach or guys who give talks, very often Jesuits. But I don't know a lot of the diocesan priests."

When he was president, Archbishop Roach recalls, "If I did not know them, I would say, 'Sorry.' If the person was already an auxiliary or a bishop I would know something about him."

Archbishop Roach reports that "I would not rank them," but that has changed. Bishop James Malone, president from 1983 to 1986, explains, "The pro-nuncio says, 'These are the names that have surfaced. Give me a list of three in order of your preference and give the reasons for your preference.' " Similarly, Archbishop May says, "These names have been proposed, and you are told, 'If you wish, will you comment on these names or, if you prefer, put in any different names, put in your own names. Then give us a terna and give your reasons for it.' So I usually come up with three names [and] tell why I think these three deserve consideration."

Some have criticized the NCCB leadership for not taking a more active role at this point in the process. One archbishop said,

When the second consultation occurs, the conference leadership ought to contact whoever represents that region on the NCCB Committee on Appointments and find out what he thinks. If that bishop doesn't know, he ought to find out.

But that step doesn't seem to occur, and whenever I hear the bishops complain about appointments, I feel that we have ourselves to blame for not using well what has been offered us.

In the past there were certain American bishops who were "kingmakers" in the hierarchy because they had unique influence in the choice of bishops. Cardinal Francis J. Spellman of New York was very influential during the pontificate of Pius XII (1939–58). While his only success in the West was the appointment in 1946 of his auxiliary James F. McIntyre to Los Angeles, in the East he was dominant. He supported the appointment of Richard Cushing as archbishop of Boston in 1944. In 1945, John F. O'Hara, another New York auxiliary, was named bishop of Buffalo, and in 1951, he became archbishop of Philadelphia. In 1947, Patrick A. O'Boyle, Spellman's director of Catholic Charities, was named archbishop of Washington.[40]

But under John XXIII and Paul VI, Cardinal Spellman's influence dwindled. In 1958, Archbishop Egidio Vagnozzi, the new apostolic delegate, made it clear to the bishops that he, and not Spellman, was in charge.

Bishop Edward F. Hoban of Cleveland, as a friend of Amleto Cicognani, the apostolic delegate, was very influential in the late 1950s. According to Monsignor Ellis,

Hoban was either directly responsible for a number of bishops or influential in starting them on their way, e.g., Floyd Begin to Oakland, Paul Hallinan to Charleston and then Atlanta, John Krol to Philadelphia, John Treacy to La Crosse, John Whealon as auxiliary in Cleveland before his promotion to Erie and subsequently Hartford.[41]

John F. Dearden of Pittsburgh and then Detroit and James Malone of Youngstown were also said to have been boosted by Bishop Hoban.

"There is no kingmaker among the American bishops today," reports the church historian Monsignor Ellis. Neither Archbishop Jadot nor Laghi had one American prelate whom they listened to exclusively. Cardinals O'Connor, Law, and Hickey are said to be the members of the American hierarchy closest to Archbishop Laghi. But one archbishop explained, "In the long run, Laghi will do a couple of things to make people happy, but then he will shift off to some other force. He is a very skilled diplomat."

Cardinal Hickey confessed to being ambivalent about having so many of his good men made bishops in other dioceses. "I'm going to hide my lists," he said jokingly. "Within about a year and a half, four major leaders were chosen to be bishops: Bishop O'Malley of the Virgin Islands; Bishop John Ricard, auxiliary in Baltimore; Bishop Donohue, in the office here for nineteen years as chancellor; and then Bishop Foley to Richmond. I'm very honored that my priests are considered to be such fine men, but, you know, just forget about us for a while." After this interview, in 1988 he lost another chancellor to Birmingham and an auxiliary to Atlanta.

The American best positioned to play kingmaker today is Cardinal John O'Connor of New York, who in 1985 was appointed to the Vatican Congregation for Bishops, a position that was held by his predecessors cardinals Spellman and Cooke.

Cardinal O'Connor is taking very seriously his work on this congregation that deals with the appointment of bishops, as will be explained later. One person in Denver quoted John O'Connor as saying he was instrumental in the appointment of Archbishop J. Francis Stafford in 1986.

During the appointment process, Archbishop Jadot reports that "the bishops of a region are most helpful for the new diocesan bishop. For an auxiliary, the bishop and the priests are most helpful." While he was apostolic delegate, Archbishop Jadot recalls that "99 percent of the time, two to five names come out strongly as the candidates. Most often there is a strange coincidence of names coming from the bishops and from the priests—seldom is there difference between them. When there is, then the apostolic delegate has to work it out."

On the other hand, input from the laity appears to be of limited value. "It is exceptional when their answers are helpful," said Archbishop Jadot. "They are usually fine answers, but they have limited knowledge." Another participant noted that "the replies of religious women are very useful whether they are commenting on candidates or the condition of the diocese."

Local Boy or Outsider

If a vacant diocese has an auxiliary, he is an obvious candidate to become the diocesan bishop, and the pro-nuncio will hear from people about the auxiliary's qualifications. But, in fact, only 10 percent of the diocesan bishops were first auxiliaries in the diocese they now govern. In 1987, only archbishops Flores of San Antonio, Pilarczyk of Cincinnati, Roach of St. Paul, and Sheehan of Omaha were auxiliaries in the archdioceses they now govern. Interestingly, all four are very popular in their archdioceses.

Despite all the work of examining the diocese and consulting with many people, often the candidates can be determined by which auxiliaries are due for a diocese. "I have to confess that they do write wonderful reports about the needs of the local churches, the profile, the resources," one participant said. "But I am afraid that the appointments are very often made on the basis of the human needs of who is waiting in line."

Normally a bishop is an auxiliary for about six years before becoming a diocesan bishop in another diocese. Campaigning for a diocese can be delicate. "There are some auxiliary bishops who talk about virtually nothing else but when they are going to get out of the morass they find themselves hooked into," said one archbishop. An archbishop will often approach the pro-nuncio on behalf of an auxiliary. "But some of the auxiliaries get so agitated that they do go and confront the pro-nuncio about it. We try to keep them from doing that, but the fact is that sometimes it happens." Some auxiliaries get promoted soon after a new archbishop arrives so that he can put in place his own men.

But some auxiliaries are never promoted. A few do not want to be diocesan bishops, but others have been passed over because of health problems or because they are judged to be poor administrators. So far, few black or Hispanic auxiliaries have been promoted to diocesan bishops. A few auxiliaries have been blackballed because of their positions on controversial issues like the ordination of women. Auxiliary bishops Thomas Costello of Syracuse, George Evans of Denver, Thomas Gumbleton of Detroit, and Francis Murphy of Baltimore were considered too liberal by Rome to be given a diocese.

The pro-nuncio also hears the views of people on whether the new bishop should be from the diocese or from outside. Someone from the local clergy is often desired in the hopes that he would be more sensitive to the local situation.

On the other hand, sometimes there is the feeling that "new blood" is needed in the diocese. Someone from outside might be freer to act without his critics claiming that he is listening only to his old friends and appointing them to offices. Archbishop John F. Whealon recalls going to Erie and to Hartford as an outsider:

I thought that having an outsider was healthy because when I went into both of them, there was some tension of clerical politics in a negative sense, factions and groups that were operating. It was healthy for them to have someone that didn't even know the people involved and then could make a much more objective judgment. So even though he would be slow in making judgments, he would be objective.

Archbishop Jadot reports that "there is usually unanimity or quasi unanimity in the diocese over the question of whether the bishop should be a local person or from outside." Another official agreed: "Generally it is one trend or another, and more often than not it is in reaction to the former bishop. If he was local, they want an outsider, and vice versa. I can't recall any case where it was divided right down the middle, where half wanted a local man and half wanted an outsider." Archbishops who are from their archdioceses are Flores of San Antonio, Lipscomb of Mobile, Pilarczyk of Cincinnati, Roach of St. Paul, Sanchez of Santa Fe, and Sheehan of Omaha.

Archbishops

The process for appointing an archbishop does not differ substantially from that of appointing any other diocesan bishop. Greater care may be taken, and more people may be consulted, but the process is basically the same. The man chosen to be archbishop is more likely to be already a diocesan bishop at the time of his appointment.

When an archbishop was to be appointed, Archbishop Jadot would consult all the archbishops. Archbishop Laghi consults some archbishops, but not all of them all the time. He consults archbishops in neighboring archdioceses or those who might have special information. "I had been under the impression that all archbishops are consulted on all archbishoprics," says one archbishop. "I have been consulted on a number of them, but not all of them." Some archbishops reported they were not consulted on the recent appointments to Atlanta, Boston, and New York.

Many observers feel that it is especially in the appointment to fill large archdioceses that Rome plays a key role. "On those biggies, Laghi always finds out what Rome wants," explains an archbishop. "Who is Rome? That is always faceless. Is it Cardinal Baum? Is it Archbishop Rigali? Is it the pope himself?"

Archbishop Justin Rigali, originally from Los Angeles and now president of the Pontifical Ecclesiastical Academy, is said to have been influential in the appointment of Archbishop Roger Mahony to Los Angeles. Cardinal William Baum, as the only American cardinal in Rome, is thought to be influential, especially since he sits on the Congregation for Bishops. One archbishop thought that Cardinal O'Connor was the pope's personal choice for New York, while Cardinal Law was Archbishop Laghi's candidate for Boston.

Many church observers argue that archbishops recently appointed by the Vatican have been more "conservative," a term I attempt to avoid in this book. These commentators point to archbishops Bernard Law of Boston (1984), John O'Connor of New York (1984), Roger Mahony of Los Angeles (1985), William Levada of Portland (1986), and Anthony Bevilacqua of Philadelphia (1987) as the Vatican's attempt to reshape the American hierarchy. Whatever the case, the current appointment process allows the pope to appoint whom he chooses, and it is likely he gives more attention to the appointment of archbishops than of other bishops.

Questionnaire

The pope in some ways faces the same problems in the appointment of bishops as the president faces in the appointment of judges. Once appointed, it is difficult to remove either a bishop or a judge. As a result, in both systems high priority is given to finding out about the candidate prior to his appointment. "Security" checks are conducted. Information on his background, education, and previous jobs is gathered. People who know the candidate are interviewed about his attitudes and views.

The scrutiny of a priest prior to being first appointed bishop is in some ways greater than it is for bishops who are being promoted. Great care is taken to find out about the priest because once he is appointed he is in until he retires at seventy-five. Bishops, on the other hand, have already been through the process once and are better known by the pro-nuncio and Rome, who have seen how they have acted as bishops.

In order to get information about a priest for the ternus, the pro-nuncio sends a confidential questionnaire on the candidate to twenty or thirty people who know him. Some of these names are suggested by the priest's diocesan bishop; others are diocesan officials or people the pro-nuncio has gotten to know personally in the diocese through his travels. Not only priests but also religious and lay people are sent the questionnaire. The laity consulted tend to be officers in diocesan lay organizations or on diocesan advisory committees. Once again, names are also taken by the pro-nuncio from those listed under the diocese in *The Official Catholic Directory*. They are told to answer the questions without seeking further data from others. Nor can they tell anyone, especially the candidate, that they have received the questionnaire.

Confidential Vatican Questionnaire on Episcopal Candidate

Please describe the nature of your association with the candidate and indicate the length of time that you have known him.

1. Personal Characteristics:	Physical appearance; health; work capacity; family conditions especially regarding any manifestations of hereditary illnesses.
2. Human Qualities	Speculative and practical intellectual capacity; temperament and character; balance; serenity of judgment; sense of responsibility.

3. Human, Christian, and Priestly Formation:

Possession and practice of human, Christian, and priestly virtues (prudence, justice, moral uprightness, loyalty, sobriety, faith, hope, charity, obedience, humility, piety: daily celebration of the Eucharist and of the Liturgy of the Hours, Marian devotion).

4. Behavior:

Moral conduct; comportment with people in general and in the exercise of the priestly ministry in particular; the ability to establish friendships; rapport with civil authorities: respect and autonomy.

5. Cultural Preparation:

Competence and aggiornamento in ecclesiastical sciences; general culture; knowledge of and sensitivity toward problems of our time; facility with foreign languages; authorship of books or magazine articles worthy of note.

6. Orthodoxy:

Adherence with conviction and loyalty to the doctrine and magisterium of the Church. In particular, the attitude of the candidate toward the documents of the Holy See on the Ministerial Priesthood, on the priestly ordination of women, on the Sacrament of Matrimony, on sexual ethics, and on social justice. Fidelity to the genuine ecclesial tradition and commitment to the authentic renewal promoted by the Second Vatican Council and by subsequent pontifical teachings.

7. Discipline:

Loyalty and docility to the Holy Father, the Apostolic See, and the Hierarchy; esteem for and acceptance of priestly celibacy, as it has been set forth by the ecclesiastical Magisterium; respect for and observance of the general and particular norms governing divine worship and clerical attire.

8. Pastoral Fitness and Experience:	Abilities, experience, and effectiveness in the pastoral ministry; evangelization and catechesis; preaching and teaching (preparation, public speaking capability); pastoral skills in sacramental and liturgical ministries (especially in the administration of the Sacrament of Penance and the celebration of the Eucharist); the fostering of vocations; sensitivity to the needs of the missions; a spirit of ecumenism; the formation of the laity in the apostolate (family life, youth, the promotion and defense of human rights, the world of labor, culture, and the media); the promotion of human causes and of social action with particular attention to the poor and the most needy.
9. Leadership Qualities:	A fatherly spirit, attitude of service, taking initiative; the ability to lead others, to dialogue, to stimulate and receive cooperation, to analyze and organize and carry out decisions; to direct and engage in team work; appreciation for the role and the collaboration of religious and laity (both men and women) and for a just share of responsibilities; concern for the problems of the universal and local Church.
10. Administrative Skills:	Accountability for and proper use of Church goods; abilities and performance in fulfilling administrative tasks; sense of justice and spirit of detachment; openness in seeking the collaboration of experts in the field.
11. Public Esteem:	Estimation of the candidate on the part of confreres, the general public, and the civil authorities.
12. Your Judgment of the Candidate: Suitability for the Episcopacy:	His suitability for the episcopacy in general; in particular whether he would be more apt as a diocesan or an auxiliary bishop; whether in an urban, industrial, rural, large, medium, or small See.

13. Any Additional
    Comments:

14. Names, addresses, and qualifications of others who know the
    candidate well (priests, religious men and women, laity), who
    are truly reliable, with good sense, prudence, and calm
    judgment.

The questionnaire was prepared by the Vatican Congregation
for Bishops and is used for all episcopal appointments that go
through the congregation. The questionnaire had been rather
skimpy, but it underwent major revision in the 1970s when
Cardinal Sebastiano Baggio was prefect of the congregation.
The questionnaire sent by the pro-nuncio contains fourteen
items, including a request for additional names of persons who
know the candidate (see above questionnaire). Although the
questionnaire is detailed, the covering letter indicates that it "is
only to serve as an orientation. . . ." The pro-nuncio asks that
the information be given "in a discursive manner so as to develop fully your observations."

Most of the questions deal with the obvious physical, intellectual, moral, spiritual, social, and priestly characteristics that
one would hope for in a bishop. It is interesting to note that
while the questionnaire does ask about the administrative skills
of the candidate (item 10), it goes into much more detail asking
about his pastoral fitness and experience (item 8). Under this
item are listed not only pastoral skills but also "a spirit of ecumenism" and "the promotion and defense of human rights."
And the question on leadership qualities (item 9) clearly indicates that an authoritarian pastor is not wanted: "A fatherly
spirit . . . the ability to lead others, to dialogue, to stimulate
and receive cooperation . . . to direct and engage in team work;
appreciation for the role and the collaboration of religious and
laity (both men and women) and for a just share of responsibilities. . . ."

The questions on orthodoxy (item 6) indicate that a priest

supporting the ordination of women, optional priestly celibacy, or birth control would not be made a bishop. But neither would a priest opposed to the teaching of the church on social justice. Archbishop Jadot explains:

> If the priest's first reaction to *Humanae Vitae* was negative—he just blew up—and later came to accept it, this would not be a major objection. But if he does not agree with the magisterium. . . . The pope has been strong on this. He wants people who agree with himself, and this is very natural. If the priest has given a lecture or written an article against *Humanae Vitae* or for women's ordination, he would have a difficult time becoming a bishop. He is saying the opposite of the magisterium.

Fidelity to the magisterium appears to be stressed today even more than it was in Jadot's time. "Orthodoxy is the big issue today. Someone who is known to be a challenger can certainly not be chosen to be a bishop," said one official involved in the selection process.[42] Orthodoxy is defined primarily in terms of loyalty to the Holy See and attitudes toward *Humanae Vitae*, priestly celibacy, and women's ordination. Bishops must be willing "to take positions not always shared by one's faithful, diocesan priests or bishops' conference."[43]

As far as can be known, this screening process appears to be successful in getting bishops who uphold traditional views. Episcopal defiance of the Vatican is rare. Survey data show that "on matters of religious attitudes and sexual morality, bishops tend to be even more 'conservative' than the clergy over 55, while on matters of ecumenism and social action, bishops tend to be even more 'liberal' than the clergy under 36."[44] This would appear to be exactly what the Vatican wants.

Pro-Nuncio's Report

After the pro-nuncio has examined the responses to the questionnaires and prepared a ternus, he writes a report (approximately twenty single-spaced pages) in Italian, extracting and synthesizing the content of the consultation and giving his own judgment. The ternus and the pro-nuncio's report are sent to the Vatican Congregation for Bishops, and no U.S. bishop sees them unless he is a member of that congregation. Normally the report gives a description of the diocese and then describes the process the pro-nuncio went through in selecting the candidates. The pro-nuncio then lists the candidates in order of his preference and describes each one. "Laghi does a good job on his reports," said a Vatican official. "He covers everything."

The pro-nuncio sends all of the documents that he has received to Rome with his report. For the appointment of a diocesan bishop this could be one hundred letters, but normally it is about twenty letters for each of the candidates. When the candidate is already a bishop, the documentation is less. In this case, the question is not whether he is qualified to be a bishop but whether he is apt for the particular diocese. On the other hand, the documentation for an archbishop's appointment can be heavy. The stack of materials for the appointment of a new archbishop in Los Angeles was two feet high. Processing the appointment can take two to four months, depending on the size of the diocese or the unanimity or tension in the diocese. Archbishop Jadot noted that "Archbishop Laghi works faster than I did on appointments, but he travels less."

Congregation for Bishops

When the documents arrive in Rome, they go to the Congregation for Bishops, headed by Cardinal Bernardin Gantin, a Vatican official from the Benin Republic in West Africa who was named prefect of the congregation in 1984. It is considered one of the most important and hard-working congregations in the Vatican curia or offices. It deals not only with appointments but also quinquennial reports and ad limina visits (see chapter 8). The working language of the congregation and its staff is Italian.

Cardinal Gantin's predecessor, Sebastiano Baggio, was a

hard-working curial cardinal who rarely missed a day in the office. Cardinal Baggio was Italian, like practically all of his predecessors since the congregation was founded in 1588. Cardinal Gantin's appointment in 1984 came as a surprise to most people in Rome, since he is not only not an Italian, he is not European or Caucasian. "Jaws dropped," says a Roman official. "He was not one of those who was rumored." Since he is from a mission country, his own appointment as a bishop went through the Congregation for Evangelization of Peoples. Despite the surprise, his appointment was welcomed by the congregation's staff.

The documents from the pro-nuncio are checked by the congregation staff person in charge of appointments from the United States to see if they are complete. This American priest, who usually serves for five years, is also in charge of appointments from Canada and Australia. Another priest handles most of Europe except Italy, which is handled by two priests. One priest handles Brazil and another the rest of Latin America. Episcopal appointments for mission countries (most of Africa and Asia) are dealt with in the Congregation for Evangelization of Peoples. Appointments for the eastern-rite churches in union with Rome go through the Congregation for the Oriental Churches or their synods.

The staff person is expected to read the pro-nuncio's report and the entire dossier. He evaluates it and offers recommendations on what should be done if there are unanswered questions, if certain people should have been consulted who were not, or if more information is needed. For example, if there was insufficient information about the candidate's orthodoxy, the pro-nuncio would receive a letter from the prefect asking for the information.

A staff person has no power, noted one official, "but he does have an awful lot of influence due to the nature of his job and the fact that his superiors cannot be expected to study the whole issue as thoroughly as that person has to." The staff works on manual typewriters. There is a photocopier and electric typewriters for formal letters, but no computers for data files or for word processing.

If everything is in order and the cardinal prefect approves, the appointment process moves forward to the congregation, which meets twice a month from October through June. The congregation in 1987 was composed of thirty-six members, appointed by the pope, who have five-year renewable terms—twenty-nine cardinals and seven archbishops. Sixteen of the cardinals are permanently stationed in Rome as part of the Vatican curia. Ex officio members of the congregation include prefects of the Council for the Public Affairs of the Church (Cardinal Agostino Casaroli, secretary of state) and of the Congregations for the Doctrine of the Faith (Cardinal Joseph Ratzinger), for the Clergy (Cardinal Antonio Innocenti), and for Seminaries and Institutes of Study (Cardinal William W. Baum).

Before the appointment goes to the congregation,[45] a cardinal *ponente* (presenter) is chosen by the undersecretary of the congregation.[46] After reviewing the full dossier, the ponente, who is usually a curial cardinal,[47] provides a summary to the other cardinals at a meeting of the congregation. The ponente, explains Cardinal O'Connor, "synthesizes, analyzes, and presents the entire picture" to the rest of the congregation.

The cardinal ponente has to be fairly fluent in the language of the country of the candidate, since only the pro-nuncio's report is in Italian. Cardinal William Baum, the only American cardinal in Rome, is sometimes the cardinal ponente on American appointments, but not always. The job of ponente is rotated in order not to overburden any of the cardinals. Cardinal Baum, for example, is also prefect of the Congregation for Seminaries and Institutes of Study and cannot devote all of his time to the Congregation for Bishops. The more complicated and controversial the appointment, the more likely the undersecretary will try to get a ponente fluent enough to understand the nuances in the documents. Most members of the congregation are capable of reading and understanding English.

When Cardinal Baggio was prefect, members of the congregation were notified two weeks before the next meeting would take place. This made it difficult for cardinals and archbishops not residing in Rome to attend the meeting. As a non-European, Cardinal Gantin is more sensitive to this problem. He sends members of the congregation an advanced schedule of the meetings to be held from October through June. Thus if a cardinal is coming to Rome on other business, he can schedule his visit to coincide with a meeting of the congregation.

Still, most members living outside of Rome do not attend. Cardinals Jean-Marie Lustiger of Paris and Carlo Maria Martini of Milan attend about once a month, but they live a short airplane ride away from Rome. The archbishop of Sydney, on the other hand, is twenty-three hours away by air and rarely attends.

Cardinal Terence Cooke and Cardinal Humberto Medeiros were members of the congregation prior to their deaths. Cardinal Cooke never attended because he did not understand Italian, the language used in the meetings. Cardinal Medeiros, who could speak Italian, attended once or twice a year when he was in Rome for other business. Also fluent in Italian, Cardinal Joseph Bernardin served on the congregation as an archbishop from 1973 to 1978 and attended meetings a couple of times a year when he was in Rome on business as president of the National Conference of Catholic Bishops or as a member of the council of the synod of bishops.

Although still working to improve his Italian, Cardinal John O'Connor gets to Rome about every other month for meetings of the congregation since his appointment in 1985. "I try to get there when an American appointment is under consideration," explains Cardinal O'Connor. As a result, he reports attending meetings that consider from 75 to 80 percent of the American appointments.

This concern for local appointments is not untypical for members of the congregation. Through most of the 1970s, Cardinal Heenan of Britain and Cardinal Conway of Ireland attended meetings of the congregation when appointments were being considered for their countries. Cardinal Heenan said that when an appointment to Upper Volta was being considered, he would "keep silence, read my papers, write my letters," but when an English bishop was being appointed, "I made clear whom we [considered] the best man."[48]

But since most of the noncurial members of the congregation usually do not attend, the decisions of the congregation are heavily influenced by the sixteen curial cardinals.

Two weeks prior to the meeting, members are given the agenda, which usually consists of the names of four or five dioceses whose appointments will be up for consideration. Until recently, only those attending the meeting were given the pro-nuncio's report. A member of the congregation from outside of Rome did not receive the report until he arrived in Rome just before the meeting. Cardinal O'Connor, however, now receives copies of all the documents in New York. If he cannot attend the meeting, he phones or mails in his vote.

At the meetings (normally on Thursdays) of the congregation in the Vatican Apostolic Palace, usually about fifteen cardinals attend, together with the secretary and undersecretary of the congregation but no other staff members. The cardinal ponente gives his report and the members of the congregation discuss the appointment under the chairmanship of the prefect, Cardinal Gantin. The language used is Italian.

Cardinal O'Connor says that he is "tremendously impressed by the objectivity, sensitivity, and concern demonstrated by the bishops on the congregation. They are deeply concerned that the world get the best possible bishops."

But some people believe that a candidate who has studied in Rome has an advantage with the congregation. Thirty-seven percent of the U.S. bishops and half of the archbishops have, in fact, studied in Rome.[49] As early as 1880, a "Roman education was seen as guaranteeing loyalty to Rome."[50] Many believe this is still true. "Some on the congregation—those very Roman—would see that as a plus factor," explains one Vatican observer.

They imbibed some of the Roman culture and tradition, and they were exposed to the universal church because of spending two, three, four, or six years in Rome. Other members didn't give it a second thought where a man studied, just that he had some theological depth as well as canonical knowledge and was orthodox and adhered to the discipline of the church, as this pope considers those two elements extremely important in the appointment of bishops.

Another observer agreed, "If they get somebody who studied in Rome, then they can say that at least he should know what he is supposed to do." Archbishop Jadot says that, while he was apostolic delegate, "no candidate was ever preferred over another simply because he studied in Rome. The fact that he had further studies would be important. I never saw a candidate preferred because he studied in Rome rather than at Catholic University" in Washington. But one study indicates some statistical evidence that "elite training [in Rome] is more important than advanced degrees in helping a candidate become a bishop."[51]

After the members of the congregation discuss the appointment, they vote. Very often (some estimate 80 to 90 percent of the time) they follow the recommendation of the pro-nuncio. This would especially be true if his views coincided with those of the local hierarchy. Cardinal John J. Wright, before his death in 1979, complained, "Now it's reached the point where everybody falls over backwards to meet the wishes of the local church. People like myself with wider experience are ignored."[52] But sometimes the congregation recommends the pro-nuncio's second or third choice. And sometimes it rejects the ternus altogether and tells him to present a new one. "Yes, some are sent back," said a Vatican official. "This reflects the Pope's concern about the choices."[53]

There has been much speculation that when Archbishop Jadot was apostolic delegate from 1973 to 1980 most of his recommendations were approved at the beginning of his term but that toward the end more of them were rejected. "Jadot was very high when Paul was pope," commented one expert on the

American hierarchy, "but he went down under John Paul." "Some in Rome," reported an official, "thought that some of the bishops appointed during his years in Washington were not completely faithful to the teaching of the church. They spoke poorly of him because they thought some of the appointments, some of those who are under heat today—Hunthausen and Gerety—were considered to be Jadot's mistakes."

An American observer noted that "in 1980 when the president of the Secretariat for Non-Christians died of a heart attack, Archbishop Jadot was appointed to replace him in a disgraceful haste in order to get Jadot out of the United States." A Vatican official, however, categorically denied this. "It is not true that Jadot was removed," he said. "He asked to leave for reasons of health."

Whatever the case, once he got to Rome, Archbishop Jadot says he was not consulted concerning appointments to the U.S. hierarchy. This reluctance of the Vatican to use an obvious source of information supports the view that he was out of favor in Rome. "I was disappointed that his expertise on the church in the United States was never drawn upon because with many he had lost favor," said one official. "He was a very controversial figure those final years. There were even many Americans in Rome who had no use for him."

The Pope

The final step in the appointment process is taken when the prefect presents the pro-nuncio's, the congregation's, and his own recommendations to the pope at a Saturday audience. The staff prepares a three- to five-page memo (*Foglio d'Udienza*) on the appointment, which the prefect takes with his recommendation to the pope in a private audience. The prefect summarizes the discussions of the congregation and reports any dissenting opinions and votes. "Ninety-five percent of the time, the pope makes his decision on the spot after the prefect explains the vacancy and informs the pope of the various options and what the recommendation of the pro-nuncio is and what the congregation's is," explains an official. "Maybe 5 percent of the time he would say, 'Let's wait a week' or 'Let me read all the documentation; let me consult some other advisers.' "

The pope can play an active role at this point, especially if he knows the candidates, as might be the case with bishops being put forward for promotions. Certainly Pope John Paul II would play an active role in appointments in the Polish church, as Pope Paul VI did in the Italian hierarchy. An official who had been in the Vatican since 1977 reports John Paul "takes a deep and personal interest in the appointment of bishops, especially to the larger sees. It is a major theme on his agenda."[54] His travels have given him personal knowledge of some dioceses and their needs. In addition, Archbishop Laghi meets more frequently with the pope, and there is more intense consultation about bishops.[55]

In the first ten years of John Paul's reign, approximately 1,200 new bishops were appointed, which averages 10 bishops a month. With much to do as pope and only a limited amount of time, he must depend on the congregation for most of these appointments. This is especially true since he travels so much. Cardinal O'Connor reports that the "overwhelming percentage of the congregation's recommendations are accepted by the pope." If the pope consistently did not like the nominees, he would eventually have to replace the people on the congregation.

The pope would also play an important role if his advisers disagreed with one another. Thus if the prefect and the congregation or the congregation and the pro-nuncio were not in agreement, the pope would have to choose whom he would follow. Similarly, if an American prelate with access to the pope made his views known, this could have an impact. Usually in such cases, the pope will ask for more study. Other times he will just decide.

More important, perhaps, is the general orientation and direction that the pope gives to the congregation, the pro-nuncio, and the bishops. Archbishop Jadot, for example, was told by Paul VI and by Cardinal Baggio to appoint more pastoral bishops in the United States, which had a reputation for bishops who were only managers. Vatican spokesman Navarro-Valls says that Pope John Paul II seeks "one element above all—a solid, intellectual knowledge of theology."[56] In his address to the American bishops visiting Rome in 1983, the pope stressed unity and fidelity to the magisterium. He said that the bishops should look for "priests who have already proven themselves as *teachers of the faith as it is proclaimed by the Magisterium of the church*, and, who, in the words of St. Paul's pastoral advice to Titus, 'hold fast to the authentic message.' "

He told the bishops,

It is important for the episcopal candidate, as for the bishop himself, to be *a sign of the unity of the universal church*. . . . Never is the unity of the local church stronger and more secure, never is the ministry of the local bishop more effective than when the local church under the pastoral leadership of the local bishop proclaims in word and deed the universal faith, when it is open in charity to all the needs of the universal church and when it embraces faithfully the church's universal discipline.[57]

Sometimes the pope's appointments are not popular. While visiting Holland in 1985, Pope John Paul II, in an unusual move, publicly defended his appointments there:

The recent appointments of bishops have deeply offended some of you who are wondering about the reasons for these tensions.

I should like to say in all sincerity that the Pope attempts to understand the life of the local church in the appointment of every bishop. He gathers information and takes advice in accordance with ecclesiastical law and custom. You will understand that opinions are sometimes divided. In the last analysis, the Pope has to take the decision. (Must he explain his choice? Discretion does not permit him to do so.)

Believe me, brothers and sisters, this suffering on account of the church grieves me. But be convinced that I have truly listened, considered carefully, and prayed. And I appointed the person whom I thought before God the most suitable for this office.[58]

John Paul's appointments have tended to be older than previous appointments. The average age of the world's bishops has increased under his pontificate from about fifty-nine in 1978 to nearly sixty-four in 1988. Another change is the increased number of religious-order bishops. More than one-fourth of his bishops are religious priests.[59]

Notification and Consent

After the pope makes his decision, the congregation notifies the pro-nuncio, who then approaches the nominee and asks if he will accept the appointment. The entire process takes four to eight months from the time a vacancy occurs until the appointment is announced.

Usually the pro-nuncio telephones the candidate or his bishop. Archbishop May received the call from Archbishop Jadot while he was shaving. His successor in Mobile, Archbishop Oscar Lipscomb, received a letter because Jadot did not know his private number. If he was willing to accept the post, he was supposed to telegraph a coded message to Washington: "Diocesan report on its way." Interestingly, in such cases the letter from the pro-nuncio does not tell the nominee the code for saying no. They presuppose he will say yes. In fact, the nominee can refuse the appointment, and about one out of twenty do. The refusing candidate usually says, "After having consulted with my spiritual father, I respectfully decline." Sometimes they can be persuaded to accept the appointment, but often there is a health problem that people were not aware of.

The extent of the secrecy involved in the process is evident in that some of appointees are honestly surprised when they are approached. On the other hand, there was wide speculation concerning the appointments to Chicago, Los Angeles, and Philadelphia with Bernardin, Mahony, and Bevilacqua mentioned in the press for those sees. If the candidate does accept,

Rome is notified and a date is set for the announcement, usually a Tuesday.

In the meantime, the nominee cannot tell anybody. Archbishop Lipscomb did not even tell his family ahead of time. On the night before the announcement, without explanation he asked his sister to gather the family at 6:45 A.M. in his mother's hospital room since the announcement would be made at 7 A.M. Mobile time. His sister's response to his request was quite natural considering the early hour: "[Expletive deleted], that is the most ridiculous thing I ever heard in my life."

Next morning when he told them that he was going to be the archbishop of Mobile, he recalls:

> For what seemed like an eternity, no one spoke. What could they say? But my mom finally gave me the first familial word of affirmation and congratulations, flat on her back in the hospital bed, she looked at me and held out her arms and said, "Well, God help us all."

This was a slightly more positive response than the mother who told her son, "It's too bad you weren't made a bishop when it still counted."

Conclusion

A number of things become clear from a description of the process by which a bishop is appointed. The pro-nuncio, as long as he maintains the confidence of the Vatican, is the key figure in the process. For diocesan bishops, he draws up the ternus, and for auxiliaries, he can influence or veto the ternus drawn up by a diocesan bishop. For example, "It did not take long for the American bishops to catch on that Jadot was looking for pastoral people as bishops," said Monsignor Ellis. "They would take people out of the chancery or academic work and make them pastors to get pastoral experience." But once the pro-nuncio loses the confidence of the Vatican, he will soon be removed.

In addition to his role in developing the ternus, the pro-nuncio is very influential through his report, which accompanies the ternus. This report is in Italian, the working language of the Congregation for Bishops. While he does send other documents to the congregation, which can be examined by members of the congregation and its staff who read English, his report is the primary document. In 1973, Archbishop Jadot was asked to translate all the English documents into Italian, but he refused because of the immensity of the task. In the 1950s the documents were all translated into Latin.

Although the pro-nuncio plays a key role in the selection of bishops, the American bishops are also very important. First, by nominating priests in province meetings, they provide the pool of candidates from which bishops are selected. Second, by drawing up the ternus for their auxiliaries, diocesan bishops have a tremendous impact on the American hierarchy. Three-fourths of all the U.S. bishops received their first appointments as auxiliaries, including 57 percent of the diocesan bishops. They also can influence the pro-nuncio's ternus with their suggestions.

A third important actor in the process is the retiring diocesan bishop or, in his absence, the administrator of the diocese. He determines how wide and thorough will be the consultations on the needs of the diocese and the qualities desired in the next diocesan bishop. He recommends to the pro-nuncio the names of people who should be consulted about the diocese and the appointment. It is said that before his own death Cardinal Spellman had requested Cooke's appointment by the Holy See.[60] Likewise, there is some suspicion that Cardinal Timothy Manning of Los Angeles supported the candidacy of Roger Mahony as his successor. As a priest, Mahony had been an adviser to Manning, who was bishop of Fresno prior to his promotion to Los Angeles.

A fourth set of actors is the priests and others who fill out the questionnaires on the individual candidates. These are primarily diocesan officials or members of committees listed in *The Official Catholic Directory*. With their answers they can make or break a candidate.

Fifth is the role of the Congregation for Bishops and its prefect. Their role appears to be primarily a check on the pronuncio. If he loses their confidence, they get him replaced. In addition, members with personal knowledge of the United States, such as Cardinal Baum, can be influential.

The American members of the congregation residing in the United States could be very influential if they attended meetings. Until Cardinal O'Connor was appointed, their attendance was rare. By making the effort to attend the meetings and to learn Italian, Cardinal O'Connor is becoming a key figure in the appointment of bishops in the United States. It is too early to tell if he is the new kingmaker, but the evidence points in that direction.

Finally, there is the all-important role of the pope. He is the one who can ultimately appoint as bishop any priest he wants. While he cannot give his undivided attention to each appointment throughout the world, he sets the tone and the criteria by which candidates are nominated and evaluated. He works primarily through the Congregation for Bishops and the pronuncio, who are well aware of his wishes. If he does not like what they are doing, he can replace them.

The selection process is not a democratic process but an institutional process that attempts through wide consultation to find a candidate who will be a pastoral bishop, sincerely concerned about the good of the people in his diocese, who is also loyal to Rome. On paper it appears to be an autocratic process. What makes it work as well as it does is the good faith of the participants, who are concerned for the good of the church. In addition, they recognize the problems that result from imposing on a diocese a bishop who is at odds with his priests and people or who is inadequate to their needs.

Besides good will on the part of the participants, the process works because of the checks and balances provided by people at various levels within the system. For example, the administrator of a diocese and a small clique of chancery officials might conceivably push a candidate who the pro-nuncio finds through his investigation is not widely supported. Or if the pro-nuncio begins appointing bishops out of touch with the needs of the American church, the American bishops, especially the archbishops and cardinals, can appeal to the Congregation for Bishops or even the pope, as they did in the case of the apostolic delegate Archbishop Raimondi. And while the power of Rome appears absolute, it is almost totally dependent upon information that is sent to it by the pro-nuncio and the American church.

Improvements?

"Few issues are of more vital concern to the priests than the manner in which bishops are chosen," reports the NCCB Ad Hoc Committee for Priestly Life and Ministry.[61] Numerous criticisms have been directed at the appointment process, especially in 1972 when "new" Vatican norms were published.[62] The president of the Canon Law Society of America wrote:

A great deal of concern and criticism about these directives was expressed at the time, noting particularly that the ecclesiology implied in the norms seemed to be pre-conciliar, but, more importantly, that the consultation process, although somewhat more liberal, was still too restrictive, and did not seem to reflect the awakening consciousness of the responsible People of God in the Church.[63]

Some want to strengthen the role of the American bishops in the process, while others would give a larger voice to the clergy and laity. Canon lawyer Ladislas M. Orsy, S.J., writes in favor of strengthening the role of the bishops.

The bishops are permitted to act collegially only during the first and abstract part of the selection process, while drafting a list of candidates. When it comes to finding the right person for a determined see, no collegial action is asked for. Each bishop is expected to submit names without the benefit of the wisdom of his brethren. And the delegate alone must take the awesome responsibility of composing the terna in preparation of the final choice by the Holy See.[64]

Critics note that, in the nineteenth-century American church, there was no apostolic delegate and the bishops of a province met to recommend the ternus for a diocesan bishop to the Vatican. Father Orsy believes that "if a see is vacant, the bishops of the province could certainly gather and deliberate in virtue of their communion about a worthy successor. No one can forbid them to do so and to send their recommendations directly to the Holy See. Bishops have rights given them by their consecration that no decree can take away."[65] Similarly, the NCCB Committee on the Selection of Bishops might meet to make recommendations when an archdiocese is vacant.

The Canon Law Society of America recommended that each diocese have a committee for the selection of candidates for the office of bishop that would receive nominations from individuals and groups.[66] One member of the eleven-member committee would be appointed by the bishop, the rest would be elected by the diocesan pastoral council—two each from diocesan priests, religious women, religious men, laywomen, and laymen.

After considering the nominees and the state of the diocese, the committee would submit its report and a list of nominees to the priests' council. The council would review the report (provide additional comments) and narrow the committee's list to not more than ten names. The report and the names would be given to the diocesan bishop who would make his own inquiry concerning the merits of the candidates proposed. At the spring meeting of the bishops in each region of the NCCB, the proposed candidates would be considered and voted on by the bishops. The results would be forwarded to the NCCB Committee on the Selection of Bishops, which would finalize the list of candidates for a particular office of bishop. In filling a particular office, the Holy See would limit itself to the three to five names submitted by the NCCB Committee on the Selection of Bishops.

Other critics would like to see group consultations about candidates so that a consensus could develop.[67] Some want the bishop directly elected by the priests, the priests' council, or a body composed of priests and laity in the diocese.[68] Such elections would be subject to confirmation and acceptance by the pope. There is wide support among priests for the election of bishops, but not among bishops. The election of the bishop by the priests of the diocese is supported by 70 percent of the diocesan priests and only 24 percent of bishops. Election of the bishop by the priests, religious, and laity of the diocese is desired by 65 percent of the priests and 24 percent of the bishops.[69]

Vatican officials and most bishops oppose making the process more democratic and public. The more democratic and open it becomes, the more "political" it will be. Pressure groups and factions will organize and thus divide a diocese. Democracy fosters campaigns and party politics. They note that those who want more democracy in the church are the same people who are not terribly happy with the candidates democracy has produced in the United States. They also argue that such a "democratic" system would be subject to pressure from undemocratic governments where the church's source of independence is Rome's control over episcopal appointments. Critics respond that the process is already political but the choice is determined by cliques influential in Rome. Nor has the current process kept totalitarian governments from interfering in appointments.

Many involved in the process believe that a major flaw in the operation of the current procedures is the fact the priests do not take it seriously. Priests can have an impact through recommending names to the bishops and the pro-nuncio and by thoughtfully filling out the questionnaires on the candidates. Lay participants are handicapped by their limited knowledge of possible candidates. They can, however, have an impact by describing the needs of the diocese and the kind of bishop they would like. The bishop must ultimately serve their spiritual needs and be their pastoral leader. The National Federation of Priests' Councils prepared materials on the selection of bishops to be used by priests' councils when their dioceses are in need of a bishop.[70]

Any selection process must ultimately be judged by the people it advances. In chapter 3 we will look at the archbishops who have reached the top of the ecclesial ladder in the United States. But first we will examine the archdioceses that they must govern.

2. The Ecclesial Environment

> Every local church, like every individual human personality, is very distinctive and very different.
>
> ————ARCHBISHOP JOHN R. QUINN

> A diocesan bishop . . . possesses all the ordinary, proper and immediate power which is required for the exercise of his pastoral office except for those cases . . . [reserved] to the supreme authority of the church or to some other ecclesiastical authority.
>
> ————Canon 381

After an archbishop is installed, he is responsible for his archdiocese. Archbishops are frequently thought to be absolute monarchs who can do whatever they want. In some areas, the archbishop's power is nearly absolute, but in other areas his power is limited. He is not exempt from moral, civil, or canon laws. His power is also limited by the financial and personnel resources he has available and by the social and ecclesial environment in which he operates.[1] Finally, he is limited by the traditions and expectations of the priests and people of his archdiocese. This chapter will examine the normative, canonical, demographic, and historical environment that an archbishop steps into when he takes over his archdiocese.[2]

Voluntary Membership

While the hierarchical structure of the church gives the appearance of coercive power, the pope can no longer send the Swiss Guard into a diocese to restore order. Nor do bishops have this option, although they can call on the civil authority if civil laws are broken through trespassing, breach of contract, theft, etc. Ultimately, church authority rests on persuasion. "The ultimate expression of effective social control" in a religious organization, as in most organizations, explains Joseph Fichter, S.J., "must necessarily be the self-control of the subject."[3]

But as in any voluntary organization, individual Catholics have the ultimate freedom to disobey, to withhold financial support, or simply to walk away. But while this freedom may act as a deterrent to some abuses of power, few Catholics today want to leave the church even when they disagree with its leadership. Likewise, while priests can and do leave the ministry after conflicts with authority, a priest's professional identity is inexorably tied to his continuing participation in the church.[4] Participation requires some degree of conformity, since the bishop decides who can continue to minister in his diocese. But ignoring regulations is also possible. For example, over half the priests under forty-six in 1969 had said Mass without proper vestments.[5] Most bishops are not going to kick a priest out except in extreme instances.

Ecclesiological Beliefs

As a normative organization, the governance of the Catholic church is strongly influenced by the beliefs, values, and opinions of its members and leadership about what is the proper exercise of authority and power. Church theology functions in a way similar to ideology in secular society. Where there is a consensus on goals, values, and norms, they are more important in setting the boundaries to appropriate behavior than law or coercion.[6] Where there is disagreement, clashes can occur. Where there is uncertainty, there will be confusion.

Although there are numerous theological disputes in the Catholic church, its members share many beliefs, a common liturgy and sacramental system, and the same Scriptures. For the current generation, the experience and documents of the Second Vatican Council are also normative. Disagreements can occur in interpreting these documents, but they provide the common text to which everyone appeals. The post-Vatican II emphasis on service, collegiality, the principle of subsidiarity, and the pastoral role of bishops has influenced episcopal behavior and the expectations of church members. For example, collegiality, which strictly speaking refers to bishops working together with the pope, has been stretched to include collegial cooperation among bishops, priests, and people working together. The principle of subsidiarity states that activities should take place at the lowest level possible in society or the church. Both collegiality and the principle of subsidiarity would argue against authoritarian and overly centralizing behavior. Even a single book, like *Models of the Church*,[7] can have an impact on ecclesiological views and behavior.

In fact, the generally positive attitude of Catholics toward the church and its leaders makes the work of bishops easier. Two out of three Catholics express either "a great deal" or "a lot" of confidence in the church, a higher percentage than for any other institution.[8] And they believe, by 61 to 36 percent, that "leadership in the church should be restricted to bishops, priests and deacons."[9] Interestingly, only 28 percent of the diocesan priests agreed with this highly clerical notion. This would seem to indicate the ability of theology to counter self-interest.

In diocesan governance, the bishop must especially deal with the views of priests, the cadre working most closely with him. While public opinion is not normative in the church, presbyteral attitudes toward the bishop's role can affect what he can and cannot do. In fact, Catholic priests are very supportive of episcopal government. In 1969, Rev. Andrew Greeley found 61 percent of the priests considered themselves members of the "bishop's team" and felt they were doing priestly work when "doing a job that has the local bishop's approval."[10] Nine out of ten priests thought that the bishop should have a very great or a great deal of influence in determining policies and actions in the diocese.[11] "Even the younger priests cast a majority vote for a strong bishop," reports Father Greeley.[12] Such views reflect a wide acceptance by priests and laity of episcopal authority.[13]

Father Greeley notes, however, that for 29 percent of clergy, the way church authority is exercised is a great problem for them. And 35 percent believed that the way church authority is exercised is a great problem to most priests.[14] They wanted a decentralization of power and decision-making influence. They supported greater power for priests' senates, auxiliary bishops, pastors, and the laity. "One must conclude that priests view ecclesiastical power as expandable rather than a fixed pie—giving someone a larger piece does not mean that others get smaller pieces."[15]

These views have had an impact on diocesan governance and how bishops exercise their power. The creation and use of consultative bodies has been in response to the desires of priests for more participation. By 1985, the percent of priests saying the way church authority is exercised is a great problem for them, decreased to 22 percent. And only 9 percent of the diocesan priests said their relationship with their bishop is a problem for them.[16]

There are undoubtedly many reasons for the decline in dissatisfaction among priests. The most dissatisfied priests have left the ministry, and young priests today appear more satisfied. The change from an authoritarian to a more pastoral episcopal style by most bishops has also helped. Consultative structures have also diffused dissatisfaction. But whatever the causes, the desire for strong bishops means that bishops can exercise leadership especially if they have a consultative style that respects the priests' council or senate. On the other hand, if priests and laity become alienated, for example by the appointment of an authoritarian bishop, the bishop will find it difficult to lead his people.

Canon Law[17]

Canon law provides the legal environment within which an archbishop must work. It both gives and limits his power. Every seminarian studies canon law. About a third of the archbishops have also done graduate work in canon law. Experience as a diocesan bishop (or as a chancery official prior to his appointment as bishop) also gives an archbishop some knowledge of the canon law. In addition, he would normally have a priest on his staff with a degree in canon law.

On the positive side, the code of canon law describes the bishops[18] as "teachers of doctrine, priests of sacred worship and ministers of governance."[19] The bishops are "the successors of the apostles by divine institution" and the vicars of Christ, not merely vicars or agents of the pope. But they must exercise "the functions of teaching and ruling . . . only when they are in hierarchical communion with the head of the college [of bishops] and its members."[20]

In short,

a diocesan bishop in the diocese committed to him possesses all the ordinary, proper and immediate power which is required for the exercise of his pastoral office except for those cases which the law or a decree of the Supreme Pontiff reserves to the supreme authority of the church or to some other ecclesiastical authority.[21]

In order to understand the limits of episcopal power, it is necessary to examine some of "those cases" that are reserved to higher authority. In fact, many cases are reserved to the pope because of Vatican concern for unity. A bishop cannot do many things even if he wants to. He cannot rewrite liturgical texts or ceremonies, ordain women or married men, or consecrate a bishop without Vatican approval. Where the code is most detailed, it articulates the limits of episcopal power. Many important decisions over doctrinal, moral, and liturgical issues are reserved to higher authority: to the pope or to the national conference of bishops. Commentators note an ongoing tension in the constitutional life of the church: the bishop is to enjoy increased decisional discretion in the daily exercise of his office; yet, he is still situated within a hierarchical structure, which stretches both above him and below him. The Pope's prerogatives must be safeguarded if he is to exercise properly his role of fostering the unity of all the churches.[22]

In governing his diocese, however, the bishop has a great deal of discretion. There is, in fact, no true separation of powers as is common in civil society.[23] The diocesan bishop is the chief legislator, executive, and judge in his diocese. The restrictions on his local authority are primarily procedural checks on possible fiscal or pastoral abuses.

On the legislative side, he is the legislative authority for the people in his archdiocese, but he may not issue legislation contrary to laws passed by a higher authority, namely the pope or the national conference of bishops. He is instructed to have a priests' council (about half of whom are to be elected members),[24] and he can have a pastoral council including members of the laity if he wants one.[25] He does not have to follow the recommendations of these councils, but he must consult the priests' council on the modification of parishes (their erection, division, or suppression), on the calling of a diocesan synod, and on the imposition of a tax to meet diocesan needs. More will be said about these bodies in chapter 3.

The bishop must also have a college of consultors (six to twelve priests from the priests' council with five-year terms)[26] and a finance council (five-year terms, and must include at least three persons "skilled in financial affairs as well as in civil law").[27] The college of consultors and the finance council must give their consent for the alienation of church property and "acts of extraordinary administration."[28] This will be explained more fully in chapter 5.

As chief executive, the bishop has wide powers over policy, personnel, and finances in the diocese. He establishes policies, creates programs, and opens offices. He appoints and can fire all diocesan administrative officials. He "must see to it that all matters which concern the administration of the entire diocese are duly coordinated and arranged. . . ."[29]

He must appoint a priest or an auxiliary bishop as vicar general who can have wide powers as his alter ego in pastoral and administrative affairs.[30] But the bishop can limit the vicar's authority by reserving as many matters as he wants to himself.[31] In Boston, Chicago, Los Angeles (under Manning), and New York, the vicars general were very powerful, but in some smaller archdioceses, they function hardly at all. The bishop can also appoint episcopal vicars with geographic or functional responsibilities.[32] Here again they only have as much power as he gives them. In large archdioceses, the geographical vicars are often auxiliary bishops. The use of functional vicars for administration is declining because lay people cannot be vicars. As a result, it is more common for these administrators to be called delegates, secretaries, or directors who have power delegated to them by the bishop.

The bishop must appoint a chancellor, who no longer has to be a priest.[33] The role of chancellor varies greatly among the archdioceses. According to canon law, the chancellor is responsible for taking care of the archives and for preparing certain canonical documents. In New York and Atlanta, he has traditionally been the chief financial officer. In Philadelphia and Los Angeles, he has been in charge of priest personnel. In some archdioceses, he is the canonical adviser to the archbishop.

In many places the chancellor acted as the chief of staff. The 1983 code of canon law, however, created a new, optional diocesan officer, the moderator of the curia, who must be a priest and is normally also the vicar general. The moderator, under the bishop, is to "coordinate the exercise of administrative responsibilities and to see to it that the other members of the curia duly fulfill the office entrusted to them."[34] As a result, if other persons are the vicar general, moderator of the curia, priests' personnel director, and finance officer, the chancellor's role is quite limited unless the bishop gives him special responsibilities.

Another official required under the new code of canon law is the finance officer.[35] He is the only administrator who cannot be removed by the bishop during his five-year term except for serious reason and after consulting with his college of consultors and finance council. More will be said about the financial administration of archdioceses in chapter 5.

As chief executive, the bishop appoints not only chancery officials but also pastors. Archdiocesan procedures dealing with the appointment and removal of pastors will be dealt with in detail in chapter 6.

Finally, there is the role of the bishop as judge. The diocesan tribunal exercises judicial functions under the bishop, but this court mostly deals with the annulment of marriages. This is a complex canonical area that the bishop usually leaves to the tribunal and its canon lawyers. The bishop's main impact in this area is making sure that sufficient numbers of canon lawyers are trained to handle the tribunal's case load. In addition, adequate office equipment and secretaries are necessary. The archdioceses of Atlanta and Detroit, for example, have developed sophisticated computerized systems that have made their tribunals more productive.

Many bishops have also set up due process or grievance panels that review the decisions of church officials in a quasi-judicial fashion.

A bishop is very powerful in his diocese, but there are limits to his power. He has wide latitude in organizing his diocesan administration and in exercising his responsibilities. He has almost complete discretion to appoint various officials and officers and to delegate to them as little or as much authority as he pleases. Even auxiliary bishops have practically no authority other than what he gives them. While the bishop is required to have certain consultative bodies, he does not usually have to listen to them. Since he determines the membership of those bodies whose consent is required for certain actions (finance committee and consultors), he can control them by appointing people who will say yes to him.

Most archbishops made little reference to canon law when I interviewed them. Canon law does not loom large in their lives, rather it is taken for granted as part of the ecclesial environment. When asked how canon law affects their lives, most began talking about their tribunal. Once appointed, the American archbishops do not spend their time studying canon law, they spend it studying their archdioceses.

The Archdiocese

Sometimes a new archbishop is familiar with the archdiocese because of past service there as a priest or an auxiliary bishop. Archbishop Oscar Lipscomb recalls when he was appointed archbishop of Mobile.

> I came into my own home town. I pretty well knew what was going on. Even more importantly, I told them at my ordination, "I know what is not going on." [I know] what can happen, where all the bodies are buried, and maybe where a few ought to be buried.

But usually—84 percent of the time—the archbishop comes from outside the archdiocese.[36] The new archbishop will have to spend time getting to know his archdiocese. Archbishop John F. Whealon, who came to Erie and to Hartford from other dioceses, says that at first he was "slow in making judgments" because he did not know the diocese.

If all archdioceses were identical in makeup, the new archbishop would find few surprises when he arrived on the scene. The contrary, however, is the case. Archdioceses are very different from one another. "Every local church, like every individual human personality, is very distinctive and very different," explains John R. Quinn, who has been archbishop of both Oklahoma City and San Francisco. "Each has its own identity."

Archdioceses vary in geographical size, in density of population, in percentage of Catholics, and in many other ways.[37] This external political, social, and economic environment of an archdiocese has an impact on archdiocesan government and on how the archbishop operates. Often what an archbishop does is in response to what he perceives to be the needs of his archdiocese.

Boundaries

Diocesan boundaries for the most part follow political boundaries. A diocese may contain a number of cities and counties, but rarely is a political jurisdiction split between two dioceses. The overlapping of civic and ecclesial boundaries makes church-government relations simpler. Experience has taught the church the value of presenting to government officials a united front, which is easier to achieve when only one bishop is in a jurisdiction. The danger of having two bishops in one civil jurisdiction was seen in the city of New York, where two dioceses antedate the unification of Brooklyn and New York cities in the nineteenth century. When New York City added to its contracts a clause dealing with homosexual rights, the church was embarrassingly divided with the bishop of Brooklyn signing the contracts while the archbishop of New York refused.

Following political boundaries does have a negative side effect. Many metropolitan areas, such as Kansas City, New York, and St. Louis, are split between two dioceses because of state and local boundaries. The church experiences the same problems governing such metropolitan areas as do secular governments. Inconsistent policies between the two dioceses cause confusion, and the duplication of programs causes inefficiency. In addition, parishioners might live in one diocese and work in another, with their psychological identity split between the two. If the public media is centered in one diocese, that will also tend to orient people away from their own diocese toward the media center. Archbishop Edward T. O'Meara of Indianapolis notes, "It is very difficult for people [in southern Indiana] who live with their whole lives oriented to Louisville to feel that their particular church is a church that includes Terre Haute, Bloomington, Richmond, and Indianapolis."

Geographical Size

A geographically large archdiocese will obviously be more difficult to govern than a smaller one. Geographic size increases the costs of transportation and communication in any organization.[38] The size of an average American archdiocese is 17,700 sq. mi., more than twice the size of the state of Massachusetts. Archdioceses vary in size from Anchorage (which, with 138,985 sq. mi., covers a fourth of Alaska) to Newark, with only 513 sq. mi. Simply visiting and getting to know the various parishes in a large archdiocese can be very difficult. Archbishop O'Meara of Indianapolis estimates that he puts 40,000 to 45,000 miles on his car every year visiting parishes in his 13,500 sq.- mi. archdiocese. Large size also hinders participation in diocesan pastoral councils. In fact, geographic size is the most common reason given for their demise.[39] On the other hand, the same factors that make the operation of consultative groups difficult also reduce the number of protests in rural dioceses.[40]

In a small archdiocese, such as Newark, San Francisco, or Chicago (all under 1,500 sq. mi.), the archbishop can drive to the most distant parish under his jurisdiction in an hour or so, depending on traffic. In large archdioceses, such as Anchorage, Santa Fe, Oklahoma City, and Denver (all over 39,000 sq. mi.), it could take all day to drive to the most distant parish. The archbishop of Anchorage, Francis T. Hurley, flies his own plane around his archdiocese. But the other archbishops travel by car. Some have chauffeurs so that the archbishop can work while traveling.

Population

The geographically large archdioceses would be impossible to govern if they also had large Catholic populations. In fact, the five archdioceses with the largest areas all have Catholic populations of under 340,000, which is about half the Catholic population of an average archdiocese. They are thus large in size but small in numbers.

The greater the number of Catholics, the more difficult it is for the archbishop to minister directly to his people. Through his surveys, Joseph Fichter, S.J., found that "the bishop in the smaller diocese has a more immediate concern about his parish priests and tends also to meet more frequently with the parishioners."[41] "More than half (57%) of the parishioners in the small dioceses, as compared to less than one fourth (23%) of the others, say that they have personally met their bishop or are on friendly terms with him."[42] Priests in small dioceses were also much more likely to say that the bishop took a personal interest in them. As a result, it is not surprising that smaller dioceses have fewer instances of protests by priests.[43]

On the other hand, large dioceses have certain advantages over small dioceses. Bigness has been shown to have many benefits in other organizations, including "easier, less expensive financing; more numerous, highly trained intellects to attack trouble spots; sustained research; and more accurately tailored and adaptable marketing systems."[44] Likewise, large dioceses usually have a larger pool of talented personnel and bigger bank books than smaller dioceses. Larger dioceses tend to have better organized and more competent chanceries. In Fichter's survey, priests in small dioceses were less likely than priests in large dioceses to rate their diocesan chanceries as efficient.

The average archdiocese has just over 695,000 Catholics, but here again there is a wide diversity. The largest is Los Angeles with 2.7 million Catholics, while the smallest is Anchorage with only 22,928.

The problem of governing dioceses with large numbers of Catholics has led to splitting them into smaller ones. Every archdiocese with over 1 million Catholics (Boston, Chicago, Detroit, Los Angeles, Newark, New York, and Philadelphia) is less than half the area of an average U.S. archdiocese. The largest in this group, Los Angeles, with 8,762 sq. mi., might someday have Santa Barbara and Ventura counties split off as a separate diocese. This would leave Los Angeles County for the archdiocese of Los Angeles. Working against such a split is the fact that the archdiocesan seminary is in Ventura County. Few archbishops want to lose their seminary if their diocese is split. In addition, an archbishop would be reluctant to split off a rich suburban county if it left him with only a poor inner-city area that was not financially viable.

Splitting a diocese makes it more manageable for the bishop. Thus, Archbishop Quinn of San Francisco reduced his administrative burden by pushing for the creation of a new diocese in San Jose even though San Jose was not demanding independence. The archdiocese of Los Angeles also spun off San Bernardino and Orange counties under Cardinal Timothy Manning. If a large diocese cannot be split, the bishop will often divide it into regional areas in order to aid governance.

Most archdioceses fall into one of three categories depending on the density of their Catholic population. First, the most highly concentrated archdioceses (Boston, Chicago, Detroit, Hartford, Los Angeles, Newark, New York, Philadelphia, and San Francisco) have 300 or more Catholics per square mile. They usually contain a very large metropolitan area consisting of a central city and suburbs. Where an archdiocese is densely populated and centered on one city, it often has a large, centralized chancery. Most also have auxiliary bishops acting as regional vicars. In the early 1970s, John Seidler found that the more urban a diocese, the more progressive the bishop regarding changes in the church. On the other hand, urban dioceses were also more likely to have priests protesting actions of their bishop.[45]

Some of these large archdioceses, like Hartford, have more than one urban center. Possibilities then arise for decentralizing the chancery staff, for example by having local offices of education and Catholic Charities. Los Angeles is attempting this under Archbishop Roger Mahony. But most archbishops fear such a strategy endangers the unity of the archdiocese.

A second category contains archdioceses with medium density, 90 to 190 Catholics per square mile. These (Baltimore, Miami, Milwaukee, New Orleans, St. Louis, St. Paul, and Washington) usually have a large metropolitan area, suburbs, and a rural area. These archdioceses also frequently have strong centralized chanceries and auxiliaries acting as regional vicars.

A third category contains archdioceses with low population density, 20 or fewer Catholics per square mile. They (Anchorage, Atlanta, Denver, Indianapolis, Kansas City, Louisville, Oklahoma City, Omaha, Portland, and San Antonio) usually have a metropolitan center and a large rural area with small towns. Here the chanceries tend to be smaller. Often there is no auxiliary, or only one. If there is an auxiliary, using him as vicar for the rural areas can cause the rural parishes to feel abandoned by the archbishop. Visiting rural parishes can mean tens of thousands of miles of traveling each year by the archbishop. Providing clergy for these small towns can also be difficult, and in these dioceses lay administrators of parishes are more common. Creating a representative pastoral council can also be difficult in these largely rural archdioceses. In the archdiocese of Omaha, for example, two-thirds of the Catholics live in the metropolitan area of the city of Omaha, but two-thirds of the parishes are outside this area.[46]

Some archdioceses (Cincinnati, Dubuque, Mobile, Santa Fe, and Seattle) have more than one metropolitan center within a mostly rural area. This encourages the decentralization of some chancery offices, such as Catholic Charities and the school office. If these centers were more populous, they would be made separate dioceses. Maintaining a sense of unity in such an archdiocese can sometimes be difficult. On the other hand, in an archdiocese like Mobile, with a small number of Catholics (66,548) concentrated in two cities, the archbishop can adopt a nonbureaucratic, pastoral style. Archbishop Lipscomb even goes to the Catholic high school football games whenever he is in Mobile. In a more populous archdiocese this would be impossible.

Religious, Ethnic, and Social Character

Not only the size, but the makeup of the population can affect the governance of an archdiocese. As part of the environment, the population can be characterized as hostile or benign,[47] homogeneous or heterogeneous, stable or rapidly shifting, unified or segmented.[48] A united, homogeneous Catholic population in a stable community is quite different from a divided, heterogeneous population with a Catholic minority in a rapidly changing community.

The activities of an archdiocese will be affected, for example, by whether it is growing or declining in population. The Catholic population of Miami skyrocketed practically overnight as a result of Cuban and Haitian refugees. More typically, there has been population growth in the South and Southwest, while parts of the Northeast have declined. Atlanta Archbishop Thomas A. Donnellan reported,

We are a growing diocese, so it has been necessary to establish about three new parishes every two years. That means a good deal of planning, a good deal of consultation with priests in various areas, and it means an active recruitment of vocations. Those would be primarily the things with which I occupy myself.

But while Atlanta is building new churches, other archdioceses (Baltimore, Chicago, and Detroit) have been consolidating and closing churches, especially inner-city ethnic parishes from which Catholics have moved to the suburbs.

In areas with large numbers of Catholics (Boston, New York, Philadelphia, and San Antonio), the archbishop can play an important role in civic affairs. But in non-Catholic areas (like Atlanta, Mobile, and Oklahoma City), the archbishop's involvement may not be welcomed unless he works closely with leaders of other denominations. Seidler even argues that the religious makeup of the diocese can influence the behavior of the bishop: the higher the percentage of Catholics in the population of the diocesan area, the less humanitarian and egalitarian his style of leadership.[49]

The various Catholic groups within an archdiocese provide both opportunities and challenges for the archbishop. The more heterogeneous the population, the more archdiocesan organizations will be created to deal with the various groups.[50] These groups must be ministered to, but they are also the groups from which come leaders in the church, both lay and clerical.

The ethnic character of an archdiocese, for example, solicits an archdiocesan response with programs and offices. Historically, the church has responded to waves of immigrants (Irish, Italian, German, Polish) with special programs and ethnic parishes. These old ethnics are now loyal, mostly middle-class, Catholics. Today, archdioceses with large Hispanic populations, such as Miami and those in the Northeast and the Southwest, frequently have vicars or offices for the Hispanic apostolate. Sometimes this vicar is an auxiliary bishop who is Hispanic. In San Antonio and Santa Fe the archbishops themselves are Hispanic.

Besides large numbers of Hispanics, Los Angeles and San Francisco also have numerous Asian and Pacific immigrants who require a pastoral response to their language and culture. Anchorage must be sensitive to Native Americans. Inner-city archdioceses are also compelled to respond to black needs, both financial and spiritual. Offices or commissions for other ethnic groups are common in multiethnic archdioceses.

How to deal with these groups and still maintain one community of faith is a concern of archbishops. Archbishop Quinn describes his strategy in San Francisco.

We respond to that in two ways: first by trying to respect and encourage the distinctiveness of each culture and language group, but second by trying to foster unity among the different groups.

When I came here and was asked to appoint a vicar for the Spanish-speaking, I did not do so. While the Spanish-speaking had certain unique claims, I felt it would probably be offensive to the many other groups, like the Filipinos and others, if the Spanish-speaking were singled out.

There is a secretary for ethnic affairs and a coordinator for the different individual groups, like the Filipinos, the Chinese, the blacks, the Spanish-speaking, and so on.

Archdioceses also have programs and offices responding to major occupation groups. Farmers are a special concern in rural archdioceses like Dubuque, Denver, Kansas City, Oklahoma City, and Omaha. The elderly and retired in Miami and the diplomatic communities of Washington and New York require special attention. An archdiocese with a large population of university students, hospital patients, or prisoners must find chaplains to serve them. Recently the church has responded to the AIDS crisis, especially in cities with large homosexual populations such as New York, New Orleans, and San Francisco.

If large numbers of people in the diocese are poor or unemployed, they will not be able to contribute a lot of money to the church. Archbishop Peter Gerety notes, "The problems of the city of Newark brought on problems for the archdiocese." In addition, poor people will often turn to the church for help. Here programs like Catholic Charities become very important. The economic decline of Newark was matched by a growth in Catholic social services.

The political climate can also affect the archdiocese. In St. Paul, Archbishop John Roach explains:

In Minnesota we are politically a liberal group and a very political group. The church is a product of this society in that we tend to be very political. When I say liberal, I am not sure what it means, but we move. Really early under Archbishop Leo Byrne, we developed an urban affairs commission here which was way ahead of its time in addressing the really hot social issues.

Chicago has the most politicized clergy and church. "When you have grown up in Chicago, politics seeps into your blood," explains the executive secretary of the personnel board in Chicago. The church of Mobile is much quieter. "We have never been picketed," reports Archbishop Lipscomb. "If pickets showed up, we would probably invite them in to lunch to hear what they had to say."

Institutional Commitments

When the archbishop arrives in his new archdiocese, he does not start from scratch. Many programs and institutions are already in place with numerous employees, including the priests and religious. Most of the churches, for example, including his cathedral, are already built, although some may need extensive renovations or replacement. These people and structures are both resources and obligations for the new archbishop.

In comparing Oklahoma City and San Francisco, Archbishop Quinn noted that in his first archdiocese there were only two Catholic high schools and a junior college, while in the San Francisco Bay area he found a wealth of Catholic educational institutions. Few Catholic colleges are run by archdioceses; most are run by religious orders. The faculties of these schools can be tapped by an archdiocese as a resource in the continuing education of both priests and laity. They can also be a source of conflict if the archbishop is at odds with their theologians. An archdiocese without these institutions will need to fly in teachers and speakers for workshops and institutes.

Some archdioceses (Chicago, Los Angeles, New York, and Philadelphia) have so many primary and secondary schools that they are bigger than most public school systems in the country. Each will need a sophisticated department of education on the archdiocesan level, and the archbishop will be responsible for their financial viability and their Catholic character. He will have to deal with numerous parents, students, and teachers. Mobile, on the other hand, has only one Catholic high school, and Anchorage has none. More will be said about Catholic schools in chapter 7.

Some archdioceses have large medical facilities. Catholic hospitals in Chicago, Cincinnati, Los Angeles, New York, and Detroit, for example, treat over 1 million patients a year. New Orleans, on the other hand, has only two Catholic hospitals treating 76,000 patients. Concerns about Medicare and Medicaid cuts, medical ethics, malpractice insurance, and hospital finances eventually reach the archbishop if the archdiocese has a number of hospitals.

Other archdioceses may have extensive social service programs in place, such as orphanages, food kitchens, housing for the elderly, nursing homes, counseling services, etc. More will be said about Catholic social services in chapter 7.

All these institutional commitments take work to continue, and they can also be politically difficult to close down. They are both a resource and a liability to the archbishop. He can use them for carrying out his ideas and plans, but he must also work to guarantee their continued existence and effectiveness. His concern would most often be expressed through separate agencies or boards of directors, but ultimately if they are archdiocesan institutions, he must worry about their financial and spiritual welfare.

Personnel

This institutional variety is matched by a variety in personnel. The larger the number of schools, hospitals, and social service agencies, the larger the number of lay and religious employees in an archdiocese. Their talent and dedication is the life blood of the local church. At the same time, someone has to deal with their problems and pay their salaries. A large number of employees calls for a professional personnel office. The lay workers might also have a union that the archbishop must deal with.

Some archdioceses have large numbers of religious women. While many religious communities were founded to do one particular ministry (education or health care), most now have sisters in various ministries. Besides teaching in schools and working in hospitals, many are involved in other parish and archdiocesan ministries. In the past, the archbishops could expect unquestioning service from these women; now the bishops must pay attention to their views and aspirations. Declining numbers of sisters have placed an added financial burden on archdiocesan institutions that in the past depended on the sisters' hard work at low pay. The religious communities themselves are facing financial difficulties because the percentage of elderly and retired sisters is increasing.

Finally, there are the diocesan priests upon whom the archbishop depends to minister in the parishes. Most of the priests who will serve during his reign are already ordained and in the parishes when he arrives. More will be said about these priests and their relations with their archbishop in chapter 5, but, obviously, without them there is no archdiocese. Without their cooperation, the archbishop can accomplish little.

In a large archdiocese, the new archbishop will also find one or more auxiliary bishops already present when he arrives. One of the first things the new archbishop has to figure out is what to do with these auxiliaries. What they do besides confirm is up to the archbishop, although there has been pressure from the pro-nuncio to make them regional or administrative vicars. As a regional vicar, an auxiliary would be responsible for a geographical part of the archdiocese, while as an administrative vicar, he would head a major agency in the chancery. But some older auxiliaries have declined such positions, preferring to be pastors of parishes.

An auxiliary, since he is normally from the archdiocese, can be very helpful to a new archbishop who is from outside the archdiocese. The auxiliary knows the background and history of archdiocesan institutions and personnel. But if the two do not work well together, it can be a very uncomfortable relationship for both of them.

Tradition and Inheritance

Besides institutions and personnel, traditions and history make archdioceses different. Some sees have had episcopal giants (such as cardinals Francis Spellman of New York, Richard Cushing of Boston, John Dearden of Detroit, and Lawrence Shehan of Baltimore) in whose shadow their successors must operate. Every archbishop is compared to his immediate predecessor. The style of his predecessor creates expectations on the part of people in his archdiocese. If they are used to seeing the archbishop at "every dog and cat fight in town," they will be disappointed if the new archbishop does not attend their organizations' dinners, graduations, or award ceremonies. An archbishop like Cardinal Cushing, who was well loved by his people and priests, is a hard act to follow, as Cardinal Humberto Medeiros found in Boston. On the other hand, Cardinal Joseph Bernardin was greeted in Chicago with a sigh of relief by his clergy and people after their negative experiences with Cardinal John Cody.

Cardinal Medeiros was also handicapped by finding a large debt (estimated at $50 million) when he arrived in Boston. Inheriting a $25 million debt from your predecessor, as did Archbishop Gerety in Newark, forces an archbishop to give a lot of attention to finances. On the other hand, finding a financially secure archdiocese, as did Cardinal John O'Connor in New York, Archbishop Mahony in Los Angeles, and Archbishop Anthony Bevilacqua in Philadelphia, can provide the new archbishop with a great deal of flexibility.

Living in the shadow of one's predecessor is even more difficult if he is still alive. With bishops retiring now at seventy-five, a retired archbishop may be living in the archdiocese with the new archbishop. But during my interviews, I never heard of a retired archbishop interfering with the activities of his successor. Much to the surprise of the local priests, strong personalities like archbishops James Byrne of Dubuque, William Cousins of Milwaukee, John Dearden of Detroit, James Mc-

Intyre of Los Angeles, Lawrence Shehan of Baltimore, and Thomas Toolen of Mobile either supported the new archbishop or kept quiet.

In Mobile, the archbishop is even supposed to take care of the weather, a tradition that started in 1927 when Bishop Toolen began a campaign of prayer after two hurricanes had devastated the city. For the next forty-two years while he was bishop, Mobile was not touched. To this day during hurricane warnings, people call the chancery to ask if the archbishop is praying. Toolen's successor, John L. May, made it through nine years until a hurricane hit Mobile. As he left Mobile for St. Louis the following year, he told his successor Archbishop Lipscomb, "Pray hard. You only get one hurricane."

Conclusion

Canon law tells a bishop in detail what he cannot do but tells him little about what he is supposed to do, except in the most general way. The specifics are mostly to protect against abuse of office and disunity in the church. But the variety of dioceses in the United States, to say nothing about the rest of the world, means that canon law was never meant to provide detailed prescription for episcopal action. Nor is size alone the controlling variable in archdiocesan governance. Organizations adapt their structures to handle constraints and contingencies.[51] In the pre-Vatican II church with a stable environment with accepted ministries ("technologies"), organizational structure was simple in spite of the size. A changing social and theological environment and new ministries have required more complex organization. Archbishops react to their environments, and this makes sense both theologically and sociologically.

The institutions, the personnel, traditions, and needs of an archdiocese provide the archbishop with the starting point of his ministry. These provide him with opportunities, but they also are restraints on his actions. He can attempt to guide the institutions and personnel in new directions to achieve his goals. To do this he must organize his archdiocesan administration in a way that fits his personality and style of operating.

3. Style and Structure

Hero, Nero, and Zero.
————Description of three archbishops

The archbishop of New York is foolishly expected to have an opinion on every subject in the world.
————CARDINAL O'CONNOR

Whenever a new archbishop is to be appointed, the priests and laity of the archdiocese are asked to describe the type of person they would like to have as archbishop. Jesus Christ would have a hard time fulfilling the expectations that people have for their archbishop.

The ideal archbishop is a pastorally sensitive administrative genius who can prophetically preach the gospel in a nonthreatening way and provide extensive social services and educational programs at low cost with few bureaucrats. He must govern in a way that is widely consultative, decisive, innovative, collegial, and orthodox, while keeping everyone happy. He must be prophetic in his concern for the poor and raise money from the rich. He must convince his priests that they are the most important people in the archdiocese without alienating religious and laity by being excessively clerical.

He should provide national and international leadership in the church without leaving the archdiocese more than two days a year. He must be a holy priest who understands the real world of budgets and finances. He must be loyal to the Holy Father, but he should not be pushed around by the Vatican. He must give every priest the parish he wants and every parish the priest it wants. And he should be ecumenical but stress his Catholic identity.

Backgrounds

While this may be the ideal, what in fact are the men like who become archbishops? Archbishops, like other bishops, mostly come from working-class backgrounds that are similar to the backgrounds of their priests.[1] Half of their fathers never graduated from high school, only 12 percent graduated from college, and an additional 36 percent graduated from high school. The average archbishop is fifty-three years of age when he is appointed.[2] He can therefore look forward to twenty-two years in office until he reaches retirement age (seventy-five). Appointing older men, such as archbishops John O'Connor to New York and Anthony Bevilacqua to Philadelphia (both were in midsixties when appointed), means that they will be in office fewer years.

Ninety percent of the archbishops were already bishops and 61 percent were diocesan bishops (the head of a diocese) when they were promoted. They had served about six years as a bishop before becoming an archbishop. Being a diocesan bishop or even an auxiliary gives a man some of the experience and skills he would need as archbishop.

Before becoming a bishop, about half of the archbishops had held a top chancery position (vicar general, chancellor, secretary to the bishop). In these positions they would learn much about church administration. But some archbishops (William Borders of Baltimore, John Dearden of Detroit, Patrick Flores of San Antonio, Peter Gerety of Newark, Raymond Hunthausen of Seattle, Francis Hurley of Anchorage, Thomas Kelly of Louisville, Daniel Kucera of Dubuque, William Levada of Portland [OR], John May of St. Louis, Eugene Marino of Atlanta, John O'Connor of New York, Edward O'Meara of Indianapolis, John Roach of St. Paul, Rembert Weakland of Milwaukee, John Whealon of Hartford) had never worked in a chancery before becoming a bishop.

Thirty-five percent of the archbishops (Borders, James Byrne of Dubuque, John Carberry of St. Louis, Dearden, Thomas

Donnellan of Atlanta, Flores, James Hickey of Washington [DC], Hunthausen, John Krol of Philadelphia, Kucera, Levada, Marino, Daniel Pilarczyk of Cincinnati, John Quinn of San Francisco, Roach, Charles Salatka of Oklahoma City, and Whealon) as priests had worked in a seminary, often as rectors. Working as seminary rector provides some administrative experience, especially in working with priests before they are ordained. Since an essential part of a bishop's job is working with priests, this is quite useful.

Finally, the archbishops are better educated than most priests but not much better educated than other bishops. About 30 percent have either a S.T.D. (the highest ecclesiastical degree in theology) or a J.C.D. (the highest degree in canon law). Most of these degrees are from Roman institutions or the Catholic University of America in Washington, DC. Half the archbishops studied in Rome. Half also studied at Catholic University. In so far as their views parallel those of other bishops, they are more "conservative" on religious attitudes and sexual morality than their priests and more "liberal" on ecumenism and social action.[3]

No one has all the qualities necessary for being a perfect archbishop. As a result, each archbishop tends to emphasize certain aspects of the job. The personality and preferences of the archbishop play an important part in determining how he spends his time and how he organizes the archdiocese. This chapter will examine a typical day in the life of an archbishop, his style of governance, and how an archdiocese's organization and structure is influenced by the personality and style of the archbishop.

A Typical Day for a Workaholic

Most American archbishops are workaholics who try to do everything in the job description for an ideal archbishop. Even those in their seventies at the time of my interviews (Borders,

Philip Hannan of New Orleans, Krol, and Timothy Manning of Los Angeles) would run into the ground a younger man trying to keep up with their schedules.

A few have been slowed down by ill health. Before or during the period of my study, archbishops with serious health problems included: James Casey of Denver and Donnellan (who died in office); Borders, Gerety, Hunthausen, Edward McCarthy of Miami, Daniel Sheehan of Omaha, and Edmund Szoka of Detroit (who had heart problems); Flores (who had an operation on his inner ear); Krol (who had an operation on his throat); Pilarczyk (who had a stroke); Quinn (who took a six-month sabbatical because of stress); and Whealon (cancer).

Most archbishops would consider an eight-hour day a rare luxury. A typical day in the life of an archbishop will begin around 6:30 in the morning after turning in at 11:30 the previous evening. Most days will be spent in the office dealing with mail, appointments, and meetings. Many evenings and weekends are given over to parish, archdiocesan, and civic functions. Sometimes these functions and meetings of committees and boards will also take the archbishop out of the office during the day.

Most archbishops find it difficult to describe a typical day in their lives. Archbishop Roach of St. Paul gives it a try:

I am not sure there is one. I will give you about as typical a day as I would have. I get up at 6:30 in the morning and get on an exercycle for twenty minutes.

I try to spend a half hour or thereabouts in prayer. Then, depending upon what my schedule is, I have Mass at home if I don't have Mass somewhere else during the day. About three times during the week I have Mass somewhere else.

Then I am in the office by 9:00 or a little bit before. The first thing I try to do in the morning is go through the NC News Service, just to see what's happened the day before.

Then I try from 9:15 to 11:00, generally, although that tends to get eroded very badly, I try to do office work, mail, that kind of stuff.

Start appointments at 11:00 and go from 11:00 to 5:00, pretty much with appointments or meetings. Then I try to get out of here at five o'clock.

If I've got an evening commitment, which is rather frequent, then I do that. About three nights a week I would have evening things. In the spring, when confirmation schedule is heavy, it is a little more than that; I'm probably out four nights a week.

If I don't have an evening commitment, I do a variety of things. I try to do a fair amount of reading. I try to do some recreational reading and some professional kind of reading. I tend to do a lot of speaking. Last night I worked, and that's not typical, until 10:30 here in the office getting ready for some talks that I've got to give.

Office Work

Office work can take up a great amount of time. Many letters the archbishop receives can simply be passed on to one of his subordinates. They will answer the letter or draft an answer for the archbishop's signature. Some archbishops have their secretaries distribute incoming correspondence, but most like to see all their mail as a way of keeping in touch. Some letters, especially those from priests, archdiocesan officials, bishops, civic and ecumenical leaders, will have to be answered by the archbishop himself.

Archbishop Gerety of Newark described the mail on his desk the day I interviewed him:

In the mail you will find all sorts of things. You will find things that relate to parish life, permissions that are being requested, complaints that are being made—somebody is mad because he didn't receive justice in the tribunal or something like that.

This morning, here are some examples. There is talk of a merger of a couple of parishes. Well, of course you will have all sorts of complaints about that. I get a lot of stuff like that.

Here is a notification—I have to be at the Serra International to celebrate Mass next week.

Here is an inquiry from the Westside Presbyterian Church; they are looking for retreat facilities.

Here is a complaint about some land we have. It's a landfill that has been smoking and the people are mad.

Here is a complaint—a letter I received from Cardinal Mayer [of the Congregation for Divine Worship] because somebody from here wrote in complaining about the distribution of the precious blood in the archdiocese of Newark.

Here Bishop Arias, who is vicar for Hispanics, sent me a copy of a letter he wrote to the parishes because we're changing our schedule of Masses. He wants to make sure that the Hispanic population gets a proper shake in the Mass schedule.

Here is another one from one of your Jesuit provincials, asking for correspondence with regards to one of your priests.

Here is another, a Benedictine who wants faculties for a couple of fellows and approval for their assignments.

Here is a request from the New Jersey Catholic Conference to approve the appointment of an educational aide down there in Trenton.

Here's another communication from the North American College in Rome notifying me that they have accepted one of our priests for their next course in the fall, and I have to see to it that he is released and all that business.

Last year we had over ninety meetings with the sisters and religious because of the Quinn Commission. We listened to them about how they felt about the "Essential Elements" [a document on religious life issued by the Vatican] and how they felt about religious life. Here is the responses from the religious.

That's a guy who wants to get laicized.

Here is a complaint about the tribunal.

I get a lot of crank letters. I've got two or three right there complaining about this, that, or the other thing. Sometimes I don't reply because they are absolutely nuts. But other times you got to at least pay attention, say, "I'll take your ideas into consideration" or some blasted thing. It depends on what it is. You don't want the people to feel that they can't approach you.

I just got through a lot of other stuff, dictating to the secretary in between appointments.

Archbishop Gerety had a busy schedule of appointments that day also:

Today [June 24, 1985] is a typical day, it has certain things happening today that don't happen every day, but in a sense it is a typical day.

I frequently start in with a breakfast meeting because some of the archdiocesan corporations are made up of laymen [who work during the day]. I have already seen three priests for various reasons [before 11:00 A.M], and I have gone through the mail, which on Monday morning can be rather heavy. After I finish with you, for a few minutes I am going to see a seminarian who's going to Rome.

We have a large number of corporations that are under the archdiocese of Newark, so I've got to be interested in all that stuff. I am on all those boards. We have an archdiocesan hospital corporation; that is an umbrella corporation that has under it three of our Catholic hospitals that are directly the responsibility of the archdiocese. I got a fairly lengthy report on their activities, finances and everything else, from the fellow who runs the corporation. We have a lot of problems in that area. So after I have a bite to eat, I am going to have a meeting about the health corporation with the vicar general and our chancellor for administration, who is on the corporation board. We got other things—cemeteries, we got womb to tomb.

And at two o'clock, after that meeting, I am going to be given a slide presentation [by city officials] of the changes that are going to take place, or at least are proposed, for Jersey City. They are of concern to us because the changes will affect the parishes.

Then at 3:30 I am going to see an archbishop from India who is here and wants to come in and shake my hand, I guess.

Then at 4:30 I have a meeting with the Foundation for Educational Alternatives, which is one of our corporations, which is a foundation to help out poor kids; and they are going to stay for dinner. That's what I am doing today.

Engagements outside the office, especially in parishes, frequently take place in the evening and on weekends. In a geographically large archdiocese this can mean late hours and much traveling. Archbishop Oscar Lipscomb of Mobile describes one of his worst weekends:

I get home generally at ten or eleven o'clock at night, if I have my wishes. If I don't, it is whenever it is that traveling brings me in, generally very late.

I was in Montgomery for a catechist day on Saturday morning. All the catechists from that area came by, and we had a big Mass. I commissioned them all as catechists. That afternoon we dedicated a new addition to the social service center in Montgomery.

The next morning [Sunday] I had Mass at a parish where I had not been for some time since a new pastor was appointed. I dealt with some personnel problems in the afternoon.

Sunday night I went up [eighty-five miles] to Birmingham and offered Mass the next morning for a lady whose husband had died, who I had known for many years. In the middle of the day, I had something else.

This was all preparatory to going on television with Mother Angelica. So I finished television live with Mother Angelica at 9:00 P.M. and at ten o'clock I left to drive [260 miles] to Mobile. I got home at three o'clock in the morning, pretty well dead.

Despite being workaholics, archbishops cannot do everything. With a limited amount of time available to them, their personalities and the needs of the archdiocese will make them concentrate on certain activities. How archbishops use their time is one way of defining their episcopal styles.

Episcopal Styles

There are many ways that bishops can be categorized.[4] One archdiocese had a well-loved archbishop who was followed by a tyrant and then by a nonleader. The priests dubbed them, "Hero, Nero, and Zero." As it turned out, when Zero retired, the priests were sorry to see him go as they realized how many things he had permitted to happen.

Catholic bishops are most frequently categorized in the press as liberals or conservatives, two categories this book tries to avoid. More sophisticated writers note that the bishops, in comparison with American society, tend to be liberal on social issues and conservative on doctrine and morals. Within these categories may be shades of differences, but they are slight compared to American society as a whole. This is shown by the almost unanimous support given by the bishops to their pastoral letters on peace and economic justice. Likewise on doctrine and morals, only a couple of bishops have publicly disagreed with the pope on women's ordination, *Humanae Vitae*, or any other major issue. In any case, this book does not attempt to fathom the theological or social views of the bishops. Rather its emphasis is on what bishops do, how they spend their time, how they make decisions.

In *Models of the Church*,[5] Avery Dulles, S.J., describes the church as institution, sacrament, communion, herald, and servant. As a result, bishops could be examined in their functions as leaders in each of these aspects of the church. Canon law refers to bishops as "teachers of doctrine, priests of sacred worship and ministers of governance."[6] Some attention will be given to the role of bishops as teachers (heralds) and priests of worship (sacrament and communion). But this book primarily examines the bishop's role in governance, as a leader in the church as an institution.

While each archbishop is an individual with unique talents and personality, it is possible to make some generalizations about governance styles of archbishops. The most valuable resource an archbishop has is his time. Even the workaholics are not able to do everything. How an archbishop uses his time is one way by which they can be described as pastors, administrators, teachers, national leaders, or a combination. Bishops are frequently classified as administrators or pastors, but this dichotomy needs more nuance. The next section will attempt to describe episcopal types. What will be described are archetypes, with examples of archbishops who epitomize these categories. But archbishops perform all of these functions to varying degrees, although they are usually more comfortable with some roles rather than others.

Civic Leader

In their local communities, archbishops are not only church leaders, they are also major public figures. Their presence is desired at many events because the archbishop can give them added credibility and visibility. For example, when the first research conference on AIDS was scheduled in New York City, the sponsors found that politicians were afraid to attend. Some politicians feared a negative reaction from the New York archdiocese. When one of the sponsors informed Cardinal Terence Cooke of this problem, he offered to give the invocation at the opening of the conference.

While trying to avoid being used for political purposes, archbishops are willing to give their presence to events that benefit the community. For example, Archbishop Flores made spot announcements on San Antonio radio and television urging people to register and vote. Many archbishops see this as part of being a good citizen and as a way of showing the involvement of the church in the life of the local community. In addition, it is useful for them to keep on good terms with civic officials whose cooperation may be needed on zoning, local ordinances, or funding for Catholic social services.

Frequently archbishops are called upon to deal with civic problems through their social services. Many archbishops have been approached by civic leaders to run programs for the homeless and the poor. Sometimes they also get involved in civic disputes directly. "Whenever there is any trouble, I am called upon to be a go-between," explains Archbishop Hannan of New Orleans. "For instance, the black militants would come and talk to me, but they won't talk to the black mayor. Then I am supposed to go and talk to the mayor about what is worrying them." After a police shooting in a black neighborhood, representatives of the black community, police, and mayor secretly met at night in the archbishop's office trying to work out their differences.

But some archbishops profess not to want to be civic leaders. "A recent newspaper article referred to me as one of the ten most powerful people in San Francisco, but as one who underused his potential to have influence," reports Archbishop Quinn. "That rather pleases me. I do not want to have that kind of influence. It is not my role. I want my religious role to be obvious and clear." On the other hand, his view of his religious role led Archbishop Quinn to be in the forefront in San Francisco on issues like sanctuary, AIDS, and the nuclear freeze.

As public figures, archbishops' support is also solicited on various public issues. Some have spoken forcefully on controversial local issues (capital punishment, public school integration, local gay rights ordinances, fluoridated water, public school health clinics, state funding of abortions, and the location of race tracks, low-income housing, shelters, and soup kitchens). They are concerned about what happens in the civic community because it can impact on the church. They also feel a responsibility to influence public policy in a direction that is moral and just. Their positions on community issues often affect how these issues are resolved. But when Catholics are a small minority in the community, it is less likely that the archbishop will be a visible community leader.

Ecumenical Leader

Increasingly, the archbishops attempt to coordinate their public activities with other religious leaders in the community. In some cities, the judicatory heads of major religious groups meet to discuss issues of common concern. These ecumenical groups sometimes take united positions on public issues. Archbishop Weakland of Milwaukee reports,

My day has as many Protestants seeing me sometimes, as Catholics. I see the Lutheran and the Anglican bishops a lot more than Catholic bishops, except my auxiliaries. We do everything together. That's important in a city like ours.

Some archbishops also encourage their parishes and agencies to work with other church groups. Some archdioceses, like Louisville, have signed covenants with other churches where they commit themselves to joint programs of prayer and social services. Ecumenical efforts are especially strong with Jewish groups in Los Angeles and New York and with mainline Protestant groups throughout the country. For the most part, conservative fundamentalist groups are not interested in cooperation except in the pro-life field.

National and International Leader

Some archbishops are not only leaders locally, but also nationally and internationally. The cardinal archbishops are called on to do projects for the national and international church. For example, Cardinal Krol was involved in investigating Catholic Relief Service and the Vatican bank and in raising funds for Polish farmers and the Vatican debt. Cardinal Bernardin is a member of the council for the synod. Cardinal O'Connor is a member of the Congregation for Bishops. Cardinal Law is working on the international catechism.

On the national level, every three years, the bishops elect a president and vice-president of the National Conference of Catholic Bishops (NCCB). Normally at the end of his three-year term, the vice-president is elected president. All the presidents of the NCCB (except Bishop James Malone) have been archbishops: Krol, Dearden, Bernardin, Quinn, Roach, and May. Archbishop Pilarczyk, elected vice-president in 1986, will probably become president in November 1989.

The NCCB elections are a good indication of which bishops are respected by their peers. The inability of Cardinal Law and Archbishop Mahony to get elected to any NCCB office in 1986 was noted by many commentators as an indication of their weak standing among their fellow bishops. The next year, however, Archbishop Mahony was elected chairman of the bishops committee on international issues.

The president and vice-president of the conference frequently act as spokesmen for the American bishops on religious and public issues. They have met with U.S. presidents and represented the American bishops at national and international meetings. They also visit Rome a couple of times a year to express the views of the American bishops to the Vatican. These jobs are in addition to bishops' work in their dioceses.

Being NCCB president, Archbishop Roach reports, took 30 percent of his time.

Being on a NCCB committee can also be time consuming, especially for the chairman. Archbishop Weakland chaired the committee drafting the bishops' economic pastoral, while Cardinal Bernardin chaired the committee for the peace pastoral. Archbishop Quinn chaired the papal commission on religious life and, with cardinals Bernardin and O'Connor, was on the committee that resolved the Seattle crisis. But some archbishops avoid national work because they want to devote all their time to their archdioceses.

Teaching Archbishop

All archbishops consider themselves teachers, but some take this role more seriously than others and are willing to take time from other duties to read, prepare talks, and write. About a third were teachers earlier in their careers, usually in seminaries. "I like to teach," reports Archbishop Roach, a former headmaster, "and very few people in the world have an opportunity to teach in the same way that the bishop does. That is a terrible burden, but it is also a remarkable opportunity, and I do like to teach."

Of all the archbishops, only Archbishop Whealon of Hartford currently teaches in a classroom. He teaches Scripture to seminarians and candidates for the permanent diaconate. Few archbishops are qualified to be academic theologians. Only five (archbishops Hickey, Levada, McCarthy, O'Meara, and Pilarczyk) of the current thirty-one archbishops have S.T.D.'s, the highest ecclesiastical degree in theology. Archbishop Lipscomb has a Ph.D. in church history; Archbishop Pilarczyk, in classics; Cardinal O'Connor, in political science; Archbishop Kucera, in education; and Archbishop Bevilacqua has a J.D. Only six archbishops (Bevilacqua, Hannan, Hickey, Kelly, McCarthy, and Sheehan) have J.C.D.'s, the highest degree in canon law. (Donnellan, Krol, and Power also have J.C.D.'s.)

Some fulfill their teaching role by exercising vigilance over the theologians at their seminaries and at local Catholic colleges and universities. Cardinal Law shocked a graduation audience by expressing the hope that Jesuit-run Boston College might become more Catholic, although he did not explain how it should do this. As chancellor of the Catholic University of America, Cardinal Hickey has been the Vatican point man in dealing with Rev. Charles Curran, the moral theologian whose views on certain moral issues were questioned by church officials. He also opposed the appointment of a dean of religious studies who, he felt, held an unorthodox position on sterilization.

But most archbishops exercise their teaching role primarily through their sermons at confirmations and other liturgies. Archbishop Kelly, being of the Order of Preachers, takes each sermon very seriously.

There is nothing more satisfying to me than to preach to a church full of people and to keep their attention. I work hard at my preaching. It is very important to get their attention and hold it and to talk to them about themselves and my experience as their bishop. That is what the pope does. I admire him most for his willingness to be present to the universal church in his preaching. And he does that exceptionally well.

Besides preaching, some bishops use confirmations as an opportunity to meet with young people to answer their questions. Before their confirmations, Archbishop Donnellan brought them to the Atlanta cathedral where they could ask him questions on confirmation or anything else.

It's fun, it takes a little time for them to loosen up and ask questions, but then you might go for two hours in which they are just asking questions. Also, since their parents are there with them, their parents ask questions. Sometimes, that is a difficult experience, but it is a fun experience.

Archbishop Hannan of New Orleans also opens himself up to questions from high school seniors, whom he meets with every year. As he explains,

I speak a very short time, maybe ten minutes at the most, and then ask them to ask me any questions they want—to make sure that they know that the church has an answer for everything and that we are approachable in every problem that they have and that we want to help them.

About half of the archbishops use a column in their arch-diocesan newspapers to carry their teachings beyond the sound of their voices.[7] As teachers they attempt to motivate and in-spire their people. Archbishop Weakland explains,

I write an article each week for the Catholic newspaper, which is very important to me as a means of communicating with people on a spir-itual level. These are not informative articles as such. They usually are more of a spiritual nature.

A few archbishops have become nationally recognized as teaching bishops through articles, pastoral letters, and ad-dresses. None has published in *Theological Studies*, the most prestigious American theological journal. Cardinals Bernardin, Krol, and O'Connor and archbishops Hurley, Lipscomb, May, Pilarczyk, Quinn, Stafford, Weakland, and Whealon have pub-lished in *America*, a Catholic periodical frequently read by the bishops.[8]

Another way of identifying teaching bishops is to see which archbishops write speeches and pastoral letters that gain na-tional attention. Some archbishops use ghost writers for early drafts of these documents, but the final version represents their views and implements their teaching role no matter who wrote it. Episcopal statements that gain national attention are usually printed in *Origins*. Archbishops Bernardin, Quinn, and Roach are cited more frequently in the author index of *Origins* than any other archbishops.[9] This is partially due to the fact that while presidents of the bishops' conference, their addresses and statements were frequently printed in *Origins*. But even discounting these official statements, Bernardin and Quinn have been quite prolific. Since becoming chairman of the com-mittee drafting the pastoral on the economy, Archbishop Weakland has been more prominent in *Origins*, as have archbishops May and Pilarczyk since becoming president and vice-president of the conference. Other archbishops whose works have been frequently reprinted in *Origins* include Mahony, Hickey, O'Connor, Stafford, Law, Bevilacqua, and Borders.

But most archbishops do not make the time for the reading and writing that the teaching role requires. Archbishop Quinn is an exception. It is not unusual for him to take a whole afternoon off to read and to write articles and addresses. He explains:

> I have a great feeling that when I get up to speak I should say something of substance. I think my mission in the church is to be a bishop, that means to me that my mission is to say something that has substance to it. So I try to always say something of substance. I try to prepare what I have to say. So I work on these things before I give them.

One San Francisco chancery official said of Archbishop Quinn, "He is more of a theologian than an administrator. He would be much better as the head of the Vatican Congregation on Doctrine of the Faith."

Media Minister

No archbishop in the United States has been as effective communicating through electronic media as have Protestant TV evangelists. A few (cardinals Cody and Szoka and Archbishop Hannan) have spent large sums developing archdiocesan television centers, but the high cost has deterred most bishops from taking that route. Cardinal Bernardin dismantled the Chicago television center built under Cardinal Cody. Many archbishops are members of the Catholic Television Network of America (CTNA), but unless the archdiocese can get local cable companies to carry the programs, they are little used except as videos for classroom and parish discussions.

A few archbishops, like Archbishop Weakland, use television or radio Masses to reach more people in their archdioceses. The Milwaukee archbishop explains:

I consider my primary task that of a teacher, and I do what I think is a lot of teaching. I tape a broadcast Mass every Sunday on the radio—eight o'clock out of the cathedral—and I work hard on that homily. It's listened to by about 70,000, so it's worth taking it as a serious chance to reach a lot of people. I find from correspondence I get that it reaches a lot of non-Catholic people who listen in regularly.

Archbishops get little training on dealing with the media. Officers of the NCCB, like archbishops Bernardin, Kelly, May, Pilarczyk, Roach, and Quinn, learned how to handle a national press conference. Most archbishops have at least a part-time press person. Archbishops tend to get good local press coverage when they first arrive in their archdioceses, but they are retired to the back pages after a few weeks. Archbishops in heavily Catholic areas tend to get more coverage than archbishops in non-Catholic areas.

No archbishop has captured media attention as much as Cardinal O'Connor of New York. His predecessor, Cardinal Cooke, was a hands-on administrator with an intimate knowledge of the archdiocese, but he preferred to work in the background and not in front of the media. Being less knowledgeable of the archdiocese, Cardinal O'Connor has delegated more responsibility to his staff, but he has known how to capture the attention of the New York newspapers and television stations and turn them into his bully pulpits. The director of Catholic Charities for New York remarked how this made a difference in his life:

Cardinal Cooke was very good on advocacy, but he tended to low key his advocacy. Cardinal O'Connor is very strong in that. He is very far up front in advocacy.

A few years ago, we were pushing for a moratorium on the [apartment] conversions, which was another way of getting rid of [poor] people and gentrifying. Cardinal Cooke was behind us and he would meet with Mayor Beame, but he wouldn't go public on it. I would be the one going public. Now the cardinal is the one going public on the moratorium.

On the other hand, the cardinal had to learn the hard way that not all news coverage is good. Cardinal O'Connor explains:

The archbishop of New York is foolishly expected to have an opinion on every subject in the world. No matter what happens of significance, someone from the media is going to ask me what do you think about it. I'm here now about two and three-fourths years, but it's taken me most of the time to learn that I don't have an opinion about everything.

I have to laugh as I reflect on my earlier days. I would come up with some kind of opinion. I would try to think it through and pray it through. I'd try to be honest about it and say what I believe. That got me into considerable trouble—saying what I really believe—because I think the media weren't accustomed to it. They assumed there would be some dissembling. They assumed there would be a political dimension to it.

When I would see the way it would be distilled and re-presented, I thought, "Why did you have an opinion about it in the first place? You really didn't have anything to say, and you said what you didn't have to say, and now you have to pay the price."

Pastoral Archbishop

Many people use *pastoral* to describe a style of being bishop, but it is not always clear what they mean. "It is easier to describe what is the opposite of a pastoral bishop," admits Archbishop Jadot, who is credited with appointing pastoral bishops. "He is authoritarian, does not ask advice, does not relate well to other people, a loner, does not like to meet other people, does not like to hear confessions or preach." When priests use the term they often mean that the bishop gets along well with his priests; he pastors them. The term also applies to bishops who get out of the office and visit parishes. The pastoral archbishops enjoy meeting people and celebrating the liturgy in parishes.

Every archbishop considers himself pastoral. Most profess that the part of their job they enjoy most is going to parishes, celebrating the Eucharist and confirmation, and meeting the people. Their most frequent complaint is that they do not have more time for this. Archbishop Lipscomb of Mobile says,

The most satisfying times to me are sacramentally oriented. I love confirmations, I love to be around giving the sacrament of confirmation, and the aftermath, to be with parents.

The opportunity for archbishops to give individual attention to people is limited, especially in large archdioceses. But they still feel it is important for the bishop to be seen by his people even if it is impossible for him to be personally involved with each person.

Cardinal Manning explained his approach in Los Angeles:

A bishop cannot be a great financial man exclusively or a great administrator or author or public relations man. But I think his presence is very important, his presence among his people, and that's what I have striven for myself mostly during my administration—to be present to as many people as I can.

Last night I heard confessions for an hour and a half in South Pasadena. I said Mass at a place we have for bag ladies on Tuesday. On Sunday I had two Masses: one at St. Mark's in Venice and one at St. Martin of Tours for different events. Saturday I had Mass at St. Andrew's in Pasadena, and so on.

I am on the road night and day. I will be at the men's jail Christmas Day and the women's jail on New Year's Day. I will be saying Mass at various rest homes during this coming week, such as, the Sisters of the Poor in Nazareth House. I go to the detention camp so that they will know who their shepherd is.

Archbishop as Administrator

American archbishops are primarily administrators, and this has been true for most of the history of the American hierarchy. Early bishops were builders of churches, schools, orphanages, hospitals, and other charitable institutions that served a rapidly expanding immigrant church. They were often criticized for being administrators rather than pastors. As early as 1878, George Conroy, Bishop of Ardagh, Ireland, after making a visitation of the American church, reported to the Vatican:

In the selection of bishops priority is given to financial, rather than pastoral, abilities. . . . Whenever there is a deliberation to choose a candidate for the episcopacy, the bishops of a province feel constrained to seek, at all costs, a man skilled in financial administration. Indeed, it has too often happened that the most valued gifts in a candidate proposed to the Holy See were properly those of a banker, not of a Pastor of Souls.[10]

Conroy failed to recognize that while the European church was living off ecclesiastical infrastructures built up over centuries, the American church had to start from scratch in a non-Catholic environment. In addition, some European bishops had little to administer because the church lost much of its property, including educational and charitable institutions, to the state in the nineteenth and early twentieth centuries. In other countries the church received financial subsidies from the state so the bishops did not have to raise money. Today American bishops are administrators of large operations built by their predecessors for which they are financially responsible. In Europe, on the other hand, "as a rule the bishop, in keeping with a concordat, has no specific financial competence. Finances are usually attended to by boards of established (state-recognized) churches. In these cases the financial administrator is the accountant responsible for the budget which he has to justify before the state church board."[11]

This has led church historian Msgr. John Tracy Ellis to remark,

I don't see any marked change in the type of bishops being appointed since the beginning of the American hierarchy. George Conroy's report is still accurate. The American bishops, unlike their European counterparts, were the holders of vast properties. It was common sense that they therefore had to be good administrators.

When looking for an archbishop, administrative skill is still high on the list of qualifications. But archbishops do not learn administration by going to school. None of them has an M.B.A., a master's degree in business administration. A couple had courses in educational administration, but that would be the extent of their formal training except for their courses in canon law.

Archbishops, for the most part, learn administration by doing it. Most archbishops (63 percent) get experience in governance by being the bishop of a smaller diocese before being transferred to an archdiocese. Working closely with another bishop as an auxiliary also is helpful. Prior to being made a bishop, almost half the archbishops (Bernardin, Bevilacqua, Donnellan, Hannan, Hickey, Krol, Law, Lipscomb, Mahony, McCarthy, Power, Quinn, Sanchez, Sheehan, Strecker, Szoka) also served as vicars general, chancellors, or secretaries to bishops. Some (Borders, Donnellan, Hickey, Hunthausen, Pilarczyk, Quinn, Roach, Whealon) gained administrative experience as seminary administrators. Archbishops Mahony and Stafford were directors of Catholic Charities. Archbishop Pilarczyk was vicar for education.

Some archbishops have had administrative experience outside of chanceries or seminaries. Archbishops Hunthausen and Kucera were presidents of Catholic colleges. Cardinal Bernardin and Archbishop Kelly were general secretaries of the National Conference of Catholic Bishops. Archbishop May was president of the Catholic Extension Society. Cardinal O'Connor was Chief of Navy Chaplains. Archbishop O'Meara was director of the national office of the Society for the Propagation of the Faith. Archbishop Weakland was abbot primate of the Benedictines. Archbishop Marino was vicar general of the Josephites.

Many archbishops enjoy the day-to-day work of administration and the challenge of problem solving and decision making, but few like to admit it. "I like to govern. I like the process of governing," confesses Archbishop Roach of St. Paul. "I like to be able to work with people and to come to a judgment about the appropriateness of an action. I like that very much."

Although most archbishops enjoy administration, others profess to actually hate it. They would prefer to spend all of their time on pastoral work. It is difficult to know how seriously to take these complaints about the burdens of administration. Their statements may reflect current theology of ministry, which is biased against administration and portrays the priest as a pastor and teacher. Or their comments may reflect the general clerical antipathy for bureaucracy and administration. Cardinal Bernardin and archbishops Flores, Lipscomb, Sanchez, and Quinn, for example, profess a dislike for administration.

Archbishop Lipscomb acknowledges,

The times that are most frustrating are the times which you least sense as being connected with priesthood or the sacrament of orders, for me anyway—desk work, administration, finance. I hate finance, who doesn't?

Because administration is such an important part of an archbishop's ministry, the simple distinction between pastoral and administrative bishops is not sufficient. It is important to examine the various styles or models of administration used by archbishops.

Innovator vs. Maintainer Models

Some archbishops have very specific ideas for innovative programs for the archdiocese. Cardinal O'Connor of New York and Archbishop Hannan of New Orleans, for example, are constantly pushing their ideas for new programs on their staffs. Sometimes they publicly announce new initiatives that are complete surprises to their staffs. Archbishops tend to be innovative at the beginning of their terms. Archbishop Mahony, for example, initiated numerous programs and reorganizations his first year in Los Angeles. Normally, these initiatives will be focused on areas of interest to the archbishop. For example, although Archbishop Hannan is full of initiatives for social services, he pretty much leaves his pastors alone.

Other archbishops, especially those who have been in office for a while, are primarily concerned with maintaining the existing programs on a sound and peaceful basis. Thus, Archbishop Strecker had many initiatives when he first came to Kansas City, KS, but now he works at continuing these programs. Other archbishops, like Manning, Whealon, and Donnellan, came to office during the late 1960s when there was much turbulence in the church. In response to a query about his major accomplishments, Archbishop Donnellan of Atlanta responded "keeping peace, with all of my flock and all of my neighbors." Simply to survive that period was a great achievement. If initiatives were to come, they would come from others.

Tolerant or Supportive Styles

Many archbishops (Bernardin, Borders, Donnellan, Flores, Gerety, Hunthausen, Hurley, Kelly, May, McCarthy, O'Meara, Pilarczyk, Power, Roach, Salatka, Sheehan, Strecker, and Whealon) are praised by their staffs not so much for their ideas and initiatives as for their allowing others to take initiative and even make mistakes. In their lifetimes, the archbishops have seen bishops oppose changes that later became accepted practices in the church. They remember how divisive it was when bishops attempted to suppress individual charisms. As a result, they are likely to permit initiatives, even those they might not agree with. These laissez-faire archbishops believe that if the initiative is good, it will succeed and help the church. If the initiative is bad, it will fail on its own without their intervention. This "permissiveness" is often misunderstood in Rome and by American Catholic conservatives.

Some archbishops not only permit initiatives, but actively support people with initiative. Sometimes the archbishop has a general sense of where he wants the archdiocese to go but is unclear about the programmatic specifics. If his ideas are to be realized, he must find creative people to flesh them out. These people must be supported by the archbishop.

For example, although very proud of Renew, a program of spiritual renewal used in many dioceses, Archbishop Gerety refuses to take any credit for it. "We got a couple of bright fellows here, that's how it started. It certainly wasn't my fault."

One of those "bright fellows," Rev. Thomas Kleissler, recalls Archbishop Gerety's role more clearly:

He wanted me to work developing parish councils. I had done it for years as a volunteer. So I said to the bishop, "It is not going to work unless you have several years of basic spiritual formation right across the diocese." He said, "OK, do that." I told you he is smart, so he pulled the trap door.

Thus began Renew. Archbishop Gerety also found and supported creative people to deal with his financial problems and to run social services. Finding such people and empowering them is one of the most important things an archbishop does.

Archbishop Weakland of Milwaukee explains how he does it:

I guess the secret is somehow sensing what needs are there and beginning to bring people together to look at them. And somebody seems to surface who has the leadership quality that you need to move it. That happens over and over again.

Hands-On Administrator or Monarch

Prior to the Second Vatican Council, practically every archdiocesan office or agency (and sometimes the people within them) reported directly to the archbishop. As an episcopal monarch in a stable environment with few diocesan agencies, an archbishop could make practically all important decisions. He could be more or less informed about everything that was going on in the archdiocese.

The explosion of diocesan programs after Vatican II made this style more difficult.[12] The monarchal approach can also get bogged down in many unimportant details. For example, in 1977 during his first week in San Francisco, a chancery official brought Archbishop Quinn the pink slip for an automobile purchased by the archdiocese. His predecessor had always signed the slips. Archbishop Quinn said, "I am here and I have a pen, so I will sign it. But don't ever bring me one of these again."

In some archdioceses, this monarchal model continued after

Vatican II. In a small archdiocese, the archbishop can be involved in supervising agencies because they are small and demands on his time are less. Some archbishops even tried to be monarchs in large archdioceses. Cardinal Cody, for example, signed all the checks for the archdiocese of Chicago.

In large archdioceses, trying to be a monarch eventually causes serious problems. As archdiocesan structures multiplied and became more complex, it became impossible for an archbishop to supervise all archdiocesan agencies. "Theoretically a year ago, sixty-seven different offices and agency heads were on a direct line of accountability with the archbishop," explained the moderator of the curia in St. Paul. "The truth of the matter is that nobody was."

Large archdioceses prove to be beyond the ability of any one person to govern directly. What frequently happened was that many agencies operated with little or no supervision. The agencies that received the attention of the archbishop were those with financial problems, with personnel problems, or with programs that the archbishop was personally interested in.

Delegator

In a small archdiocese, if an archbishop likes administration, he can be very much involved in the day-to-day work of the chancery by directly supervising agency heads. He can also get involved in the supervision of the parishes. And in an archdiocese like Anchorage or Mobile, with few Catholics and a small archdiocesan structure, the archbishop's administrative responsibilities do not get in the way of his pastoral inclinations.

In large archdioceses, with large agencies and bureaucracies, there is the need to delegate or the archdiocesan apparatus will grind to a halt. Also, if an archbishop does not like administration or has heavy commitments outside the archdiocese, he must delegate his administrative work load or he will become very frustrated, as was Boston Cardinal Medeiros, who hated making decisions. The style and preference of the archbishop will determine how much authority and responsibility he delegates to other officials in the archdiocese. All archbishops claim that they delegate, but some delegate more than others.

Archbishop Donnellan of Atlanta said, "If you are going to be an administrator in an archdiocese, it is necessary that you delegate a good deal, that you trust the people who work with you and that you are not hesitant in correcting mistakes." Donnellan was willing to let his subordinates make decisions in their areas:

> You try to get competent people, you look for reports on what is going on, you occasionally check. But by and large, the idea is to make sure you have competent people and let them make their decisions and let them do their own administration.

For Donnellan and many archbishops, being kept informed is the key to the process:

> I'm not enthusiastic about surprises. I like to be kept informed, but I generally leave them to do things in their field. I like to be informed, but I don't need to be consulted. They are free to make their decisions, but I like to know what is going on.

Some archbishops, on the other hand, talk of their subordinates making decisions, but it often appears that their "decisions" are whether or not to recommend something to the archbishop. Thus, Cardinal Krol of Philadelphia explains his administrative philosophy:

> I expressed my philosophy of administration in these terms [pointing to a plaque]: "I would rather you do it yourself." That is the responsibility of leadership, to train people to make responsible decisions.
>
> When I first came here, I got a lot of this, "whatever you want." "It isn't what I want. You are in charge of that department, tell me what is needed. I may have to say no thirteen times, but the fourteenth time I might be in the position to say sure. But you tell me."
>
> That's the only way you can train responsible leadership for the church is by giving them responsibility. And I tell them, "You have

to make the decisions and if you are wrong, I'll rap your knuckles, that's all, I'll fire you. Is that acceptable?" "Yeah, sure." And they do.

Differences in administrative style are most easily seen when there is a change in archbishops. Cardinal Cooke, for example, was very much involved in detailed decision making in New York, while Cardinal O'Connor has been much more of a delegator. Cardinal Cooke was able to immerse himself in detail because he had spent practically all his ministry in administration in the New York archdiocese. Cardinal O'Connor, on the other hand, knew little about the archdiocese before he arrived.

Archbishops who like to get involved in administrative detail, according to their staffs, include cardinals Cooke, Krol, and Hickey and archbishops Kucera, Salatka, and Whealon. Normally this style is only possible in small archdioceses. And sometimes it is necessary because skilled administrators are simply not available for the archbishop to delegate to. Archbishops who delegate, according to their staffs, include Bernardin, Borders, Donnellan, Flores, Gerety, Hannan, Hurley, Kucera, Lipscomb, May, McCarthy, O'Connor, O'Meara, Pilarczyk, Quinn, Roach, Szoka, and Weakland. But even these archbishops involve themselves in details of matters they are interested in. Most archbishops pay attention to problem areas and delegate areas that are stable and noncontroversial.

Structures

An archbishop needs governance structures that fit his personal style and the needs of his archdiocese. An archbishop who wants to be involved in administrative detail will need a different structure from one who prefers to delegate. In a small diocese, an archbishop can have frequent personal contact with every agency administrator and pastor. In a large archdiocese, this will be impossible.

Structure is the internal differentiation and patterning of relationships in an organization.[13] Structure is an attempt to achieve bounded rationality, which is especially important when facing uncertainty and complexity. "By delimiting responsibilities, control over resources, and other matters, organizations provide their participating members with boundaries within which efficiency may be a realistic expectation."[14] Structure also facilitates coordinated action by the interdependent elements of an organization.

The structure of an archdiocese is influenced by its mission, its ministries, and its environment as well as the desires of its leadership. Many large and medium-sized dioceses have undergone reorganization recently. Reorganization has been necessary because of expansion of the archdiocesan agencies with new ministries responding to new demands since Vatican II. The archbishops want to lessen their administrative load while at the same time improving supervision, coordination, and accountability. Diocesan reorganization has also responded to desires for better lines of communication for both vertical and horizontal communication.[15]

Regional Vicariate Model

As an administrator, the archbishop is responsible for supervising both archdiocesan parishes and agencies. If the archbishop does not like administration or does not have the time for it, he must delegate some of his administrative responsibilities. In large archdioceses, delegating responsibilities is imperative. The larger the number of parishes, for example, the more difficult it is for him to supervise and coordinate them. In populous archdioceses the trend has been to establish regional vicariates under auxiliary bishops. Priests can also be episcopal vicars, but bishops carry more weight. Baltimore, Boston, Chicago, Detroit, Dubuque, Los Angeles, Newark, St. Paul, and Washington have regional vicariates under auxiliary bishops. The vicariates are further divided into deaneries. Smaller archdioceses with less than two auxiliaries are more likely to simply have deaneries under the archbishop.

What kind of authority and responsibility these vicars and deans have is up to the archbishop. For the most part, they represent the archbishop in the parishes. At a minimum, they are the archbishop's eyes and ears, even if they cannot always solve problems by speaking with the authority of his voice. Priests or parishioners with complaints can see them. They can act as ombudsmen with the archbishop and the chancery. They can also be sent by the archbishop to investigate complaints or problems. Often they convene meetings of pastors and others in order to facilitate cooperation and coordination among parishes in their area. More will be said about parishes in the next chapter.

Department or Secretariat Model

Besides parishes, the archbishop must supervise and coordinate archdiocesan agencies. The larger, the more numerous, and the more complex the agencies, the more difficult this becomes. The growth in the number and complexity of these agencies in large archdioceses has forced archbishops to group them in departments supervised and coordinated by department heads who report to the archbishop. Thus, when Joseph Bernardin became archbishop of Chicago, he reorganized the archdiocese and placed archdiocesan agencies under six directors or secretaries (they can be vicars if they are priests) for administrative services, community services, educational services, financial services, pastoral services, and personnel services. This provided the model for reorganizations in Boston and St. Paul, although they combined financial and administrative services into one department.

The earliest secretariat system was established by Cardinal Francis Spellman in New York. Spellman needed such a structure because of the size of the archdiocese and his many interests outside the archdiocese. After Vatican II, secretariats were also established in Baltimore, Detroit,[16] Newark, and Washington.

Under this secretariat model of governance, usually four to seven administrators oversee different parts of the archdiocesan bureaucracy and report to the archbishop (or to the vicar general). The three most common departments are for finances (sometimes called administrative or central services), education, and social services. Some archdioceses also have departments for pastoral services or ministries (liturgy, marriage preparation programs, parishes, chaplains, Renew, lay organizations), personnel (lay ministry, clergy personnel, vocations, seminary) and/or ethnic affairs.[17] But the existence of finance and personnel offices does not necessarily mean that all financial and personnel matters go through these offices. In large archdioceses, sometimes large agencies, like the schools office or Catholic Charities, have their own finance and personnel staff.

Some agencies are difficult to place in a department. Many programs have pastoral, educational, and financial components. RCIA (Rite of Christian Initiation of Adults), Renew, the diocesan newspaper, and youth ministry are pastoral and educational. Should youth ministry go in education or pastoral affairs or, if it is aimed at poor teenagers, in social services? Some programs, like family ministry, pro-life, have both pastoral and social dimensions. It is especially the constituency-oriented offices (youth, family, blacks, Hispanics) that are hard to place and yet are most in need of coordination with other diocesan agencies.[18] Thompson argues that organizations group positions to minimize coordination costs.[19] Units with the greatest interdependence are placed in the same department. Placing units together in a central building is another means of fostering coordination, but it can also distance agencies from their clients.

Sometimes there is a "tupperware" department for leftover agencies (public relations, newspaper, cemeteries, tribunal) that do not fit neatly under other departments. Often an agency is placed in a department for political reasons (who works well with whom) rather than out of any logical order. One archdiocesan liturgy office, for example, is under the chancellor because the priest director would not work with the woman who heads the department of ministries.

All matters dealing with their agencies are first dealt with by the department heads. They are responsible for supervising and coordinating the agencies and settling conflicts within the department. They also attempt to coordinate their work with other department heads and to settle conflicts through negotiations and compromise. This process becomes cumbersome when departments only communicate through their directors. More successful is coordination through informal interdepartmental communications or through lower-level task forces consisting of persons from a number of agencies from different departments that are concerned with the same issue. What they cannot settle goes to department heads who must resolve the dispute or take it to the archbishop. The department heads are also responsible for implementing his decisions in their agencies.

The secretariat or departmental structure makes a large archdiocesan organization more manageable. For example, when Cardinal Law became archbishop of Boston, he found fifty-four agencies reporting directly to him. This was too many for him to supervise and coordinate effectively. After the reorganization, there were only seven: social services, pastoral services, education, community relations, health care services, ministerial personnel, and central services.

Archbishop Weakland of Milwaukee explains the advantages and disadvantages in this kind of system:

> The idea is to give me a chance to be freed up a bit. I know I couldn't cover all the bases without that [departmental] structure. The fear is that a structure like that gets too bureaucratic, too impersonal, and too large. My job in all of that is to provide direction, vision, and priorities.

Some archbishops have been reluctant to adopt the secretariat model because they are concerned about how the chancery bureaucracy is perceived by the priests. Archbishops fear that the priests will see the secretaries as simply another layer of bureaucracy. Pastors often complain that the secretariat system creates a clique of highly paid bureaucrats who get between them and the archbishop. In addition, archbishops in smaller archdioceses do not feel so great a need for this kind of structure. And in small and medium-sized archdioceses, a secretary often is also a pastor or director of an archdiocesan agency. As a pastor, he often provides more liaison and credibility with the priests than actual supervision of the department.

Cardinal James Hickey, who set up a secretariat first in Cleveland and then in Washington, is pleased with the way it works. But he notes some of the systemic difficulties.

I have to be sure of three things: first, that letters get answered; second, that problems don't get lost in intersecretarial, sempiternal committee work that never gets called up. Things can get lost going back and forth or sitting on somebody's desk. There's only one name on the letter and that's mine. If something doesn't happen, if the pastor doesn't get an answer, he doesn't blame the secretary for this or for that. "Old Hickey, down there, he isn't doin' anything, he doesn't care about us."

The third problem that I find with this secretarial system is a subtle tendency to let Daddy do it, to sort of pass it up without recommendation, or to pass it up without prior consultation.

I can get a recommendation from one secretary, and I'd say, "Well, did you talk to so-and-so?" Well, then I end up referring it, and that makes work for me instead of doing work for me. To use the famous Bishop [Albert] Ottenweller [of Steubenville, OH] funnel metaphor, I can have eight funnels coming down over my head: black concerns, Hispanic concerns, education, social concerns, parish life, support services, secretary for the clergy, secretary for religious women—and they all come down on top of me.

At our staff meeting this year, organizationally, that was the point I brought out most clearly. I said, "I don't want to make this sound crass, but basically you're helping me do my work. If instead of your helping me do my work, you are eight people creating more work for me, then the whole thing's in reverse." There's a tendency to do that, to sort of dump things on my desk. And I don't like things dumped on my desk. It should go to a pertinent person.

Vicar General/Moderator of Curia Model

But after delegating supervisory authority to geographical vicars and to secretaries, the archbishop "must see to it that all matters which concern the administration of the entire diocese are duly coordinated and arranged. . . ."[20] This coordination and direction can be done either by the archbishop or by the vicar general acting as his alter ego. The archbishop can also appoint a moderator of the curia, who is usually also a vicar general, "to coordinate the exercise of administrative responsibilities and to see to it that the other members of the curia duly fulfill the office entrusted to them."[21] In the past, this role was sometimes performed by the chancellor or the bishop's secretary, as Cardinal Hickey explains how it was when he was a priest.

My job as the bishop's secretary [in Saginaw, MI] was to coordinate all these things and to get people to talk to one another and to come to the boss [Bishop Stephen Woznicki] with a reasonable consensus or at least a couple of options, with recommendations, so that he could make a decision knowing the facts. Maybe it wasn't always the right decision, but he knew the facts, and he wasn't blindsided by someone coming in that he hadn't heard of.

The power of these officials varies tremendously from archdiocese to archdiocese. A vicar general "possesses that executive power in the entire diocese which belongs to the diocesan bishop in law, that is, he possesses the power to place all administrative acts with the exception of those the bishop has reserved to himself or which in law require the special mandate of the bishop."[22] A powerful vicar general could make many decisions and free the archbishop by taking on most of his administrative responsibilities. But if the archbishop "reserves" to himself most of the power, the vicar general can be a figurehead.

If the vicar general is powerful, other officials in the chancery report to him, he might chair cabinet meetings, and if something must go to the archbishop, it goes through him. The vicar general is the one who coordinates and supervises the department heads or secretaries. The vicars general play important roles in many of the large archdioceses like Boston, Chicago,

Detroit, Los Angeles (under Cardinal Manning), Newark (under Archbishop Gerety), New York (when Bishop O'Keefe was vicar general), Philadelphia (in Cardinal Krol's last years), San Francisco, and Seattle.

The motivation for having a powerful vicar general can be that the archbishop wants more time for long-range planning, for pastoral work, or for work outside the archdiocese. Or it can simply be that the archbishop prefers being brought solutions, not problems. He may dislike conflict and confusion and want matters clarified before they reach him. A strong vicar general can also serve a sick or elderly archbishop.

If an archbishop wants to spend most of his time in pastoral work, he will need someone who takes care of the day-to-day administration. Both Cardinal Manning and Archbishop Quinn found it necessary to have powerful vicars general who would take care of most of their administrative duties. Cardinal Manning's vicar general (Msgr. Benjamin Hawkes) was technically only for finance, but since most things cost money, he exercised sweeping powers in Los Angeles. Archbishop Quinn went through two reorganizations of his San Francisco chancery until he found the structure and a vicar general that suited his needs. In such a system, the vicar general acts as the chief operating officer and supervises and coordinates the archdiocesan agencies under the general policies set by the archbishop.

Chief Executive Model

Most archbishops' administrative styles are more like Jimmy Carter's than Ronald Reagan's.[23] Most archbishops feel at home in administrative work and find it difficult to give up. In these cases the vicar general or moderator of the curia plays a less prominent role than in the case of an archbishop who does not like administration. For example, the quotations above indicate that Cardinal Hickey as a priest exercised a coordinating role for his bishop, but no one does that for the cardinal today.

At the time of my visit to St. Paul, the chancery had been

recently reorganized and was still developing. The vicar general and moderator of the curia explained:

> In fact, Archbishop Roach is still the chief operating officer. It is a question whether he will give up that. He is so much an administrator. It is in his bones, and he is so damn good at it.
>
> What I have done is take a whole lot of sweat off his back, because I do meet regularly with each of the divisional directors and do monitor the smooth coordination. And I settle fights, I am starting to ameliorate wars between divisions.
>
> But Roach is still the chief operating officer. He runs those cabinet meetings; I am not running those meetings. It is really clear. Theoretically, he did say a year ago that eventually he wanted to be able to be out of this office two or three days a week and concentrate more on the parish side, the pastoral side. I will wait and see.

Some archbishops have simply refused to have a moderator of the curia. As Archbishop Weakland of Milwaukee explains, "I don't have a moderator of the curia. I just don't want anybody between myself and. . . . How many layers of administration can you have? It just seems unnecessary to me. But I do have a kind of cabinet."

Individual vs. Cabinet Style

Once he has a staff in place, the archbishop has to figure out how to coordinate and direct it. A number of archbishops (Bernardin, Borders, Hickey, Hunthausen, Hurley, Law, McCarthy, O'Connor, Pilarczyk, Roach, Sheehan, and Stafford) meet weekly or monthly with their staffs. Usually these meetings are with their cabinet, consisting of the department heads (education, social services, finance, pastoral, etc.), the vicar general, chancellor, moderator of the curia, and archbishop's secretary. Sometimes included are the head of the tribunal and directors from offices of planning, minority affairs, and public relations. Frequently an official wears more than one hat. Archbishops who use cabinet meetings are frequently seen as collegial by their staffs. Archbishop Roach, for example, has a regularly scheduled cabinet meeting each week and a monthly meeting with the heads of all the archdiocesan agencies. Cardinal O'Connor has weekly meetings with about thirty members of his staff.

Harry Fagan, associate director of the National Pastoral Life Center, explains that many people, especially priests, find long weekly staff meetings an abomination.

> People on the outside of a chancery have a tendency to put down bureaucracy. God knows, it is still the palace guard. But, if you're running the archdiocese of Washington, roughly a $125 million-a-year corporation, it is impossible to run a corporation with that kind of payroll without all kinds of meetings and all kinds of paper and all kinds of reports.
>
> I don't think we like to see our church reduced to a business, frankly, and it just drives us crazy when we hear an archbishop having a weekly meeting of his secretariats that lasts all morning. But I think we should compare it to a small business of a couple of hundred million dollars.
>
> With the proliferation of ministries and agencies and offices these days, they almost have to do that. You don't know what the hell everybody is doing unless you meet. Most of these guys have gone from a system of sixty to seventy people reporting to them directly to having created some kind of middle management. That middle management only works if you meet with them and say, "Yea, do that," or "Don't do that," or something like that.

But many archbishops prefer meeting individually or in very small groups with those involved in a particular issue. This is the style, for example, of archbishops Donnellan, Hannan, Kelly, Krol, Kucera, Lipscomb, Mahony, May, O'Meara, Quinn, Strecker, Szoka, and Whealon, who do not have regular cabinet or staff meetings. These archbishops believe that larger groups slow down decision making and involve people who do not necessarily have any expertise in the issue being discussed. Others, like the late Archbishop Casey of Denver, simply do not work well in groups.[24]

The pre-Vatican II church did not have much need for cabinet meetings or other types of committee meetings. Most decisions did not require the pooling of knowledge or expertise, so they could be made in a hierarchical structure. Coordination did not need to be fostered, it could be commanded. But today, what happens in one archdiocesan agency can have an effect on another. Coordination is needed on scheduling of events, drawing up budgets, planning joint projects, and developing common policies and procedures. A program like Renew, or a program aimed at helping families, needs the cooperation of all archdiocesan agencies (schools, parishes, liturgy office, social services, newspaper, etc.) if it is to be successful.

Archbishops, like most priests, have no training in committee work. And only in recent times have they had experience in operating through committees. Most do not like committee meetings, others hate them. "If I seem to have an animus against meetings, I do," comments Archbishop Lipscomb of Mobile. "There is one good thing about being a bishop. You can't control all of them, but there are lots of times when you can say, 'No, we do not need to meet.' "

Even archbishops who take their cabinets seriously, like Archbishop Roach in St. Paul, appear to have meetings more out of conviction that it is the right way to operate than through a personal preference. Often the meetings are more important as a means of communication than of decision making. And frequently the archbishop learns nothing new at a meeting, but the meeting enables the members of the chancery to find out what everyone else is doing. Meetings also contribute to chancery morale by providing face-to-face encounters with the archbishop.

Consultative Bodies

Archbishops also use their cabinets as a consultative body on issues not necessarily related to the work of the departments.[25] In a large archdiocese, he would also meet with his auxiliaries or regional vicars. Baltimore invented the acronym COVAS (Committee of Vicars and Secretaries) for a joint meeting of the cabinet and regional vicars.

Archbishops feel more comfortable consulting with these groups than with other consultative bodies. They are smaller groups, which makes consultation easier and more confidential. These officials are his appointees, they are knowledgeable in their areas, and they have a greater than average knowledge of the whole archdiocese. In addition, they are available on a regular basis, often working in the same office building. Archbishops who meet monthly with their staffs include archbishops Borders, Flores, McCarthy, O'Connor, Sheehan, and Sanchez. Those meeting more frequently are archbishops Hickey, Hunthausen, Hurley, Law, Pilarczyk, Roach, and Stafford.

Consultation with groups outside the chancery has become an important part of church governance in the United States. Some archbishops are very good at it and use it as a means of forging a consensus on an issue. Cardinal Bernardin's style is very consultative. A few archbishops seem to enjoy the consultative process. Archbishop Weakland reports,

What takes up much of my time in administration are the meetings with the archdiocesan pastoral council and the priests' council. I meet with both executive boards as they prepare the meetings, and I meet with both councils when they have their full meetings. I enjoy those two groups. They're different in character, they have different interests, different approaches. But I think it's important to hear both. And I enjoy going to those meetings.

Since the Second Vatican Council there has been a remarkable growth in consultative bodies in the Catholic church. Canon lawyers stress that these bodies are consultative and not deliberative—they advise the decision maker, they do not make decisions unless he specifically delegates this power to them. On the other hand, one study found that "by law they behave like advisory groups, by inclination like interest groups."[26]

Diocesan consultative bodies required by canon law are the priests' council, the college of consultors, and the finance council. In addition, most American dioceses would also have a diocesan pastoral council, a board of education, and a priests' personnel board. Many bishops also have cabinets. The board of education, the personnel board, and the finance council will be described in later chapters. Here we will examine the role of the consultors, priests' council, and the archdiocesan pastoral council.

The College of Consultors

The college of consultors is the only diocesan consultative group that predates the Second Vatican Council. The college is made up of six to twelve priests appointed for five-year terms by the bishop.[27] The new code of canon law requires that the consultors be members of the priests' council. But the bishop can choose his consultors from the elected, appointed, or ex officio membership of the council.

When the 1983 code went into effect, a number of archbishops simply appointed their existing consultors to the priests' council. Others, in an attempt to integrate the two consultative bodies more closely, made the elected executive committee of the priests' council their college of consultors. This made the consultors a more representative body, and it also cut down on the number of groups the archbishop had to consult by merging two consultative groups.

The role of consultors today is confused because of the creation of new consultative groups. Their unique role today is the selection of a diocesan administrator who runs the diocese during the interregnum between the death of an archbishop and his successor.[28] In the past, some bishops used the consultors as an informal priests' personnel board as is still done in the archdiocese of Kansas City. According to canon law, the college must be consulted on certain financial matters and acts of extraordinary administration (see chapter 5), but the bishop must also consult the newly mandated finance council on the same matters.[29]

The college of consultors is an old institution in search of a new purpose. Some archbishops consult them on confidential matters that they do not want to bring to the full presbyteral council. But even here, an archbishop has other sources of confidential advice: his auxiliaries (if he has any), the finance council, the personnel board, the executive committee of the priests' council, and his cabinet. In a number of archdioceses, the college rarely meets and for all practical purposes has become nonfunctional. One study found that bishops have chosen not to use the title "diocesan consultors" in 15 percent of the dioceses and have not convened the consultors in at least an additional 25 percent.[30]

Presbyteral Council

The Second Vatican Council told bishops they should listen to their priests, "consult them and have discussions with them about those matters which concern the necessities of pastoral work and the welfare of the diocese. In order to put these ideals into effect, a group or senate of priests representing the presbytery should be established."[31] These priests would be "collaborators of the bishop in the government of the diocese."[32] Such consultation and collaboration was seen not only as a source of good advice but also as a response to a feeling of powerlessness among the clergy that had led to morale problems and protests.[33]

In the United States, prior to Vatican II, no such bodies existed, but in March 1965, before the council ended, a priests' senate was organized in the diocese of Worcester. "By the end of 1966 some 45 senates were functioning, and a year later 135."[34] The creation of these senates was overwhelmingly supported by the priests.[35] A few were organized and met without the bishop's approval. Most were recognized and more or less encouraged by the local bishop, but he could ignore it if he wished.

Vatican II provided no details on how these senates were to be organized. Each diocese drew up its own set of statutes, which were approved by its bishop. The 1983 code of canon law established rules governing their membership and authority and changed their name to presbyteral councils. The archbishops almost always attend the meetings of the priests' council, whereas they did not always attend meetings of priests' senates.

All the members of the old priests' senates were usually elected, but the new code says "about half" of the presbyteral council is to be elected.[36] The rest can be ex officio members designated by the council's statutes or members appointed by the archbishop. Most archbishops have interpreted "about half" to allow the vast majority of the membership to be elected. The elections are usually by geographic districts (e.g., deaneries), by ordination class among the priests, or by a combination of the two.

There is some ambivalence about the representative character of these elected council members. They are encouraged to meet with their constituents to get their input and to communicate the results of council meetings. Sometimes during council discussions the archbishop will ask whether their views reflect those of the priests in the region. On the other hand, members are also told to look beyond their constituencies to the good of the entire archdiocese.

In some cases, where the elections are by deaneries, archbishops have made the elected members deans to give them added status and power. As such, they become not only channels of communication between the council and the priests, but also diocesan administrators. They also can be leaders and coordinators in their deanery on local issues. Some priests object that this overburdens the representative with too many jobs. Theoretically, conflicts could also arise between a priest's administrative responsibilities as a dean and his responsibilities as a councilman. On the other hand, merging the positions gives more status to both and eliminates duplication.

Normally, auxiliary bishops, the vicar general, and the chancellor are ex officio or appointed members of the council. Some bishops have appointed the priest members of their cabinet to the council where they can provide information and be forced to listen to the views of others. Other bishops have their cabinet attend the council meetings as resource persons, not as members, which more clearly separates the legislative and executive functions of governance. On the death of the bishop, the council ceases to exist until it is reestablished by the new bishop.

The presbyteral council has only a consultative voice, but the archbishop "is to listen to it in matters of greater moment."[37] These matters would include, according to the *Directory on the Pastoral Ministry of Bishops,*

the holiness of life, sacred science, and other needs of the priests, or the sanctification and religious instruction of the faithful, or the government of the diocese in general. . . . It is the task of this council, among other things, to seek out clear and distinctly defined aims of the manifold ministries in the diocese, to propose matters that are more urgent, to indicate methods of acting, to assist whatever the Spirit frequently stirs up through individuals or groups, to foster the spiritual life, in order to attain the necessary unity more easily. They ought, finally, to deal with equal distribution of funds for the support of clerics, and also with the erection, suppression and restoration of parishes.[38]

The bishop *must* consult the presbyteral council on several issues:

the advisability of a synod (c. 461 §1); the modification of parishes (cc. 515 §2; 813); offerings of the faithful on the occasion of parish services (c. 531); norms for parish councils (c. 536); the construction of a church or the conversion of a church to secular use (cc. 1215 §2; 1222 §2); and the imposition of a diocesan tax (c. 1263).[39]

The old priests' senates elected their own officers, usually a president and vice-president, and set their own agenda. According to canon law, the bishop is the president of the presbyteral council and determines its agenda.[40] Most archbishops allow an elected chairman to run the meetings, which might occur eight to ten times a year. The agenda of the meetings is usually drawn up and discussed at a meeting of the archbishop with the executive committee or the officers of the council. Few archbishops will veto agenda items, although they will discourage bringing up controversial items over which they have no control, e.g., priestly celibacy or the cases of Charles Curran and Archbishop Hunthausen.

When they first came into existence, priests' senates and councils concentrated on priestly concerns: priests' morale, salaries, stipends, health insurance, automobile expenses, automobile insurance, pensions, retirement, retreats, the process for appointing pastors (personnel boards, tenure, etc.), continuing education, due process for disputes with the bishop, rectory living conditions, and the relations between pastors and associates. Most councils have a committee on priestly ministry that studies and makes recommendations on such issues.

Many of these issues made the councils look like labor unions negotiating with management over pay and working conditions. In fact, what the priests were seeking was not significantly more money but a more professional relationship in what had been a very paternalistic system. For example, in the past the bishop or a diocesan hospital would normally take care of a priest who was seriously ill, but there were always horror stories about priests stuck with huge medical bills. Likewise, there was a desire for greater equality between priests in rich and poor parishes, and between pastors and associates.

Once these issues were dealt with, many councils moved on to social justice issues. Numerous resolutions were passed on abortion, racism, housing, welfare reform, nuclear weapons, Vietnam, Central America, South Africa, boycotts, etc., most of which would be defined as politically "liberal" and were in keeping with (or to the left of) the positions taken by the National Conference of Catholic Bishops. Some of these resolutions had specific relevancy to local conditions; others were in response to national or international events. For the most part, these resolutions were not very controversial in the council because they did not demand anything more than a letter to a public official from the bishop or the priests' council. Priests might be encouraged to preach on peace or justice on a particular Sunday, but such recommendations were always optional.

In some dioceses, the priests' senate or council was an important initiator of pastoral programs following the Vatican Council, especially if the bishop was a benign nonleader. In these cases, the natural leaders from the clergy could take charge with the bishop's acquiescence. This is a time-consuming process that may burn out these leaders who have other full-time jobs.

Bishops have also asked their councils' advice on the establishment of parish council guidelines, the implementation of RCIA, whether or not to do Renew or some other parish renewal program, and the implementation of liturgical reforms. Archdiocesan mission statements have also been prepared or critiqued by presbyteral councils, as have proposals for reorganizing the archdiocesan administrative structures. Some councils have also been involved in planning for the day when there are fewer priests.

With the switch from a priests' senate to a canonical presbyteral council, some priests feared that they would lose control because of the bishop's ability to appoint members and control the agenda. Some argue that it is no longer a priests' council but the bishop's council. In some cases, it is said, the bishop controls the agenda to repress controversial topics and maintain control. But other archdiocesan observers believe that the councils are working better than the senates because as canonical bodies the archbishops and priests take them more seriously. A 1974 study found that 29 percent of the council officers felt that it was a great problem that the bishop had given no real decision-making power to the council, but an even larger percent (52 percent) felt that getting grass-roots input was a great problem.[41] In many archdioceses, turnouts for council elections have exceeded previous turnouts for senate elections. This perceived improvement may be due to the experience archbishops and priests gained while working in senates rather than due to any change in structures.

Pastoral Council

Most archbishops have also formed archdiocesan pastoral councils in response to the Second Vatican Council's call for greater lay involvement in the church:

It is highly desirable that in each diocese a pastoral council be established over which the diocesan bishop himself will preside and in which specially chosen clergy, religious, and lay people will participate. The function of this council will be to investigate and to weigh matters which bear on pastoral activity, and to formulate practical conclusions regarding them.[42]

The first council was formed in Richmond in 1965. By 1983, at least 36 percent of the dioceses had councils.[43] Although the 1983 code of canon law says pastoral councils should be established "to the extent that pastoral circumstances recommend it,"[44] the code gives few details on how these councils should be organized. As a result, they vary in organization, size, procedures, and frequency of meetings.

The median size of diocesan pastoral councils is 33, with the largest being Omaha with 407 and the smallest Beaumount with 15 members. The councils, especially the larger ones, make use of committees to do work and prepare reports for the full council. Because of the existence of presbyteral councils, the emphasis in pastoral councils has naturally been on lay input, although they are, in fact, composed of priests, religious, and laity. The laity account for two-thirds of the members of each council: 32 percent are laywomen and 34 percent laymen.[45] Often a layperson chairs the meetings of the pastoral council, but sometimes the archbishop chairs them to show that he takes it seriously.

The membership of the councils is "to be so selected that the entire portion of the people of God which constitutes the diocese is truly reflected, with due regard for the diverse regions, social conditions and professions of the diocese as well as the role which they have in the apostolate."[46] They can be appointed, but one study found that 70 percent are elected by deanery councils or similar representative bodies.[47] The priest representatives are normally elected by the presbyteral council and the religious representatives elected by the religious. Lay representation tends to be on geographic regions with some special rules for special constituencies like minorities and young people. In a small archdiocese, like Mobile, lay representatives may be chosen from each parish. Experience has shown that better communication with the parishes results if the representatives are the presidents (or at least members) of the parish councils. In a large archdiocese, regional councils often elect members to the pastoral council, but communication between the regional councils and the pastoral council has been difficult.

George Wilson, S.J., who has been a consultant for a number of pastoral councils, prefers councils that are appointed after input from a broad range of nominating mechanisms. He has found democratically elected councils difficult to work with.

> Experience seems to be showing us that the method of electing parish "reps," who then gather to elect deanery or regional "reps," who then become the diocesan council, does not in fact produce members competent or attitudinally suited to play the serious role of leadership in development of a diocese, i.e., in determining its goals and policies.[48]

Others would agree that working with democratically elected councils is difficult, but that they better reflect the real church as required by canon law. All would stress the importance of council members seeing themselves as concerned for the common good of the diocese and not simply as representatives of a particular parish, region, or group: priests, religious, blacks, Hispanics, women, rural, etc. "The pastoral council is meant to be *representative* of the whole people of God without the members being considered necessarily *representatives* (deputees) of a specific constituency."[49] Successful councils usually have orientation programs for new members.

The council's responsibility is "to investigate under the authority of the bishop all those things which pertain to pastoral works, to ponder them and to propose practical conclusions about them."[50] Most councils meet at least quarterly. Some of the very large councils meet annually as assemblies with an executive committee meeting monthly. The agenda of the pastoral council is usually set by the executive committee. Often the archbishop will ask the pastoral council to discuss and react to documents from the National Conference of Catholic Bishops or from Rome. For example, many archbishops asked their councils for reactions to the early drafts of NCCB pastoral letters on peace, on the economy, and on women. They also asked help in responding to material sent out prior to the 1980 synod on the family, the 1985 extraordinary synod, and the 1987 synod on the laity. Such discussions are both educational for the council members and helpful to the archbishop in preparing his response.

Pastoral councils have dealt with internal church issues (parish councils, financial policy, lay salaries, due process, religious education) and issues of concern to the wider community (abortion, advocacy programs for minorities, peace, and justice). Pastoral councils have also been involved in preparing archdiocesan mission statements. Sometimes these mission statements are preceded by archdiocese-wide surveys and parish discussions. Archbishops hope that these mission statements will help set priorities for the archdiocese, but usually these statements are so general and mention so many topics that they are little help in setting priorities. On the other hand, some archbishops refer back to these statements frequently in discussions about priorities and budgets. Often the process and discussions in the pastoral council are more important than the mission statement itself.

Most archbishops admit that their pastoral councils do not work well.[51] Some complain that their councils get involved in administrative issues rather than policy questions. Nor is the relationship of the council to other consultative groups clear. Some have conflicts with school boards over school policy.

Communications between the pastoral council and other entities (diocesan agencies, priests' council, school boards, regional councils, and parishes) has been weak. Most are too large and act too slowly to be working groups. And they usually meet only three to eight times a year. Their members are heterogeneous groups with varied educations, backgrounds, and interests. They are unsophisticated theologically, and they are uninformed on many of the topics they discuss. On the other hand, they do reflect the church, which is not a homogeneous group of experts.

Archbishops report that the pastoral council functions best as a feedback mechanism. An archbishop hears most often from people who write letters, people with complaints, people who want him to do something, or people who work directly for the church. A council allows the archbishop to hear from a representative group of people in the archdiocese. From the pastoral council, the archbishop gets feedback on how well programs are serving the people. Council members can be especially vocal about those parts of the church that touch their lives or the lives of their children: what goes on in parishes and schools. They are also good at reacting to proposals for new programs or policies. The council can give the archbishop a feel for how people will react to the proposals.

Archdiocesan Synods

A consultative body dating from the fourth century is the diocesan synod. A diocesan synod "is a group of selected priests and other Christian faithful of a particular church which offers assistance to the diocesan bishop for the good of the entire diocesan community."[52] Synods do not meet on a periodic basis but only when called by the bishop after consulting with the presbyteral council. The 1917 code of canon law mandated a synod every ten years. In fact, they were rarely called, and the 1983 code dropped the requirement.

Ex officio members of a synod include auxiliary bishops, vicars general, episcopal vicars, the judicial vicar, members of the presbyteral council, the rector of the seminary, deans, a priest elected from each deanery, and some superiors of religious communities. Lay and religious members are also chosen by the pastoral council in a manner and number to be determined by the bishop.[53] The members are not simply invited but "obliged to participate" and may not send proxies or substitutes.[54] The legislation enacted by the synod must be approved by the bishop before it can take effect.[55] Others, including non-Catholics, may be invited as observers.

The *Directory on the Pastoral Ministry of Bishops* suggests five ways a synod can assist the bishop for the good of the local church: "(1) adapting laws and norms of the church universal to local conditions; (2) setting policy and programs of apostolic works; (3) resolving problems of the apostolate and administration; (4) giving impetus to projects and undertakings in the diocese; (5) correcting errors in doctrine and morals, primarily by providing authentic teaching."[56]

During the period of this study, some archdioceses were having or planning synods (Los Angeles, Miami, Milwaukee, New Orleans, New York, St. Paul). The New Orleans synod developed a manual of policies and procedures that implemented the new code of canon law. But most synods have attempted to be more pastoral. In St. Paul, the synod was seen as the culmination of a process that started with a program of priests' renewal and Renew in parishes. In other places (New York and Los Angeles), the synods were used by new archbishops to get grass-roots input and to set goals and priorities.

Often it was not clear why the work of the synod could not be done by an ongoing archdiocesan pastoral council rather than by a one-shot synod. Archbishops argue that the synods involve more people and are taken more seriously than the pastoral councils. In addition, the preparation for synod meetings tends to be much more extensive than for pastoral councils. Many synods are preceded by surveys, parish discussions, and work by commissions and committees.

But the results of a synod are often predictable. People want good parish liturgy, they want affordable Catholic schools, and they want programs that will keep their children on the straight and narrow. They also want programs to take care of the elderly and the poor. But the synods rarely bring together the expertise needed to achieve these goals, nor do they solve the problem of limited resources. After the statements are written, the people go home and the archbishop and his cabinet are left with the problem of implementation.

Another difficulty is the relationship of the synod to the other consultative bodies. One expert recommends the following division of labor.

1. Diocesan synod: sets the vision or general direction, expresses the spirit of the diocese by enacting basic policies.
2. Diocesan pastoral council: does pastoral planning to implement the vision over a period of time.
3. Presbyteral council: advises the bishop on governance questions in the diocese, implementing the pastoral plan in practice.
4. College of consultors and finance council: provide advice and at times must consent for various financial transactions.[57]

Despite their limitations, consultative bodies are important sources of advice and information for bishops. In order for a council or synod to function well, certain prerequisites are needed. First, there must be a level of trust between the council members and the archbishop so that free discussion can occur on any item. Having an executive committee prepare the agenda and having someone other than the archbishop chair the meetings protects the archbishop from giving the appearance of manipulating the council. Some archbishops sit back and listen in order to encourage free debate. Others prefer to join the discussions. A bishop's willingness to argue for one position and then publicly change his position as a result of the discussions also builds trust. In some instances, the fact that the bishop listens is the most important thing that happens at synod and council meetings. If he projects a sympathetic concern, people will be more accepting even if he cannot or does not do anything.

Second, the archbishop has to bring important issues to the councils. Councils that depend solely on agenda from the grass roots often get sidetracked on peripheral issues. The grass roots are not always sufficiently informed so that they can pick the most important issues for consideration.

Third, councils need someone to do, not only their secretarial work (minutes, correspondence, mailings, etc.), but also other staff work such as research and planning. Good council members, both priests and laity, have full-time jobs and other commitments. Normally, staff assistance will have to come from chancery officials. Some archdioceses have a planning office or an office of councils that works with consultative groups. These staffs also provide an important link between the various consultative bodies.

Fourth, if a council is going to discuss a topic like education for which there is an archdiocesan office, the director of that office must be present to listen and answer questions. The presence of the director speeds discussion and improves communications. Council committees also need support and help from the archdiocesan staff.

Fifth, council members need a training and orientation program so that they understand how the diocesan structure works and their role in it. Confusion and misunderstandings can result when people think a consultative body is like a secular legislature. *Robert's Rules of Order* is not helpful for bodies desiring consensus rather than confrontation. On the other hand, discernment models from religious communities are not always helpful since they require a sense of community that takes more time to create than is usually available.

Finally, the councils need means of communicating with their constituencies on the regional and parish level.

Conclusion

Not all archbishops are alike. Their personalities and preferences influence how they govern and what they do. Their leadership styles do have an effect on their archdioceses. John Seidler, in studying conflicts between priests and bishops, found "the one overriding determination of the diocesan climate is the ordinary. His policies are reflected in a unified and buoyant clergy, or a splintered and disgruntled one."[58] The clerical climate improved when the bishop had a progressive attitude toward change and when he had a humanitarian and egalitarian style of leadership. "By contrast, leadership that was inward-looking, disciplinarian and edict-dominated has great likelihood of provoking dissent, or bringing on disunity and grievances."[59]

But in order to govern well, bishops must establish and use structures that fit their personalities and styles. These structures must not only respond to their styles but also to the characteristics and needs of their archdioceses, as was explained in the preceding chapter.

In the next four chapters we will examine how archbishops govern some of the more important parts of their archdioceses. It is impossible to examine every aspect of archdiocesan governance. Rather the focus will be parishes, finances, personnel, schools, and social services. Throughout these chapters we will see how the personality and preferences of an archbishop interface through archdiocesan structures with the needs and characteristics of his archdiocese. Chapter 8 will examine the role of the archbishop outside his archdiocese.

4. Parish and Regional Governance

What does it take to keep the archbishop happy? Wine, women, and song.

———PRIEST, St. Louis

Unless the pastor is turned on with something, your program is going to end up in file thirteen.

———DIRECTOR OF PLANNING, Louisville

The ministry of the church is carried out primarily in parishes, the geographical units into which a diocese is divided.[1] Here new members are baptized, and their Christian life is nurtured and celebrated through the sacraments and other parish programs. This chapter will look at how archbishops influence parish life. Bishops and chancery officials often describe their role as supporting and supervising the work that is done in the parishes. Many also speak of encouraging the parishes to work together.

The bishop influences what happens in a parish in a number of ways. Most importantly, he trains seminarians, ordains priests, and appoints pastors, as will be explained in chapter 6. He also oversees the parishes' financial administration, as will be explained in chapter 5. He can also set a tone for the archdiocese through pastoral letters, newspaper columns, sermons, and addresses to parish personnel. He can exhort and encourage certain activities and discourage others.

Diocesan Policies

The bishop can also mandate archdiocesan policies and procedures that must be followed in the parishes. These policies and procedures can apply to the spiritual, sacramental, educational, and financial life of the parish. Some archdioceses, like Philadelphia, have a manual or a collection of policies and procedures for pastors. "Cardinal Krol loves this book," explains the controller. "He thinks it is the greatest thing since apple pie. Every time he assigns a new pastor, or when the newly ordained get assigned, he hand-delivers a copy and says 'This is required reading now. You read this and follow it.' "

The establishment of rules and routines that constrain the actions of subsidiary units in an organization is a normal method of control and coordination.[2] Such standardization requires a stable environment and a high degree of certainty that the rules and procedures will result in the desired outcomes. Mandated policies vary greatly from diocese to diocese. Much of the material will simply repeat the Vatican or national regulations dealing with issues such as the liturgy and sacramental life of the parish. Some will expand on these regulations, for example, what music may or may not be used at weddings, or what preparation is required before someone can receive the sacraments of penance, Communion, confirmation, or matrimony. Some policies regulate the administration of the parishes. Most archdioceses, for example, require pastors to have parish councils. Other policies will apply to church finances or to the parish school.

These policies are not usually made in a vacuum. Normally the policies are developed through a consultative process involving the bishop's cabinet, priests' council, pastoral council, school board, or other groups. Often they are modeled on policies developed in other dioceses.

But bishops do not establish policies to cover every contingency. Such an attempt would be counterproductive and would treat priests as bureaucrats rather than as professionals. Policies dealing with the spiritual life of the parish are less detailed except when dealing with preparation for and admittance to the sacraments, especially marriage. Policies tend to be made in response to past problems or conflicts. They are also written to answer the questions most frequently asked of chancery officials. The most detailed policies tend to cover finances (budgets, construction, collections, etc.), personnel (salaries, hiring, firing, etc.) and legal obligations (contracts, taxes, insurance, etc.). These are all areas with secular parallels. More will be said in later chapters about diocesan policies and procedures affecting finances, personnel, education, and social services.

More recently, archbishops have attempted to coordinate by planning, which is a better response to a changing environment than standardized rules and routines that are adopted for the archdiocese.[3] As will be seen below, through parish visitations they have also encouraged coordination through mutual adjustment or coordination by feedback.

Complaints

Establishing policies is one thing; getting them implemented is quite another. Publishing policy statements will not make good parishes. The bishop must give to the parishes support, encouragement, and correction where needed. To do this, he must first find out what is going on.

Archbishops hear from parishioners. "They have no hesitation about writing letters," explained Archbishop Donnellan of Atlanta, "so you get a variety of complaints. There is no problem about things being brought to your attention." Most bishops pay serious attention to their mail. They like to see incoming letters before they are routed to the appropriate offices.

Most of the mail from parishioners is negative. These letters have to be kept in perspective by the bishops since "an astonishing 88 percent [of Catholics] approved of the job their priests were doing; only 9 percent disapproved."[4] "Just like letters to the editor, they are mostly critical," reports one archbishop. "Those who are satisfied never bother to write." This same archbishop said, "It used to be that the left wing of the church were the ones unhappy. I hear nothing from them anymore, it is the right wing that you hear from most. It is mostly in the way of complaints on liturgical matters. They are hyper-critical. It is a minority, a vocal minority, and a very active minority."

Some of the right-wing writers send copies of their letters "to Cardinal Joseph Ratzinger [prefect of the Vatican Congregation for the Doctrine of the Faith] or Cardinal Augustine Mayer [prefect of the Vatican Congregation for Divine Worship]," complained one archbishop. "I used to answer those, but now I don't. If they want to correct something in this diocese, fine, tell me and I will correct it. Or I will explain that this is an option and that the priest can do that."

Besides complaints about sermons and liturgies, often the complainant feels he or she was treated unfairly by the pastor. A parish school will also be a source of complaints. Sometimes the complaints deal with the personal conduct of the priests.

In responding to complaints, most archbishops prefer to have the problem dealt with at the lowest level possible. A complaint about a pastor might be passed on to a chancellor, priest personnel director, regional vicar, or dean who would then investigate the complaint and get the priest's side of the story.

Bishop Leo J. Burst, vicar for clergy in Milwaukee, explains how he deals with complaints over the phone:

> The main thing is to listen, to let the person talk. See what it is. Sometimes it is not serious at all. Sometimes he didn't like what the priest said in the sermon. A lot of it involves school problems. Some teacher's contract was not renewed. Great turmoil over that.
>
> Sometimes the best thing is to get the person to talk to the priest directly. And that will handle it. Sometimes the best tactic is to stall a little bit, and it will all go away by itself.
>
> Generally, we call the priest and tell him this has come to us by phone, just to let him know. Then you always get a different side of the story.
>
> The main thing is to pass the buck as much as you can. If it is a school issue, contact the school office. Otherwise you get swamped under if you try to handle everything yourself. No use trying to solve all the problems in the world by ourselves. That would be dumb.

Depending on the nature of the accusation and the number of previous complaints against the pastor, the complaint will be taken more or less seriously. "If it is a very serious thing, then you have to take more serious actions," says an archbishop. "And if it is something gravely serious that could cause scandal to the church, then you have to take drastic action. You have to tell them that I'm not going to allow them to continue until we see a psychologist or whoever in the community would have to deal with this."

Some archbishops, like Donnellan of Atlanta, will not take the complaint seriously unless the person is willing to put it in a signed letter that can be shared with the accused to get his side. If the complainant insists on remaining anonymous, the matter will usually be dropped. Other archbishops prefer not to reveal the name of the person complaining. One archbishop explains:

It might be somebody complaining that a priest was maybe crude or inconsiderate in a given situation. It might be that somebody thinks that he is drinking too much. It might be a priest showing some kind of misconduct that others have a right to complain about in his personal life or in his ministry.

Generally, a word to the wise is all that is needed. I tell the priest that "I don't think I have to reveal the source. I'm telling you what the complaint is, and I have no way of knowing if it is an objective thing or purely subjective by way of the complainer. You were reported to have done this or not done that. I'm not judging you, I don't know how reliable that person is. But you know whether you did this or not."

Sometimes the priest will be noncommittal and not say yes or no. I am not asking them to say yes or no, I just want to get this information to him. If this happens again, then I will have to ask him, "Is this true?" and get down to the nitty-gritty. If he denies it, then, OK, he denies it. But I'm not discounting the complaint either.

Most bishops and chancery officials appear to be biased in favor of the priests. This reflects their desire for due process (he is innocent until proven guilty) and their reluctance to take sides against a fellow priest. On the other hand, serious problems often first surface through complaints addressed to the bishop.

Regional Governance

Some archdioceses have so many parishes that it is impossible for the archbishop to supervise and support them directly. Archbishops of populous archdioceses have responded by dividing their archdioceses into regional vicariates overseen by episcopal vicars who are usually auxiliary bishops.[5] The auxiliaries spend much of their time visiting parishes.

Archbishops recognize advantages and disadvantages to the vicariate system. The advantage is having someone close to the scene, familiar with the local situation, who can represent the archbishop. If the vicar is an auxiliary bishop, his representative value can be very strong. The vicar is also an important communication channel who can inform the archbishop about the needs and problems of his vicariate. The disadvantage of the vicariate system is that the priests often see it as another layer of bureaucracy separating them from the archbishop. In addition, the actual power and authority of the vicars is frequently limited and ambiguous.

Population size is a more important variable than geographic size in fostering regional vicariates. For example, Newark, the smallest archdiocese in area but one of the largest in population (1.3 million Catholics), is divided into four vicariates, each headed by an auxiliary bishop, coinciding with the counties of Bergen, Essex, Hudson, and Union. Baltimore, Boston, Chicago, Detroit, Dubuque, Los Angeles, St. Paul, and Washington also have regional vicariates overseen by auxiliaries. The vicariates are often further divided into deaneries.

How to divide the diocese geographically is a debated issue. Often vicariates and deaneries follow city and county boundaries. Most also attempt to join parishes with similar economic or demographic characteristics, because they share common interests and problems. When they meet as a unit, they can discuss their common concerns and develop common policies and programs.

In some dioceses, like Detroit, there is an attempt to construct vicariates that reflect the diocese as a whole. Rather than placing urban parishes in one, suburban in another, and rural in a third, each vicariate would contain a mix. This pie-shaped model is defended on the grounds that it forces everyone to remember that they are one church. It also encourages twinning between rich and poor parishes. On the other hand, their vicariate meetings are not very productive because the people do not share common concerns and find it difficult to work on common programs. In Detroit, for example, the school office tried working with the vicariates, but "it doesn't work," reports the superintendent of schools. "The city schools have different needs than the suburban schools."

Archdioceses with only one auxiliary usually do not have a vicariate system because of the fear that the region given to the auxiliary would feel abandoned by the archbishop. For example, an archdiocese with one major city and a large rural area could not officially give the rural area to the auxiliary while leaving the city under the direct supervision of the archbishop. Many rural areas already feel they do not get enough attention from the archbishop, and leaving them to the auxiliary would exacerbate things. Unofficially, an archbishop may, in fact, ask the auxiliary to give more time to places distant from the see city.

But even some populous archdioceses, like New York, Philadelphia, and Hartford, with a number of auxiliary bishops, do not have them acting as regional vicars. Archbishop Whealon decided against using vicars in Hartford, although he wondered if he had made the correct decision. He explains:

I can see a plus in the vicar system in that it does permit a close supervision of almost everybody down the line. People reporting to people who report to the bishop.

On the other hand, the drawbacks are that it sets up middle men between the priest and the bishop; that leads to resentment on the part of priests. It develops a flood of mimeographed materials sent out to people who have to do the work anyhow—the parish priests. It can easily establish a person in the middle who feels supported by neither side. Further, it builds up bureaucracy in a dramatic way. It builds up expenses.

I am going to stay away from it as long as I can, but I am just not sure that this is the way it should be. I think it is a necessity in New York, Boston, and Chicago. But is it a necessity in Cleveland, in Erie? I just don't know.

Power and Influence

What powers a vicar has varies among archdioceses. The archbishop usually reserves to himself the really important decisions—priest personnel assignments, large expenditures, the closing or opening of a school or parish, etc. Normally, the archbishop would consult the vicar before making a major decision affecting his vicariate. Some vicars have input into these decisions by sitting on the priests' personnel board, the finance council, the archbishop's cabinet, and/or other advisory bodies. Often it takes time before the priests and people recognize the vicar's role. "It took almost two years before people would accept their decisions as authority," reports Archbishop Borders of Baltimore, where one of the first regional systems was set up. In addition, if the auxiliary is seen to have no influence in important matters, the pastors will not take him seriously.

Vicars are especially concerned about who will be made pastors in their vicariates. If they sit on the personnel board, their input is direct. They will bring to the board the needs of their parishes and the desires of their priests. If they are not on the board, the priests' personnel director or the archbishop will have to get their input.

Some vicars do have extensive financial jurisdiction over the parishes. For example, a vicar in Detroit reviews the parish budget and can approve any project that costs up to $50,000. Even when the vicar does not have the authority to make the decision, often the archbishop or the vicar for finance will consult him about the situation in the parish.

In Los Angeles, Archbishop Mahony established regional offices for vicars that included officials from Catholic Charities and other archdiocesan agencies. How these administrators will relate to their archdiocesan supervisors and to the vicar is not clear. But most archbishops are opposed to setting up minichanceries in the vicariates. As a result, the relationship of the vicars to the archdiocesan chancery is often unclear. He is someone the administrators should listen to respectfully, but the priests' personnel director, the superintendent of schools, and the director of finances report to the archbishop not to the vicars. The vicar may see chancery officials infrequently unless the archbishop has joint meetings of his regional vicars and his administrative directors.

Under these circumstances the vicar's power is often based on his ability to persuade the archbishop, chancery officials, and pastors to go along with his proposals. The vicars tend to describe themselves as conveners and coordinators of pastors or other local groups with common interests and problems. They often act not as decision makers but as facilitators who help groups work toward consensus. Some vicariates, for example, have developed common sacramental preparation programs used by all the parishes in the vicariate. Others have developed joint social or educational programs.

The vicars also act as lines of communication between the parishes and the chancery, especially the archbishop. They can interpret and explain policy to pastors and be a channel of feedback to the central administration. Vicars can also act as ombudsmen by supporting parish interests before archdiocesan agencies. In addition, many diocesan agencies are finding the vicariate meetings an efficient and effective way of communicating with parishes. Communication is very important when a regional organization and an archdiocesan agency are working on the same problem. For example, school consolidation would normally be worked on by both the school office and a deanery or vicariate organization.

As a result, the regional vicar is often the man in the middle, which allows him to influence decisions but not make them. Since he would rarely disagree publicly with his archbishop, he may have to defend policies he disagrees with. He is often inaccurately seen by the parishioners as a man of immense power (after all he is a bishop). On the other hand, pastors realize that he can often be circumvented on important issues. In short, the man is more important than the office. If he is listened to by the archbishop and respected by the priests, he can be very influential. But if he fails to persuade others to his point of view, he will be very frustrated because he has little power to impose his views.

The importance of the man in the job became clear in 1985 when the priests' council in the archdiocese of New York considered a proposal to divide the archdiocese into four vicariates. Under Cardinal Terence Cooke there were seventeen vicars (priests and bishops) who had been given their positions and then told not to do anything. Cardinal O'Connor found upon his arrival that vicars and priests were very dissatisfied with this system. The council proposal would have transformed the old vicars into deans and then established new vicars over larger areas of the archdiocese. This proposal received wide support in the priests' council until the members began to think about who would be their vicars. Since in most cases the auxiliary bishop residing in the vicariate would be the vicar, the members of the council could guess who would be their vicar. This gave enough priests second thoughts so that the proposal was sent back to committee for more study.

Often the vicariates are further divided into deaneries. The deans do on a smaller scale what the vicars do in their regions. They act as facilitators and coordinators in their deaneries. For example, they might help coordinate Mass schedules and penance services in their deaneries. They often act as consultants and lines of communication for the vicar. But since the deans are full-time pastors, the time that they can give to being dean is limited.

Parish Visitations

Archbishops do not like simply to sit in their offices doing paperwork. They believe that visiting parishes is an important part of their ministry. Some archbishops only visit a parish for a special event like confirmation. They either have no time for anything else or they feel that it is best to leave the pastors alone to do their jobs. Other bishops will make a special pastoral visit independently of confirmation. This practice has been encouraged by the Holy See.[6] Such visits provide a bishop with information and feedback that can improve his supervisory and coordinating activities.

When visiting a parish, the archbishop or auxiliary bishop can be a role model for priests in the way he preaches and celebrates liturgies. "They have to hear me preach well," explains Archbishop Kelly of Louisville. "For me to wing it in their presence is to allow them to do the same."

In St. Louis, pastors quickly learned that Archbishop May wanted women to be involved in his liturgies as either eucharistic ministers or lectors when he visited a parish. He also liked singing and encouraged Communion under both species. As the priests' underground newsletter put it: "What does it take to keep the archbishop happy? Wine, women, and song."

Even a confirmation visit can tell the bishop a lot about the parish. The bishop can gain much information about the parish simply by observing how well the liturgy is prepared: Can the choir sing? Can the readers be understood? Is there an offertory procession? Are there extraordinary ministers of Communion? If the parish did not prepare well for the bishop's liturgy, it is likely that they are unprepared for most of their liturgies. "If you go for a confirmation," Archbishop Donnellan of Atlanta explained, you have the opportunity to observe how the altar boys function, what the rectory looks like, how the sacristy is, and so on. You have an opportunity to observe the parish and to talk to the pastor.

Besides liturgical ceremonies, the archbishop can observe other things about the parish during his visit. How do the people interact with the parish priests and staff? How well do those confirmed answer his questions? What do people say to him at the reception? Archbishop Lipscomb of Mobile recalls being approached at a reception by a young child who has just received confirmation.

[She] is in tears, not because she has received the Holy Spirit, but because she cannot serve Mass.

Here is her chance to confront the bishop up close. That is what she has been waiting for all during her confirmation, to ask the bishop about why she can't be an altar boy.

There is somebody who has got the preparation and instruction of those children all mixed up if they have made this kind of value so paramount in their lives as to cause drastic warps in their faith life.

In an official full-day pastoral visitation, the bishop will meet with the parish council and the parish staff, especially the pastor and the associates. If there is a school, he would also meet with the principal and even visit some of the classes. "The kids go home and tell their parents, 'The bishop was there. He talked to us,' " explains Archbishop Kucera of Dubuque. "It is corny, but I always tell the little kids, 'You go home and hug and kiss your mother and father, and you tell them: This is from the archbishop. He thanks you for sending you to a Catholic school.' "

After visiting each classroom for five minutes, Archbishop Pilarczyk of Cincinnati meets with the teachers and the religious education teachers for forty minutes to an hour. "I ask them what they like about their school, what they would like to see going on in the next five years or so," he says. "The same thing about the CCD [religious education] program. [I listen to] whatever they want to say. I try to encourage them to be teachers because the church needs teachers."

Archbishop Pilarczyk also meets with the parish staff, which could include the principal, director of religious education, youth minister, liturgy minister, organist, pastoral minister, permanent deacon, and others.

> I meet with them as a group. I thought of meeting them individually, but then I decided that wasn't such a good idea because one could be afraid of what the others are going to say.
>
> I ask everybody to tell me what they do, and we just go around the circle. 'I do this and this and this.' But the pastor will say, 'Yeah, but you also do such and such.' It's a nice thing.

In the evening, the bishop will usually have dinner with the priests. "My thinking is that there has to be a time when priests have time with their bishop," says Archbishop Pilarczyk. Then there would be a liturgy and afterwards a meeting with the parish council. Archbishop Pilarczyk also asks the council, "What do you like about your parish and what would you like to see going on in the next few years?"

In such a visit, the archbishop has more time to listen to people's concerns and ask questions about what they are doing. He also can learn their reactions to archdiocesan programs and agencies: Are they really serving the parish or simply getting in its way? But such visits are time consuming. Many archbishops complain that they do not have enough time to do these visits properly. In bigger archdioceses, the archbishop cannot make long visits at many parishes; the auxiliaries will have to bear the brunt of most parish visitations.

Closing Parishes

A serious problem currently faced by archbishops is population shifts that have left many old inner-city churches empty as Catholics moved to the suburbs. These huge plants are expensive to run for a few families, but closing them is very controversial. Not only do the parishioners want their parish kept open, former parishioners who have moved to the suburbs often have sentimental attachments to these churches. This is especially true of churches built by strong ethnic communities. The problem is further exacerbated by the fact that the parish may now contain black or Hispanic Catholics who will feel abandoned by the church if the parish is closed.

"We had a nine-month process, working with the people," recalls the secretary for planning in Baltimore where two parishes with only seventy-five parishioners were closed. "The end result was still the same, they believed it was a betrayal." In both cases there were neighboring parishes within three or four blocks.[7]

Similarly in Detroit, controversy surrounded the announcement in October 1988 that forty-three inner city churches, serving ten thousand parishioners, would be closed the following June. The announcement, which affected one-third of the city's parishes, followed a five-year study of the archdiocese. Church officials noted that there are only 48,800 Catholic households in the city, down from 104,380 in 1976. Over the past seven years, the archdiocese had subsidized urban parishes and their schools to the tune of $19 million. In 1981, when the archdiocese closed one parish, parishioners occupied the church and it took sixty police officers to clear the site for demolition.

Rather than stir up a hornet's nest, the archbishop will usually leave the parish alone as long as it is not a serious drain on archdiocesan finances. But the decline in the number of priests and the need for them elsewhere puts additional pressure on the archbishop to act. He will also have to consider closing small rural parishes. To "take a priest out of a small rural parish that has had one for 150 years can be devastating," notes the Baltimore secretary for planning, especially if there is no nearby parish where the people can go.

Archbishops have attempted a number of different strategies to deal with parish closings and priest shortages. Probably the least successful is the executive fiat from the bishop closing the parish. Many bishops have had to back down in the face of strong opposition to such announcements. Sometimes the archbishop will indicate to the parish that when the current pastor retires he will not be replaced.

Where the archdiocese has a number of such parishes, as in Chicago, Cincinnati, and Detroit, the archbishop will attempt to develop a systematic way of dealing with the parishes. Often this will involve extensive consultation with priests and parishioners prior to any decision. Plant surveys will be made to determine which church buildings are in the best condition. Census data will be used to show historical trends. Urban planners will be consulted on the future of the neighborhood. Spread sheets projecting annual income and expenditures will be distributed.

Ideally, the parishioners will be convinced that they would be better off consolidating with a neighboring parish. More realistically, they will recognize that the decision was not arbitrary. "There is always going to be pain," admits the secretary of planning in Baltimore.

No matter how careful, how sensitive, how long the process, how much effort, how many people are involved, when the actual closing comes, there is a lot of hurt. You try to be sensitive and do everything you can and plan, study, get data, make a case. But ultimately, somebody has to say, this is dying. Dying is tough.

Some archbishops are trying to get their people ready for fewer priests. In Chicago, the personnel office projects that the number of priests will decline from 850 in 1984 to 600 in 1990 for 444 parishes. Places with two priests would have one, and some with one would have none. When this information was shared with twenty-four sample parishes, the responses were surprising. The director of personnel reports:

The most liberal parishes said, "So we may not have priests. We will be a faith community. We really don't need priests. We will be leaders ourselves."

The most conservative parishes said that "priesthood is absolutely essential because we have to have Mass. So change the rules about who becomes priests." Old ethnic Polish parishes said, "Why don't they ordain the nuns? Then we will have enough." We were not prepared for that kind of response.

Cincinnati has a parish-based planning program called, "For the Harvest," that appears to have been successful.[8] Archbishop Pilarczyk describes it:

It has three components. One is, what's our parish all about and what should we be all about? The second component is, what are we going to do when we don't have as many priests? And the third component is, how can neighboring parishes work together?

The first component is a self-evaluation tool. [The second is] a fact they're going to have to deal with, and most of the parishes have come to grips with ways to deal with it. The third is revolutionary because of the mind-set of many pastors: "I have been sent by God to be pastor here; our parish will do everything." To depend on another parish for anything was viewed as a failure.

In Norwood there are three parishes with a consolidated school. If we were starting over, we wouldn't have three parishes, we would have one. Those pastors got together about a year ago, about the time that "For the Harvest" was just getting underway. They revised their Saturday and Sunday Mass schedules so that nobody's would conflict with anybody else's. They hired a common director of religious education for the three parishes. They exchanged bulletins. A parishioner from any of those three parishes can go to any of the other two, put his envelope in the basket and the envelope is returned to the home parish. Amazing!

Despite all the studies and consultation, closing a parish remains one of the most difficult things a bishop has to do.[9]

Lay Ministry

With the decline in the number of priests, some bishops are appointing lay administrators to parishes rather than closing them. Seventy of the 167 dioceses responding to a NCCB survey have parishes with nonpriests as administrators. Fifty-one dioceses said they had parishes with Sunday services conducted without a priest.[10] In 1988, the Baltimore archdiocese announced that nine of its 153 parishes (three in each of the three vicariates) would be headed by pastoral administrators. In the Portland archdiocese, Archbishop Power appointed lay administrators to two parishes, both women, one a religious, one a lay catechist.[11] This is most common in small towns or rural areas where the distances are too great for people to drive to another parish. Depending on his or her abilities, the lay administrator becomes for all practical purposes the pastor. He or she visits the sick, prepares people for the sacraments, and counsels people in the parish.

Some parishes will be visited once a week by a priest who says Mass. Others might be visited only once a month. When a priest is not available, the lay administrator will conduct a service that will include a Liturgy of the Word (prayers, songs, Scripture readings, and a homily) much like that at a Mass. This will be followed by a quasi-eucharistic prayer (without the consecration) and a Communion service using already consecrated bread. At the time of my interviews there was concern that the new archbishop of Portland, William Levada, would reverse this trend by employing retired religious and foreign-born priests. Supporters of the program wanted to learn from the experience of having lay administrators in a few parishes before the inevitable time when twenty to forty parishes had no priest.

The increase in the number and kinds of lay ministries has resulted, not simply because of the decline in the number of priests and religious, but also because of the growth in the number of parish programs and an increased awareness of the role of the laity in the church. Numerous volunteers teach religious education to children, run social programs, and participate in various parish committees. Eucharistic ministers, for example, take Communion to the sick and shut-ins.

A recent phenomenon of parish life is the increasing number of full-time professionals employed by the parish. Lay people were first hired as teachers in the parish school and as book-keepers. But the number of ministries has expanded tremendously. Many parishes have religious education directors for organizing and running catechetical programs both for adults and for children not in the parochial schools. These directors supervise and coordinate the volunteer teachers.

Some parishes also have liturgical ministers who train and coordinate musicians, singers, eucharistic ministers, servers, and lectors. They also plan and organize weddings, funerals, baptisms, and the Sunday liturgies. Pastoral ministers are also involved in marriage and baptismal preparation programs, as well as in marriage counseling. Youth ministers are employed to run programs for young people, and social ministers run programs to help the poor and underprivileged. Some large parishes have business or plant managers. The number of lay ministers varies tremendously around the country. More appear in archdioceses that are feeling the pinch of the clergy shortage.

"We have about 185 full-time, full-blown parish ministers in this diocese, and that's unusual" reports Archbishop Roach of St. Paul proudly. "We have about 85 full-time youth ministers."

At first these ministries developed with little encouragement or control from the chancery, especially in archdioceses where parishes had the financial resources and freedom to take the initiative. Later the archbishop and the chancery began to take notice of these ministries to encourage or control them. Chanceries also became involved in response to complaints and calls for help.

Complaints came that people without training were hired to do religious education. "You get a mixed bag of very well qualified and not too well qualified people," explains Archbishop Roach. "We tended to move very quickly to meet those needs. You spend the first three years hiring and the next three years trying to clean up your act, getting rid of the people you shouldn't have hired. But for the vast majority, we've done pretty well." As a result of these complaints, some archdioceses established guidelines for hiring religious education directors and other lay ministers.

Other complaints came from pastors of poor parishes who had their personnel stolen by richer parishes who could offer higher salaries. Parish employees would complain that they were fired without cause by a new pastor. The IRS would complain that taxes were not being withheld. Someone would get injured and sue the parish and the archdiocese, and the archbishop would find out the employee was not covered by any insurance. All of this raised questions about how detailed should be diocesan regulations covering lay ministers and employees in parishes.

Pastors also came to the chancery asking for help. Where do you find a good religious education director, youth minister, etc.? Are there any sisters looking for work? They also requested legal advice on taxes, contracts, and insurance. Should you fire someone accused of child abuse if there is no proof? Can the archdiocese run workshops or training programs for parish ministers?

All of this has led to the founding in some archdioceses (Baltimore, Chicago, Miami, Newark, St. Paul) of an office for lay ministry or a personnel office. These offices have become resource centers and clearinghouses for job applicants. Application forms are filled out, transcripts, letters of recommendations, and other information are collected, and candidates are interviewed. Sometimes diocesan standards will be set for certain positions, for example, requiring a degree in religious education for a religious education director.

The ministry office will then make available to approved candidates a list of parishes looking for people. The candidate then approaches the parish, is interviewed, and ultimately hired or not by the pastor. The ministry or personnel office might also draft contracts and propose salary scales, but usually the parish can pay more than the scale if it wants to. The ministry office will also run or organize workshops and training programs for parish ministers.

For many of these ideas, the ministry office did not have to reinvent the wheel but was able to borrow many policies and procedures from the archdiocesan department of education, which had many years of experience processing teachers' applications.

Most dioceses also have deacons, who are canonically clerics, not laymen. Since most of these deacons are only part-time workers in the parish where they live, they have not had as much impact as full-time lay ministers. Responding to complaints that deacons are simply glorified altar boys, the archdiocese of Hartford now requires that a candidate have a contract with his pastor giving him primary responsibility for a ministry in the parish before he can be ordained a deacon.

Archdiocesan Programs

Besides working directly with parishes and through his vicars, the archbishop also oversees numerous agencies that provide programs for the parishes. Some agency programs are independent of the parishes, but many either serve the parishes or need their participation to be successful. For example, the liturgy office may have workshops to train lectors and eucharistic ministers, while the education office might have workshops for catechists. Or a social justice program may need the participation of parish volunteers to achieve its goal. The archbishop is often the man in the middle between the pastors and agency heads. Agencies want to use him to twist arms so that the parishes participate in their programs. Pastors often give him an earful about what they think of the programs.

Pastors complain that archdiocesan offices often create more work for them rather than serving them. What they get in the mail from these offices is a list of things that they are supposed to do or that they are supposed to get their parishioners to do—parish-based programs to fight abortion, feed the hungry, to dialogue with other faiths, to improve liturgy, to reach out to the unchurched, to work for peace and justice, etc. The last thing that the pastors want is something else to do.

In addition, bishops are sensitive to the complaints of pastors about the amount of paper they receive from chancery offices. The pastors are at the bottom of a paper funnel that collects encyclicals, pastoral letters, reports, newsletters, and statements from offices in the Vatican, from the National Conference of Catholic Bishops, and from the local chancery. The more they receive, the less likely they are to read it. This is a Catch-22 problem, however, since the pastors also complain when something happens and they are not informed or consulted.

Chancery officials see pastors as the "narrow neck of the funnel," explains the director of planning in Louisville. "Unless the pastor is turned on with something, your program is going to end up in file thirteen." Some agencies "develop a great program, put it in the mail to all the parishes, and then go home," he complains. "Until the customer uses it, it isn't a sale. If you don't get it down to the parishioners, you haven't done anything." Some agency heads believe that the pastors will use their programs only if the archbishop gets behind it. But the archbishops realize that they can't push everything without losing credibility. Other agencies try to bypass the pastors and work directly with lay leaders in the parishes. This can also lead to angry pastors if they are not consulted or if they do not like what is going on.

A program that has proven very popular with archbishops is Renew, a parish renewal program originating in Newark. Often it has been the archbishop who has pushed most strongly for Renew because of the good things he has heard about it from other bishops. Where the archbishop has not been enthusiastic, Renew has not been adopted or it has not been implemented. The biggest obstacle to Renew is usually the pastors who see it as just another program to be added on top of what they are already doing. Those who see it as an opportunity to develop new leadership in the parish are more easily won over.

Conclusion

Although parishioners rarely see their archbishop, he has a tremendous impact on the life of their parish. It is impossible for an archbishop to minister directly to the thousands of people in his archdiocese. These people are reached primarily by the priests and other ministers in the parishes. The archbishop can exhort and encourage, he can lay down policy and regulations, and he can visit parishes. But the ministry must be done by others. In a large archdiocese, even the supervision of the parishes will have to be done by a vicar. In addition, through various archdiocesan offices, he can offer programs to the parishes. But he has to be sensitive to the ability of the parishes to absorb these programs.

None of this can happen unless the parishes and the archdiocese have money to run their programs. The next chapter will examine how an archbishop supervises parish finances and how he finances archdiocesan operations and programs.

5. Finances

Any diocese can give to the People of God only what the People of God can pay for.

———MSGR. BENJAMIN G. HAWKES

While money isn't everything, it's probably better than holy pictures for paying people's salaries.

———ARCHBISHOP O'MEARA

Without financial resources, the church, like any other organization, cannot do very much. Money buys food, clothing, shelter, and office supplies. It pays salaries, rent, telephone, and energy bills. Money cannot buy everything, especially the supernatural goals the church holds dear. But efficient and effective use of financial resources make the achievement of these goals a possibility.

Every archdiocese is a multimillion dollar operation. The smallest archdiocese, Anchorage, has a budget of $1.5 million for its central offices. The revenues of the New York archdiocese, including parishes, exceeded $264 million in fiscal year 1983. The endowment and deposit and loan funds of the archdiocese totaled more than $172 million. The plant facilities, evaluated at cost, were more than $811 million. Across the Hudson River in the poorer archdiocese of Newark the figures are still big. At replacement value, the 250 parishes plus schools are evaluated at over $1 billion. The annual operating budget is close to $100 million with 10,000 employees.

With operations of this size, financial administration is important and takes professional expertise. Even smaller archdioceses require careful administration to husband limited resources. A single financial mistake can be devastating to a poor archdiocese. For example, in order to give the University of Albuquerque a chance to become self-sustaining, the archdiocese of Santa Fe took it over. When it eventually closed, the archdiocese was left with its $6 million debt.

Most bishops have no training in financial administration. If they were lucky, they learned a little about church finances while working in the chancery before becoming a bishop. In addition, most archbishops got experience administering a smaller diocese before being put in charge of an archdiocese.

To help him in financial administration, the archbishop has a finance officer, who is usually one of the most influential persons in the archdiocese. In the past, these officials were usually priests, but now they are more often laypeople with training in financial administration. Frequently, an accountant is hired away from the accounting firm that audits the archdiocese's books.

The finance office collects revenues, pays bills, manages the cash flow and investments, and negotiates contracts for construction, insurance, and salaries. The finance officer is also the principal financial advisor of the bishop. "I am in charge of everything that has a dollar sign in front of it," explained the late Msgr. Benjamin G. Hawkes, vicar for finances in Los Angeles.

The degree of professionalization and the size of the finance staff varies from archdiocese to archdiocese. In general, large archdioceses usually have larger and more professional staffs than small archdioceses. In a large archdiocese, economies of scale may permit specialists to handle real estate transactions, investments, fund raising, insurance (health, property, and liability), pensions, accounting, purchasing, cemeteries, etc. In a small archdiocese, the finance officer may be the only professional on a staff that includes bookkeepers and secretaries.

Besides size, the financial condition of the archdiocese has an impact on the size and professional character of the finance office. An indebted archdiocese, like Newark, is more likely to improve its financial administration than a financially stable archdiocese that feels no pressure to clean up its finances. The Newark director of finances recalls that when he arrived "some of the more rudimentary controls or rudimentary business techniques were nonexistent."

Finally, the retirement or death of an old archbishop or finance officer may bring about changes in financial administration. While these experienced men may have carried the financial and administrative history of the archdiocese in their heads, their successors must build a professional system to understand and control finances.

Parish Finances

In examining archdiocesan finances, it is important to distinguish between the parishes and the other archdiocesan administrative units. Parishes are supported almost entirely by revenues collected from their parishioners. The average Catholic contributes $320 to the church each year, or 1.1 percent of his or her annual income.[1] This money is used to maintain the parish plant and to support parish personnel. In the New York archdiocese, 97 percent of the revenues collected in a parish stay there for parish programs, including the parish school.

Dioceses are organized under civil law in different ways depending on state laws. Over half the dioceses in the United States, including many archdioceses (like Atlanta, Chicago, Louisville, Los Angeles, Miami, Mobile, San Francisco, St. Louis, and Washington) are organized as a corporation sole, where, without a board of directors, the bishop is the legal owner of all the parish and diocesan assets.[2] Other dioceses are organized as a corporation aggregate. In these archdioceses (like Hartford, Minneapolis, New York, St. Paul), each parish is a separately incorporated nonprofit corporation with the bishop and/or his appointees as trustees or members of the board of directors. For example, the bishop might be the head of the parish corporation with his vicar general, the pastor, and a couple of laypersons as trustees. Other parts of the archdiocese are also separately incorporated: high schools, seminaries, hospitals, cemeteries, Catholic Charities, chancery, and other institutions and agencies. Ordinarily, the archbishop would be the president of all these corporations.

The civil and canonical legislation covering church finances is complex. The laws ensure that the bishop maintains control over church funds. The laws also require that money given for a specific purpose generally be used for that purpose. The bishop is ultimately responsible for seeing that the funds of the parish are used wisely and for the good of the church. On the other hand, if someone donates $1 million to a parish for a new church, the bishop can not use it to help build a new high school.

How much autonomy parishes have over their funds varies from archdiocese to archdiocese. In most archdioceses the parishes are very independent; in others the archdiocesan finance office holds a tight reign. In some archdioceses, such as Los Angeles, the finances are highly centralized, while in others, like St. Paul, they are decentralized.

Parish Budgets and Annual Reports

All archdioceses require that a pastor submit a financial report to the chancery at least once a year. These reports allow a minimal form of financial control and provide statistics for an unaudited financial report. In addition, they are used to calculate assessments paid by parishes to the archdiocese.

Typically, the reports show the income and expenditures of the parish for the concluded fiscal year, but the sophistication of these reports varies. Most would give a breakdown by major categories: income from collections, tuition, bingo, and other fund-raising events; expenditures for salaries, utilities, insurance, repairs, etc. All of this would usually be on a cash rather than accrual basis.

Some archdioceses have developed more sophisticated parish accounting systems that aid in the control and management of expenses. Most reports would try to separate the income and expenses of the school from other parish income and expenses.

This would be useful in deciding tuition charges. But such accounting "is subject to the pitfalls of bookkeepers estimating what goes where," according to the archdiocesan controller in Louisville. Direct expenses for the school, such as salaries and supplies, are easily separated. Joint expenses, like maintenance and utilities, are sometimes difficult to allocate, especially for multiple-use buildings.

Many archdioceses also require that the parish draw up a budget projecting the income and expenses for the coming year. Most archdiocesan finance officers admit that these budgets and annual reports are not closely examined unless a parish wants to borrow money or unless it is receiving a subsidy from the archdiocese. The Chicago director of administrative services confesses that, with limited staff, "the ones that are reviewed are the ones that need the financial help from us. Those that don't, get away with murder because you concentrate on what is draining your cash. We can have rich places that are very sloppily run."

Besides looking at parishes that need money from the archdiocese, the finance office examines the budgets and reports to find parishes with financial problems. The finance office of Hartford explains what he looks for:

If the parish is operating at a deficit, that is a problem. We look at it to see why. That is the number one red flag.

Another might be that the subsidy to the school is growing and their reserves are getting down to zero. We would probably let them know that the day of reckoning is coming. Those reserves are not going to last. They had better anticipate the school problem.

We might see a parish has borrowed money, and if we haven't given permission for that we would want to know what that was all about. It might have been an expenditure that we hadn't given permission for.

Most of our annual reports do not present problems. On the contrary, a number of them call for a letter of commendation for the pastors who did a great job making ends meet.

More and more archdioceses are requiring that the financial report and the budget be reviewed by the parish finance council. Archdiocesan finance officers hope that these councils will give the budgets and reports the kind of scrutiny that the finance office does not have time for.

Sophisticated Oversight

With the advent of computerized accounting programs, a few archdioceses attempt to give greater scrutiny to parish budgets and reports. For example, the budget projections can be compared with the financial figures from previous years to pick out large increases or decreases. A parish budget can also be compared with budgets from similar parishes so that unusual expenditures can be found. In St. Louis, the director of finance hopes to use a new accounting system to compare heating bills. "If it is out of whack, look at it," he says. "Find out where the leak is."

Newark developed an accounting system to oversee parish finances. The director of finances explains the system he set up:

First we had to make sure that the information being submitted by the pastors had financial credibility. Some pastors had been known to "forget" to report something now and then, whether it be the candle money or something. We developed a uniform set of financial reporting standards so that we could compare all parishes on the same basis.

We then began to accumulate data bases in the computer on all the parishes so we can compare your last year's actual figures with this year's budget. [We would tell a pastor,] "It is totally unrealistic that you are going to lose 50 percent of your Sunday collections in one year. So let's correct the numbers and look at it realistically."

As a result, we are able to establish the reputation that no one is pulling any wool over our eyes, and we start to get good data.

Archdiocesan review is easier if the parish accounts are computerized in a format that is compatible with the archdiocesan accounts. The Washington archdiocese, for between $8,000 and $10,000, will provide a system to a parish that includes hardware and software for word processing, envelope accounting, financial accounting, and census data. These are all compatible with the archdiocesan system so that the parish can send in a diskette rather than a written report.

Some archdioceses have not developed sophisticated parish accounting procedures because they do not think that it is worth the effort. The Louisville archdiocesan controller notes that some people

want to set up all kinds of cost centers in a parish. That is a needless thing. Obviously, almost all of your cost centers in the parish are losing propositions, that is the nature of the game. You don't eliminate a CCD program because the fees aren't covering it.

You have to determine what apostolates and ministries the parish is going to be involved in on the basis of something other than money. Then the total picture has to deal with what resources are available.

Likewise in Cincinnati, the director of finances questioned the value of closely scrutinizing parish budgets.

Unless a parish gets into trouble and asks us for help, we don't normally require a budget from them. We would have to put on a lot more staff to look at their budgets. Even then, from our remote position, it is difficult to determine whether budgetary items are correct or not.

Church A may have very high ceilings, so the budget for utilities might be unbelievable. Church B may have low ceilings, only uses the church on certain days, and uses a convent chapel on other days. Their utility costs may be unbelievably low. Yet both may be accurate. It is impossible to know that from this remote location.

Sophisticated accounting systems are expensive and need well-trained parish and archdiocesan staffs to implement them. These systems are usually opposed by pastors who see them as bureaucratic impositions on their time and energy. The bishop will have to expend political capital selling the system to the pastors, and many bishops conclude that the money saved by such a system would not be worth the cost in money, time, and popularity.

In some cases, because of long years in office, the bishop or the finance officer knows more about the parishes than could ever be put in a computer. The difficulty with this personalistic system is that the information disappears when the individual dies or retires. In Los Angeles, the finance officer, Monsignor Hawkes, was practically a one-man operation. After his retirement and death, he was replaced by about five professionals who had to build a system from scratch.

Archdiocesan Auditors

A few archdioceses (Baltimore, Detroit, New Orleans, Philadelphia, Washington) have internal auditors who check to make sure that the parish financial report reflects reality, but this normally happens only when a parish gets into financial trouble or after a new pastor is appointed. One auditor in a metropolitan, midwestern archdiocese says she found inadequately prepared bookkeepers, improperly prepared financial reports, and even embezzlements by unscrupulous bookkeepers.

After finding the problems, the main task of the auditor is to educate the pastor and the staff. She recalls, "It was a matter of working with the pastor, so that he was much more comfortable with the financial structure of his parish and the parish as it related to the diocese."

Auditing parish books goes against the grain in most dioceses. The St. Louis director of finances did not think auditing parishes was a good idea.

I will never have an auditor on the staff to go out and find something wrong in the parishes. That is an adversarial relationship, they are there to find something wrong. I don't think that is a good attitude.

Every pastor has his own little cookie jar, some money put away for the rainy day. Everybody knows it. Why have somebody go out and say, "Aha, we found the cookie jar." As long as it is within reason it is OK.

In Chicago, the director of administrative services began doing random audits of about 10 percent of the parishes each year. This did not last long.

A couple of the pastors who I know pretty well said, "I understand why you are doing it, but any way you cut it, it comes across as an element of suspicion."

I found out that the young auditors would find that somebody hadn't checked a bank reconciliation or someone had presigned checks—venial sins at the most. They were never finding loose money or anything significant, so I abandoned it. All it did was create more work for the parishes, with also a little bit of the taste that they weren't trusted.

On the other hand, if there is a real problem or if the parishioners request an audit, he sends a public accounting firm to do the job rather than use his own staff. "I like it to be a dispassionate third party," he says. Nor does he use a large firm. "They are full of young kids right out of college who can get eaten alive by a sophisticated pastor who knows where to hide things." He would use middle-size accounting firms with experience doing parish books. "They can't be fooled very much because they are used to doing the books."

The most useful time to look at parish finances is when a new pastor is appointed. "The new man has the certainty that he is starting out with a verifiable set of books," explains the controller in Philadelphia. The auditors can also help the new pastor who is not responsible for the problems in his parish. The Detroit director of finances, who has a staff of ten internal auditors to examine parish books, explains:

We say to the new pastor, "This is what is in your parish, and this is what should be. You did not cause this; you are being asked to turn it around." We return in six to eight weeks after the pastor has received the audit report to check where they are on compliance. Then we send a memo to the regional bishop.

Permission to Spend

A very common expenditure control mechanism is the requirement that a pastor get archdiocesan approval for any construction, renovation, or contracts costing over a specified amount, usually between $3,000 and $10,000. In some archdioceses, the archbishop must sign any contract over a specified amount, for example, $10,000 in Washington.

In many archdioceses, the expenditure limit applies only to capital improvements. Recurring costs of running a parish—salaries, utilities—are simply paid by the parish. "If they want to build or remodel, they have to come in for approval," explains the director of business affairs in Portland. "If they want to spend $40,000 a year on religious education, or buy a new organ or a vehicle, there is no approval needed. If they've got the money, they do it." Requiring the pastor to get permission for capital expenditures not only controls expenses, it also controls permanent alterations to the parish plant.

Some archdioceses control not only how much is spent but how it is spent. In Los Angeles, if the pastor got permission to spend money on a particular project, he would be told what contractors or vendors he could use. In Dubuque, on the other hand, pastors would not have to pay attention to the recommendations of the archdiocesan finance office. "They are getting permission for the boiler, but we can't tell them the quality," complains the finance officer. "Only with the advent of local parish councils has there been any restraint on the local pastor who doesn't know a BTU from a carrot."

But the major failure of this control mechanism is that it gives no attention to one of the biggest expenses of parishes: salaries. Thus a pastor might have to get permission to buy a $5,000 computer but not to hire a $30,000-a-year religious education director. As dioceses get more sophisticated in reviewing parish budgets, this control mechanism will become less important except for major parish projects.

Major Parish Projects

If a parish is planning a major construction project, such as a new building or renovation, it will have to get the approval of the archbishop. Approval is also necessary if the parish is going to borrow money either from the archdiocese or from a bank.

Every archdiocese has policies and procedures governing major building projects. In Oklahoma City, Kansas City (KS), and St. Louis, for example, the parish must have 50 percent of the funds necessary in hand before starting the project. The parish plans will usually have to be reviewed and approved by an archdiocesan building committee and by a liturgical committee if the construction involves a church. Their recommendation will then go to the archbishop.

Depending on the archdiocese, the preparatory work for the construction project would be done by the parish or by the finance office. In the centralized approach, the proposal is submitted to the chancery, and the finance office does most of the work in analyzing its merits and feasibility. The finance office personnel, which might include an architect and/or an engineer, draw up a plan to implement the proposal, including contracts for competitive bidding. If the request is approved, the finance office hires contractors for the parish and negotiates a loan if necessary. Once construction is started, the finance office may even have someone supervise the work.

In the decentralized system, most of this has to be done at the parish level, although archdiocesan approval will always be necessary. The finance office in St. Paul meets with the pastor, the architect, and the chair of the parish building and finance committees.

Prior to their coming, I ask that they have a basic floor plan, a sketch of the building, and a ten-year spread sheet on how they are going to be able to handle this additional debt and operating costs while at the same time maintaining their present programs.

This has two great advantages. Number one, it indicates to us whether or not that parish will be able to handle it. Number two, since they have gone through the process, it is their program, not one we have imposed on them. Therefore, they can get a great deal of ownership.

Our bottom line is, show us you can do what you propose then we will give the permission.

While I was visiting St. Paul, one parish dropped its church renovation plan because its ten-year spread sheet projected an unrealistically heavy burden for the parish. The finance director did not have to say no, his system forced the parish to face reality.

Cardinal John Krol in Philadelphia had a more direct approach. In twenty-six years as archbishop, one hundred new churches were built in Philadelphia, and he took an active role in their planning. He explained how he dealt with one pastor:

One of the professors from the seminary became a pastor, and he was like a little boy with a new toy. He had ideas. He had an idea for classroom space. He was going to monkey around with the old buildings, trying to make adjustments.

I said, "No. You want to do all kinds of things and put up some more chicken coops over here. Concentrate right now on one thing and have a fund drive. And what you are going to do is put up a beautiful church at street level.

"You see the level of the street? The ground falls, tapers down. So naturally the church will be at this level, so that underneath, without excavation you have a big hall. You want to have bingo, you want to have meetings, you want to have whatever. Concentrate on that. You live in that old farm house as a rectory; the people will appreciate that. But you do this.

"Now having done that, you have a lot of place to work. The old church is convertible into classrooms. You can tie this and you can tie that and what not. But now you have a solid permanent building.

"Having that, because of the inadequacy of that home of yours, when you pay off this or get into a manageable financial condition, the rectory is the next project. And by that time, you may have to replace some of those old buildings and classrooms. So you put up nice new buildings."

Under a centralized system, the archdiocese can encourage a pastor to do more, as in the above case, or less. In the Los Angeles parish where I grew up, the chancery chopped one of the church's towers out of the pastor's plan. Monsignor Hawkes of Los Angeles explained, "We believe that the have's should help the have-not's. We do not believe that a suburban parish should have sixteen classrooms when an inner-city parish cannot afford or cannot have eight."

Often the archdiocese has a building commission composed of pastors and laypeople that reviews construction plans. In St. Louis, the director of the building commission tries to control the height of new churches. "We try not to go higher than twenty-four to twenty-eight feet from floor to ceiling because of energy costs," he says. "You don't want to heat a fifty-five-foot building."

Sometimes the building commission might encourage the pastor to think bigger than he is proposing. For example, in St. Louis the building director recommended that a parish build more classrooms than were requested by the pastor. "The area is growing," he told the archbishop. "Why don't you suggest they build six instead of four. Financially, they can handle it." Sometimes the pastors think small because they believe it will be easier to get archdiocesan approval and also because they do not want to raise the money.

Bids and Contractors

For large expenditures, the archdiocese will usually require that a parish take at least three bids. Depending on the sophistication of the finance office, the bids would be examined to see whether a more economical deal is available and whether the contract protects the parish's interests. The building commission has "saved immeasurable amounts of money by requiring bids," reports the chancellor for administration of the archdiocese of New Orleans.

Frequently a pastor says this parishioner will do it for this amount. "He wants to help the church." We say, "That is wonderful. To make sure that he knows he is helping the church, we will get two other bids." Surprising the number of times the parishioner's is not low!

We had a recent case of $10,000 to repair air conditioning. We sent a man down there. All it needed was freon. Roofing, the same thing. Sometimes a variant of $20,000 to $30,000.

Some archdioceses, like Los Angeles, limit certain types of work and purchases to specific contractors or suppliers. While in Los Angeles, I witnessed one pastor being chewed out by Monsignor Hawkes for having some parish volunteers paint the inside of his church rather than using an approved contractor. Likewise, the building director in St. Louis would try to talk pastors out of using certain prize-winning architects. "They get the prize, but you pay for it," he says.

There are arguments for and against archdiocesan control of parish expenses. The experience and expertise available in the central finance office is almost always greater than that available to a local pastor. In addition, the finance office can look out for the good of the entire archdiocese. On the other hand, the central office cannot know the needs and conditions of the local parish as well as the pastor and the parish council. The ideal system draws on the strengths of all the participants so that through consultation and dialogue a better result occurs than if decisions were totally centralized or totally decentralized.

Archdiocesan Banking

Besides being concerned about how parishes spend money, archdioceses also monitor what parishes do with their savings. Most archdioceses have a system encouraging parishes to deposit funds with the chancery. The archdiocese acts like a bank and pays interest to the parishes on these funds.

Archdiocesan banking is often adopted when an archdiocese faces severe financial difficulties. In Louisville it started during the Depression when the banks took a holiday. They refused to pay out money to depositors but demanded payment on loans to parishes. Bishop John A. Floerish arranged to consolidate the deposits so that he could pay off the loans.

Centralized banking was implemented on a massive scale in the New York archdiocese under Cardinal Spellman. When he arrived in 1939, he found that the archdiocese and its parishes were $26 million in debt to New York banks.[3] But while some parishes were in debt, others had money on deposit in these same banks. By pooling together the deposits of the solvent parishes under archdiocesan administration, he was able to pay off the banks and internalize the debt.

More recently, Archbishop Gerety established a central bank in Newark after he arrived and found a $25 million debt. He made the program optional, but offered interest rates and services to parishes that were competitive with local banks. In six years deposits went from zero to $34 million.

A great variety of archdiocesan policies and procedures govern these banking systems. Depositing funds with the archdiocese is mandatory in some archdioceses (Baltimore, Chicago, Cincinnati, Detroit, Los Angeles, New Orleans) and optional in others (Atlanta, Omaha, Mobile, New York, Philadelphia, St. Paul). Some archdioceses pay parishes a competitive rate of interest on their deposits, while others pay them very little. They also vary on how much of the parish's funds have to be deposited with the archdiocese.

In Los Angeles, for example, all Sunday collections and other income are deposited in an archdiocesan account in the name of the parish, which is paid 6 percent interest on its deposits. Money is transferred to a parish checking account by the archdiocese when it is needed.

In Chicago and San Francisco, a parish is supposed to deposit "excess funds" with the archdiocese. In Chicago, excess funds are defined as anything more than a month's operating expenses. The archdiocese invests the funds and returns 60 percent of the earnings to the depositors and keeps 40 percent for the archdiocese. Thus if the investments earn 10 percent, the parishes get 6 percent.

In St. Paul, on the other hand, the system is voluntary, and no significant parish deposits are with the archdiocese. Parishes have their own savings accounts and investments. The director of finances in St. Paul explains:

> Our parishes tend to say, "This is ours." And so we don't get the sharing of surplus funds with which we could do many things if we had them. We have encouraged it, but it has never really come to be very much.

When the banking system is not mandatory, it is difficult to attract deposits if a parish can get a higher return elsewhere. In Portland, the director of business affairs notes, "During 1981–83, we lost a lot of parishes because they could put it in 14 percent and 15 percent CD's" while the archdiocese was only paying 8 percent.

The vice chancellor for finances in New York explains how he responded when parishes wanted to withdraw their funds.

> We went to the files and found out that the parish over the years had been a borrower. So we wrote a very nice letter saying that "it is not a bank, it is a reciprocal situation whereby one parish helps another parish. You are probably not aware of the fact that your parish in 1943 got a $240,000 loan and you only paid 3 or 4 percent interest on that." That was the end of that.

Optional systems can attract deposits if they offer competitive interest rates and service. The Atlanta archdiocese received $5 million of deposits by paying parishes the same rate that they would get from six-month Treasury notes, with the addition of day-to-day liquidity. Newark also attracts parish deposits by offering competitive interest rates and additional services such as NOW accounts and investment management services. In addition, aggressive leadership of the archbishop made clear where he wanted parishes to deposit their money. The director of finances explains:

Archbishop Gerety played a key role. The pastors don't know the staff, but they do know the ordinary. Archbishop Gerety said, "I am the one who has to go out and deliver this. If it is going to be successful, I am the one who is going to take all the credit. I guess I've got to take the opposition too."

He called together a pastors' meeting, and we introduced all of these programs. He talked about how important this is for the current and future financial viability of the church of Newark.

He was the one who constantly kept reminding people. If he was somewhere, he would say, "How do you like the program? You in the cash management program? You in the investment management program?"

Despite promises to the contrary, some pastors fear that they will not be able to get their money back from the archdiocese when their parishes really need it. The Portland director of business affairs reports, "There is still a perception that if they deposit the money, we will steal it. Paranoia is out there."

Even in archdioceses where the banking system is mandatory, sometimes pastors will hide the money. Since few archdioceses have internal audit controls, this "nest egg" is usually not found until the pastor dies or a new pastor is appointed. One director of finances tells of a new pastor bringing him a briefcase containing $80,000 that had been hidden in the rectory. "The old pastor was not trying to take care of himself," he says. "He just wouldn't send it downtown, and he wouldn't trust banks."

There are advantages and disadvantages to such a banking system. Most prosperous parishes prefer the decentralized system that gives them more control over their own finances. Some argue that this power is necessary to develop a sense of local responsibility. In addition, parishes can often get a better rate of return than is available from the archdiocese. The fiscal officer of the Hartford archdiocese, which does not have an internal bank, reports, "From the PR point of view, of keeping the troops [pastors] happy, there is a big advantage to leaving the money on the local level even though there are some investment advantages to pooling."

A centralized banking system allows money to be handled more efficiently. With pooled funds, experts can recommend better and more diversified investments than are available to parishes. The higher yield from these investments can be used to support church ministries.

Most importantly, the money deposited with the archdiocese can be loaned out to parishes and other archdiocesan agencies at lower rates than they would be able to get elsewhere. The archdiocese thus replaces the bank as the middle person between parishes with surpluses and parishes with debts. In Newark, the first $25,000 deposited with the archdiocese was loaned to an inner-city parish so it could pay its bank loan. The bank had charged 1.4 percent over prime for ten years and the parish was never able to pay back any of the principal. Under the terms of the new loan, the parish paid the same amount to the archdiocese, but that amount included the amortization of the loan over a ten-year period.

How much interest an archdiocese charges a borrowing parish varies tremendously. Archdioceses with mandatory deposits and low interest payments to depositors loan money at the lower rates of interest. In Los Angeles, borrowers were charged 5 percent rate, while depositors were paid 6 percent even when commercial rates were three to four times higher. In Milwaukee, on the other hand, the archdiocese charges one point above the prime rate. Frequently, borrowing parishes will be charged 1 percent more than an archdiocese pays to parishes with deposits. This 1 percent spread is supposed to cover administrative costs.

Some archdioceses loan out to parishes all of the money on deposit. Others keep some in case a parish wants its money back. The St. Louis archdiocese has $44 million on deposit and $20 million loaned out. The rest is invested. On the other hand, Dubuque actually loaned out $6 million to parishes while only having $3 million on deposit from parishes. Normally the loans must be paid back within ten years in order to make the money available to other parishes. In addition, says the Detroit director of finance, "they will have another project in that time."

If the archdiocese does not have enough money to loan, the parish will have to borrow from a bank that might charge two or more points over the prime rate. By guaranteeing the parish loan, the archdiocese can get from the bank a more favorable rate than a parish would get on its own. "It is our cheapest way to assist them," explains the St. Paul finance officer, "because we get favorable interest for them that way." The archdiocese of Washington, for example, negotiated a line of credit that was .5 percent under prime. But the result can be that the archdiocese is guaranteeing millions of dollars in loans. "It looks staggering to see $20 to $30 million that we are guaranteeing," admits the St. Paul finance officer. "But we have gone over the finances of the parishes, so the risk is minimal."

New Parishes

Besides dealing with renovations and existing expenses, growing archdioceses have to start and build new parishes. Archdiocesan policies and procedures for opening a new parish are aimed at ensuring its financial viability. In a poor archdiocese, getting funds to start a parish would be up to the new pastor. But a better-off archdiocese can come to the assistance of the new parish. In Los Angeles, Monsignor Hawkes explained:

When we start a new parish—we do one or two a year—the cardinal gives the parish the property. Then we build what we think the place and the location needs. That would be a rectory and a multipurpose building for a church. Half of the multipurpose building might provide four classrooms, but it could also be used for Sunday Masses.

What it usually costs is $2 million, and the diocese gives the parish up to $1 million. That is the only way the people can handle it. Five percent on $2 million is a large portion of your collection for interest.

It would be $100,000 a year, that's $2,000 a Sunday. How can they do that and cover the maintenance and pay on the principal?

Services to Parishes

Large archdioceses frequently have financial services that can help parishes. The archdiocese might run benefit programs for parish employees (both lay and clerical), including medical insurance, worker's compensation, and pensions. Archdiocesan attorneys might be available to deal with legal questions. Larger archdioceses also might have in-house consultants on energy conservation, construction, purchasing, or other matters. Boston, for example, has a specialist on heating, while New Orleans has a specialist on air conditioning. In Baltimore the archdiocese has a professional consultant to help parishes with building and maintenance. If a parish needs a new roof, boiler, or renovations, the consultant would write the specifications and help them with bids.

Centralized purchasing, for example, can achieve economies of scale through large purchases or through providing suppliers with a large market by advertising through a special newsletter. "On simple school furniture," explains Cardinal Krol of Philadelphia, "we can get it at 40 percent of normal cost. That operation runs on an average of $30 to $40 million, and all we charge is about a quarter of a percent, which maintains the staff of buyers." Similarly, the archdiocese of Washington reduced the per-unit cost of installing double-paned windows by contracting for it on a large scale.

Insurance

During my interviews, finance officers were especially concerned about insurance costs. Churches need property, casualty, and liability insurance as well as health insurance for their employees. Archdioceses normally have centralized insurance programs rather than letting each parish buy its own.

Insurance coverage is less expensive when purchased at the archdiocesan level.

The cost of insurance has skyrocketed in recent years. Archdioceses have experienced 100 to 500 percent increases in a single year while not being able to get the same amount of coverage. In Cincinnati in a two-year period, the insurance premium went from $600,000 a year to $1.3 million. "Last year [1985] we had a $10 million umbrella that cost $18,750," reported the Atlanta finance officer. "The figure we were quoted for renewal for only a $4 million umbrella was $80,000. Ten times per million [dollars of coverage]!"

Liability insurance recently has become a special problem. Sometimes no one is willing to insure an archdiocese because of its involvement in schools, day care, and youth programs. The archdiocese of San Francisco had trouble getting an insurance company to cover its athletic programs. The finance officer explains:

> We are in the business, which is a highly risky business, of doing things with kids. We have schools, summer camps, altar boys, buses, CCD, all these things where kids are involved. Nationally, insurance claims where kids are involved are big, big claims. You are getting huge sympathy verdicts out of juries. A kid can be climbing on a slide in a playground and fall off and break a foot and it is a $40,000 settlement. Those things add up. The church is a deep pocket, and they go for it.

In response to increased costs, finance directors are examining numerous options for insurance. In Washington, DC, the archdiocese changed insurance companies when its provider lowered the liability coverage from $50 million to $1 million. The new company offered coverage up to $25 million but excluded coverage for child abuse, trampolines, and numerous other things.

Archdioceses are also doing risk assessments to see how they can limit their liability. The director of business affairs in Portland explains some of the issues they are examining:

More and more people want to use church facilities because other people have turned them down. We want to be a good citizen, we want to be active in the community, support things. But every time we let someone come in and use our facility, we open ourselves up for lawsuits. If someone slips and falls, it is because a tile was loose.

Ten years ago, nobody would think of suing the church. Now we are the first ones they think of. We are perceived as being wealthy.

Youth outings! You heard about the accident on Mt. Hood [where students from an Episcopal school were killed on a school-sponsored outing]. We have youth ministers who like to go on rafting trips and camping trips. They have school buses in the parish which they take. Well, who is driving the school bus? Usually a volunteer or the youth minister himself. Who is maintaining the school bus? For the most part it sits there and is used spasmodically. What shape are the brakes in?

There is more concern over the use of alcohol at parish events, wedding receptions. Oregon, like most states, has cracked down on that—very tough laws. The liability has been extended back to the source.

How do we deal with all those issues? How can we transfer liability from us to someone else?

We will no longer allow parishes to just rent a bus and insure it under our program. Now we say, if you rent a bus, you also have to acquire the liability insurance through the bus company. It is costing them $200, $250 for insurance. The parishes are all upset. They are going to have to be upset; that is the real world.

Some archdioceses have cut costs by no longer insuring old buildings at replacement cost. "We would not want to rebuild it anyway," explains one finance officer. More and more archdioceses are also going the self-insurance route. The general feeling is that insurance company premiums include a percentage for profit and administration. In addition, self-funded health insurance programs can be designed with the church's needs in mind. "It is easy to say we disallow immoral procedures," reports the Cincinnati director of financial services. On the other hand, Cincinnati is generous in covering mental illness and chemical dependency. "Our feeling is that that individual needs it worse than maybe anyone else."

Few archdioceses would risk total self-insurance. Frequently they will be self-insured for the first $100,000 per fire or accident with reinsurance for higher amounts. Dubuque is considering total self-insurance for property. Rather than buying insurance, it would use the premiums from the parishes to build a reserve fund. For general liability, the director only wants to buy coverage for anything over $700,000. "We got $1 million worth of premiums a year," he explains, "and our average loss in fifteen years is only $330,000." On the other hand, Dubuque closed down its self-funded health insurance program for teachers and went to Blue Cross/Blue Shield because it could reduce family premiums by $600 a year.

Helping the Poor Parishes

Most parishes are self-supporting and do not need help from the archdiocese. Even a poor parish, unless it has a school, can usually support itself until it needs a major repair. If a parish is in trouble, the archdiocese will usually come to its rescue. A number of archdioceses have programs to give financial aid to poor, usually inner-city parishes and schools. The Los Angeles archdiocese, for example, aids thirty-six parishes in meeting their operating expenses. Chicago helps seventy parishes with $8.5 million annually, most of which goes to parish schools. Philadelphia helps twenty-two parishes with $1.8 million. New York has a similar $7 million program.

Often a committee of pastors is responsible for reviewing the requests and dividing up the money. This works well because the pastors are knowledgeable in parish finances and can advise the parishes as well as give them money. In Miami, the committee will visit the parish, review the plant and finances, and make recommendations on what the archdiocese should do for the parish. "That is helpful to us," says the Miami vicar for temporalities, "because it is not the central office making decisions. It is local pastors on behalf of parishes. They identify the problems and solutions."

Sometimes the financial problems are caused by incompetent financial administration, but often the parish is poor and the congregation is small. Inner-city parishes with large old churches and few parishioners are financial losers. Likewise, an inner-city parish with a school is frequently in trouble, especially if enrollment declines.

But such programs are possible only if the archdiocese has money to distribute. In dioceses where the money is decentralized in the parishes, twinning of rich and poor parishes is encouraged. Here a rich parish would help a poor parish directly rather than through the diocese. The advantage of such a system is that it is personal and can bring the parishioners directly in contact with each other. On the other hand, it is also dependent on personal relationships between pastors, and the money might not go where there is the greatest need.

Revenues for Archdiocesan Programs

Archdioceses run other programs besides parishes: cemeteries, hospitals, high schools, social services, seminaries, the chancery, and other agencies. Few programs are self-supporting. Cemeteries can be money makers, but schools only partially cover their costs through tuition. Some programs, such as social services, are also able to get grants from governmental or private agencies. But most programs need at least some money from the archdiocese. Getting revenue for archdiocesan programs is essential if the archdiocese is going to be more than a collection of independent parishes.

Archdiocesan revenues mostly come from three sources: assessments on parishes, special collections in parishes, and income from investments. Most of the revenue usually comes from the parishes either through special collections or through assessments. Only a few archdioceses (like Chicago, Los Angeles, New York) have significant investment income from endowments created by past gifts. Sometimes no longer needed property can be sold and turned into an endowment as recently happened in Portland. If parish funds on deposit with the arch-diocese are not loaned out, they also are invested.

Almost every archdiocese has an assessment or tax system that collects money from the parishes.[4] Sometimes referred to as the cathedraticum, its original purpose was to support the bishop and his chancery. Some archdioceses have only one as-sessment, while others have assessments for various purposes. Like any tax system, the assessments are often complex and controversial. The assessment is normally a percentage tax on income with consideration given for whether the parish has a debt or a school.

The systems vary from archdiocese to archdiocese. Many have complicated formulas for determining what income is taxed at what rate. Income never includes tuition, but it may or may not include things like bequests, investment income, special collections (that the parish does not keep), and profits from fund-raising activities like bingo. Most archdioceses have tax systems that are proportional—they tax all parishes at the same rate. A few, like Washington, have tried progressive rates that tax the richer parishes at a higher rate.

For example, the Los Angeles archdiocese assesses 1 percent of ordinary income. Ordinary income excludes special collec-tions, estates, and gifts of property or stocks. This is the cath-edraticum that "nowhere meets the cost of the chancery," ac-cording to Monsignor Hawkes. In addition, he reported:

We assess the ordinary income of the parish 3 percent for semi-naries. They are subsidized in excess of $1 million a year. And we assess our parishes 4 percent of ordinary income to cover our thirty-four high schools. So our total assessment is 8 percent.

St. Paul in 1980–81 had a 7.5 percent assessment on income less $150 per student in the parish school. In Newark, the cal-culation is a bit more complex. The maximum percentage is 12 percent on total revenues. There is a reduction of 1 percent for a parish school and a further reduction of 1 percent for a parish or school with a mortgage. There is a 1 percent surcharge on investment income if the funds are not in the archdiocesan investment management program.

One advantage of the percentage formula is that as parish incomes go up each year, so does the revenue for the archdiocese. A few archdioceses do not use percentage formulas but simply assess each parish a set amount. Unless there is a process for raising the amount each year, the archdiocese finds it difficult to keep up with inflation.

The New Orleans archdiocese has no assessment formula. Once the archdiocese decides how much money must be collected, the individual assessments are set by a committee of pastors who take into consideration parish income, expenses, debts, and other factors. Archbishop Hannan explains, "The pastors know the capabilities of each parish, they know their peers, though they argue with them."

Raising assessments is as controversial in the church as raising taxes in civil society. Pastors are practically always against raising assessments. The moderator of the curia in St. Paul says the pastors "scream, yell, moan when you raise the allocation one percentage point like we did this year. It went from 7.5 to 8.5 percent."

Archdiocesan Appeal

Besides the assessment, most archdioceses also have one or more special collections in the parishes. These archdiocesan appeals are structured in various ways. Often the money collected through the appeal goes for social services, education, and popular programs that have good fund-raising potential. Less glamorous programs, like insurance, utilities, the finance office, the tribunal, and the chancery office, are paid for by the assessment.

Sometimes there is one big collection for a multitude of programs. St. Paul, for example, has an archbishop's appeal that is collected on specified Sundays in the parishes. The trend appears to be toward one multipurpose collection so that people are not "nickeled and dimed to death." How this money is divided among archdiocesan agencies is an important part of the budgetary process. Normally from year to year, there will not be significant changes in the proportion going to the bigger programs like education and Catholic Charities.

But some archdioceses have separate collections for programs like the seminary, Catholic Charities, Catholic education, etc. Specified collections are one way of letting parishioners determine archdiocesan priorities. Cardinal Krol explains how he let people in Philadelphia vote with their check books:

All our collections are specified. We give the people an opportunity [to decide]; what we collect is sent to that specific thing. It isn't necessary to make priorities because we follow the policy of truth in advertising and respect the wishes of the donor. If we ask for this, and they give it for this, then that's what it is supplied to.

In some archdioceses, the collection occurs on a specified day, and whatever is collected goes to the archdiocese. In other archdioceses, the parishes are given a mandatory goal for the appeal. If they do not reach it in the collection, the money will have to come from other parish funds. If a parish goes over its goal, some archdioceses allow them to keep all or some of the money, while others require that all the money be sent to the chancery. Boston is unique in that neither the assessment nor the appeal is mandatory. The Detroit and Washington archdioceses are unusual in soliciting through direct mail campaigns.

Normally, the appeal goals are changed only incrementally, usually by adjusting them for inflation. "The individual goals of the parishes are done with a look at history and a look at the financial ability of a particular parish," explains the Louisville controller. "It is a seat of the pants thing." Raising appeal goals is not popular with pastors. The St. Paul moderator of the curia reports:

The annual Catholic appeal every year tries to raise the goal for every parish, especially those that did very well last year. They [the pastors] raise hell, scream, yell, and moan and have all kinds of appeal processes if they are not heard right.

In San Francisco, the priests' council voted to freeze the archdiocesan appeal target for a year and the archbishop reluctantly accepted their recommendation, which meant that many budgets had to be cut. Both archbishops and pastors appear to be reluctant to ask their people for more money. In addition, Bishop William McManus argues that it is in professional fundraisers' self-interest to set goals low so that they are achievable.[5] In any case, Catholics, in fact, contribute a smaller portion of their income to their church than do Protestants and Jews.[6]

It is sometimes argued that bishops act conservatively in order to please large contributors. In fact, churches are primarily funded by small contributors. Large donors are more likely to give to hospitals, colleges, and cultural institutions than to churches. Bishop McManus reports that "development directors in several dioceses who responded to an inquiry of mine about their recently successful fund-raising ventures all said that the local bishop's credibility—his openness to suggestions, follow-through on commitments, and high visibility in the diocese—is essential to enlist pastors' and parishioners' cooperation with a diocesan fund drive."[7] In Seattle, officials note that contributions to the archbishop's appeal continued to increase despite Archbishop Hunthausen's public statements on peace and justice and his conflict with the Vatican.

Budgeting for Archdiocesan Programs

Most of the current archbishops remember serving under bishops who operated without budgets. With only a few archdiocesan agencies, the budgetary process was simple prior to the 1960s. When someone needed money, he asked the bishop, who would say yes or no depending on his personal preferences and whether there was any money in the bank. Often the bishop himself wrote the check.

Social services, however, proliferated in the late 1960s and

1970s. The same period saw an increase in the number of diocesan offices, many of which were devoted to goals set by the Second Vatican Council: liturgical renewal, ecumenism, family life, adult religious education, minority affairs, peace and justice, etc. Although they raised some of their money from outside sources, these new agencies also competed with the schools for archdiocesan money just at the time school costs were increasing because of the replacement of low-salaried religious teachers with more expensive lay teachers. In the 1980s, lay ministries also entered the competition for church funds.

Budgetary problems arise because no archdiocese has unlimited resources and many have very limited resources. Monsignor Hawkes, late vicar for finances in Los Angeles, put it bluntly: "Any diocese can give to the People of God only what the People of God can pay for." Although some archdioceses were run in the red in the past, today no archbishop wants to have an unbalanced budget and that leads to conflict over limited funds. The moderator of the curia in St. Paul reports, "The archbishop worships fiscal accountability, which is not bad. A balanced budget, that's his rule. They almost killed each other around here last year because the budget committee couldn't get a balanced budget."

One of the early steps in the budgetary process is projecting revenue. Since the archbishop almost always demands a balanced budget, income projections determine the size of the archdiocesan budget. Projecting income is more or less difficult depending on whether appeal goals are mandatory and how assessments are calculated. Normally all categories are adjusted upward slightly. Sometimes income is conservatively projected to be the same as the previous year, which is an informal way of providing for unforeseen contingencies. During a local or national economic downturn, income projections may even be lowered because of the fear that people will have less to give.

In Newark, some expansions in the budget were made contingent on the achievement of fund-raising goals. The director of finance tells an agency head, "Look, we achieved a goal of

$3 million last year. Given all the factors we will probably get $3.4 million, but we are not sure about the $400,000 increase." The programs covered by increased revenues cannot be initiated until the revenues come in.

There is no easy way to judge among the various requests for money. Hard choices have to be made if the budget is to be balanced. Every archbishop and finance officer is looking for the magic budgetary process that will guarantee the most efficient use of church funds for the most important church priorities while at the same time keeping everyone in the archdiocese happy. No one has found this magic formula, which is not surprising since neither has any government or philanthropic agency.

A few archdioceses say that they have adopted budgeting systems that have been tried in the federal government: PPBS (planning, programing, budgeting system used in the Johnson administration), management by objectives (Nixon administration), or zero-based budgeting (Carter administration). Many who do not have these systems wish they did. Hardly any of the participants seem to know that these systems did not produce miraculous results in Washington.

In the minds of most archdiocesan officials, the ideal budgetary process begins with the drawing up of a mission statement that establishes the priorities and goals of the archdiocese. Once priorities are decided, they believe that the budgetary process will be an easy calculation of the most efficient way of reaching these goals. Agency heads will draw up their budgets with these goals in mind. They will be reviewed by their supervisors and an archdiocesan budget committee that will make recommendations to the archbishop.

The difficulty is that these mission statements usually are abstract and general in tone. They favor Catholic education, social justice, family life, youth ministry, care for the elderly, concern for minorities, continuing education for priests, parish renewal, adult education, etc. Any mission statement that does not cover all of these bases would not be backed by a consensus in the archdiocese. As a result, to the outsider, the mission statements are comparable to political party platforms—a wish list without priorities.

To those who participated in drawing up the mission statement, however, it has more meaning. They know the politics behind each phrase, who pushed for it, who opposed it, why it was changed, how much it was debated, how seriously it was considered by those who adopted it. As a result, the process of drawing up a mission statement is often more important than the product.

The archbishops recognize that they cannot relax after the mission statement is written. Archbishop Weakland of Milwaukee explains, "The budget process is the way in which you take your vision and goals and try and make them concrete." But translating the mission statement into budgetary terms is not easy. Archbishop Roach of St. Paul notes, "Our 'Five-Year Vision' is more than just a piece of paper. We work at that, very unevenly, but we do work at it."

In St. Paul, the planning committee attempted to translate the mission statement into quantifiable budgetary terms. The more often an agency was mentioned in the five-year plan, the higher its priority. "It could mean as many as 10 percentage points of annual budget," says the moderator of the curia. "Sounds as arbitrary as hell, but that was one way they did it." One of the problems with this system was that the tribunal, utilities, debt service, and other essentials not listed in the vision document still had to be paid for. In Baltimore, in attempting to quantify priorities, the archbishop's cabinet gave points to each program depending on how they judged it on a series of criteria. The most humorous result was that the archbishop's house came out as a low priority not to be funded.

After the mission statement is written, agencies are asked to submit with their budgets an explanation of how their goals and objectives fit into the mission of the archdiocese. They are also asked how their programs will fulfill their goals and objectives. The director of planning in Louisville admits that the mission statement is an umbrella designed to cover everything "we can or should be doing in the diocese." It is in writing the objectives and programs of agencies that things get concrete and restrictive. "It is not really the top, it is the bottom that is important," he says.

Agency heads can find this process threatening because it allows others to pass judgment on the legitimacy of their work. In fact, there is little indication that these processes have had major effects. The process is most beneficial to new archbishops, new cabinet members, and budget committees because it helps them learn what the agencies are doing or supposed to be doing. But here it is really new leadership, with a new agenda, that is forcing change, rather than a budget system. After a few years of this process, the production of goals and objectives by agencies becomes routine. Old copies are pulled out of the files and updated.

Budget Committee

Most archdioceses have an agency's budget first reviewed by the agency's board of directors if it has one. Then it is reviewed by the director of the department the agency reports to. Finally, an archdiocesan budget committee examines revenue projections, agency budgets, and the total financial picture of the archdiocese. Although the archbishop still has the last word, using a committee is perceived as being more democratic and collegial. Sometimes the committee is composed of chancery people, for example, the archbishop's cabinet. Chancery officials bring expertise to examining the budget but also vested interests.

Some archbishops try to get outsiders, both lay and clerical, to review the budgets. The logical group under canon law would be the finance council, but usually its members are chosen for their expertise as accountants, lawyers, and financiers, not for their sensitivity to pastoral issues. In addition, they are usually too busy with other financial issues (insurance, investments, real estate, construction, audit) to give enough time to the budget. Often a separate budget committee representing a better cross section of the archdiocese is preferred. The committee might include members of the priests' council and laypersons and religious from the archdiocesan pastoral council.

When an outside group closely examines agency budgets and programs, conflict can arise. There can be a gap "between all of the vested service people and the volunteers who are supposedly exercising ecclesial oversight," explains the St. Paul moderator of the curia. "There has to be a bridging between them, because historically we have had two camps, and there is a lot of blood spilled between them."

If an archbishop does not have the time or desire to examine each office budget in detail, the recommendations of the budget committee carry great weight. In addition, if he follows its recommendation, the committee can also take some of the blame if people are unhappy with the final budget.

Archbishop Weakland of Milwaukee explains how his budget committee works.

I have nine people on the budget committee—six lay and three priests. The three priests are appointed by the executive board of the priests' council and the other six, the lay people, I appoint.

The delegates from the various departments present their portion of the budget to this board. The board then looks at each department's budget, looks at the composite budgets, and then recommends to me what they think the income is going to be for the next year.

[They point out] the areas that they don't think are too solid, where they think some questioning should be given. They give me the options where they think something will have to be cut or money will have to be raised or whatever so as to balance the budget. They end up giving me a pretty good account of what they think is happening or could happen for the next year.

Percentage Increases and Cuts

When the budgets submitted by the various agencies are totaled, they usually exceed the amount of money available. In order to avoid this, some archdioceses simply instruct their agencies not to increase their budgets more than a set percentage. The director of business affairs in Portland admits, the budget process is "not very sophisticated, mostly taking last year's budget and adjusting it for inflation without much thought to what our priorities should be." In St. Paul, despite attempts to use the vision statement for priorities and budgeting criteria, spending increases in 1985 were simply limited to an across-the-board percentage. "The projected income was such," explains the finance officer, "that that was the only way we could have balanced the budget."

If agencies are allowed to propose what they think they need, the total will always exceed the income available. Then the proposed budgets must be cut. In Omaha, the finance officer says,

> We don't want to get into the situation where we tell them, "Cut this program or that program." We wait until after they submit their budgets and see how much the budgets add up to. We see it is going to be short this much money, then we have to cut. Just cut 1.5 percent.

This approach is simpler to administer than examining each budget and deciding what to cut. It also has the appearance of fairness since everyone is hurt equally. Archbishop Gerety of Newark explains:

> Deciding what to cut in the budget is very difficult. So you just have to slice. We did it on an across-the-board basis. Of course that caused a lot of problems, but nevertheless we had to do it. You take the bull by the horns and say, "There is so much pie; now you fellows go ahead and slice it up."

In a detailed review of items in the budget, the archbishop and the budget committee exercise control over what an agency does with its money. Under a block grant system, the archbishop delegates to subordinates the decisions about how the money in their agencies is used. They can expand one program and cut elsewhere. The directors, rather than the archbishop or the budget committee, are forced to make the difficult choices. "That is why you hire a director," explains the director of planning in Louisville. If he chooses projects that are worthless, "he is going to have egg on his face. If he is going in the wrong direction, then he or she won't be around very long."

Cutting budgets is very difficult. All agencies are doing or proposing worthwhile things, and all have employees and constituents who will be hurt by the cuts. Since a high proportion of the archdiocese's budget goes to salaries, any significant cut must eliminate personnel. The preferred way of doing this is not to replace someone when they retire or quit. In addition, reorganizations are sometimes aimed at reducing duplication and saving money. But often cuts are aimed at nonpersonnel expenses like travel, workshops, and so forth.

The Hard Choices

When the hard choices have to be made, an archdiocese will first recognize that certain expenses are simply unavoidable. In Newark, the archdiocesan finance office categorized expense items by whether they were fixed or variable. Insurance, utilities, debt service, contractual obligations, the archbishop, and auxiliaries were considered fixed expenses. "You can't ask the bank to wait for two months," explains the finance officer. "If we want to expand, we can only expand after we have absorbed fixed expenses."

Even in Washington where there is an attempt to use zero-based budgeting, the process is applied only to "optional" or new programs. "You can't zero base the tribunal," admits the secretary for support services. "Canon law says there is going to be a tribunal. The administrative budgets are those things that we consider to be givens." In such a system, however, the debate is over what should stay for close review. As the secretary for planning and management in Baltimore notes, "It is hard to get agreement on what should stay and what shouldn't."

Second, there will be a determination of salary increases that will eat up much of the increased revenues. "Let's say our income goes up $1.5 million, and you give a raise," explains Bishop Robert Banks, vicar general of Boston. "The raise, depending on what it is, is going to take about $500,000 to $750,000. So that leaves you very little to fool around with."

Third, new programs or expenses will get greater scrutiny than old programs. Often they will be cut or postponed if the budget is tight. Cutting existing programs, firing existing staff is more difficult than postponing hiring or major purchases, like a new car.

Finally, when existing programs are judged, a multitude of variables come into play. Attempts to establish quantifiable criteria for judging programs have been unsuccessful. "You have to do it by intuition," says the director of planning in Louisville. As a professional planner, he admits that relying on intuition rather than quantifiable criteria makes him uncomfortable. But trying to quantify everything does not work either. "If you are going to get everything down in numbers and add it up, get a computer," he says, "you don't need people." But people do not find choices between programs easy to make. "You can spend more money in Catholic Charities, or is Catholic education more important?" he notes. "There is no answer. You have to look at what they are doing and not doing. What would they do if you provided them more resources?" In fact, the proportion of funds going to various ministries does not change radically from year to year.

Often an important input for the archbishop in this intuitive decision is what he hears about a program from important constituencies like the pastors. If they bad-mouth the program, he will decide the money is being wasted. Also important will be his judgment of the program director. If he has the archbishop's confidence, his program will not be cut but might expand. But expansion can also depend on the availability of qualified personnel especially in smaller archdioceses. A program might be desirable, but the archbishop will not fund it until the right person is found to direct it. "That is where you bump your head most of the time," says the director of planning in Louisville.

Paying Off a Debt

Some archbishops found deficit spending and large debts when they arrived in their archdioceses. "Any bishop who goes into a diocese which has serious financial problems is terribly compromised," says Archbishop Hurley of Anchorage. "Until he gets that under control the entire pastoral operation is in jeopardy. You run into the factual problem of no money, then the necessity of getting money from the locals."

Archbishop Gerety found a $25.5 million debt in Newark. Cardinal Medeiros reportedly found a $50 to $80 million debt in Boston. For these archbishops, the first matter on their agenda had to be paying off their debts. In Newark a number of high schools had been built and not completely paid for. There were also heavy expenses in the social service area. At the same time the archdiocese was losing wealthier parishioners to the suburbs. In addition, there were rumors of financial incompetence and mismanagement.

Archbishop Gerety's first move, he says, was to form a finance committee of "people who know what they are talking about" to assist him. Next, he had "to convince people that what we were trying to do was something credible, that we were trying to put the archdiocese on an even keel financially. We had to cut budgets, we had to consolidate a bit. We had to negotiate with the banks, we had to convince the banks that we could pay it off if they gave us a reasonable interest rate."

Newark's $25.5 million debt came due on January 1, 1984, at a time when interest rates were very high. If the loan was renewed, the existing 7 percent interest rate would more than double. The finance officer told the archbishop, "If we don't get that principle down to a level we can manage, you will find that any new revenues you generate will go to additional interest expenses" and "the banks would have owned half the church in Newark."

The finance office also negotiated with parishes that owed money to the archdiocese or the banks. "We reached 172 agreements with parishes, addressing everything from past-due assessments, self-insurance premiums, pension obligations, loans," reports the finance officer. Some parishes were so poor or so heavily in debt that pastors had given up hope. The archdiocese eventually wrote off $10 million in debts owed it by parishes so that pastors could "see the light at the end of the tunnel." Newark met the deadline by increasing revenues, reducing expenses, and by internalizing the debt through its deposit and loan fund.

But sometimes an archbishop is forced to go deeper in debt. Archbishop Hannan was installed in New Orleans in October 1965, shortly after Hurricane Betsy destroyed six churches and badly damaged every other archdiocesan building. In addition, a number of high schools were under construction.

"The first Christmas I was here," Archbishop Hannan recalls, "the priest in charge of finances told me that $1 million was due on January 1 on our indebtedness and we didn't have a dime." He got the banks to give him sixty-day notes to cover that. "Then, through the centralized financing, I paid back those sixty-day notes," he says. "In order to complete these high schools we had to run the bank debt up to $37.5 million. That made a real big problem for the future, but that was the only thing to do."

As the case of New Orleans shows, debt was not always a bad thing. The debt that Archbishop Hannan inherited from Archbishop Cody was at only 5 percent interest. When other interest rates went up, the archdiocese wisely kept these loans as long as it could.

Financial Restrictions on a Bishop

There are few canonical restrictions on the power of a bishop over diocesan finances. Canon law, which is the same for bishops and archbishops, aims at conserving the patrimony of the diocese and at avoiding debilitating debts.[8] Canon law requires that the bishop get the approval of his finance committee before alienating church property worth over $500,000. *Alienation* is a technical term that means the transfer of the ownership of property from one person to another. A sale of property is not an alienation unless the proceeds are transferred to another person or institution. The alienation of property worth over $1 million requires the approval of the Holy See.

In the strict sense, alienation applies to real property and to funds invested for a specific purpose by proper ecclesiastical authority or by the intention of the donor.[9] On the other hand, money, stocks, bonds, certificates of deposit, or other securities not designated for a specific purpose do not come under the alienation rules. Thus, by only "temporarily" assigning money to various funds or endowments, a bishop can avoid the alienation rules if he later wants to withdraw the funds.

Canon law also requires that the bishop obtain the approval of his finance council and college of consultors for acts of "extraordinary administration." Extraordinary actions have traditionally included "land purchases, construction of new buildings or extensive repairs on old buildings, leasing or renting property for longer than nine years, the opening of a cemetery, long-term investment of any kind of capital, the establishment of a school or institution, and taking up special collections."[10]

Their approval would also be needed for incurring indebtedness (without corresponding increases in assets of the diocese) that exceeds $500,000. The Holy See's approval is needed for indebtedness exceeding $1 million. But since most indebtedness does result in an increase in diocesan assets, e.g., a new church or school, Vatican approval is rarely needed for a loan unless it is to cover operating expenses.

The American bishops consider seeking permission from Rome on financial matters to be impractical and feel that the $1 million ceiling is too low. At the November 1985 meeting of the NCCB, they recommended increasing the maximum amounts to $5 per capita of the Catholic population of a diocese up to a ceiling of $5 million. They also asked the Holy See to empower the pro-nuncio to allow expenditures beyond the maximum limit when recourse to the Holy See is difficult. The Vatican considered the recommendations were "inappropriate" and said no.

Other restraints on episcopal financial power are financial disclosure and external audits. In 1984 about 70 percent of the dioceses made their financial reports public.[11] Of these published reports, 78 percent were done by CPA firms. Audited dioceses had larger populations, revenues, and revenues per Catholic. The books of most archdioceses are audited, and the audit and management letter are usually reviewed by the finance committee.

The American Institute of Certified Public Accountants and the National Conference of Catholic Bishops have recommended a set of accounting principles and reporting practices for dioceses.[12] Although there are some technical disagreements between the two groups, both recommend the use of fund accounting and the accrual basis for financial reporting. All "indicate that essential disclosure information is to be found in the Balance Sheet, the Statement of Activity, the Statement of Change in Fund Balance, the Statement of Change in Financial Position, and the Footnotes."[13] One study found that on a 100-point scale, dioceses scored 60.5 on disclosure.[14] Interestingly, population size did not affect disclosure scores. Dioceses using CPA firms had higher scores. Dioceses experiencing financial stress also tend to disclose more to satisfy creditors and donors. The Vatican Bank and PTL scandals are apt to encourage fuller disclosure in the Catholic church.

Canon law does not mandate external audits or specific reporting practices, but it does require a diocese to "render an account to the faithful concerning the goods offered by the faithful to the Church. . . ."[15] Typically, the archdiocesan newspaper will publish all or part of the audit. To most nonprofessionals it is unintelligible, and it elicits few letters. But whenever the newspaper decides not to publish the audit, letters come in asking what they are trying to hide. Further confusion results from the fact that when an archdiocese has many corporations, the financial report for the central offices does not give a total picture of the financial condition of the archdiocese.

Conclusion

Every archbishop must spend a good deal of his time on finances. Even in Los Angeles where finances were delegated to a powerful vicar for finances, Cardinal Manning would have to pay some attention to finances. "It is completely delegated [to me]," explained Monsignor Hawkes, "but I do nothing of any magnitude that I do not advise him of before I do it."

Decisions to build a church or school, to sell or buy a large piece of property, to increase salaries, to borrow money would all be brought to the archbishop. Frequently, state law requires his signature for such actions. The annual budget, especially major changes in expenditures for programs or services, would also come to him.

The archbishop might de facto delegate many financial decisions to a finance director or to a budget committee, but there is no question in anyone's mind that he has the authority to make the decisions himself. Some archbishops delegate for theological reasons—they believe in consultation and shared responsibility. They also delegate because they want to spend their time doing something else. Often delegation is a strategy to avoid the conflict that surrounds the scramble over limited funds. It is easier to be a unifying force in the archdiocese if a committee or finance director is blamed for making the unpopular financial decisions.

But despite all the financial problems faced by archbishops, most agree that finances are not their biggest headache, it is personnel. Even financial problems are often symptomatic of personnel problems. "You find out the problem is people not money," explains the finance officer in New York. "If you got the people, money is secondary. If they are innovative, take initiative. . . . Money that could be spent better is shoring up personnel situations all over the lot." In the next chapter, the archbishop's role in personnel will be examined.

6. Personnel

The biggest problem for any archbishop running a diocese is to get the right people in the right place.

————ARCHBISHOP GERETY

Priest personnel—those are the most difficult, the most delicate, the most sensitive decisions I have to make in the course of the year.

————ARCHBISHOP SALATKA

The most important influence a bishop has over his diocese is through the recruitment, training, and assignment of personnel to parishes and diocesan agencies. Most archbishops and chancery officials agree that personnel is their greatest concern. Dedicated and trained laypersons, religious, and priests are necessary to the operation of an archdiocese. They staff the parishes, schools, hospitals, and other archdiocesan institutions. If the personnel are hardworking and creative, these institutions will flourish and provide a structured basis for the religious and spiritual life of the people in the archdiocese.

Although there is some support for a personnel system that treats priests, religious, and lay employees the same, most dioceses have different policies that apply to priests, religious, and lay employees. Priests and religious, for example, usually are paid less than lay employees. In the past, sisters were paid less than priests, although this injustice is becoming less common.

Priests' Personnel

As far as the archbishops are concerned, the key personnel issues relate to the diocesan priests. This is not to denigrate the importance of the religious and laity, but simply to indicate that most of the personnel issues that reach an archbishop concern his priests. Most lay and religious employees of an arch-diocese are hired by and report to someone other than the arch-bishop—a pastor, a school principal, or the administrator of a hospital or of another archdiocesan agency.

On the other hand, all diocesan priests are assigned by the archbishop to their jobs whether it be in a parish or other church institution. In addition, diocesan priests pledge obedi-ence to the bishop and his successor. Their commitment to the diocese is unqualified. Religious normally can serve their or-ders in other dioceses, and a layperson can seek employment elsewhere. Finally, if the priest has a personal problem, it can become the concern of the bishop. As a result, bishops consider clergy personnel issues special.

In dealing with priest personnel issues, bishops and person-nel directors are always trying to balance the good of the priest with the good of the diocese. In a sense, the personnel prob-lems and opportunities faced by a bishop are similar to those faced by any family business. A family business thrives on the dedication and enthusiasm of the family members who are will-ing to work long hours at low pay. Dean Hoge, for example, found that "Catholics pay much less for religious leadership than Protestants." He estimates that "the institutional cost of a full-time priest averages $26,376 at the local level plus $1,428 at the diocesan level (plus $1,039 for continuing education)." The cost for Episcopalians would be "$45,005, followed by Lu-therans, $39,059, and Methodists, $35,308."[1] But in a family business you do not fire Uncle Charlie because he could be replaced by someone more efficient. The head of the family must simultaneously be concerned for the welfare of the busi-ness and the members of the family, even when these conflict.

Similarly in the church, the bishop must be concerned about the good of the parishes and also the good of the priests. The dedication and commitment of the vast majority of the clergy gives life to the church. But the less successful priests are not simply replaceable parts in a machine. It is almost impossible for a bishop to fire a priest. And even if he could, there is not

a large pool of priests waiting to replace him. As one archbishop explains, "By and large, you do the best you can with
what you've got to work with."

Priests' Personnel Office

Dealing with clergy personnel issues is considered by church
administrators as the most difficult job in an archdiocese. A
comprehensive personnel service would deal with recruitment,
screening, selection, assignment, training, development, evaluation, support, counseling, crisis intervention, retirement,
and termination.[2] A large diocese might have different people
working full time on many of these functions, but in smaller
dioceses many functions would be performed by one person
or by part-time personnel. In most dioceses, for example, recruitment would be taken care of by a part-time director of
vocations. Training is done in seminaries either inside or outside the diocese.

In the past, the archbishop usually dealt with postseminary
personnel issues directly, with the help of his priest secretary
or chancellor. Since Vatican II the number of priests helping a
bishop with this work has grown. Today most archdioceses will
have a personnel board to help advise the bishop on assignments. Large dioceses might also have a priests' personnel director, vicar for clergy, director of continuing education, and
vicar for retired priests.[3] In smaller dioceses some of these positions might be held by one person or the jobs might be part
time. In Milwaukee, Archbishop Weakland considered the personnel office so important that he placed his two auxiliary bishops in charge of it.

The National Association of Church Personnel Administrators notes that in the business world a rule of thumb "is that
one personnel specialist should be on the staff for every 100
persons served."[4] By such standards, church personnel offices
are understaffed considering the large numbers employed by
an archdiocese.

The creation of personnel offices was overwhelmingly supported by the priests in the mid-1960s.[5] Confusion and unrealistic expectations often are present when the creation of a priests' personnel office is considered. Should the priests' personnel director be an administrator, counselor, ombudsman, mediator, or all of the above? Some confusion arises because the bishop and priests sometimes have different expectations for people in the personnel office. For example, are they representatives of the bishop to the priests or of the priests to the bishop? Or both? "I have my own expectations of what I should be doing," reports one personnel director. "The bishop has expectations of what I should be doing, and every priest has expectations. At times there are unreal expectations placed on us."

Bishops usually perceive the personnel director, like his secular counterpart, as someone who can help the chief executive with assignments and personnel problems. Often, however, the personnel office has been created at the instigation of the priests' council because the council feels the bishop is failing to hear the needs and desires of the priests. The priests hope that a good personnel person can act as an intermediary between the priests and the bishop. They may also want him to fulfill other roles. The vicar for clergy in Hartford noted that besides being involved with assignments, "The priests wanted the vicar to be a mediator, advocate, confidant, someone with whom they could share their problems."

In fact, most personnel directors represent the bishop to the priests, but they also conscientiously attempt to look out for the needs of the priests. In all the archdioceses, it is clear that the personnel director works for the bishop even in cases where the bishop allows the director to be nominated by the priests. Even the elected personnel boards see their role more as advising the bishop than as representing the priests.

In an effort to deal with the multiple personnel roles, some archdioceses (Chicago, Newark, Milwaukee) distinguish between the priests' personnel director, who deals with assignments, and the vicar for clergy, who deals with priests' problems. Diocesan priests like this distinction because they do not want the person who deals with their personal problems to have anything to do with their assignments.

But even with this distinction, it is still unclear whether the vicar for clergy should be a counselor helping the priests or an authority figure intervening in the name of the bishop. As a result, they can be caught between the expectations of the priests and the expectations of the bishop if their job description is not clear. For example, how much of what the priests tell the vicar can be passed on to the archbishop? In Chicago, the vicar for priests would not pass on to the archbishop information without the priest's consent if the priest came to him. But if the archbishop initiated the contact because of his concern for the priest, then the priest is told that anything he tells the vicar can be passed on to the archbishop.

Some people working in priests' personnel believe that there is need for at least three persons: a counselor/advocate whose only concern is the priest's welfare, a personnel director concerned about assignments, and a vicar who challenges, evaluates, intervenes, or corrects priests in the name of the bishop. Cardinal Hickey in Washington has his chancellor deal with complaints about priests rather than his vicar for clergy or priests' personnel director. "I would not give it to the secretary for parish life or the secretary for clergy," he says. "I don't want to prejudice the program or the secretary. I don't want his or her credibility chewed up."

On the other hand, priests are biased against any bureaucracy that separates them from their bishop. In Cincinnati at a priests' convocation the men appeared to favor an ombudsman, but when they were later surveyed, the response was negative. "On further reflection they saw it differently," explains the priests' personnel director. "It wouldn't help things that much just sticking another person in the bureaucracy."

But in many dioceses, the priests' personnel director has all these multiple and sometimes conflicting roles. Some of this is inevitable because it reflects the multiple and sometimes conflicting roles of the bishop, who must be simultaneously concerned with the good of his priests and the diocese.

In any case, a priest dealing with personnel is a man in the middle. It has been recommended that he have skills in several fields: theology and pastoral care, church teaching and policy, professional personnel administration, and counseling and behavioral science.[6] But most have had little or no training in professional personnel administration or in behavioral science. They tend to be pastoral men with interpersonal skills and good judgment who are respected and trusted both by the bishop and their peers. After they are appointed, they get on-the-job training.

Many have found the job very burdensome. Sister Christine Matthews, O.P., director of the National Association of Church Personnel Administrators, reports:

> The personnel directors know it all [the virtues and vices of the priests]. They find it a tremendous burden. They find that their relationships with the other priests change. I have had one say to me, "I am not invited to the same parties. The whole relationship changes. In six years when this is over, I won't forget all of that stuff, and I will be treated the same way."

One personnel director told how his appointment affected his friendships among the clergy.

> I have a priest who is a nervous wreck every time I call. I am not calling except to talk to him about something else. I went by to visit one day because I was nearby. He said, "Why are you here." "I just came to say hi." "Are you sure?" he asked. I said, "Yes, no ulterior motive at all." His term as pastor is nearing its end, so he knows that one of these times I am going to call for that reason.

On the other hand, many priests involved in personnel work experience it as a fulfilling ministry. "I really enjoy the opportunity to be pastor to priests," says Bishop Richard Sklba who is co-vicar for clergy in Milwaukee. "There is something so gratifying about that pastoral ministry. They are very good guys.

Almost everybody is praying hard and working hard. The chance to sit down and spend time together is very gratifying."

Despite the ideal of a comprehensive personnel program, the primary concerns of priests' personnel directors are the assignment of priests and crisis intervention. Most of their time is spent on assignments and on priests with problems. Concern for continuing education often takes a back seat to these primary concerns except where a person's sole responsibility is to encourage priests to update their training. What has made all of these personnel issues even more difficult is the shrinking of the personnel pool.

Shrinking Personnel Pool

The decline in the number of priests has church administrators very concerned because it is making clergy personnel issues even more difficult.[7] The shortage of priests is only just beginning to affect the church, but already 34 percent of Catholics have personally experienced a shortage of parish priests.[8] And it is going to get worse, much worse. One national study estimates that there will be half the number of active priests in the year 2000 as there were in the 1960s.[9]

Projections on the supply of priests are being done in many archdioceses. Portland, for example, is projecting thirty to fifty priestless parishes by the year 2000. Archbishop Whealon of Hartford reports, "I had a study done by our insurance people that indicates that the 500-plus priests that I had when I came here in 1969 is gradually being reduced so that at the end of the century there will be 360 active priests. At the same time the average age is going up steadily, relentlessly in fact. Priests are fewer, older, having many health problems."

The impact of the shortage in the large urban dioceses (Boston, New York, Philadelphia, Washington) has been lessened by the large numbers of priest students or teachers at educational institutions who help on Sundays. But even in the large urban dioceses, the effects of the shortage are beginning to be felt as there are fewer associate pastors to help in parishes.

"In the last nine months," explained the Philadelphia chancellor in 1986, "we have had fifteen parishes where we could not replace an assistant pastor when he was transferred. We have had a number of priests forty-five and older suffering heart attacks and getting seriously ill. Not so much burnout as unexpected heart attacks."

But some personnel directors do not consider the shortage of priests their biggest problem. "My biggest problem," reports one personnel director, "is that I have people I cannot place. They can't get along with the staff at the parish; they have different ecclesial models of the church or they won't fit in with the lay staff or lay participation. Of the sixty moves this year, there were five or six I can't fit anywhere. I spend 80 percent of my time on these." This problem is not simply with older priests. Some personnel directors complain of newly ordained priests who did not fit in.[10]

Priests' Problems

Unassignable priests and priests with other problems are a major concern of bishops and personnel directors. Bishops are especially concerned about priests who leave the ministry or get in trouble. "I can ride with almost everything except the priest not taking advantage of the grace that's available to him and this leading to misdirectedness," said Cardinal Krol of Philadelphia. "I can shake off almost anything, but when it comes to things of that nature, you wake up at two o'clock in the morning, and you have been thinking of it all night long."

Cardinal Manning of Los Angeles also admitted worrying about similar problems at four o'clock in the morning. "That's when they surface, the problems of personnel. Our Lord had his disciples around him, and they had their problems, and Jacob had problems with his sons. Those are probably the hardest things to reconcile."

Every archbishop's secretary told me that if a priest telephones and wants to see the archbishop, he gets in as soon as possible. "Any priest who calls can see the archbishop," says the secretary to Archbishop Roach of St. Paul. "I will ask if it is an emergency or whether it can wait. I don't ask for details, although they often give them to me. If it can't wait, I will bounce a staff person, who can see the archbishop later, so that he can see the priest." Archbishop Quinn of San Francisco gives to his priests the numbers of the private lines that ring in his office and residence so that they can reach him without going through a switchboard or secretary.

Most archbishops, even those who on the surface seem gruff, have a reputation for being very good at dealing with a priest who comes to him with a problem such as alcoholism, drugs, gambling, or a failure in celibacy. One personnel director described his archbishop:

> He is very formal, demanding, insists on 100 percent obedience. But if a man is in trouble in any way, any kind of trouble, trouble with the law, drinking or drugs, women, anything—he is the most kindly, understanding, helpful man you would ever hope to have on your side.
>
> If he can help you come to terms with whatever the problem is and you come back to active ministry, then the whole thing is off the record like it never happened. There is no grudge held, no "Well, we can't trust him anymore." He is very fair.

The priest with serious moral or legal problems is the rare exception. But when these problems do surface, they take a great deal of the bishop's and personnel director's time. A number of personnel directors felt that, at the time of this study, their work in this area was especially high because they were dealing with problems that had been ignored by bishops in the past. In any case, if the priest approaches the archbishop before there is a public scandal, usually all can be forgiven and dealt with if the priest is willing. Here the bishop is not an employer, but a father or the representative of the forgiving Christ. If the priest reforms (and sometimes even if he does not, as long as it does not become public), he can continue in his ministry.

Many archdioceses also have policies and procedures for intervening to help priests with problems of substance abuse.[11] Often the intervention team is headed by priests who are already members of Alcoholics Anonymous. In one archdiocese, the intervention team even talked to the archbishop about his drinking problem.

Programs of counseling and therapy are offered and willingly paid for by the bishop. A variety of treatment options are available in larger archdioceses that would include AA, counseling, and treatment programs such as Guest House, which specializes in alcoholic priests. Bishops willingly spend money for treatment. In New York the personnel director says that any decent program will cost $30,000. He says he has an open-ended budget for this purpose. After treatment, it is common for a priest to return to his ministry.

The major exception today is in cases of child abuse. In the past, because of ignorance, some bishops were lenient in dealing with priests who sexually abused children. There was little understanding of the problem as an illness and a crime or of the archdiocese's liability as an employer. In 1986, however, a jury awarded $1 million in damages to the family of an abused child which had to be paid by the diocese of Lafayette (LA) because the bishop knew the priest had problems and moved him to another parish where he abused more children. Additional payments were made to thirteen other families in out-of-court settlements. Insurance companies quickly added an exclusion for child abuse to their contracts with churches or at least placed a cap on their liability.

Few bishops will risk that kind of liability in the future. Bishops all across the country, under the guidance of their lawyers, quickly established policies and procedures for reporting and dealing with accusations of child abuse by any church employee. Some lawyers recommended against dealing with the parents lest any sympathy or help be considered an admission of responsibility. Stonewalling, however, often angered the parents into the suits the lawyers were trying to avoid. Most dioceses found that the parents are primarily concerned with getting help for their child and with making sure no other child is abused. When the diocese is forthcoming, the parents usually prefer not to sue lest further damage be done to the child. The Christian response proved to be the smart response.

But getting evidence of child abuse if the children or parents do not come forward is almost impossible. One personnel director describes the problem:

> When it blows, it blows all over the place. You think there are two families, then forty families come out of the woods just angry as heck. But you never have concrete data until something like that happens. That is what is so bad about it. You got insinuations, you got kids that will say, this might happen, nothing happened. You really don't know.
>
> The kids are afraid for their parents, afraid of being disloyal to the church or father. They are not going to say anything. We had a kid who came back much later as an adult.
>
> Today we don't know, but there are a lot of red flags. How do you handle those without barging in and ruining somebody's reputation? People find out in a hurry.
>
> We have a couple of possibles, but you don't ever have data on which to really act. We did take two out of circulation and put them into counseling. There was no hard-core evidence, parents or anything, but always insinuations that this happened or that happened.
>
> Psychologically, they are hard nuts to crack as far as admitting any need for help. Both of these denied the whole works. I suppose you get a little paranoid when you see a guy with a couple of servers on a trip or in a car. It is dangerous.

Priest Morale

Although they take an inordinate amount of time, priests with serious legal, moral, or psychological problems are the rare exception. The bishop must also be concerned about the rest of his priests. A major concern of the bishops since the early 1970s has been the morale of their priests. Bishops worry about low morale because it is bad for the priests, bad for the church, and bad for the bishop. Priests with low morale are unhappy, they do not work well, and they are less likely to support and follow the leadership of their bishop. And they may leave the ministry.

In fact, the morale of priests is higher than comparable American males who are married and much higher than unmarried males.[12] But low morale among any priests is a concern of bishops. The causes of low morale are many.[13] In the past, priest morale problems often centered around conflicts with authoritarian bishops and, for associates, conflicts with authoritarian pastors.[14] The appointment of bishops sensitive to priests' concerns under Archbishop Jadot did much to neutralize this area of conflict, so that in 1985 only 9 percent of the diocesan clergy said relationship with their bishop was a problem for them.[15] New structures (personnel boards and priests' councils) and new governance styles after Vatican II also have improved relations between bishops and priests. Surveys have shown that priests' "self-esteem, work satisfaction and morale all increased between 1970 and 1985."[16] But feelings of being overworked and lonely remained at the same level as 1970. Recently, however, the appointment of more conservative bishops has led some American priests to fear a return to authoritarian governance. These bishops would more quickly step in to stop experimentation that goes beyond what would be permitted by Rome.

Low morale is also caused by loneliness and the desire to marry. Surveys have found that many priests favor optional celibacy, but most recognize that this option will not be available in their lifetime. Celibacy "is a real problem, especially as we have more priests living alone," says the executive secretary of the Chicago personnel board. "Priests [are] working longer and longer days and saying, 'who really loves me, who really cares about me, or what kind of relationships do I have that really matter?' "

The numbers of men leaving the priesthood and the decline in the number of vocations is also troubling to priests.[17] The same Chicago priest notes:

The same number of people [about 9 per year in Chicago] have taken leaves of absence in the last few years, but the quality has changed. In the past, guys would take leaves and you kind of say, "I always thought that would happen. It was obvious that he was not happy; he is struggling with a lot of stuff."

But this year, some of the really best priests have taken leaves of absence. People I really respect, this is really what a priest is. And he says, "I want to take a leave of absence." That has been very, very hard.

The bishops find this depressing also. "The hardest thing of all is when a priest is leaving," reports Cardinal Hickey of Washington. "I mean, I die a little bit every time. It just saddens me to see this man in whom there is so much promise and so much hope. If it were a thoroughly bad person . . . but that's so rare. When you see a man leave, you just say, 'Did I fail him? Did the church fail him? What happened here?' That's my greatest sorrow."

Recent media attention to pedophilia and homosexuality among the clergy have also contributed to low morale.

Priests' morale is also affected by changing concepts of what it means to be a priest today and by their lifestyle and work. The identity and roles of priests prior to Vatican II were fairly clear and stable. Priests in the past normally lived in a milieu where they received the unquestioning respect and reverence of their parishioners. They administered the sacraments from the church to which people came. The pastor was boss. He knew what was good for his people, and they accepted his leadership. He had a theology that was unquestioned.

Today, the role of the pastor is not clear, because it has changed and is still evolving. While survey data does not support the notion that priests lack a clear idea of what a priest is or have been negatively affected by theological change in the concept of priesthood,[18] the practical implementations of these ideas may be more problematic. How is he supposed to be a leader and at the same time a member of a team? Is he a teacher or a coordinator of ministries? Is he supposed to minister to parishioners or facilitate ministers who do that? And what is the role of the associate pastor in all this?[19] Is his time being wasted in administration? Should he be involved in the school or religious education program? Is he supposed to be sympathetic or prophetic? Should he spend his time in one-on-one counseling or dealing with large groups? Which groups in the parish should he reach out to—school children, teenagers, young singles, engaged, newly married, families in crisis, the sick, elderly, grieving, dying, blacks, Hispanics, ethnics, Yuppies, churched, unchurched, Protestants, Jews, altar guild, Boy Scouts, Girl Scouts, altar servers, St. Vincent de Paul Society, athletes, the poor, unemployed, homeless, drug addicts, abused women? Since he cannot do everything, how should he budget his time and energies? And how does he say no to those he cannot serve?

Today, the pastor must deal with a parish council, questioning parishioners, and expectations that he be all things to all persons. And all of this is happening at the same time priests' numbers are fewer and their average age is rising. In Chicago, "there is a growing concern over the huge parishes that we have," says a priest working in personnel. "What does it mean when there is just one priest or two priests to run that? You have a funeral every day, three or four weddings on Saturday. How do you revive yourself, keep yourself alive and alert in that kind of situation?" Between 1970 and 1985, the number of priests complaining of too much work increased slightly (9 to 11 percent) as did the number complaining of unrealistic demands and expectations of lay people (8 to 16 percent).[20] This is especially true of younger priests.

While few priests want to go back to the old ways, many experience frustrations their predecessors never dreamed of. Not infrequently they suffer from burnout and stress.[21] Part of this stress comes from the inability to have a private life. The expectation is that priests are always on duty. In addition, parish rectories have become less homes for the priests than offices and meeting places for parish activities. Some would prefer to live elsewhere. "Priests under forty are finding it intolerable," explains the personnel director in Chicago. "They live in public buildings. It is living above the store, and they can't stand it anymore. They are not with people they want to live with. It offers neither privacy nor community."

Their morale will be especially low if they think those in authority do not understand or appreciate their problems.[22] A number of priests dealing with personnel expressed shock at the pope's speech in France declaring that the priests' identity crisis was over. "I feel really bitter about those kinds of statements coming out of Rome," says one priest. "I have felt so much of the personal pain of really good men who have tried so hard to do a good job, and I see what they are going through. And then to hear that there is no crisis, that is really bad."

Another personnel director says, "What the pope said is just absurd. I am stunned by that remark, because it is just so ignorant. Diocesan priests, we have no idea what our charism is. How we fit in. The morale is abysmal. Bishops are denying it, or they are paralyzed by it. You have someone like the pope saying that it is all over. That is idiotic. Just idiotic. He is just poorly informed."

Some archbishops, especially older ones, admit that they were not sensitive to priests' problems. They grew up in the Depression and the Second World War; they were used to a life of obedience and sacrifice. When they faced problems, they gritted their teeth and bore it. They also began their ministry in a time when most questions had a simple answer. They enjoyed being priests, were successful, and reached the top of their profession.

As a result, some, such as archbishops Donnellan and Whealon, did not realize until late in their careers how important it was to work at improving priests' morale.

Archbishop Donnellan of Atlanta explained:

I grew up in a tradition that said, "Here I am Lord, send me." I found the priesthood a wonderfully happy experience, and my class-mates have been very close to one another and supported one another so that I was probably not sensitive enough to stress.

I am inclined to say, "Hey, look, the average guy out there with a wife and children and a job has more stress in a week than we have in a month." There is a lot of truth to that, but just because you don't feel that much stress, doesn't mean that it isn't there for other people. Maybe that is an area that I should have been more sensitive to.

Likewise, Archbishop Whealon of Hartford at the conclusion of a 1985 Emmaus, a renewal program for priests, confessed in his homily:

The major lesson which I take from Emmaus is the need, in the 1980s, to affirm priests. That may sound to you younger men like a self-evident truth. Let me explain to you why this is something new. The training of my generation was not to work for or expect human praise. Priests did their best, for Christ and the church, and were not singled out for praise by either their bishop or their fellow priests.

But I now see this situation as not good, because in the 1980s a brother can feel unsupported, isolated, not understood. A bishop needs to be available to his priests, to encourage and thank and love and affirm them. If a bishop only says thanks to his priestly co-workers and encourages them, he has spent a good day. But how to do that, with knowledge and sincerity and without deflating the value of words of gratitude—that is a challenge.[23]

A similar admission was made by Archbishop Weakland of Milwaukee. As a Benedictine, "I thought that the diocesan priests liked that individualism. 'Don't touch me, let me alone, let me do my own thing.' I didn't understand soon enough the enormous amount of strokes they need and the care they need. So I mishandled the priests for a few years."

How a bishop is to relate to his priests is a complex problem. He is both their boss and brother. The old style bishop was aloof and clearly the boss. Some bishops avoid having friends among their priests lest they be accused of favoritism or cronyism. Despite his desire to affirm priests, for example, Archbishop Whealon would not attend dinners in honor of priests— "You would have to go to all of them."

Archbishops have tried a number of strategies and programs for improving morale and communications with their priests. Archbishop Whealon was one of the first bishops to support team ministries in the parishes and his primary motivation was improving the morale of younger priests who were not pastors. Workshops and sabbaticals and other forms of continuing education are also seen as helpful in aiding priests' morale and ministry.[24] The Emmaus program tries to help the priests' spiritual development and to foster a feeling of solidarity among the priests. In Hartford, three groups of priests did this program, and the archbishop went through the program with all three groups. Another program, "Ministry to Priests," was used in New Orleans, and again the archbishop attended each one.

To improve communications between priests and their archbishop, the Chicago archdiocese had "overnights," jokingly referred to by the priests as pajama parties, which began at noon and went to noon the next day. At these affairs Cardinal Bernardin invited a group of priests of varied ages (e.g., everyone ordained in a year ending in five). The day involved a "state of the diocese" address by the archbishop together with a no-holds-barred question period. Discussions were also organized to improve communications between priests of various ages. Time also was available for the priests to simply relax together.

A strategy used frequently by bishops when they first come to their dioceses is to go around to the deaneries or vicariates to dialogue with their priests. Archbishop Quinn did this when he first came to San Francisco as did archbishops Levada of Portland and Law of Boston in their archdioceses. Others have invited small groups of priests to lunch or dinner at the archbishop's house so that they could talk informally.

In New York, Cardinal O'Connor late in 1986 decided to set aside one day a week to see any priest who wanted to see him at his residence. "I'll be available to priests all day long at the house," he explained. "It will be like a barbershop. They can come without appointments."

Priests' morale involves many issues outside of the bishop's control, but he can do much to improve it or make it worse. Sensitive listening and sincere love and respect for his priests is essential. "A bishop's relationship with his priests is all-important," comments one archbishop, "but it is not all that easy to establish a level of trust or understanding [where priests accept] a decision where you can't really share all the reasons for it. A bishop can't do a thing without his priests. You shouldn't do things just to please them, I guess if you wanted to you couldn't. But you should be honest with them, open with them. If they ask a direct question, you give them a direct answer. Don't say, 'That is none of your business.' "

Assignment of Priests

An area about which priests are especially interested is the assignment of priests to parishes. The appointment of priests to parishes and diocesan offices is a major preoccupation of bishops. "The toughest thing about being a bishop," says Archbishop Sheehan of Omaha, "is making the appointments." In making assignments, bishops want to take into consideration the needs of the priests and the needs of the diocese. Balancing these needs and getting the right man in the right job is the problem.

Another archbishop, for example, recalls the trouble he had finding a priest secretary.

The first man I had as secretary was absolutely hopeless. He was one of the most interesting fellows I ever met in my life, but he was totally hopeless as a secretary. He just couldn't get himself organized, but, boy, could he talk about philosophy or theology or Rahner or Schillebeeckx. I used to love to ride with him, but he was hopeless.

Then I got another secretary to succeed him. But here again he was a very fine pastor subsequently and a very wonderful priest. But as secretary you cannot become emotionally involved in the people who are calling you up all the time. They get hundreds of calls and people are complaining about this and that. And this guy would be falling apart. So he went on to better things. I named him a pastor.

Finally, after three tries I got the best secretary in the world, just perfect for the job.

In order to help them put the right person in the right spot, archbishops have set up various systems and procedures. Many have a priests' personnel director who gathers information on the parishes and interviews priests for various positions. But Archbishop May was reluctant to appoint a full-time priest to personnel work in St. Louis:

I have dealt with personnel matters in three different situations. I was director of the personnel board in Chicago, and then worked on personnel in Mobile and here.

I'm concerned about expectations. Everybody feels that this approach or having certain policies and having a personnel board is going to create a situation in which everybody is going to be satisfied. They've all been consulted; therefore, they're going to be in a place that is fulfilling them, and so on.

You raise expectations, and then it will never, never be that way. There's a greater disillusionment very often when you do all those things and still there is a great deal of disappointment.

Chancery officials consider working on priests' assignments to be the most thankless job in the diocese. It is impossible to give everyone the assignment they want, and suspicions and complaints abound among priests over personnel assignments. In response to these complaints, many members would agree with Archbishop Hunthausen of Seattle: "It would be important for every priest in the diocese to have a stint on the personnel board so that they would know how hard it is. It is easy to stand out there and criticize it."

Archbishops feel that priests will complain no matter what the system is. A new priests' personnel director told this story about a conversation with his archbishop:

[I said to the archbishop,] "I really want to run this office in such a way that guys will have no complaint."

The archbishop laughed and roared, "Shame on you!"

I said, "What do you mean, 'Shame on me'?"

"Shame on you, I thought you loved your priests!"

I said, "I do."

"Cripes," he said, "you want to take away their number one pastime."

Personnel Board

Most archbishops have instituted an elected personnel board (sometimes called committee, commission, or council), consisting of about seven priests, to advise them on the assignment of priests. The establishment of these boards often came in response to requests from the priests, but how well they work depended on the style of the bishop.[25] Most bishops have come to depend heavily on these boards in the appointment process. "All that used to be done by the bishop," explains Archbishop Kelly of Louisville. "I don't know what else he could do; he could spend his whole life doing that. What is more, I would make bad judgments if it was all up to me. The priests' personnel board is the greatest invention of Vatican II."

The written procedures usually recognize that the archbishop can bypass the board if he wants. "Anytime I want to I can bypass this process and make an appointment," says Archbishop O'Meara of Indianapolis. "But obviously, if I would do that very often, why have them? Implicit in that is that you can do it, but you really won't."

A few archdioceses do not have elected personnel boards, for example, Philadelphia (under Cardinal Krol), Newark (under Archbishop Gerety), and Kansas City (under Archbishop Strecker). "Our priests will take an appointment from the bishop," explains Cardinal Krol, "but if it's [from] a personnel committee, they are resentful, they are cantankerous, they complain." In Newark and Philadelphia, the auxiliary bishops acted as a personnel board, meeting with the archbishop and the personnel staff. In Kansas City the board is appointed by the archbishop.

Surveys have indicated that priests, in fact, overwhelmingly favored personnel boards as early as the mid-1960s.[26] Although most priests like the idea of personnel boards, some priests bypass them, especially in a small diocese. In Mobile the chairman of the personnel board remarks:

> Some priests say, "I made my promise to a bishop, I didn't make it to a board, and I will deal with the bishop." A lot of guys when they have to do with appointments, they talk to the bishop. Sometimes things get settled that the board doesn't have a whole lot of definite input into. But this is a small archdiocese, and after all, we are advisory. There is nothing iron clad about our "rights."

Most priests prefer personnel boards to the old assignment process that was totally dependent on the archbishop and his appointed staff. The old system was attacked for being insensitive to the needs of the priests and for being subject to cronyism. Personnel boards are seen as being more democratic and more sensitive to the views of the priests. In addition, if a priest does not relate well to the priests' personnel director or the bishop, he can usually find someone on the board he can talk to.

Personnel boards are usually elected directly by the priests. Normally, each age group elects its own representative, but sometimes the age group nominates candidates and the entire presbyterate votes on all the candidates. In a few archdioceses (for example, in Los Angeles and Indianapolis), the members are elected by the priests in particular geographical areas.

The board members serve as volunteers while holding down other full-time jobs. The staff work in a large diocese is done by a full-time personnel director. In a small diocese it might be done by the chairman of the board or by a chancery official who works part-time on personnel.

The archbishops have found boards to be a good source of

advice. "We have a personnel board, elected by the priests, that is simply fabulous," reports Archbishop Kucera of Dubuque. "I take no credit for it because it was here when I arrived. It has done a tremendous job in being sensitive to the needs of the priests and the parishes. Working with them is a pleasure." Being new to the archdiocese and not knowing the priests, he found the board especially helpful. "Listening to these people talk filled me in very quickly," he explains. "It gave me a background on who's who, and the nuances were much more easily viewed."

But even when the archbishop is from the archdiocese, he usually finds the board helpful. "The personnel board certainly has brought to me special dimensions of priests' capabilities and priests' weaknesses when we are making appointments that I would not have had knowledge of," explains Archbishop Lipscomb, a native of Mobile.

"Our job is to match the skills and abilities of the priests with the needs of the parish and the diocese," explains the director of personnel for the St. Paul archdiocese. In order to do that, the personnel director and the board must have information on the parishes and the priests.

Desires of the Priests

In 1960, 50 percent of the pastors and 84 percent of the curates said that they were "simply told to report" to their current assignment without being consulted.[27] Today, this would be atypical. What the St. Paul personnel board does to gather information about the desires and needs of the priests is more common:

In January we send out a letter asking the priests if they want to move, if they want to be interviewed by the board, how they are getting along with their pastor (or associate). About 80 percent of them answer the questionnaire.

We first interview those who want a change, then those who want to be interviewed simply to keep us informed about what is going on. Then we look at those who did not answer the questionnaire, and, if we have not interviewed them in three years, we do so.

Formally surveying the priests about their interest in moving and the type of parish they are interested in helps personnel boards match up the needs of the diocese with the desires of the priests. Some boards also have interviews with the priests, although this is usually left to the personnel director.

In Milwaukee the personnel office uses an interview procedure constructed by Development Dimensions International to measure skills, especially management skills, of the priests in order to match them up with the right parish. For example, to examine a priest's staff leadership ability, the office might ask him the following:

What approach do you use to work with the parish council when one of its committees is to consider a new idea or policy? What ways have you found to make your associate pastor or parish employees' jobs easier and more rewarding? Tell me about the toughest groups in the parish that you have had to get cooperation from, and what did you do to get that cooperation? Can you think of a parish project or policy (not necessarily your own) that was successfully implemented because of your efforts? What changes have you tried to implement in your own area of responsibility as pastor, and what have you done to get these changes underway?

The Milwaukee personnel director defends using an interview procedure developed by business: "We look at pastors and priests as managers of a lot of things. The skills required in any position are basically the same. It is how you apply them. There is a set of questions for each skill category. It basically measures behavior in given work situations."

Open Listing

In the past, a pastorate would become open if a pastor died, retired, or moved. A pastor's death would be known to all the priests, but often his retirement or transfer was kept secret by the chancery until after a replacement had been found. Priests complained that this system favored "insiders" or people with friends in the chancery. It did not treat priests equally or fairly. In addition, this system was considered paternalistic because it presumed that those in authority knew what was best for a man without even asking him.

Now the trend has been toward *open listing*, where all the priests of the diocese are informed of an opening through the diocesan newspaper or through a special mailing from the chancery. Any priest may apply for the position if he wishes. A financial and historical profile of the parish is given to anyone interested in the parish so that he can decide whether or not he wants to apply.

The first advantage of this process is that it provides the bishop and personnel board with information on the specific desires of the priests. They do not have to guess whether a priest would be willing to go to a particular parish. Through the applications that they receive in response to the open listing, they know which priests are interested in which parishes.

Second, many personnel directors feel that open listing treats priests as mature adults who should have something to say about their lives. It requires that the priests take initiative rather than waiting to be told what to do. "It has been psychologically healthy for priests to take some responsibility for their own lives," explains a director, "instead of sitting back and waiting to be recognized by authority. Obedience as a genuine call to a difficult service is a very important spiritual part of our lives, but the passive stuff that it frequently creates is very unhealthy."

Or as another personnel director says, "It is very mature because it puts ownership on the men involved. You make your own bed, you lie in it." The Louisville priests' personnel director notes that open listing "takes some of the blame off of the board and the archbishop for making a decision that affects their lives. Now the priests have to make a decision that affects their lives or at least let us know which way they are thinking."

Some archdioceses (Atlanta, Baltimore, Indianapolis, Kansas City, KS, Mobile, Philadelphia, San Francisco) do not have open listing. Cardinal Krol of Philadelphia explains, "We don't advertise vacancies. To me that is a kind of helpless leadership. I think you have to fill places, and unpleasant places."

Some priests object to open listing in principle. "Some of your better people, for spiritual reasons as well as psychological reasons, feel they should not apply," explains the chairman of the Omaha personnel board. "It is a matter of principle or just fear. Sometimes spiritual: 'If the Lord wants you to do it, the bishop will ask.' But how is the bishop ever going to know if you don't say something?"

In some small dioceses there is fear that open listing would be destructive to priestly camaraderie. The priests' personnel director in Louisville says that the priests were reluctant to go to open listing. "They are afraid of competition, afraid of dog-eat-dog type stuff." A member of the personnel board in Kansas City, KS, reports:

We are a small archdiocese and guys know each other pretty well. They all know resources are limited and the parishes are limited. To pit guys—have them bid against each other for a parish—could end up being pretty destructive.

But he admits that "some guys would like to know that so-and-so is going to be moving, so they would know some other things might be possible."

But even in those places without formal open listing, a priest can still request an assignment if he knows about it, although this was not common in Philadelphia. In Kansas City, a member of the personnel board notes, "Obviously word gets around about some of the places that are going to be open." In San Francisco, the personnel director explains, "The archbishop has said that people can let him know if they are interested in a particular opening, which means that we, in fact, have a modified open listing."

In places that have open listing, some priests just tell the personnel director that they are open to a variety of assignments. The Seattle personnel director reports:

We had a good number of priests who said, "Yeah, I am interested in a move. I am not committed to any one particular parish. If you see a place where you think I might be good, I want you to know I would be willing to talk about it." That freed us up a lot.

Those dioceses that do not have open listing must face the issue of when in the process a priest should be consulted about a specific assignment. Everyone would agree that it is best to consult the priest as soon as possible about his general preferences and needs. But when it comes to asking him whether he would be interested in going to a particular parish, the key question is, do you consult him before or after conferring with the archbishop?

Some prefer to consult the man first. These personnel directors see no reason to propose to the archbishop an assignment that the priest is going to oppose. In addition, they feel that the archbishop should know what the views of the priest are before he makes up his mind. If this is the procedure followed, then the personnel director must stress to the priest that no decision has been made and that other priests are being consulted for the same position. On the other hand, some personnel directors prefer to get tentative approval from the archbishop before approaching a priest. They do not want to raise false expectations among the priests that may not be fulfilled.

One difficulty with this consultation is that sometimes the appointment falls through. The Atlanta personnel director reports:

It can raise expectations. But it is made clear, and all the priests know that it is only a feeler, only by way of trying to work up a cohesive slate that will work all the way around. They know from past observations that most of the time it doesn't work out the way they were first approached.

A few weeks ago, we approached a young priest about making him a pastor in a small church in the mountains. I called him; he was all gung ho. Then something else happened that did not involve him at all, and we ended up sending someone else. He may be disappointed, but I think it also flattered him and encouraged him because he realized that even in spite of his young age, he is needed and wanted. Obviously, there will be other offers.

Regional Vicars

Another problem of priests' assignments is how to relate the work of the personnel board to the desires of the regional vicars, especially if they are auxiliary bishops. The vicars want the best priests in their regions and would oppose the appointment of a man who would cause problems. As a result, there are fights among the vicars and fights between the vicars and the personnel board over assignments. When there are disagreements, the archbishop has to find a solution or choose sides.

In some archdioceses (Detroit, Miami, and Washington) the regional bishops sit with the personnel boards and participate in their deliberations. The personnel board chairman in Detroit reports that this works well:

The role of the regional bishops is crucial because they are the ones who are actually preparing for the meetings by looking at their region and all their priests, meeting personally, individually with those whose terms are due, getting a sense of what those priests are like, what their own desires are, how they want to be assigned. It is based on that information that we proceed in the assignment process.

The elected priest members of the board have equal say with the bishops at the meetings. They will add or subtract. But what the bishops do is very important. Plus they have the personal element too. They are the ones who are in touch with these priests, to communicate that they did get it or they didn't.

Problems are more frequent where the bishops do not sit in on the personnel board meeting. In one such archdiocese, a regional bishop questioned the appointment of a priest in his region. When the personnel board made the recommendation anyway, he asked, "What is the point in asking us?" The appointment was then put on hold so the auxiliary could review the matter. When the priest asked the personnel director why the decision was taking so long, he was told the vicar had some problems with the appointment. At this the auxiliary exploded and complained to the archbishop, who agreed that the priest should not have been told this since it would cause resentment against the vicar under whom the priest would have to work if the appointment did go through.

Confidentiality

This example raises the question of how much secrecy should surround personnel decisions. Personnel boards have been criticized by some as incapable of keeping secrets. Archbishop Gerety, when he was bishop of Portland, Maine, heard in casual conversation in a rectory the results of the personnel board meeting he had attended earlier that day.

Most boards brag that there are no leaks. One director noted, "You got some guys out there who are good at guessing. Many times they come up with the right answer, and everyone thinks that somebody must have leaked it."

Another director agreed that often the guesses are on target:

I go home, and one of the associates where I live tells me what we did that day. Often he is either on target or a step ahead. I tell the priests, "I listen closely to the rumors so that we know what to do in the personnel board, because you guys are spending all this energy thinking it up, we might as well take full advantage of it."

Everyone would agree that a priest's personal reputation should be protected in the process, but how much does he have a right to know about who opposed his appointment and why? Most boards keep their internal discussions confidential and tell the man that it is the decision of the board as a whole. But as will be explained later, boards have difficulties explaining why a priest did not get a position.

Many times a pastor wants it kept confidential that he is applying for a new parish. Problems can arise if a priest's parishioners find out that he has applied for another parish— "Why do you want to leave us?"—especially if he does not get the new post. "The man wants to move but doesn't want to put his parish up for open listing until he knows what he is getting," reports the chairman of the Omaha personnel board. "You are in a Catch-22. You know that, if you open list his place, you would get all kinds of movement, but you can't do it. We had two of those this year. If you could just get the movement started, you open up a lot of things for a lot of people."

Some priests, after getting a new post, prefer to blame the archbishop for their move. "He gets up in the pulpit and says, 'I really don't want to leave, but the archbishop says I have to,' " says the chairman of the Omaha personnel board, "when the buzzard really asked for a change. Then we get all kinds of letters. You can't say he is a liar."

In another archdiocese, the archbishop was rather philosophical about being blamed.

A pastor wrote twice and said, "I might be ready for a change." But when it came time to speak to the people, "Well, the bishop wanted me to move."

The bishop must be willing to take full responsibility for the unpopular decision. That just goes with being the top authority.

If we want to have the authority that enables us to make decisions, even unilateral decisions on occasion, we also have to be willing to accept that perception on the part of the people when you cannot explain all of the reasons that you do what you do. There are times when you have to exert it that way, so we can't play the game both ways.

Secrecy breaks down when the priests begin to be consulted about specific assignments. "Once you start feeling these guys out, then there is no more secrecy," explains the personnel director in Atlanta. "Everybody then knows probably who is going where. Of course, they usually get it wrong. Within twenty-four hours everybody knows what the board is proposing, but they never know why."

Presence of the Archbishop

Another debated issue is whether the archbishop should sit in on the meetings of the personnel board. Whether he does or not depends primarily on his own inclinations, but there are disagreements over which is the best policy. Some people argue that he should not participate so that he can act on appeals from priests who disagree with the board. If he participated in the decision, it would be more difficult for him to be an unbiased judge of an appeal.

Many board members, on the other hand, believe that they can act more efficiently with the bishop present. In Washington, the archbishop and his auxiliaries began meeting with the personnel board in December of 1985. The personnel director reports:

Before, we would meet and we would make recommendations, memos would go to the archbishop and the auxiliaries. Maybe three days or a week would go by, and then we would find out, "No, we are not happy with this suggestion."

By meeting with them, if there is anything that they know that would preclude a certain appointment, we hear it right away. We have done in three hours what would have normally taken us two or three weeks to finally clarify.

One archbishop tried not meeting with the board for a couple of months but found that unsatisfactory. "I felt the need to find out why they were presenting this man for that job or that parish," he says. "I would have to go ask the board and go over these suggestions. I felt that I would be better served if I were part of the discussion so that I would know exactly why they were proposing this person for that location."

The level of participation by archbishops at the meetings varies. Some take an active role and influence the outcome by their questions, comments, and proposals. Others are less active and let the board or the personnel director take the initiative. In describing Archbishop O'Meara's style, the personnel director in Indianapolis reports, "Normally he tries to sit back and listen and let us come to consensus. But if we are going in a direction he is not going to be able to live with, he jumps in. He doesn't feel it is fair to let us agonize over these things when he knows it will not go. He makes an effort to stay out of the discussions until we have come to a consensus."

Sometimes the bishop takes a leadership role and the board reacts to his suggestions. This is common in small dioceses. The chairman of the personnel board in Mobile notes:

Technically, the board handles all the spade work and comes up with a name or two. That is the theory. But in practice very often the initial recommendation of somebody for a particular parish may come from the top [the archbishop]. It is brought to the board and the indication is that this is what the top wants. Unless some real powerful objections can be raised, that ends up being what it is.

It is not like he comes to the well to take water out; he knows what he wants before he gets there. We are a very small archdiocese, and very often he will know some of the people better than the board.

If the archbishop meets with the committee, he can hear their deliberations and know the reasons behind their recommendations. He can respond immediately with questions and comments. "We meet with each other and we change each other's minds," says Archbishop Lipscomb of Mobile, explaining the process. Sometimes, as in Atlanta, the archbishop will attend part of the meeting. "They meet for about two hours," explained Archbishop Donnellan, "and they call me in, and we go over what they have been meeting about."

Attending personnel board meetings is difficult but important work according to Archbishop Hunthausen of Seattle:

It's time consuming. It is very, very frustrating, and it's hard work. I don't find it easy to deal with the lives of other people. We are so restricted in what we are able to do. You have so many priests and so many appointments and so many needs. And to try to put the right person in the right place, it's a struggle. It's never easy, and it's never absolutely ideal.

Is it important that I go to that? Yes, I think it is. The only other way is to let them struggle and to come back to me with a package, and then I say yes or no to it. I would be hard pressed to say no to anything that came back unless it was a glaring something or other there. If that were so, I would feel the responsibility of pointing out quite at length to the personnel board that had worked so hard why I would want it to be different. So I feel the need to be part of it.

Some archbishops do not attend the personnel meetings because they do not like that kind of work. Others fear that their presence might be overpowering. "I just think they act better without me," says one archbishop. "I am an inhibiting presence here, not because of me [laughter], but because my predecessors dealt with a strong hand here. If I sat in on such a meeting I just know that they would feel that I was there to tell them what I expected them to endorse. That is the last thing in the world I want."

When an archbishop is present, some board members say they are uncertain whether the archbishop is sometimes playing the devil's advocate or whether he is putting forward his true beliefs. It takes time for board members to figure out the archbishop's style and just how hard they can push him. One St. Louis member admitted, "At first I thought I would be hesitant. Now if he says, 'What about Fr. Jones going here?' I wouldn't hesitate to say, 'You can't be serious. He has had a problem with this, this, and this.' I never thought I would do that with the archbishop, but he never holds that against you." Another member agreed, "He not only allows it, he welcomes it. He enjoys being challenged. We had one member who was extremely outspoken."

In some archdioceses where the archbishop does not attend the personnel board meetings, he meets with the personnel director before the board meeting so that the director can bounce ideas off him before the meeting. Archbishop Kelly of Louisville says, the personnel director

talks to me before they make their final recommendation. He finds out what I think, but it is just another opinion. I want them to make their judgment. That is very important to me. I don't think I have ever overridden them on anything.

But sometimes when they were surfacing possibilities, I would say "No, not that one and not that one and not that one. He is having trouble." Or "He is too good for that," or something like that. So they take those into account.

Similarly, the Atlanta director noted, "The chairman has already spoken to the archbishop before the meeting. That is where he would rule out the totally impossible or hopeless." Or as the Newark personnel director put it, the archbishop "will let you know even before you come to a meeting that he has some problems. The vicar general will say, 'He is having some problems with X as the first choice there.' So we back off or we decide to build a case." Rarely is a board inclined to make a recommendation that it feels the bishop will reject.

Assignment of Associates

In the assignment of priests, it is necessary to distinguish between the assignment of associates and pastors. A newly ordained priest hardly ever is appointed a pastor. He is usually assigned to a parish as an associate or assistant pastor where he works with a pastor. Typically, the associate assignments are all made at the same time in the spring. In the past, having two or three associates in a parish was not uncommon, but today this is becoming rare. Depending on the number of priests and parishes in a diocese, a priest could remain an associate for one and a half (Santa Fe) to twenty-five years (Boston).

Everyone involved in the process says that special care is taken in the first assignment of a priest to get him a parish where he will have a good working relationship with his pastor. Parishes with serious conflicts among the parishioners or staff will not get a newly ordained priest. "For newly ordained priests," explains the St. Paul personnel director, "we try to find the best situations we can." "A good assignment," explains another personnel director, "is one where there is a good community (or at least a potential for it), a collaborative staff, and a pastor who is not an ogre."

Sometimes this involves moving the current associate to a less desirable parish to make room for the newly ordained priest. "We want the good parishes for new priests," explains the director of priests' personnel in San Francisco, "so after a new priest has been there a few years, we have to move him out to make room for another new priest." This reverse seniority occurs because the archbishops and personnel people believe that a new priest should have a good experience of his priesthood during his first years of ministry. "We see this as an extension of their training," explains one personnel director.

Part of this training also involves working in a variety of situations. In some dioceses this could include working in the inner city, suburbs, and rural areas. "We like to give them a variety of experience," explains the San Francisco personnel director, "so the associates move about every three to five years."

In general, the fewer the number of associates, the greater their voice in determining their assignments. In some archdioceses, an associate has a virtual veto over his placement in a parish. Nor will an associate be sent to a pastor who does not want him. Some associates would find working for certain pastors intolerable, while some pastors would rather hire a lay associate than get a priest who does not fit in. "We try not to put people together who we think would have a conflict," explains the chairman of the personnel board in Miami.

In the past, associates were simply assigned. But many people feel that bad relations between pastors and associates led many associates to leave the priesthood during the 1960s and 1970s. In addition, with so few associates today and so many parishes with openings, it is usually not difficult finding one that wants him and that he likes. But one personnel director complained, "We have people going to places where they are not needed, where their skills are not being used. Before they had nothing to say, now they have too much to say."

The solution to that problem in some dioceses is to offer to associates only the parishes that really need help. For example, in Chicago the placement office must approve the open listing of a parish for an associate. "Every parish can't be on the open list," explains the executive secretary of the personnel board. "Otherwise the forty most popular parishes would just pick up another priest. If what the pastor is really saying is 'I need a youth minister, therefore I want an associate pastor,' we will suggest he hire a youth minister."

One problem with this approach is that the least attractive parishes tend to be those without money to hire lay ministers. Many inner-city pastors want an associate because he is cheaper than a lay minister. The Hispanic caucus in Chicago complained, for example, that the personnel board was not doing enough to attract men to the Hispanic parishes. In addition, a parish with a "bad" pastor is not going to attract a "good" associate, thus leaving the parishioners with little recourse except transferring parishes.

Assigning associates requires that the personnel director act as a matchmaker first by advertising openings and then by attempting to fit pastors and associates together. This is not always easy. In Newark the personnel director explained,

[If you wanted to be an associate pastor here] I would say to you, "These are twelve places that are open. Here is the data sheet on each one of them. Feel free to go visit and come back to me and tell me what you think. I will check it out to see if they are interested, and if we can strike up the marriage between the two of you, we will move on the recommendation. If there is any problem, we will just have to keep going back to the drawing board until you and they click."

For some priests this is a threatening process. "Some pastors are just not good at attracting personnel," reports the executive secretary of the Chicago personnel board. "Many pastors do not possess the interviewing skills you need for this new system. It is going to be very frightening and create a lot of worry and concern. A lot of associates are like that too."

In the absence of open listing, for the appointment of an associate in San Francisco, the committee would first check with the archbishop. If he approves, they ask the pastor to see if he would accept the associate. "Then we check with the associate to see if it is OK with him. If either says no, the process stops there, and we have to rework it. One such change can have a domino effect on the other assignments."

Appointment of Pastors

Seniority

The goal of practically every diocesan priest is to be the pastor of his own parish. Once again, bishops and personnel directors attempt to match the desires of the priests with the needs of the diocese. In the past, seniority was very important, as would be expected in an organization with low pay where it is difficult to establish objective merit criteria.[28] Even today, all other things being equal, consideration is given to seniority and to pastors whose terms are up or who want to move.

Archbishop Sheehan of Omaha explains, "With regard to appointments of first pastorates, we pretty much go down the list. The priests know who is the next one eligible for a pastorate. If we jump anybody, that creates a lot of discussion around the diocese. So we follow the seniority list pretty well for first assignments."

Sometimes a younger priest will get the position because no one else wants it. Thus, in Chicago, priests have to wait twenty years to become a pastor in a suburban parish, but one can become an inner-city pastor in only ten years. Being either black or Hispanic or knowing the language of the parishioners can also push one ahead of one's seniors.

But there is sympathy for the man who has been an associate for a long time. One personnel chairman spoke of a classmate:

> He has lived under other people's direction, whim, fantasy, rule, under their table, under their secretaries, under their cooks, for twenty-three years of priesthood. Now we have to take that into consideration when we are appointing. He might not have snap in the liturgy, but he has certain experience, and he has also personal need to get his own, to be able to be his own boss at some point.

When seniority is not followed, it can cause hurt feelings. "Some priests are hurting very much because they are not pastors yet," acknowledged a personnel board chairman. "And yet we have some younger guys, maybe seven years younger, who are loud and pushing, and you tend to give the noisy wheel the oil. And these other priests are demoralized and feel, 'well, gee, I have had some tough assignments, and I haven't complained, and here comes this Johnny-come-lately, and he is going to be given a parish. Why?' " Other personnel directors disagree and stress the needs of the parish over seniority. Survey data shows priests agree that promotion to a pastorate should be based on ability rather than seniority,[29] but ability is difficult to measure.

How long he has to wait for a parish varies from diocese to diocese. In San Francisco, Chicago, and Boston a priest can look forward to being an associate for twenty or more years before becoming a pastor. In Washington, DC, it would be fifteen years; in Baltimore, Miami, Omaha, and Milwaukee, around twelve years. In Denver, Kansas City, and Louisville, it would be eight or nine years. But in Anchorage, Portland, Santa Fe, and Seattle, it would be less than five years. As the number of priests declines, priests will become pastors sooner.

Limited Terms

Most archdioceses, following the national norm, have adopted a six-year term for pastors.[30] The terms are often renewable, but after twelve years the pastor must usually move to another parish unless he is close to retirement. "It developed because pastors were assigned to a parish, and then they were difficult to remove if things weren't going well," explains the Boston secretary for ministerial personnel.

Some archdioceses (like Denver and Kansas City) have shorter terms for rural parishes, especially for young priests. "Many of the rural pastors were younger priests going out on their first pastorate," explains a member of the personnel board in Kansas City. "The idea that they were going to be in this little rural parish for ten years was a heavy thing for a lot of them." The Denver vicar for clergy agrees: "Our country parishes are very isolated. It is fine for three years."

The issue of terms for pastors is hotly debated. Under the old code of canon law, pastors were irremovable without cause although some dioceses had an indult (exception) from Rome to have set terms for pastors. Under the new code, national conferences can permit terms of office for pastors.

Traditionally, it has been argued that leaving a pastor in a parish indefinitely enables him to develop close ties with his people. He knows his parishioners intimately, and they grow to trust and depend on him. He might baptize a person as an infant, give him first communion, and then marry him as an adult. "The pastor is akin to a father of a family," explains one priests' personnel director. "You build a family spirit, a community spirit, and then you do violence to that by taking the head away. Others would say, 'Well, we all get stale and stagnant if we stay in something too long, therefore it is good to move.' I suspect those arguments will continue to go on for a while."

"A lot of guys don't like terms," explains the Seattle personnel director. "They say, 'If it is going well, why ruin it?' The other side of it is, 'If you have done such a good job here, the diocese may need you somewhere else.' "

Critics of the old system argue that it takes two years for a priest to get to know his people. The next six years he is very creative. After that he gets in a rut. "There is no stimulation, and that applies to every program in the parish," says one personnel director. "Some priests cannot handle certain programs in the parish, so they are not done. The parish has a right to them. If you get a turnover, certain other programs might fall by the wayside, but you also get these other programs that have been denied."

One bishop reports, some priests "come forward and say, 'I would like a change.' They go to a new parish, and they get a second spring, a new life, new problems to deal with, not the same old nagging ones that have bothered them for ten years at the other parish." Those who support a set term argue that the parishioners who do not like a pastor will at least know that he will not be there forever. Personnel directors tend to favor tenure. "It gives us predictability," explains one director. In addition, it allows changes without the changes being considered negative judgments on the pastor.

On the other hand, a bishop explains, "People don't like to see their priest moved. They get at home with the priest, build up confidence, and they get comfortable. There is a very personal relationship that develops between a priest and his people. If he is going to be wrenched up every eight or ten years, people are not going to form that tight relationship. However, in the mobile society that we live in, people will move from one parish to another."

Some of the consequences of limiting terms for pastors are only just beginning to become apparent. In St. Louis, the chairman of the building commission notes that pastors with limited terms tend to postpone construction or major maintenance programs (like a new roof on the church). They prefer to leave the problems for their successors. For example, in St. Louis a number of churches were built with the idea that they would become gyms when a real church was built later. These buildings are now in need of renovations, reports the director of the building commission.

We have parishes that write in to be renovated. I suggest to the archbishop, the parish can handle the debt, I think they should build a church and then make this present place a gym as was originally intended.

He will suggest that to the pastor. We have cases where the pastor pleaded no. And [the archbishop] gave in to him. The pastor in time is transferred, a new man comes in, and he is down here saying, "Why did they let him do this? Why didn't they make him build? This is crazy." The guy is griping and complaining.

We are running into that where men are figuring they are not going to be here too long. You are not popular if you start asking [parishioners] for money, so why sweat it? Pretty up the place, don't bother the people. Let the next guy worry about it.

Limited terms for pastors also have consequences on parish staffs. With a change in pastors, the staff can provide continuity in parish services. But a new pastor may find on his arrival that the staff does not fit his needs or goals for the parish. If the staff cannot adapt to his style and goals, he may have to replace them with other personnel. And then his successor may not like the staff he assembled, and the process is repeated. If the staff have contracts or due process procedures, replacing them may be difficult. In any case, firing members of the parish staff is almost always traumatic for the parish community.

Rev. John Kinsella, an expert on priests' personnel issues, opposes set terms of office for pastors.

I don't think the rhythm of the needs of parish communities are always in sync with the cycle. I would want more flexibility, if I was personnel director or bishop, to make judgments based, not on calendar, but on needs.

In some parish communities, there is a strong need for stability and longevity. In other parish communities, you need someone to come in and do a short job and get out. Or you may need someone to come in and spend a long period of time.

Also the abilities of priests to perform are so different. We have long distance runners, and we have some short distance runners. Some guys can go in and do a bang-up job in two or three years, and then they are bored to tears for the next three years.

Other guys start real slow. Nobody likes them for the first couple of years, they gain credibility very slowly and strongly. The longer they are there, the better they get.

That difference of personality and work patterns and the needs of communities ought to be the factors that you make judgments about and not the administrative convenience of putting people on a cycle.

I think it has been used by bishops—like retirement was used—as a way of getting rid of problems rather than making the more responsible decision that someone should be out of an assignment.

Whatever the merits of the debate, a term of office for pastors clearly increases the power of a bishop over his priests and his parishes. It increases the number of personnel decisions that have to be made. It also enables the bishop to move an incompetent pastor who under a nontenured system could be in a parish for decades. A system that moves everyone makes it possible to move the problem pastors. Parishes share the good as well as the bad pastors.

Most archbishops favor terms for pastors, but few are willing to push the idea on their pastors without the support of the priests' council. Support for limited terms has usually come from younger priests who see it as a way of quickening their advancement. "The fact that a man stayed forever in a parish discouraged the younger priests," explained Archbishop Donnellan of Atlanta. Personnel directors favor it because it provides time frames for planning. They can look ahead and know when vacancies are coming up.

The Needs of the Parish

Finding the right man for the right parish is the goal of the personnel board and the bishop. Not all parishes are the same. They can be large or small, urban, suburban, or rural. The ethnic, social, and economic characteristics of the parishioners vary. For example, some would require the knowledge of Spanish or another language. Some have liberal and active congregations; others are more conservative. Some parishes have programs with numerous people involved; others do not. Some have schools or large lay and religious staffs; others do not. Some have financial problems. Some have young families; others might have nursing homes or retirement communities in the parish.

The Louisville priests' personnel director explains how the social backgrounds of the parishioners can affect the kind of pastor they would want.

> If they are middle-management-type folks who want a strong say in what is going on in that place, he is going to have to have some skills in dealing with the parish council. Or if lower-income, blue-collar workers, they might be content with him leading the show. Or sometimes the upper-middle-class parishes are more content with a pastor who will make the decisions and lead the way, because they are used to telling other people what to do and being told what to do.

A lot can also depend on the style of the recent pastor. A radical change in pastors could be upsetting to a parish that had grown to expect a certain style. The secretary for ministerial personnel in Boston describes different types of parishes in the archdiocese:

> In some parishes the laity are very much involved in the activities of the parish. Where the pastor has been a strong leader, there could have been minimal lay involvement or a lot of lay involvement.
>
> [In] other parishes, the pastor has been not only collaborative with the laity but has taken on a level of collaboration where his role is not that dominant or strong. Parishes where there have been problems need a priest to come in who has a capacity to heal. Some parishes call for a very warm type of priest. Other parishes don't call for that. You can be reserved, more Puritan in your approach.

The personnel director often gathers data for a file on the parish under consideration. Financial data can be gotten from the finance office. Demographic and sacramental statistics are also usually available. In addition, a written report on the parish can be prepared by the parish council, the retiring pastor, and/or the regional vicar.

For example, in Cincinnati, the parish council is given four questions. According to the priests' personnel director, "they are asked to name the three most important things they think happened in their parish; the three things they are happiest about; the three things they consider the greatest needs; and a couple of qualities they are looking for in their pastor. They discuss [this,] summarize it, and write up a response. It helps them to assess themselves as a parish." These can be examined both by the personnel board and by the priests who are thinking about applying for the position.

In some archdioceses (Boston, Chicago, Cincinnati, Hartford, Louisville, Milwaukee, Washington) the parish will be visited so that the parish council, staff, and parishioners can be interviewed by the personnel director or someone from the board to find out what kind of pastor is desired and needed. In Hartford, this is done by the archbishop himself. Archbishop Whealon reports:

I and the vicar for priests talk to representative laity of the parish with no priests present. We go over the statistics with them and ask them if the statistics are reliable. We go over the condition of the church and the parish with them and talk about the needs of the future and what they would like to see in the priest appointed there. That interview with the laity is always most interesting and educational.

In large archdioceses, the deans or regional vicars might be involved in these visitations.

Some personnel directors feel that these parish visits are a waste of time. "It sounds good, but I have done six of them, and they all sound the same," reports the personnel director in Washington. But he admits, "It does also bring to light things that we had no idea about, maybe divisions in the parish that the previous pastor had been able to keep away from us but suddenly will crop up at a public meeting like that."

One thing that the personnel directors try to avoid is turning the visit into an evaluation of the current pastor. Parishioners are also discouraged from proposing specific names for their new pastor. But that can be difficult in a small archdiocese like Anchorage where there are only twenty-two parishes. "It is hard for a parish to sit down and say what kind of person they need without naming priests," reports the Anchorage vicar general.

When people are asked what kind of pastor they would like, the results are not always helpful. "The job description was always the same," explains the Denver vicar for clergy. " 'He has to be a man of prayer, a good administrator, a good liturgist, a good communicator, a good preacher, has to work with the parish council, he cannot be threatened by us, has to love people, has to mingle with the people.' Jesus Christ couldn't fulfill the job description, but it was always the same. So we felt it was a waste of time." In Chicago one parishioner said the parish needed a cross between Lee Iaococca and St. Francis of Assisi.

In Seattle, the parish is asked about its needs and goals. "We didn't want a pastor profile because it ends up looking like Christ with an MBA," explains the Seattle personnel director. "We have a few of those, but not very many." But even here "it is hard to keep the people's expectations down. Once you let them talk about their needs, they want to give you names of people who they know would be excellent. And you go back to the board, and you already have him stuck in a big parish."

Some who have visited parishes still think it is worthwhile. "When I first took this job," says the personnel director in Portland, "I was not convinced that people really cared, as long as somebody came and there was Mass. This is not true. People are passionate about their clergy. Passionate about their parish. There is a face on these statistics. When you come back, the personnel board and the bishop need to know that."

In a few cases "high expectations led to disappointment when the man arrived," explains the executive secretary of the personnel board in Chicago. "But for the most part, people feel that they are heard and are part of the process. They can laugh at themselves at the end of the meeting and say, 'God, are we unrealistic.' " On the other hand, he also found parishioners who believe the consultation is a sham. "It is real hard for people to believe that we don't already have the guy picked out. 'He is probably packing while the meeting is going on,' people say to us. 'We know you already know who it is.' "

The priests' personnel director in Louisville has found visiting the parishes useful. He and a member of the board interview the pastor, the staff, and the parish council. He explains, "We have a set agenda: the strengths and weaknesses of the parish, goals, what leadership qualities would be needed in a pastor, where they are liturgically, how they function as a staff if it is a big place. Is it a shared responsibility model or is it a team model or is it 'do what the pastor tells you'?"

In Portland the personnel director turns the tables on the parish and asks them, "Why would a priest want to come here?" "The tendency today is for the parish council to express themselves very forcefully about the priest they want," says the Cincinnati priests' personnel director. "I say, 'That is a two-sided coin.' They don't think of that too much. You can get a climate where priests just don't want to go. They consider it an unhealthy, adversarial climate. Who wants to go into that?"

The personnel directors who are most pleased with visiting the parishes have multiple goals. They are attempting to get a feel for the attitudes of the parishioners as well as gather factual information about the parish. Asking the parishioners about what are the good things happening in the parish, what are the improvements they would like to see, and what type of pastor they want—these are not simply questions of fact but get at the emotional spirit of the community.

Some personnel directors also see this as an opportunity to educate the parish. "They are not just an isolated group of folks but part of a larger church that also has needs," says the priests' personnel director in Portland. "We may not have the right person; we may not be able to find a pastor. The common perception is that there is this huge pool and that all we have to do when one is gone is to arrange to have the next guy who will be perfect."

In Seattle the director spoke of "walking the line between our tradition, which puts all the weight on the bishop assigning and sending and nothing on the folk, and the Protestant tradition of the folk having the power. We are trying to find that line that keeps the best of both." In fact, there is little support among priests for the Protestant model. Only 23 percent of the priests believe that parishes should be able to "choose their own priest from among the available ordained priests."[31] A larger percentage (40 percent) of the priests thought that parishes should be allowed to "help choose the priests who come to serve them." The laity liked the idea, with 55 percent in favor and 22 percent opposed.[32]

Desires of the Priests

In the past, after being an associate for a number of years, a priest would be made a pastor of a small parish. Then, as he proved himself, he would gradually move up to larger parishes, until he finally attained the ideal—a large city parish with a school, three assistants, and convent. "This was retirement," jokes one bishop, "because the first assistant would run the whole place, and the pastor would come down like the deity and bow and smile at the people at Christmas."

Today that ideal is desired by few priests. A pastorate is no longer a benefice; it is a heavy responsibility. The larger the parish, the more difficult it is to administer. Large parishes have large staffs that have to be supervised and coordinated. Many people and organizations compete for the pastor's time and attention. Smaller parishes are now preferred to larger ones.

Every personnel director interviewed indicated that many priests also have second thoughts about taking a parish with a school. "There are a lot of guys who don't want a parish with a school," reports a board chairman. "What I keep hearing is 'I don't want a parish with a school,' " says the Louisville priests' personnel director. " 'I had a parish with a big school. I don't want another one. I have paid my dues.' Not everyone. There are still people who want it. But many are afraid of places that are big, complex, that require a lot of coordination. Some feel that they don't have the skills to do that, and most of us don't." Father Greeley found that 20 percent of the priests believed that the elimination of the Catholic school system would be a helpful change.[33]

Schools increase the administrative burden on a pastor who has to deal with a school board, principal, teachers, and parents. Schools also require him to raise money to cover the deficit of the school. One director explains, "An urban parish with financial limitations trying to support a school that has had a history of internal conflict—that type of parish would be difficult to fill."

One personnel director describes the ideal parish as "500 to 700 families, lots of organizations, a parish council that knows what it is doing and isn't going to pick at me too much, and money in the bank." Another personnel director jokingly says, "The ideal assignment is no debt, no school, no associate, no nuns, and no work." On the other hand, the Cincinnati priests' personnel director argues that there is no ideal parish today. "It depends on the individual priest," he says. "What he perceives to be the ideal parish, [what is] his energy level, his theology of church, etc."

One problem with open listing is that sometimes no one will apply for a parish or those who do apply are not considered fit by the personnel board. In these cases, the personnel director will have to talk someone into considering the parish. "We may call in a couple of guys who have skills for the kind of parish that is open," says the Portland personnel director. "When you call them, they usually say no. The priest may feel that I am just trying to get my slate filled." The personnel director invites them to his office to talk it over and explain why they should not be the one. Eventually, he may tell them, "Well, you had better get your arguments lined up, because I am going to recommend you to the board. Do you want to come in and put your case forward?" But if they continue to be opposed, they will not be appointed.

Even under an open listing system, personnel boards make clear that they will not limit themselves to the people who apply. "About 13 percent of the time we will have to go out and invite someone to take a particular parish," explains the personnel director in Newark. "No one asked, or those who asked are just not even coming close."

Recruiting is often necessary for inner-city black and Hispanic parishes. Even more difficult are parishes whose neighborhoods are in transition. "In Washington, we are facing changing parishes" reports the personnel director.

A lot of preppies are moving back into the inner city and chasing good black folk further out. They have to move beyond the beltway. Suddenly a suburban parish moves from being totally white to totally black, or there is a mixture there. You have to have a man who has had enough experience to balance those two groups of people, keep them both happy.

Once it becomes stable, either as a totally integrated parish or all black or all white, you can turn it over to another pastor who doesn't want the headaches of the transition.

Another director mentioned the difficulty of finding priests to serve in parishes that also serve large hospitals.

Out of the way, small parishes can also be hard to fill. "A majority of our parishes are out in the boondocks," explains the personnel director in Santa Fe. "We have a parish in the country now that is empty for eight months. It is too small (200 families) for a young, energetic priest, and it is too far out in the country for an older priest who needs hospital and medical help."

Sometimes geography plays a role also. Priests, like anyone, like to be near their family and friends. In the Mobile archdiocese, the priests in Mobile do not want to go to Montgomery, and the priests in Montgomery do not want to go to Mobile.

Recommendation

After examining the parish and the available priests, the personnel board will make its recommendation to the archbishop. Most boards operate by consensus and vote only as a last resort. A few, usually ones that have a large number of appointments to process (like Chicago, New York), vote in various ways. In New York, for example, if there are twelve candidates, the board members cast weighted votes: one for their preferred candidate and twelve for their least preferred candidate. The man with the least votes is at the top of the list.

The boards want to match up the right priest with the right parish. "You would like to see every parish alive, in tune with Vatican II, where the priest is happy and content to be there and the people are happy to have him," says the Cincinnati priests' personnel director. "That is the ideal and what you are trying to work toward. But in the imperfect world we live in, we don't have that always."

The personnel director in Louisville attempts never to send a parish backward:

Obviously you don't always have the people to send it as forward as you would like. But you don't take a parish that has all kinds of lay ministries going and bring in someone who wants to do it all himself. You can't jerk them around like that. We will avoid that at all costs, even if it means bringing in someone who has not been pastor before.

The chairman of the personnel board in Omaha agreed. "We made a mistake a few years ago by going from a radical on one side to an ultraconservative on the other," he reports. "The poor people just got racked. This side lost and this side won and the 80 percent in the middle didn't know where they were."

Gradualism rather than revolution in leadership is preferred.

"You try to succeed a fellow with someone who can bring in his own innovative ideas and build on what is there," explains the chairman of the Omaha personnel board. "We have had experience where you have a team that works well, and you have a pastor come in who doesn't want any team. Then you come to a screeching halt. You try to avoid that. Try to avoid a situation where you are making a radical change unless you have a person who is prudent enough and wise enough to bring that along gradually."

The choice when there are many applicants is not always easy. One director explains:

A good percentage [of the candidates] get discounted right away because you hear what the parish council is asking for and you see what they are moving toward. Right away, as the guy gets interviewed, he doesn't seem to grasp that. It doesn't take much to have certain people rise to the fore.

When it gets down to how you [rank the candidates] one, two, three, it begins to get like the Olympic skating championships. The one who has shown the least faults rises. You can objectify all you want, but at the end there is a gut feeling. Something feels good about this that goes along with all the data.

Personnel people will say you should have objective things to look at, but we don't evaluate our priests every year to see how they are doing in the parish. If you call their friends in the parish to find out how they are doing, most of the time you get, "Oh, terrific guy."

Sometimes a man is not chosen because replacing him in his old parish would be difficult. A board might also think that a man deserved a particular parish because of his past assignments. The chairman of the personnel board in Mobile describes how these factors influenced the decision of his board on an assignment:

One of the considerations would be, what is this fellow doing right now? Will it be easy to replace him where he is?

In the last set of changes, one priest who wanted the parish was the one who had seniority. But he is in a fine new parish which he has built up, and the question there right now is whether they ought to get a school or not. There were things that were going on there that would be set back until the new man got adjusted. And the board felt that there was nobody to replace him there.

The other man being considered had had a few tough assignments. The board felt that this would be a break for him, something where he wouldn't have to struggle quite as much as he had had to struggle for the previous twenty years. He wouldn't have any financial worries, he could concentrate on his work. His tenure was up over a year already. He ended up getting it, and I feel he deserved it.

A lot of intangibles make us come to our conclusions, too. I am not saying that this is the best process in the world or that it is as equitable as it could be. But most people accept it, and we have fairly well matched the needs of the parishes with these people.

If a parish has a school, that could affect the decision. "Sometimes the difference between a fellow getting a place and not getting a place was the feeling that he wouldn't want to keep the school going," explains a board chairman.

The existence of a parish staff can also make a difference. "If a parish is functioning well with a team ministry," explains the chairman of the Omaha personnel board, "we try to be sure that we have a person who can continue that, work with the team, pastoral assistant. If the parish is not doing anything, we try to turn that around with some leadership."

The choice of the new pastor can depend on what the board thinks is possible in the parish. The Cincinnati priests' personnel director explains:

Is it a parish that is still pre-Vatican II? Do you want it to become a Vatican II parish, or are you willing to let it be what it is because you don't have a whole lot of hope that the community is going to move from where they are?

If you think it should become a Vatican II church, you wouldn't want to put someone in there who would just run roughshod over the people making it a Vatican II church. You might send someone in who will move it forward but not try to convert it overnight. That would be an example of matching.

The personnel director in Louisville describes a mismatch in an upper-middle-income parish with 1,200 families and a staff of four or five people, principal, director of religious education, youth minister, music director—all full-time, paid people—and a parish council that is active and committees going and a large physical plant that needs attention. The pastor is a good old boy who doesn't know a damn thing about human resource management and preaches on a level that is very simple and not sophisticated, not at the education level of those people.

That is a mismatch; it won't work. It will get him in trouble. He will be unhappy, and they will be unhappy. He might do fine at a lower- or middle-income blue-collar parish. They might love him.

In most archdioceses, the archbishop is given only one name for the parish. In some of the larger archdioceses (Baltimore, Boston, Chicago, Newark, New York, San Francisco, Washington), he is given more names, usually three. If more than one priest is recommended, the board will rank them by their preference. One New York director favored their system of submitting three names so the archbishop would be able to *choose* a priest and not have to reject one of his priests.

In many dioceses, however, the boards are finding it more and more difficult to come up with three candidates they can realistically recommend for a position. There are just not enough priests available.

In many archdioceses the personnel board tries to make most of the appointments in the spring of the year. Newly ordained priests begin their ministry in the spring. In addition, the school year and fiscal year end in spring. Constructing a slate once a year was the tradition because of the domino effect of every appointment. If pastor X dies, and he is replaced by an associate from a large parish, then the associate must be replaced, and so on until you run out of people. Or if pastor X is replaced by pastor Y, then a pastor must be found for Y's parish.

Constructing a slate is becoming more difficult. A participant in New York complained of complications when planning a slate:

> You may get a terrific pastoral plan for an area: A is going to B, B is moving. . . . Then this guy dies. All of a sudden all that work and planning goes out. The angel of death can change the plan. One death affects what you had ready for five or six places. Very frequently you are like an air traffic controller: Can you get them to come down in different places at once?

The slate approach also makes it difficult to open list all appointments. Sometimes a priest will consider moving if the board makes him an offer he likes, but he does not want his parish open listed until he has his new assignment. If he does get a new parish, it is often impossible to open list his old parish if it is filled on the same slate.

Some archdioceses have moved away from the slate approach to a rolling system where each vacancy is treated separately as it occurs. First, the parishes are filled that have become vacant because of retirements, deaths, or the expiration of the pastor's term. Then, if pastors or associates have been moved to fill any of those vacancies, their parishes are open listed and filled in the next round.

The difficulty with this approach is that it can disrupt the plans of the parish from which the man is pulled in the middle of the year. Parish councils and staffs want the announcements as early as possible. As a result, boards and bishops like to announce most appointments in the spring, to the extent that is compatible with open listing.

Archbishop Appoints

However it is done, if the archbishop does not meet with the board, he will be given the board's recommendation and usually some background information on their decision. He will be informed of who applied for the position, what the board recommends, and what the vicars recommend and why.

Archbishop Quinn of San Francisco explains how he works with his personnel board:

The personnel board has the authority to interview the priests, to speak to them, and to discuss possible assignments. But no assignment is ever made until I am informed and approve of it. And I don't always approve of what the personnel board proposes.

Sometimes they give me a list of three names for a parish. I send it back and say, "I don't think any of these are acceptable, and I want you to reconsider it." That doesn't happen every time, but it does happen, because I know the priests, and I know the parishes, too. I feel that it is ultimately my responsibility and a very important one.

Everyone agrees that the archbishop ultimately makes the appointments. But in most archdioceses, he accepts 95 to 99 percent of the board's recommendations. Part of the reason for this high percentage is that archbishops often involve themselves in the appointment process before the board makes its final recommendation. In addition, boards are usually reluctant to recommend someone they know the archbishop would not accept. But sometimes he does not accept the recommendation because of confidential information that he cannot share with the board.

The secretary for ministerial personnel explains how the system works in Boston:

[Cardinal Law] usually accepts the list as the board presents it. It happens in one out of four parishes you would see the list change around a bit or a person taken off or added.

If he doesn't accept the list as the board presents it, it could be for certain reasons. One could be that he thinks someone on the list has seniority and therefore probably should be considered before others. He might think that the person on the list is really needed in his current position and that it would create much more difficulty for the diocese to take him out of that position. Or he would know some personal reasons why he should not be in this parish or not be a pastor, information that would not be known to the personnel board.

And most archbishops agree with Archbishop Sheehan of Omaha that "the toughest thing about being a bishop is making the appointments."

Saying No to the Bishop

Canonically, a priest promises obedience to his bishop and must go where his bishop sends him. But in fact, if a priest says no, the bishop will usually accept that. "It could be his health, could be family, could be personal, could be spiritual, any number of reasons why the guy might not want to," explains a personnel director. "He might have been to Guest House [a rehabilitation program for alcoholic priests] and found sobriety in his current parish."

But even when the reason is not substantial, the archbishop will usually respect it. "We found that if you move a pastor to a place that he has no desire to go, you have nothing but trouble," reports the director of personnel in Portland. "The people soon come to realize that this man does not want to be here. We have a problem. He is not effective."

In the open listing process, the archbishop is offering the position to someone who sought it and, as a result, he does not have to worry about the person declining the post. If the archdiocese does not have open listing or if the priest did not apply for a parish, often the personnel director will sound him out before he is approached by the archbishop. "You don't want the bishop to nominate him and have him go through the embarrassment of saying no to his bishop," explains a director.

But most priests will not say no to their bishop. Archbishop Lipscomb recalls when he had to ask a member of the Mobile personnel board to leave a position he wanted for another:

I needed this priest in this particular spot. He was the logical one except he had already been given an assignment to some place else.

I prayed over it. I said, "I am just going to ask him to do this. If he says no, then it is no."

[At the meeting] we were going over these things and this slot wasn't exactly fitting. I said, "I have prayed over this, and we all know you are the best person."

"Bishop," he said, "I know the reason I am not in this slot is that you all have already given me the other parish. But I know that I ought to be there. . . . If that is what you think, I'll do it." So that's what we did.

In one small archdiocese, the archbishop and the board put together a slate, but one man balked at first. Although he had been talked to by the personnel director, the archbishop says,

He thought the only one being considered was his assistant and not himself. He was running a good parish; people liked him. He was good on the participation, had the Renew program, all of the qualities I needed desperately in another parish that had been so terribly restricted that the place was ready to burst.

He was really distraught. I went to see him myself and explained to him why. He put it very well: "It is my problem, not your problem. I have to learn to cope with this myself." Six months after he moved, he was very happy where he was. I moved him to the same type of parish, same type of people. Because they were so pleased with having an open priest, they rallied around like nobody's business, and he did some nice adjustments there.

But even if the priest can say no, the archbishop cannot always give a priest what he wants because sometimes it is simply not available. Archbishop Salatka relates:

I don't have all that great a choice for what the priests can do. They would like to do something different than what I have available, some of them. It is really a struggle. You try to take into consideration their preferences, their abilities as the personnel commission sees them, and also our needs. And invariably I have to wind up saying, "Well, Father, I know what you want, but this is what I have." That's a hard thing to do, probably the hardest decision I have to make in the course of the year.

In Philadelphia, where another style prevails, saying no to the archbishop is not an option. Cardinal Krol tells his priests,

We can be guided by your preference, but the dominating factor is the need of the people, not your pleasure. You were not ordained to be served, but to serve. And you have to serve the whole diocese.

But most archbishops have concluded that the more consideration given to the priest's preferences, the more productive he will be as a minister. Friendly persuasion by the personnel director and the archbishop, they believe, is more effective in the long run than an executive fiat.

If the people involved in personnel work do their jobs properly, the number of refusals is usually low. The Detroit chairman of the personnel board reports:

> There were times when we got very bogged down by a few refusals. Other times it has gone rather smoothly.
>
> This year most priests accepted. That is partly because the regional bishops have done their work, the elected members of the assignment board have done their work. They made an effort to know the priests. They talk to the priests. The exchange is pretty good. So when you come to the meeting and we make these decisions, we have a pretty good sense of where most priests would be, what they would be interested in.

The Bad News

When a number of priests want a parish, only one can get it. Although the archbishop makes the final decision, the board also shares the blame and complaints for decisions that cannot please everyone. It is much easier on the bishop if the committee, rather than the bishop, has to tell a man he is not capable of being a pastor. Some boards are even willing to take the blame for decisions made by their archbishops. A board member reports:

> The most difficult part of this job is dealing with the dissatisfaction of the clergy with our decisions. They think we pick the names out of a hat. They will say, "How the hell did you come to that decision?"
>
> Sometimes it is because of confidential information that we cannot share. Sometimes it was a decision of the archbishop that we did not recommend. There is no point in us passing the blame on to him. We are many, so we can bear it better.

The executive secretary of the Chicago personnel board agreed that informing the candidates who did not get the parish is difficult.

There is not a whole lot that you can say. We don't give real specific reasons about why Fr. Smith was better than Fr. Jones. We just say that the process has been concluded, the Cardinal has made his choice. If they ask why, it is "we felt that this particular person was the one best suited for this parish."

It really is gut wrenching. You have to call priests that you know really well. You feel really bad for them. Sometimes this was the candidate that you wanted to get it. Some guys are devastated because they were convinced that they were going to get it. They are just stunned by it. Other priests who have applied for a number of parishes and been rejected reach the point where they finally explode. They are really angry.

Dealing with the applicants who do not get the position is the hardest part about the open listing process. This is especially true of applicants who have been turned down numerous times. The chairman of a personnel board explains:

Let's say ten people apply for this parish. They are putting their priesthood on the line. They are putting their reputation on the line, because obviously the people on the board know who are applying and the word gets out.

Only one gets the parish. So the morale problem. Let's say you wrote in for twelve parishes in a row and got refused each time, where would that put you?

There is a great reluctance to honestly tell priests why they are negatively perceived by the board, the bishop, and others. In St. Paul, the personnel director explains how the board would deal with a man who it did not feel should be a pastor:

I sit down with him, and the board meets with him to talk about his wishes. We talk about whether he has done well so far and how realistic his wishes are. It is tough to say to him, "You aren't fit to be a pastor, and you should look for another associate position."

He will then get discouraged and talk to the archbishop, who comes to me and says, "Can't you find him a parish?" Then I will have to tell the archbishop, "The board doesn't see him as pastor material."

In San Francisco the difficulty of dealing with rejected candidates led to the dropping of the open listing system. "There were too many hurt feelings when a man would apply for every one and get turned down," explains the San Francisco personnel director.

But many personnel directors believe that priests should be honestly told how they are perceived by the board, especially if they will never get a pastorate. "I think they should be told. They should be given reasons," says one lay personnel director. "I find that they [priests' personnel board] play games, and I can't stand that." Another director agreed, "If we sin in the whole system, it is that we are not honest with people. One of the ways we frequently sin is in not being honest and candid in our evaluations, whether they are formal evaluations, informal evaluations, estimates, popular judgments about persons."

Many archbishops do not like this approach. Archbishop Whealon of Hartford explains:

I don't think that it is good to tell a man that he will never become pastor. I like to keep hope alive if there is any, however slight, possibility of hope there.

It is a competitive situation that we have. If a priest has really not updated himself, if he cannot relate well to the people, he has a difficulty now in being assigned. It is an occasion to tell him that he needs to do some updating of himself. Or it is an occasion to tell him that he did well on the interview but don't give up. It is just that someone with greater seniority or someone with a better aptitude for this place was chosen.

Sometimes, it is a discouraging experience but still, I think, better than the old system that would assign any priest to a parish whether he was qualified or not.

Father Kinsella, an expert on personnel issues, says, "If I could send personnel directors or bishops to school, I would send them to school to learn how to speak candidly, gently, and caringly in a supportive, pastoral way, but honestly, about the way people are judged."

Evaluations

Everyone agrees that the weakest part of the priests' personnel system is the lack of any systematic evaluation of a priest's work in his parish. In most archdioceses there is no real evaluation of a priest's work. Even those who favor evaluating priests disagree on how it should be done and who should receive the results. When priests' councils vote in favor of evaluation, it is usually voluntary and offered as a means of personal growth. Often, as in Newark, they feel the results should be given only to the priest himself and not to those dealing with assignments. In Milwaukee, it is up to the priest whether the information is given to the personnel board.

A few archdioceses (for example, Newark and Milwaukee) have developed extensive evaluation instruments that include interviews with the priest and surveys of his parishioners. These would examine his ability to work with various groups in the parish (young, old, parish staff and organizations, ethnic groups) as well as his skills in administration, liturgy, preaching, counseling, outreach, etc.

In Milwaukee the evaluation takes place every five years and all but fourteen priests have gone through it at least once. It begins with a questionnaire by which the priest evaluates himself and his performance. The same basic questionnaire goes to twenty parishioners and ten priests chosen by the priest. "Most of them praise the priest to the sky, a few are very critical," explains Auxiliary Bishop Brust. The bishop believes that the self-evaluation of the priest is the most helpful. "There is more in there than in all the stuff that thirty people put together. He has insights about himself that those others don't have."

The results are tabulated and summarized in the personnel office. A specially trained priest meets with the priest. "He interviews the priest," reports Bishop Brust. "He says what he read in all these interviews without revealing any names. The upshot is the priest is asked to make a couple of resolutions for the future. Better care of his health, a little shaping up spiritually, more regular prayer life, especially reading and continuing education."

The interviewer then writes up a summary of their discussion that is reviewed by the priest who can add his own comments. They both sign the document, which goes to the archbishop, but it can only go to the personnel board with the approval of the priest. So far all the priests have authorized giving it to the personnel board.

"It came out of the perceived experience that priests need a chance to hear that they are doing well," explains Auxiliary Bishop Sklba of Milwaukee. "They need an opportunity to hear one or two areas of suggested change. They need a structured way to hear it that is growth oriented rather than just negative."

As part of the assignment process, sometimes the candidates are interviewed by the priests' personnel director or a member of the board. As a person involved in the process in Newark explains, "We have about five areas that we concentrate on for pastors: pastoral experience, administrative ability, leadership in terms of being able to share responsibilities, liturgy, and outreach to people. We have an outline we follow so that the interview is structured."

In the process of making assignments, personnel boards must make judgments about priests. One complaint about personnel boards is that sometimes priests are judged by their peers in terms of their past rather than their present.

"I see a difficulty of people knowing how a man is doing today as opposed to how he was in the seminary," explains one director. "A lot of superstars in the closed life of the seminary, do not function well in parishes. And nonfunctioners in the seminary, when given a chance in ministry, have really grown wings. We remember a lot of people from how they were seminarians, and that is not a true picture now."

"Sometimes they don't see each other afterwards," explains Bishop Sklba of Milwaukee. "They remember those associations and don't allow each other to grow. I would never like to be judged by the things I did twenty years ago."

This is not, however, a problem limited to members of the personnel board. Archbishop Lipscomb of Mobile admits, "I came out of this presbyterate, and I feel I know them fairly well. The danger is that I stereotype them, not giving scope for their growth or changes in their needs even. And that has been to my grief." Sometimes a priest returns a changed man from a sabbatical. "They still remember the last time when he was difficult to communicate with," explains one vicar for clergy. "I will say, 'Hey, wait a minute, when was the last time you talked to him? Don't make him hostage to an earlier situation.' "

The problem is accentuated in dioceses that do not have any formal evaluation process. Sometimes the members of the board have little data to go on. One personnel director admitted,

There is a kind of seduction built into the system, when you have a group of priests together and say, "You have to give us your best advice about Charlie."

If they don't know a whole lot about Charlie, they will repeat what the common estimate of Charlie is. It may be accurate. I have seen sometimes when it is incredibly accurate. I have seen other times when it is an incredible injustice to people.

But again, this is not a problem endemic to personnel boards. It was also true before there were boards, when the bishop would consult with his chancery staff about appointments. Without formal evaluations, a pastor's reputation can sometimes be based on rumor, hearsay, and the presence or absence of complaint letters to the bishop.

But even once the evaluation is completed, there are few ways of rewarding good priests. They do not receive merit pay increases, and even symbolic rewards like being promoted to monsignor are few and far between. In Detroit each year an outstanding priest is chosen by the priests' council and rewarded with a sabbatical. But the best most good priests can hope for is a word of thanks from their bishop and congregation.

Sometimes being a good priest can simply produce more work. One Chicago priest told the executive secretary of the personnel board that "the way you get rewarded in this diocese is, if you have done a good job, you get a bigger pile of shit to deal with." The secretary agreed, "If you are in a parish and deal with all these problems, then the board will look at you and say, 'Hey, this guy really handles problems well. We will give him more problems to handle.' On the other hand, if you are on the verge of falling apart, everybody is moving in on you saying, 'How can we help?' " This is a problem with a system based more on charity than merit.

Comprehensive Personnel Office

Most of this chapter deals with clergy personnel issues for the simple reason that these are much more likely to reach the archbishop than personnel issues dealing with lay or religious employees. For lay and religious personnel, the archbishop gets involved in determining personnel policy (salaries, benefits, grievance procedures, etc.) but not assignments except for high-level administrators.

The directors of the National Association of Church Personnel Administrators (NACPA) believe that the ideal is to have a comprehensive approach to church personnel systems.[34] They urge the church to adopt personnel policies that ordinarily will apply to all persons in the same work environment. "What we are advocating is that dioceses have comprehensive policies so that the policies apply to everyone," explains Sister Christine

Matthews, O.P., director of NACPA. "There are not different policies for religious than there are for clergy, than there are for lay employees."

To have such a system would probably require a cabinet level personnel department to oversee all personnel issues in the archdiocese. "What we advocate is that the diocese have a comprehensive personnel office," says Sister Matthews. This office would help establish policies and procedures that would apply to all agencies, including schools, Catholic Charities, and parishes. Such a comprehensive personnel department would deal not only with lay employees but also with priests and religious. This is the case to some extent with the personnel departments in Baltimore, Chicago, Cincinnati, Newark, and St. Paul.

Only recently have some archbishops begun to develop comprehensive personnel policies for their archdioceses. In the past, lay personnel were treated separately and differently than religious and priests. In addition, lay personnel policies and procedures have been for the most part decentralized. Each parish, school, or diocesan agency could have its own personnel program.

Typically, the church agencies with the most employees, the school office and Catholic Charities, have been the first to develop sophisticated personnel policies for lay employees. Because of the size and complexity of schools and social service agencies, personnel policies and procedures had to be developed in order to maintain order and morale. Developing personnel programs here was easier because these agencies have secular counterparts on which the church could model its personnel procedures and policies. In addition, church employees in these agencies were aware of how their counterparts in the public sector were treated, and they would lobby for similar benefits.

Since personnel decisions were decentralized, different personnel policies usually developed in different parts of an archdiocese. The policies in the schools would be different from the policies in Catholic Charities. This led to unhappiness when employees doing the same type of work (for example, secretaries) found that they were being treated differently depending on which agency employed them.

At the same time, the administrators of some small diocesan agencies (including parishes) got into trouble for not observing simple personnel requirements like contracts, withholding taxes, or liability insurance. This could lead to problems with the government or employees that end up in court.

All these problems, plus the rapid growth in the number of lay employees, bring personnel issues to the attention of the archbishop. In many cases, he and the archdiocese are legally responsible for what is done in an agency. As a result, some archbishops are establishing personnel offices or departments to coordinate and supervise personnel issues in the whole archdiocese.

An archdiocesan personnel office usually begins in the finance office, where it initially deals with salaries and benefits (medical, retirement, etc.) of lay persons in the central agencies. Depending on the expertise of the personnel director and the desires of the archbishop, it can grow into a more comprehensive office that would screen job applicants, help develop job descriptions and evaluation procedures, establish salary guidelines and grievance procedures, run workshops and training institutes, and provide advice on personnel issues to department heads.

Conclusion

A number of things become clear in examining the role of archbishops in personnel decisions in their archdioceses. First, the size of the archdiocese affects the degree to which the archbishop is involved in personnel issues. Normally, the smaller the archdiocese, the more actively he is involved.

For the most part, the personnel issues that reach him are those that deal with diocesan priests. He hires and fires relatively few lay or religious employees in the archdiocese, but he is directly involved in the assignments of every diocesan priest. He gets involved in lay and religious personnel issues when systemic problems are brought to his attention by his top administrators or by complaints from lay and religious employees.

In reaction to the arbitrary exercise of authority in the past, bishops are now more conscious of the need to consider a priest's needs and desires prior to an appointment. Although a priest does not always get the assignment he wants, practically all personnel directors admit that a priest can refuse an assignment if he wants to. This is especially true of pastors, but even an associate will not normally be sent to a parish against his will.

Since everyone agrees that personnel issues are the most difficult and controversial questions that reach an archbishop, it is not surprising that attempts are made to make these decisions easier and fairer. Archdioceses all across the country are experimenting with new policies and procedures, trying to find the magic formula that will get the right priest in the right parish and keep everybody happy.

Personnel offices, personnel boards, tenure policies, open listing, and other procedures have been tried with varying success. These have arisen not only to make the process fairer and more responsive to the priests but also to make a difficult job easier. Some priests complain that they are simply bureaucratic procedures that get between them and their bishop. Some places have had a bureaucratic tendency to set up procedures that will make the work of the personnel director, board, and bishop easier.

As Father Kinsella notes:

Policies and standards and systems guarantee a certain amount of justice and equity and consistent treatment, and that is why they are valuable—not because they make life easier, but because they guarantee consistency and some equity. Balancing that off in terms of personal response, personal care, genuine response to people in need— that is an art form, not a science. You just make decisions in those kinds of situations that are on the level of art, sizing up a situation and trying to make the best decision.

It is also clear that some of the best priests in the archdiocese are placed in clergy personnel work. But most archbishops are reluctant to staff their personnel offices adequately. These priests tend to be overworked and as subject to burnout as any priest they are trying to help.

7. Catholic Education and Social Services

About the only thing I can get on the front page of the local newspaper is the closure of a school.

———ARCHBISHOP KELLY

Because of federal budget cuts, we are opening shelters, soup kitchens, and we are back to the things we did before the Roosevelt administration.

———DIRECTOR OF CHARITIES, Hartford, CT

Archdioceses run many programs, and it is impossible to examine all of them in this book. This chapter will examine the two largest archdiocesan programs: education and social services. The first is primarily a parish-based program, while the second is usually run independently of the parishes. Both programs began as a response to the needs of poor Catholic immigrants in a hostile environment. The programs grew in size and quality and now compare favorably with similar programs run by state or private agencies. They have also expanded their services beyond the Catholic community to the public at large, especially the poor.

Supporting and overseeing Catholic education and Catholic social services is an important responsibility of the archbishop. It is a difficult job because these are large and complex organizations, but it is made easier by the fact that these are usually the most professionally organized and managed programs in the archdiocese. The superintendent of schools and the director of Catholic Charities normally have more management training and experience than other archdiocesan administrators. In addition, the programs have secular counterparts from whom they can learn and to whom they can be compared.

Although these programs are very different, the concerns of the archbishops are focused on similar issues in both programs: governance, finances, and Catholicity.

Education

There are 7,659 Catholic elementary schools, 1,391 high schools, and 233 colleges and universities in the United States.[1] Most of the colleges and universities are run by religious orders independent of the local bishop, but 60 percent of the high schools and practically all of the elementary schools are the responsibility of the bishops. Although the number of schools has declined since its peak in 1966, archdioceses still run some of the largest school systems in the country, sometimes larger than any public school system in their state. The Chicago archdiocese has 12 high schools with 5,409 students and 345 elementary schools with 116,509 students.

While all archbishops view Catholic schools as the ideal, they also recognize that most Catholic children are in public schools.[2] There are almost 2 million children in Catholic elementary schools and 708,000 in Catholic high schools, but there are 3 million elementary students and 804,000 high school students in parish religious education programs (CCD). Most of these students are taught by volunteers. These programs are judged to be ineffective by 37 percent of the religious education directors who run them.[3]

A difficult problem facing any archbishop is how to stress the importance of Catholic schools without seeming to denigrate the importance of religious education, and vice versa. If he constantly harps on the importance of Catholic schools, those involved in religious education will feel slighted. If he puts more resources into religious education, the school people will feel he is getting ready to abandon Catholic schools.

The archbishop is ultimately responsible for the education programs of the archdiocese. He must be particularly concerned about governance (who decides what), finances (how much does it cost and how is it paid for), and the Catholicity of the education programs.

Governance: Archdiocesan Offices

In his concern for governance, the archbishop must structure the archdiocesan offices to deal with both Catholic schools and religious education programs. Most archdioceses have a separate office for each. In some archdioceses (like Baltimore, Chicago, Cincinnati, Indianapolis, Milwaukee, New York, Philadelphia, Washington) a vicar or secretary for total education or Christian formation has under him a superintendent of schools and an archdiocesan director of religious education. He might also have under him the seminaries and offices for youth ministry, campus ministry, lay ministry, and family ministry.

The idea of one education department flowed from attempts to implement the bishops' pastoral letter on education, "To Teach as Jesus Did," which stressed that there was one educational mission. Sometimes there is a cooperative atmosphere between the school and religious education offices, but sometimes each office goes its own way until a conflict arises over scheduling, policy, or resources. Cooperation and communication are further inhibited when the offices are in different buildings as in Louisville. The secretary for education or the archbishop attempts to resolve disputes and improve communication and cooperation between the two offices.

Some superintendents of schools complain about the secretariat system because it places someone between them and the archbishop. Because of their size, complexity, and importance, Catholic schools have many problems that require the archbishop's attention. Every superintendent wants direct access to make sure the archbishop understands his position on school issues. "In our system, the schools are but one division of many," complained the superintendent of schools in Newark who later quit. To communicate with the archbishop "you fight up through the secretary of education, then he fights up through the vicar general and chancellor. The layers of bureaucracy can fog some of the thoughts that are given." To alleviate this problem, some secretaries for education will bring along the superintendent when they see the archbishop about a school issue.

In some archdioceses (like Atlanta, Denver, Dubuque, and St. Paul), the secretary may also be the superintendent of schools. In small dioceses with limited resources, the religious education office may simply be one or more persons who also deal with the religion curriculum in the school office. This is unsatisfactory to those involved in religious education who fear they will get short shrift despite the fact that they teach more Catholic children than do the Catholic schools.

None of these organizational structures is ideal. They work only if the people get along with each other and respect their separate ministries. If they do not, someone, either the archbishop or his vicar, will have to bridge the gap or replace the people.

Most archdioceses have a board of education that advises the archbishop on educational policy.[4] Some board promoters want them to be independent like public school boards, but in most cases board proposals cannot take effect without the approval of the archbishop. Although a board is technically only consultative, the archbishop may delegate to it much authority by, in fact, rarely overruling it. Confrontations are rare since the bishop keeps control over board membership and influences board proposals as they are being developed. Some archbishops take an active role as chairman of the board of education, but most do not attend their meetings but leave them to their vicar for education or their superintendent of schools. The education office staffs the board, preparing agenda, reports, and minutes. It also acts as liaison between the board and the archbishop. Archdioceses with successful boards tend to have training programs to educate board members to their role.

Some archdioceses (like Atlanta, Baltimore, Cincinnati, Denver, Indianapolis, Milwaukee, Mobile, Omaha) have one board for both schools and religious education, while others have separate boards for each. While a number of vicars and archbishops praise the joint boards for providing a comprehensive overview of educational policy, superintendents of schools and archdiocesan directors of religious education often complain that they do not get enough time with the joint boards.

After trying boards of total education, the archdioceses of Kansas City and Seattle set up separate school boards. The board of total education "was an unwieldy board," according to the Kansas City superintendent of schools. "You really didn't get a lot accomplished and the schools were always accused of taking all the time."

"The needs were so different," reports the Seattle superintendent. "The time being spent, particularly on school crises, was so out of proportion that they chose to have different boards." Joint boards devote most of their time to school issues because they are constantly pressing.

Boards have been active in drawing up or revising educational policies and procedures. They provide a good sounding board to give community reaction to ideas or questions from the vicar for education or the superintendent of schools. Sometimes they are involved in the opening, consolidating, or closing of schools. Often they are concerned about personnel policies and finances: school office budget, teachers' salaries, tuition, and fund-raising. Some boards also serve as appeal panels for fired teachers or principals.

Religious Education

The religious education office oversees and encourages the religious education program in the parishes. Its small staff usually divides up the archdiocese by regions or by grade levels. One or more persons may be responsible for training catechists and/or supervising directors of religious education in parishes. There are an estimated five thousand professional religious education directors in the United States (defined as a full-time employee with a master's degree in theology or religious education with at least three years experience). Most (83 percent) are women.[5]

In some archdioceses (like Baltimore, Cincinnati, Indianapolis, Omaha, Mobile, Washington), the religious education office is responsible for both the parish catechetical program and the school religion program. In other archdioceses, the school office has its own religious education staff. Having the religious education experts in one office is thought to be more efficient, but some school officials do not like this approach. "You isolate religion out of the curriculum, make it something that happens in the schools but not a total part of the school," says Rev. Stephen O'Brien of the National Catholic Education Association. "Secondly, the superintendent of schools doesn't have authority over the religion curriculum, which is bad because that is in his critical area."

In Baltimore, the religious education office develops programs for the schools, but the superintendent implements them. The religious education staff dealing with schools sits in on meetings of the school office and provides lines of communication between the two. The superintendent and principals are responsible for the entire curriculum in the schools, and if they opposed a religious curriculum plan, it would not be adopted. The Baltimore superintendent thinks that their system works well although he was worried at the beginning. "It's the way we relate to each other that makes it work," he says. "We meet every two weeks and share everything. Everyone supports each other. When you have a problem, they are there to help you."

Some archdiocesan offices of religious education (like Washington) have broad authority to determine who can be hired as directors of religious education in parishes, what training is necessary for catechists, and what texts can be used. For example, most archbishops require that the textbooks have imprimaturs in order to ensure their orthodoxy. A few also require that the parish director of religious education have a degree in theology or religious education.

Some also require that catechists go through a training program and become certified. "Unless the catechists are trained," explains the director of religious education in Miami, "you have someone teaching Trent, another teaching Vatican I, and another teaching Vatican II, or Vatican III!" Often there are levels of certification, one for beginners and the last being a master catechist who helps other catechists.

In other archdioceses, the religious education office makes recommendations, but the pastor does what he wants. Sometimes strict requirements are not imposed because so few qualified people are available. In archdioceses with few Catholic colleges, requiring a degree in theology or religious education for parish directors of religious education may be unrealistic. In addition, there is a limit to what can be demanded of volunteer catechists. Training programs and workshops for catechists are provided, but not mandatory.

Most religious education offices act as a clearinghouse or placement service for people interested in getting jobs as parish directors of religious education. Some archdiocesan religious education offices interview and screen people who want to be parish directors of religious education. Most offices have a resource center with books, films, videos, and other teaching materials, or they may share a resource center with the school office. "We have 350 video tapes," reports the director of education in St. Paul. "The smallest parish can have the best speakers, people like [the Scripture scholar] Ray Brown."

Religious education offices constantly try to get pastors and parishes to take religious education more seriously. Some pastors cut corners by hiring young, inexperienced people as youth ministers and directors of religious education. Adult religious education is often nonexistent, although the RCIA program for adult catechumens has been very successful in a number of archdioceses. Some religious education offices also run, or help parishes run, sacramental preparation programs (pre-Cana, pre-Jordan).

A delicate job of archdiocesan religious education offices is to mediate disputes between pastors and directors of religious education. Disputes can occur over the program itself, but also over salaries, benefits, responsibilities, and authority. When the chips are down, the pastor almost always wins, but the office tries to defuse disputes by facilitating communications and understanding. Job descriptions and model contracts are drawn up by the office for use by pastors and parish education committees.

Sometimes conflicts arise between those running the religious education and those running the school. The classrooms may be used after school for the religious education program. The sacramental preparation programs for both groups of children must be coordinated. And if a religion teacher in the school is also the director of religious education in the parish, he may be getting contradictory instructions from different bosses.

Conflict can also occur over parish funds. The director of religious education in Louisville notes that "we have had parishes that were happy with the DRE's [directors of religious education], really profited from them, but it came to the point where they said, 'We can't afford it.' I blame it mainly on the financial drain that the schools have put on the parish." Improving religious education usually means spending more money. If the parish is pouring lots of money into the parish school, resources may be limited. The pastor has to referee these disputes, but sometimes the archdiocesan offices get involved.

Religious educators can also be caught in the middle in areas that are disputed in the church today. According to the Denver secretary of education, they "get caught between what parents want to do, what the parents experienced, what the current theology is saying to them, what canon law might be saying, what Rome might be saying, what the bishops might be saying, all of which might be somewhat different."

School Governance

In every archdiocese, schools are one of the largest and most complex ministries. Somehow, policies have to be determined and implemented on a wide range of issues affecting students, faculty, and administrators: admissions, expulsion, tuition, hiring, firing, salaries, textbooks, curriculum, insurance, maintenance. The power of the various actors (archdiocesan board of education, vicar for education, superintendent of schools, unions, principal, pastor, parish council, parish education committee, teachers) are different in different archdioceses. "In spite of its image as a hierarchical organization with universally enforced norms, the church's policies and practices of governance and accountability are neither uniformly defined nor universally practiced in Catholic schools," reports Lourdes Sheehan, executive director of the National Association of Boards of Education at the National Catholic Educational Association. "What really happens in schools depends on personalities, policies, and politics at the local level."[6]

The school office, headed by the superintendent of schools, is usually one of the larger offices in the archdiocese, but it is always smaller and less powerful than a comparable public school office. The Denver superintendent of schools has a staff of three people although a local school district of similar size (13,000 students) has a central office staff of fifty.

Normally the office will be divided in two parts, one dealing with primary schools and one with high schools. Some (like Detroit, Los Angeles, New Orleans) have staffs that are responsible for schools in different parts of the archdiocese. In Indianapolis, the superintendent of schools explains that each of her

thirteen staff members [has] a number of schools under their jurisdiction. They go out and interview the principals of all our schools, go over their goals and objectives for the year, try to establish contact. If the principal needs some consultation, this person is the one that they call on.

In Indianapolis, most of the thirteen staff persons also have a curriculum specialty. A school office may also have persons dealing with finances (although this is usually handled by the finance office), government relations, and staff development. The school office will also act as a clearinghouse or placement service for people seeking jobs as principals or teachers.

Archdiocesan school offices have less power over parish schools than their public school counterparts have over public schools. But some archdiocesan school offices have more power than others. Determining at what level decisions should be made is not easy. "For tuition, teachers' salaries, hiring, selection of books, for the whole range of school issues," explains the Washington superintendent of schools, "there is no magic point where you can draw the line and say, 'Everything on this side of the line is parochial and everything on this side is diocesan.'"

Some archdioceses are more centralized than others. When control is decentralized, superintendents speak of a federation or "system of schools" as opposed to a "school system," which is more centralized. In a centralized system, the approval of the superintendent of schools would be required for the hiring of a principal. School policies, procedures, curriculum, textbooks, and testing would be mandated. Officials from the school office would visit and evaluate schools.

In a decentralized system, the school office staff is small. For example, in Cincinnati the office has only two persons. The pastor hires whom he wants as principal, with or without consultation with the parish school board. "Guidelines" might be issued by the school office, but the pastors and principals can ignore them. "It is to their advantage to follow the guidelines," explains the director of education in St. Paul, "because the guidelines can be on very difficult and technical matters, and they need the help."

Various factors push archdioceses toward centralizing power while other factors push toward decentralization. Decentralization is encouraged by the principle of subsidiarity that calls for decisions and work to be done at the lowest possible level. Pastors, principals, and local boards of education are presumed to know their schools and want what is best for them. Without their active involvement, the schools will not survive. Nor are school offices sufficiently staffed to govern schools directly. Normally, the superintendent is not trying to take control away from the parish staff but trying to get them to take their responsibilities more seriously.

The involvement of the laity on local school boards has also been a decentralizing influence. Although these boards are advisory, participation brings a sense of ownership that is hard to override. In addition, to the extent that parish schools are locally financed, they have a great deal of autonomy. Pastors pay the bills and therefore control their schools. Most observers agree "the important decisions regarding personnel and finances are largely made at each individual school; the diocesan superintendent of schools plays a lesser role than the public school counterpart in that position."[7]

On the other hand, many factors, such as the hierarchical structure of the church, encourage centralization. Government laws and regulations (everything from fire regulations to sex discrimination laws) tend to encourage centralization, because the school office will act to make sure the schools comply. If the schools are accredited, policies and procedures are more likely to be uniform and supervised by the school office. Archdioceses also tend to play a larger role in regional or consolidated schools, because there is no one parish to take responsibility. And when faced with difficulties, the pastor or principal often turns to the school office or archbishop for help. Schools with financial problems ask for archdiocesan funds, and outside funding means more outside control. If a number of schools have financial problems, the archdiocese will likely mandate planning and budgetary procedures.

And when conflicts arise, someone often complains to the school office or the archbishop. Angry parents will write the archbishop. A fired teacher or principal will appeal to the archdiocese. School conflicts can also develop into law suits and insurance claims for which the archdiocese may be liable. As a result, archdiocesan policies and procedures are developed to protect the archdiocese on matters like hiring, contract renewal, firing, liability, etc. Often pastors and principals welcome archdiocesan guidelines on complex and controversial issues because they relieve them of the responsibility and the burden of working out their own policies and procedures. The more complex the area, the more likely the central office has more expertise than the local school.

The replacement of religious by laity has also encouraged more centralization. In the past, religious communities saw to the training, selection, and supervision of sisters working as teachers and principals in parish schools. Local pastors and school boards do not usually have the expertise to carry out these responsibilities for their lay faculties. Concern about the qualifications and Catholicity of lay principals and teachers has increased the archdiocesan involvement in their selection, inservice training, and supervision.

Also encouraging greater centralization are archdiocesan school boards. After examining an issue, a board is apt to recommend an archdiocesan program or policy. Superintendents recognize that a recommendation from the board carries more weight than one that simply comes from their office. What superintendents and archbishops might be afraid to do on their own because of local opposition, they can more easily do on the recommendation of the archdiocesan board of education.

Catholicity

The primary function of the school office is to supervise and support the schools' academic and religious programs. Most archdioceses have curriculum experts who can help teachers in curriculum development and the choice of textbooks.[8] The school office primarily works with the principals in the hopes that they will then lead their schools. In some archdioceses, school officials visit and evaluate schools. In others (like Indianapolis, Santa Fe, Washington), the schools are visited by accrediting teams from the state or private school associations as a means of guaranteeing their academic quality. Most superintendents are happy with this arrangement. But in some localities, the relations between the Catholic school office and public school administrators are not good. "We are fighting with the state," reports the Omaha superintendent of schools. "They make life difficult every chance they have. They act like the sooner we close, the better."

Even where the relationship is fairly good, state accreditation means that the Catholic schools must follow the state's philosophy of education. "If you become accredited, you must meet their criteria," explains the superintendent of schools in Denver, "and their criteria don't always fit into what we might perceive to be in the best interest of our schools." For example, a state may require teachers to be locally certified even though they already are certified in another state. This is especially a problem for religious who during their lives teach in a number of states.

The school office pays special attention to the religion curriculum. As with religious education programs, archbishops require that religion textbooks have imprimaturs to ensure their orthodoxy. While one adult text (*Christ Among Us*) had its imprimatur removed at the insistence of the Vatican, texts for children have been for the most part noncontroversial, except when they deal with human sexuality. Some conservative Catholics have objected to any sex education in Catholic schools.

More problematic are the teachers.[9] In the past, the bishops simply trusted the nuns to teach orthodox doctrine at a time when there was little dissent in the church. Today, many who teach religion in Catholic schools are lay. A few have theological degrees, but others have little or no formal training in theology, especially in archdioceses (like Oklahoma City) with few Catholic colleges. A few archbishops are concerned about the theology the teachers may have learned at some Catholic colleges, but mostly they are concerned about teachers who have limited knowledge. Often the school office or the religious education office will run workshops and training programs for religion teachers. Some archdioceses require teachers to be certified as catechists.

The issue of Catholicity goes beyond a simple concern for orthodoxy. Sometimes it is simple neglect. One religious education official describes visiting a school with the archdiocesan superintendent. After sitting in on classes they met with the principal.

> I said to her point blank, "If I didn't see a crucifix in each classroom, I would never know this was a Catholic school." You know what her answer was? "I know it."
>
> She had been principal for five years. She walked into a bad situation facultywise, so her emphasis for five years has been to build up her faculty in everything but religion.
>
> So I looked at her and said, "So you have five groups of children who are not Catholic out in the community now."
>
> "Oh, but I am going to get to it this year."
>
> When we walked out the door, the superintendent and I wondered if we should padlock it.

Religious educators speak of the school as a community of faith.[10] Besides the academic instruction, liturgy, prayer, and Christian service are part of the faith community's life. Since the key person in the school for making this happen is the principal, many archdioceses require that principals be practicing Catholics because to be a leader of a faith community takes more than academic and administrative competence. For the same reason, some superintendents are reluctant to hire as principals qualified persons who have spent all of their lives working in public schools.

Some superintendents also organize workshops to indoctrinate new teachers with the philosophy and theology of Catholic education.[11] A number of dioceses use programs developed by the National Catholic Education Association. "We have 5,500 teachers, and there is always a turnover of teachers," explains the superintendent of schools in New York. "We have to constantly educate them to the purpose of Catholic schools." One archdiocese requires that all teachers be certified catechists even if they do not teach religion.

The Catholicity issue is more complex in inner-city schools where a majority of the black students are non-Catholic. Catholic schools are the most successful evangelizing tool available to the church in the black community. At the same time, the schools try to respect the religious freedom of non-Catholic parents and their children. Most schools teach the Catholic faith to both Catholic and non-Catholic students. Other denominations are treated with respect, and grades are based on knowledge and not belief.

Another recent issue confronting Catholic schools is what to do with unmarried pregnant students and teachers. The traditional response was to throw them out of school because they have been involved in activity unacceptable to Catholic teaching. According to this view, for the school to do nothing would be to condone the activity. On the other hand, some now argue that such policies encourage abortions by punishing those who do not have an illegitimate child aborted.

Finances

A major problem confronting Catholic schools is financing.[12] Although Catholic schools are run more cheaply than public schools, they constantly have trouble making ends meet. "Our school budget—for parochial schools, twenty-nine diocesan high schools, and the seminary—runs $105 to $110 million each year," explains Cardinal Krol. "So we are a bit busy trying to meet that budget." Some archdiocesan school offices (like New Orleans) review and approve parish school budgets. Usually school budgets are not examined at the archdiocesan level unless the parish or school is requesting archdiocesan funds (see chapter 5).

Once a school is built and paid for, the major cost of running a school is labor: salaries and other personnel costs amount to over 75 percent of a school's budget.[13] Other big items would be insurance and utilities. Catholic schools in the past were heavily subsidized by the low-cost labor of religious women. The decline in the number of sisters has necessitated hiring lay teachers, who cost much more than the sisters ever did. Increased employment opportunities for women also mean schools must pay more to attract good teachers. In addition, the church is becoming aware that it must practice what it preaches about just salaries.[14] But the higher the salaries, the higher the cost of running the schools.

Teachers' salaries are sometimes set by the school and sometimes by the archdiocese. In a few archdioceses (like New York, Philadelphia, and San Francisco), high school teachers' salaries are set through collective bargaining between the archdiocese and the teachers' union. When the school sets the salary, the archdiocese often offers optional guidelines.

Salaries are set with one eye on public school salaries and one eye on tuition. Catholic school teachers are almost always paid less than public school teachers. Some Catholic schools pay 90 percent or better of the public scale, but others pay much less. In New Orleans, some inner-city schools were paying 50 percent of the city scale. "If we can keep our teachers in this diocese at 75 percent to 80 percent of the public school system," says the New Orleans superintendent of schools, "I think we are in excellent shape." The Washington archdiocese pays teachers only about half of what public school teachers receive. As a result, 40 percent of the lay teachers have less than three years' experience as teachers.

Most teachers prefer teaching in parochial schools. But where the pay differential is too wide, the parochial schools lose their more experienced teachers to the public schools. "Unless we do something about the teachers' salaries, we are going to lose all of our schools anyway," says the superintendent of schools in Washington. "The simplest way to handle the teachers' salary issue is to charge the parents more money in tuition."

Tuition is a major revenue source for Catholic schools, accounting for 43 percent of their revenues, up from 39 percent twelve years earlier.[15] To increase revenues, a school must attract more students or raise tuition. There is great reluctance to increase tuition charges. "If we charge the parents more money in tuition," says the Washington superintendent, "we run into the problem of becoming elite and driving people away." If tuition increases cause enrollments to decline, then revenues will fall. "If the enrollment in an eight-room school is less than 150," explains the director of school planning in Washington, "it is going to be in financial trouble."

Proponents of higher tuition point out that some parents pay more for child care than Catholic schools charge for tuition. "People will tell you how when they went to school, tuition was $20 a family," recounts the superintendent of schools in Detroit. "Yet they will pay $1,600 for preschool at commercial day care centers and then complain because the Catholic first grade is $600 or $700."

Many poor parents are willing to pay high tuitions to keep their children in a Catholic school. In the archdiocese of Washington, inner-city parents formed committees to recruit students and to collect tuition from nonpaying parents. They realized that without these measures their schools would close.

Most parishes are able to subsidize their schools with money from the Sunday collection. Nationwide, 46 percent of the school budget is covered by a parish subsidy.[16] A school with children from a neighboring parish will sometimes get help from that parish, too. The parishes with the biggest collections, however, tend to have affluent parishioners who could afford the tuition anyway. The small collection of a poor inner-city parish will be of little help to its school.

How much money a parish should give its school is a debated issue. The more money going to the school, the less money is available for other parish programs. In addition, if a parish charges significantly less tuition than a neighboring parish, families with school children will transfer to that parish. A few archdioceses (like Mobile, Milwaukee, and Newark) put a limit on the percentage of the school budget that can come from the parish or on the percentage of the parish budget that can go to the school. On the other hand, school officials point out that a good portion of this money would not come to the parish if it did not have a school. For example, parents would not run fund-raising activities like bingo if their children were not in the school. And some parishes require parents to "donate" a certain amount to the church if their children are in the school.

The archdiocese, if it has money, can also be a source of funds for parish schools, as was explained in chapter 5. Archdiocesan money can sometimes keep a borderline school open, but a school in serious trouble will eventually close. "We make a huge effort to keep open all of our inner-city schools," says Archbishop Hannan of New Orleans, "because the black ministers and the blacks in general have told us that is the greatest contribution we can make to them." But some archdiocesan officials wonder how long Catholics will be willing to support inner-city schools whose black students are predominantly non-Catholic. Schools with Hispanic students stress the Catholic character of their students when competing with black schools for archdiocesan funds.

In most cases, parish and archdiocesan subsidies are simply given as grants to the school for general operations or capital improvements. Some school finance experts argue that subsidizing operating expenses is inefficient. They believe that the schools should charge full cost for tuition and then use these subsidies for scholarships. Under this system, those who can afford it will pay full cost; those who cannot, would be eligible for scholarships.

Although this may be an intellectually rational system, politically it is hard to sell. "Just the words *full cost* really can scare a lot of people," explains the superintendent of schools in Baltimore. Wealthier parents, who also contribute to the parish, object to significant increases in tuition. Middle-class parents complain of the humiliation of applying for financial aid. School finance experts note, however, that these same parents have no qualms about applying for financial aid when their children go to college. So far, archdioceses have been more successful implementing such programs on the high school level rather than in elementary schools.

Finally, state and local governments may be sources of funds for parochial schools, although Supreme Court decisions have made this very difficult. Typically the funds have been given for school lunches, secular textbooks, transportation, nurses, guidance counseling, remedial mathematics and English, bilingual education, and state-mandated testing programs. In New Mexico, accredited Catholic schools receive about $5,000 each for textbooks from the state. The New York archdiocesan schools received about $3 million a year (mostly for English as a second language and guidance) until the Supreme Court ruled that these programs could not be run in the Catholic schools but had to be done off campus.

Closing and Merging Schools

Schools get into financial trouble when enrollments decline and tuition income falls. "We don't close any schools," explains Archbishop May of St. Louis, "but people do when they no longer send their kids to them. If there is no enrollment, we have to consolidate or close that school. That wasn't our decision, it was the decision of the parents."

Especially hard hit have been rural and inner-city schools where population changes have meant fewer school-age children, fewer Catholics, or fewer parents who can afford the tuition. Sometimes a change in school administration or policy makes the schools less attractive to the parents. Whatever the cause, unless the enrollment decline is reversed, the school will become a bigger drain on parish and archdiocesan finances.

Many archdiocesan school officials believe that with proper leadership no school need close unless there are simply no children in the neighborhood. "Population and enrollment should be the basic reason why schools are closed or merged," says the superintendent of schools in Washington. "But finances and personalities often get tossed into the ring. Even the poorest of schools have created ways to continue where there has been a will and enthusiasm to do it." He found that schools are closed "because a principal comes in who can't deal with people, and the parents decide they are going to switch rather than fight." Others blame school closings on pastors and principals unwilling to deal with the financial and enrollment aspects of the school.

If the enrollment decreases, the financial viability and the academic quality of the school suffers and the school may have to close or merge with a neighboring school. Closing schools is very controversial. Some archdiocesan officials consider it even more traumatic than closing a parish. The decision to close a school very often leads to picketing the archbishop by parents, students, and alumni of the school. If the school is in the inner city, its closure will be decried as another example of the church's lack of concern for blacks and Hispanics. When Archbishop O'Connor arrived in New York, he found a number of schools that were waiting for approval to close. He refused because he did not want to become known as the archbishop who closed schools his first year in office.

No school closes without the approval of the archbishop, but sometimes the situation is so desperate by the time it reaches his desk that the decision is inevitable. In the worst-case scenario, the first sign of trouble comes in the spring when a new pastor requests a subsidy to cover a large deficit for the current school year. This comes as a complete surprise to the archbishop, because the finance office is not monitoring the parish and school finances. An examination of the parish and school books reveals that the previous pastor consumed the parish savings to keep the school open. In addition, he postponed maintenance to cut costs. The school building needs major repairs, and the Environmental Protection Agency wants the asbestos removed from the school at once. Meanwhile, early registration shows a significant decline in enrollment for the coming year. The pastor thinks that the situation is hopeless and wants to cut his losses and close the school immediately. His announcement comes as a surprise to the faculty and parents who were not consulted or kept informed about the situation. If the school is to close, the decision should be made quickly so that students and faculty can make plans for the coming year.

If the school and finance offices are monitoring the parish and the school, the archbishop should not be surprised by a last-minute crisis. Rather he will be faced with a situation that gradually gets worse. If the pastor and principal are consulting and sharing information with the parents and other parish leaders, they too will be aware of the problems. Some archdioceses have an involved process that must be followed before a school can be closed: Open hearings must be held; the pastor, parish council, and school board must concur in the decision; neighboring parishes must agree; the decision must be announced a year in advance; and every effort must be made to find other Catholic schools that will accept the students. Such procedures do not eliminate the pain, but they do make the decision-making process more open.

But an open process can also have negative effects. Publicly discussing the problems of a school and its possible closure discourages donations and encourages parents to put their children in other schools. "The word, 'viability study,' uttered no louder than a whisper in the bottom of a cellar in an inner room was enough to kill the enrollment in any school," reports the superintendent of schools in Newark. As a result, she instituted a three-year process requiring all schools to forecast and plan their futures.

Often the decision is not to close a school but to consolidate it with a neighboring school. This strengthens the financial and academic viability of both schools by combining their enrollments. Consolidating or clustering schools (as was done in Baltimore's inner city) requires significant archdiocesan planning.

Ideally, the best building at the most central location becomes the consolidated school, but preferences of pastors and parishioners and local finances play an important role.

The problem with consolidated schools, according to the superintendent of schools in Detroit, is that "everybody's school is nobody's school." The governance and financing of a consolidated school requires a clear understanding of the relationship of the two parishes to the school: what students can attend, what do they pay, how much do the parishes subsidize the school, what say do the pastors have in hiring and school policy, and how are disputes settled? Unless there is a clear, written agreement on these issues, problems will arise. For example, the pastor will say that the student may live in his parish, but the parents do not come to church or do not contribute. He therefore refuses to subsidize the student's education. Frequently troubles arise when new pastors arrive on the scene who were not involved in the original consolidation.

Principals and Pastors

Everyone agrees that the principal and pastor are the two key people in a parochial school. The most helpful thing that an archbishop can do for a parish school is appoint as pastor a priest who is sympathetic to Catholic education, as was discussed in chapter 6. "I get really nervous in the spring before the priests' appointments until I know who is going to be in those schools," confesses the superintendent of schools in Omaha. "As the pastor, so goes the school. You can see a turnaround overnight, positively or negatively."

The other key person is the principal. "If you have a key administrator," explains the New Orleans superintendent of schools, "a good leader, who knows what Catholic education is about, knows how to work with the finances, knows how to work with the local school board and work with the pastor— if he or she has those qualities, we are off to a good start."

Principals are appointed in many different ways. The principal of a regional school (with students from two or more parishes) will often be hired by the school's board. If a religious community has responsibility for the school, the community will appoint the principal from among its members. If a parish school is not the responsibility of a religious community, the pastor will appoint the principal under whatever guidelines are set by the archdiocese. The restrictions range from practically none to the requirement that the superintendent of schools approve the appointment, as happens in New Orleans. Sometimes the archdiocese requires that the principal have certain credentials or experience. The pastor's choice might be restricted to a list of approved candidates who have been screened by the school office, as is the case in New York. Or the archdiocese may require that the parish board of education be involved in interviewing and selecting the principal.

Even if he is free to select whomever he wants, a pastor will sometimes ask the school office for help in hiring a principal. The school office usually has a list of people looking for positions as principals. In addition, it can advise him on ways of proceeding that will protect him from making a bad choice. However the principal is chosen, he or she and the pastor must be able to work together for the good of the school. If there is conflict between the principal and the pastor, the school office can act as mediator, but ultimately the pastor will win unless he is moved or the archbishop intervenes.

The Archbishop

An archbishop cannot spend a great deal of time running the school system or the religious education programs, but he needs to keep informed on Catholic education because the tough decisions and problems eventually end up on his desk. The religious education director of Miami explains the things he would take the archbishop:

Certainly the opening or closure of any program, the financial status of programs, the trends in programs, the Catholicity part, any problems that might arise, any community involvements. On the other hand, the archbishop might come with various requests for involvement of the department in some area, whether it be in pro-life or in the drug scene.

On the school side, opening, closing, or consolidating schools must always have an archbishop's approval as would any major fund drive or borrowing. Schools with financial difficulties or conflicts will be brought to his attention. Major changes in policy concerning finances, personnel, or the religious character of schools will need his approval. "There is no clear-cut rule as to what goes to the archbishop," explains the St. Louis superintendent of schools. But any problem "that could either cause media attention or an upheaval in the parish would be appropriate for the archbishop to know and not be caught by surprise."

When he does turn his attention to education, an archbishop can have a tremendous impact. Although many schools are closing, some archbishops (Hannan of New Orleans and Strecker of Kansas City) are opening new high schools. Others encourage pastors in new suburban parishes to open elementary schools. But often the initiative must come from the parishioners. "If there are enough people wanting a new school and willing to assume the responsibilities," said one archbishop, "then we will back them up." Even in closing schools, archbishops can help by encouraging planning so that the closure of one school benefits others.

Depending on the funds available to them, archbishops can also help schools financially. "Szoka is very strong for schools," reports the superintendent of schools in Detroit. "He has put a ton of money into schools." A number of archbishops (Bernardin, Hickey, O'Connor, Sheehan) have attempted to raise money for endowments for Catholic schools although these efforts have not yet had a significant impact. Archbishops can also make decisions that will cost schools money. Shortly after arriving in New York, Cardinal O'Connor committed the archdiocese to raising teachers' salaries.

The day-to-day operations of the schools will be left to others, but the archbishop needs to approve questions of policy. For example, although he would not be involved in the hiring of principals (except for diocesan high schools in a small archdiocese), he would approve the policies and procedures governing the hiring and firing of principals. Any change in policy that will be mandated will be approved by him, especially if it affects the relationship of the pastor to the school. Often these policies are recommended by school boards whose meetings the archbishop rarely attends, although he usually controls who is appointed to the board.

One of the most important positions filled by an archbishop is that of superintendent of schools. He needs to find an experienced, hardworking but diplomatic person whose vision of Catholic schools is similar to his. The superintendent is the key person for the archbishop in working with the archdiocesan board of education, pastors, and principals.

The superintendent of schools often comes to the archbishop for help and advice in dealing with pastors, especially if the superintendent is not a priest. The archbishop knows the priests better than the superintendent, and the archbishop's power of persuasion is greater. "If I have a principal problem, I handle it right here," explains the Atlanta superintendent of schools, who is a religious woman.

But if it is a pastor problem, I take it to him because I do not want to get caught in the middle between him and one of his priests. He will ask me some hard questions, and he will say, "I will talk to Father for you." I have had many things cured there—in one instance, the removal of a pastor.

Finally, the archbishop can support Catholic education by his presence at liturgies, graduations, workshops, and conferences. Archdiocesan educators will invite him to speak at important meetings of teachers, catechists, and parents. Articulating a vision of Catholic education in homilies and speeches is seen as part of the teaching role for the archbishop. Simply thanking and encouraging teachers in their work is also important.

Catholic Social Services

The Catholic church runs innumerable social service programs for the poor, sick, hungry, homeless, handicapped, emotionally disturbed, unemployed, teenage runaways, unwed mothers, battered women, abused children, refugees, alcoholics, drug addicts, prisoners, victims of AIDS, and others in need. The variety of programs is extraordinary. Some programs occur in large institutions like hospitals, nursing homes, orphanages, and low-cost housing units. Others are run out of neighborhood centers, shelters, foster homes, group residences, day care centers, and parishes. Some programs give emergency assistance at a time of crisis, others attempt long-term solutions to problems through counseling, education, and preventive services.

When added together the Catholic church is the biggest nongovernmental provider of social services in the United States. In 1987, the 646 Catholic hospitals treated over 40 million patients.[17] In 1986, Catholic Charities agencies provided services to 8.7 million individuals including 2.6 million families. The largest number of people (5.2 million individuals and 1.4 million families) received emergency and food services. Counseling was provided to over 700,000 individuals and 300,000 families. Over 240,000 individuals and 90,000 families received refugee resettlement and immigration services. Over 100,000 individuals and 50,000 families were helped by pregnancy services, and almost 4,000 adoptions were processed. Support services (day care, respite care, home health care, homemaker services) were provided to over 600,000 individuals and over 200,000 families. The agencies provided housing services to over 180,000 individuals and 119,000 families. Out-of-home care services were provided for 182,000 individuals (of whom almost 150,000 were children) and almost 120,000 families.[18]

Some of these programs are run by professionals, others by volunteers, and most by a mix of the two. Of the over 170,000 individuals providing services in Catholic Charities agencies, 79 percent are volunteers and 15 percent are paid staff. Over half the volunteers have some specialized training. Of the paid staff, 60 percent are professional, 12 percent are managerial, and 19 percent are clerical and support staff.[19] Professional expertise is required for refugee resettlement, health care, marriage counseling, psychological counseling, and therapy. Often these programs and their staffs are certified by the state or professional associations. "We insist that every Catholic service in the diocese be licensed even though state law exempts them," says the director of Catholic Charities in St. Louis. "If they can't qualify for a license, they ought to be out of business, because it's minimum standards." Certification helps ensure the archbishop and outside funding sources that the programs are being run on a professional basis.

Part-time volunteers also help in numerous programs and are especially active in soup kitchens, shelters, day care, the St. Vincent de Paul Society, various youth programs, shut-ins visitation, crisis centers, and hotlines. Sometimes professionals volunteer their time as in Washington where two hundred doctors and dentists donated their services to the homeless. Renew and other programs since Vatican II have stimulated numerous parishioners to get involved as volunteers in various social ministries. Providing training for these volunteers is an important function of the professional staff. A few volunteers end up working full time, as in St. Louis where a woman volunteer runs a shelter for the homeless.

"One of our roles in Catholic Charities is to provide opportunities for people to serve," explains the St. Louis director. The volunteers are seen, not simply as free workers, but also as people to be influenced. In Baltimore, the director of Catholic Charities found that preaching to parish groups about social justice "bored people to death." Instead, he set up a program for parishes that involves close to three thousand volunteers who prepare and serve one meal a month in their food program. These volunteers are primarily from the suburbs "where they don't come into contact with the poor on a regular basis," he says. "They get to see who they are. They are not evil ogres; they are human beings. They have dignity like everybody else. It gives an understanding of what social justice and social policy is all about in this country."

More than any other church organization, Catholic social services must quickly respond to environmental factors. The programs emphasized in different archdioceses vary, and they also vary over time in a single archdiocese depending on community needs and the funds available. The need for orphanages, for example, has declined with the number of orphans and the rise of alternative programs. At the same time, increased numbers of elderly have called forth a response. "When I first came in, a lot of money went to child care," recalls the director of Catholic Social Services in Philadelphia, "that was reduced each year to more and more services to the elderly."

In 1970, the San Francisco Charities programs were primarily counseling and child welfare. "Now those components represent less than 15 percent of our activity," reports the director. "There was major growth in parish social ministry, aging services, community organizing, immigration services, housing development, prison visitors, and emergency programs like food programs."

Taking care of the immediate needs of the poor, hungry, and homeless has always been a concern of the church. When the government took responsibility for these needs during the New Deal and Great Society, Catholic Charities emphasized professional programs for counseling and child welfare. These programs attempted to go beyond emergency help and tried to provide long-term solutions through counseling, therapy, and training.

But as a result of the Reagan administration budget cuts, "We are seeing increasing numbers of people knocking at our door for alms, for financial help," reports the Hartford director of

Catholic Charities. "We are opening shelters, soup kitchens, and we are back to the kinds of things we did before the revolution of the Roosevelt administration." In Philadelphia, a Catholic shelter was opened for bag ladies. "Then women [in psychiatric hospitals] were deinstitutionalized [by the state]," reports the director of Catholic Social Services. "Then we got battered women and children who didn't have anywhere to go."

Besides social service programs, the church has also started or supported advocacy programs aimed at changing unjust social structures through education, community organizing, and lobbying. "It is not enough to take Mrs. Jones and her three kids out knocking on doors trying to find her an apartment," explains the director of Catholic Charities in Hartford. "Housing is a major problem and needs legislative attention."

Sometimes these advocacy groups are parish-based community groups. Some are coordinated out of constituency-oriented offices like an office for black or Hispanic Catholics. Sometimes they are centered in a peace and justice commission whose aim might be "consciousness raising" among the public, especially among Catholics. These programs can be very controversial because they challenge the political and economic status quo. In Mobile, when Catholic Charities "tried to do civil rights work directly, openly, there was a direct effect on fundraising," recalls the director.

As a result, advocacy agencies are usually kept separate from service agencies like Catholic Charities, lest they endanger the funding of traditional programs. "Charities offices do a lot of begging," explains the San Antonio director. "You can't make people mad and get their money. We're better off separate. If the social justice people raise hell, that's tough. Be mad at them, don't be mad at us." At the same time, the two often work informally together, with the service agencies providing programs for those being represented by the advocacy groups.

When the social programs of an archdiocese are all added together, they often make the church the largest provider of social services in the state, second only to the state government itself. In Chicago, Catholic Charities has 192 services, an $80 million budget, and about 3,200 employees. If the spending of independent Catholic agencies were included, the figure would be higher. The New York director of Catholic Charities estimates that total spending on Catholic social services in the archdiocese exceeds $1 billion a year, $600 million of which would be in hospitals.

The archbishop is ultimately responsible for the social services done by the archdiocese. As with the schools, his primary concern is over governance, finances, and Catholicity. He is also concerned about how the programs fit into the overall priorities of the archdiocese.

Governance

Catholic social services are organized and governed in a variety of ways. Some programs, like hospitals, are separately incorporated with their own boards of directors. In the past, a majority of the board members and the administrators would be religious, but today they are often lay. These independent boards (which may or may not include the archbishop or his representative) set policy, hire personnel, and are legally and financially responsible for the program.

Some archdioceses prefer independent organizations for which they are not legally or financially responsible. Even a program started by an archdiocese might be spun off as an independent entity. In Miami, Catholic Charities started a program for runaway teenagers. "We found that the exposure to liability in that program is so great," explains a Miami official, "that we separated the program from our services. We're now running it independently." On the other hand, if they are Catholic organizations, in the public mind they are often identified with the archdiocese for good or ill.

If an independent organization is self-funding and avoids controversy, the archbishop will usually leave it alone. Although he lacks legal authority over separately incorporated organizations, if they want archdiocesan money or his support in getting outside funding, he can set conditions. For example, in Philadelphia a Hungarian home for the aged was told it would have to accept any Catholics, not just Hungarians, if it received archdiocesan money.

Likewise, in Hartford, the archbishop sent the director of Catholic Charities as a "consultant" to an institution that suddenly ran a $160,000 deficit after having balanced budgets for years. "They view us as intruders giving them advice that they don't necessarily want, like all wages have to be frozen," explains the director of Catholic Charities. "We are not trying to take them over. We try to be as diplomatic as possible. Nobody wants to see them go under, but nobody wants the diocese to suffer a major embarrassment either because of significant indebtedness or poor management or whatever it might be."

There are also social programs under the direct legal control of the archbishop. The boards of directors of these organizations would be advisory to the archbishop, who would appoint their members. They would make recommendations on policy, finances, and personnel, but he would have the final say. The budget of these programs would be reviewed as part of the archdiocesan budgetary process. New programs would need the archbishop's approval, especially if they cost more money. The top administrators would be chosen or approved by him or his representative.

During the 1960s and 1970s there was a tremendous growth in the number and size of social service programs. Greater resources and increased demands from the environment stimulated diversification of services and expansion to new clientele, as would be normal in any organization.[20] Some agencies, especially those that were self-financed, operated without much archdiocesan supervision of their work and finances. As the number and size of these organizations grew, archbishops began to worry about controlling these complex multimillion dollar operations that seemed to be off doing their own thing. They also feared that these organizations were losing their

Catholic identity. When government cutbacks forced these agencies to seek more and more archdiocesan money, archbishops became concerned about controlling costs, eliminating duplication, and coordinating services.

When the directors of these programs reported directly to the archbishop, he rarely had time to supervise them. Today, many archbishops have vicars or secretaries for social services to coordinate and supervise all of the social service programs of the archdiocese. Often (as in St. Paul) these secretaries are also the directors of Catholic Charities, usually the largest archdiocesan social service agency.

Catholic Charities often acts as an umbrella for a variety of archdiocesan organizations and programs. The staff of Catholic Charities might be organized by geographical regions (e.g., different counties or vicariates) or it might be organized by services (to children, to elderly, to homeless, to parishes, etc.). It might also include administrative staff, such as a business manager and grants writer.

"The desire of the archbishop," explains one director of Catholic Charities, "is to streamline the human services network of the diocese so that there is a cleaner chain of command and greater accountability and better coordination of services." It is usually through the budgetary process that the archbishop or his delegate asserts control. Thus, if an organization wants money, the archbishop requires them to report their activities and finances to his vicar. Even if an agency is legally independent, its desire for archdiocesan funds will often make it conform.

Besides financial problems, complaints can also bring an organization to the attention of the archbishop. Complaints may come from pastors, donors, employees, or clients of the agency. If the complaints are serious and well founded, he acts on them personally or through his administrators if the organization is under his control. If it is an independent agency, he will try persuasion. If he does not succeed, he may distance the archdiocese from any legal or financial responsibility for the organization.

Finances

Catholic social services is a multimillion dollar operation in all but the smallest dioceses. Across the country, the total income to Catholic Charities agencies (which do not include all Catholic social services) was over $600 million in 1986. The largest amount, 45 percent, comes from government fees and grants. This is followed by church sources (20 percent), program service fees (17 percent), and United Way (10 percent). Of the church money, less than half comes from diocesan grants or the Catholic Charities appeal.[21]

In archdioceses, the pattern is similar. For example, the St. Paul Catholic Charities gets only $800,000 of its $10 million budget from the archdiocese. In Philadelphia, the Catholic Charities drive raises about $6 million from the parishes and United Way provides another $2 million. With third party payers and government contracts, this is parlayed into about $75 million. A few Catholic Charities are almost totally dependent on the archdiocese for funds. The Louisville Catholic Charities, for example, gets 90 percent of its $1 million budget from the church.

Most organizations do some fund-raising. The Catholic Charities in St. Paul raises an additional $350,000 through a membership campaign. Certain programs, like those dealing with children, raise money more easily than others. Food and clothing drives can also receive popular support. If a program has a popular cause and a charismatic leader, like Covenant House in New York and Boys Town in Omaha, fund-raising is easier.

Some programs (hospitals, nursing homes, counseling centers, adoption agencies) receive some money in fees from the beneficiary, his insurance company, Medicare, or Medicaid. Fees for people without insurance are usually based on the person's income. But "there are always people who fall through the cracks," explains the director of Catholic Charities in New York. "If an illegal alien gets sick and goes to the hospital, he has no money or insurance. He can't apply for Medicaid; the government would toss him out of the country. So there is always a certain amount of free care or charity care for the poor."

Some programs can get government grants or contracts. Often a government will fund the program because it realizes that the church can do the program more cheaply and efficiently, with less politics. Money for resettling refugees comes from the federal government. "The bishop called me in April of 1975 and said, 'Vietnam has fallen. How many refugees can we take?' " recalls the Mobile director of Catholic Charities. "I agreed to 100. We got 3,200."

A number of states purchase services from Catholic Charities for delinquent or handicapped children. "Primarily we get from the state government monies for residential care of children— dependent, neglected, delinquent, abused children," explains the St. Louis director of Catholic Charities. "These are youngsters that the local juvenile court has taken into custody away from their parents." Similarly, after a court case stopped Louisiana from exporting mentally retarded children for treatment in Texas, the state asked Catholic Charities to start a program for them. Also in New Orleans, "We use about fifty of our schools for the federal program of giving hot lunches to the elderly in the neighborhood," reports Archbishop Hannan. "The federal government has asked us to begin a program of feeding 8,000 elderly in their homes."

Low-interest government loans have also financed numerous nursing homes and homes for the aged. Low-cost housing run by the church agencies is also financed through low-interest loans from the U.S. Department of Housing and Urban Development (HUD). In New Orleans the mayor told the archbishop that the city was not going to do anything about housing and that he wanted the archdiocese to take responsibility for it. Similarly, three cities near Seattle asked the archdiocese to run low-income housing for the elderly, "because we understand that you will be here and you won't disappear," they told the director. In New Haven senior citizens asked the archdiocesan office of urban affairs to take over the nutrition project for the elderly because it had been politicized by city politicians.

Sometimes Catholic Charities benefits from government programs because no one else wants them. "We got the first Head Start programs, the first Neighborhood Youth Corps programs going in Alabama," recalls the director of Catholic Charities in Mobile. "We ran these programs when nobody else would touch them." But in other places, Catholic Charities might have to compete with other providers for the funds.

United Way also funds some social programs run by the church, especially programs for children, elderly, and families in need. The level of cooperation with Catholic social services varies from community to community. The more Catholic the area and the more professional the Catholic Charities, the more likely it is to get major funding from United Way. In Indianapolis, the archbishop gives a matching corporate contribution to United Way for contributions from archdiocesan employees. Sometimes, as in Baltimore and Los Angeles, the archdiocese agrees to not have a separate Catholic Charities fund drive when it participates in United Way. Sometimes this money goes to Catholic Charities as a block grant (as in Baltimore), in other cities each program must apply individually.

The type of programs funded varies from area to area because of local needs and the preferences of the people in charge of the local United Way. For example, Catholic Charities in Indianapolis and Omaha could not get United Way funding for family counseling, whereas in Hartford, Catholic Family Services gets about half its money from the sixteen United Ways in the archdiocese.

Some United Ways are having nonprofits bid against each other. For example, a United Way will say, "We have $100,000 for counseling. Who will provide the most hours of counseling?" The competition for United Way money is getting fierce. "Organizations that have traditionally been funded by government sources," explains the director of Catholic Charities in Hartford, "are beating down the doors to get into United Way. But the fund drive is barely adequate to keep pace with inflation for existing members." Sometimes the United Way avoids controversy and supports traditional programs like Boy Scouts, Girl Scouts, and recreational programs.

Some archdioceses (like St. Louis) have made it clear that if Planned Parenthood gets funding from United Way, they will withdraw from the program. In St. Paul, the archdiocese does not request much United Way money for its unwed mother program because, "if the United Way supports that too much, then the abortion people will want their share," explains the director of Catholic Charities. The Miami archdiocese has no such problem. "They are very receptive to our needs," explains one church official. "The Catholic church has a strong voice in Dade County."

In Philadelphia, United Way and the archdiocese had an agreement that it would not fund anything in conflict with the teaching of the church. "Some feminist-abortion groups screamed that we were controlling United Way," recalls Cardinal Krol. They pushed United Way to adopt "optional giving" whereby the donor can indicate what institution he wants his money to go to.

We wrote to United Way that we did not want the change. But they pressured, so we yielded. The fact of the matter is that the optional funding has benefited no one as much as the Catholics. So they had the nerve to come and ask whether we would want to back away from it.

We said, "Look, this was not part of our agreement. You proposed it, we objected. Finally, for your sake, we agreed. Now you are asking us to damage ourselves by pulling away. We will not do it."

Programs funded by the archdiocese are often programs that no one else will fund. For example, many residents oppose shelters or soup kitchens because they encourage "undesirables" to stay in their neighborhoods. Politicians will back away from such opposition. In addition, advocacy programs that challenge the political and economic status quo are not popular. In Seattle, the Hispanic Legal Action office is funded with money raised by the archbishop.

Sometimes an archdiocese will temporarily finance a program until it gets started and can find other funding. For example, Catholic Charities in St. Louis opened a halfway house for alcoholic women with archdiocesan money in the hope that others would pick up the funding. The San Francisco Catholic Charities opened a shelter for homeless youths. "Public funding wouldn't touch it, they wanted nothing to do with these kids," explains the director. "We ran it for two years on a nickel and a dime. This was a church basement operation, yet every night it sheltered twenty kids who, if they weren't with us, were going to be out in the street turning tricks." After proving that the program could work, they got the state government to fund it. "If we can prove the effectiveness of a program, we get the public sector to buy it," he says. "Then we get to move our limited charity dollars over to whatever the next thing is that needs doing."

An archdiocese will also fund programs with a special Catholic character. In St. Paul, the annual appeal funded a program for unwed mothers, a social justice program, and the divorced and separated center. It is difficult to get nonchurch money to finance parish outreach programs. Offices for black Catholics, Hispanics, and other ethnic groups are usually funded by the archdiocese because they deal with both social and religious concerns. In Newark, the archdiocese funds religious education programs for the handicapped done by Catholic Community Services. Likewise, in Louisville, church funding supported a parish outreach program and a pastoral ministry to the sick and elderly.

Finances determine to some extent what social services are provided by the church. If outside funding can be found for a program, the archbishop will rarely object to it unless he fears being stuck with the program when the funding ceases. Some people complain that some agencies will do programs that can get funded rather than programs that meet needs. One director described an agency that had been providing elderly care for fifteen years. When funding for elderly care was cut, "they started looking around" and found the state was willing to fund a program for latch-key children. "Because they need money to survive, they will go where the money is," he says.

But expensive programs without outside funding are a problem. A number of Catholic Charities have de-emphasized one-on-one counseling. "You just can't afford to do that," explains the St. Paul director. "It is too expensive." On the other hand, some archdioceses, like Baltimore, have been able to keep their counseling programs because of fees and funding through United Way. St. Louis recently opened a family counseling center in an affluent section of the archdiocese that is financed by the local parishes.

Some archdioceses had to admit that they could not afford to provide adequate services to the handicapped. San Antonio Catholic Charities, after funding a one-person office for the disabled for a few years, concluded that an office without supporting staff was "just a front." The position was transferred to the religious education office so it could hire a specialist on religious education of the handicapped. "It is all we can do," explains the director of Catholic Charities. "There are a lot of city, state, and county programs for the handicapped." Programs requiring large professional staffs require money from government and other sources.

Money from government sources is never certain. "Government ideas change," explains Bishop Martin Lohmuller, vicar general of Philadelphia. "If the government decides that it is going to provide these services directly instead of purchasing them from voluntary agencies, then we are just out of business." Most Catholic Charities were hurt by Reagan administration cutbacks. "We have experienced $2 to $3 million in cuts since 1982," reports the director of Catholic Charities in New

Orleans. "Before 1982, 90 percent of our money was from the government and about 8 percent from United Way. Now we are running about 70 to 80 percent government, 8 percent United Way, and the rest of the money we raise ourselves."

A reduction in government funding can be devastating for individual programs. The Connecticut department of mental health gave the Hartford Catholic Charities a grant for services to Hispanics. "They cut the grant," reports the director, "we cut the service." Sometimes an archdiocese can keep a program going temporarily. "If we see a deficit and we know six months from now there is going to be another source of revenue," says the Hartford director of Charities, "then we scramble like the dickens to keep that program alive for six months until the other flow starts. But if we look down the pike and don't see anything coming, that program goes."

When the state told the Newark director of Catholic Community Services that it was no longer going to fully fund a residential program for eighteen deinstitutionalized persons, she told them she would close it. "They didn't believe I was going to give up $100,000," she recalls. But keeping the program would require taking $15,000 to $20,000 from other programs that she felt had a higher priority. "We closed the program. The end result was they gave me almost as much money to do other kinds of things and the people have been put into boarding houses."

Similarly in New York, "We have closed six or seven child care centers since the 1970s," says the director of Catholic Charities.

They are just losing money and they are not going to be able to recoup. You can cut staff, but if you cut staff to the point where you are not providing quality service, it doesn't make sense. There are 10,000 children under care today. Fifteen years ago, we had 50,000.

Philadelphia had the same experience where, because of federal block grants to the state, "the money allocated for child care is becoming more limited," reports the director of Catholic Social

Services. Despite the needs of battered and abused children, "we closed a lot of specialized programs. Anything that required psychiatric supervision and therapy. They are costly services. I am not going to cut the quality of service, so we end up cutting the number that are served."

Outside funding can also mean outside control. The administrator of Catholic Charities in Chicago describes the typical pattern in dealing with state funding:

> They always come in very good the first year, because nobody else has done it and we are willing to take it on. The third year, the government is starting to get finicky with a lot of red tape about it. Then the fifth year, the government wants to run it themselves.

The Chicago Catholic Charities had serious disagreements with the state department of family and children services. "They are underfunded, so they would do a more shallow intervention with children than we would want to do," explains the administrator of Catholic Charities. And "we have a family orientation. Some of our programs return 90 percent of the kids to their families within eighteen months. The state is much more towards severing parents' rights. Unfortunately, it often comes through as a power struggle or a financial struggle, but the root of the thing has been a philosophical struggle."

In New York there was conflict between the city and the archdiocese over Executive Order 50, which prohibited funding to organizations discriminating against homosexuals. "We are not concerned about how many homosexuals are in the program," explained Bishop O'Keefe, then vicar general. "We never ask anybody. The question is, who is going to run these agencies?" Similarly, there have been court challenges to giving preference to Catholic parents in the adoption of Catholic children.

Catholicity

Recently many archbishops have become concerned about the Catholic character of the social services provided by their archdioceses. All archbishops would agree that Catholic agencies should not be involved in activities contrary to church teaching. In a counseling center, for example, Catholic identity requires "that nobody who works there will counsel children in a way that would violate Catholic teaching," explained Bishop O'Keefe. "You don't have to believe, but you can't send kids to an abortion mill." Likewise, in Hartford, the Catholic Charities must check with the archbishop before allowing anyone other than a validly married Catholic couple to adopt a Catholic child.

Some social programs downplayed their religious character or their church connections in order to get outside money. "Because 80 percent of our dollars came from government funding," explains the director of Catholic Community Services in Newark, "people became intimidated or felt that we had an obligation to somehow deny our church orientation. I absolutely disagree. We help people on a nonsectarian basis, we hire people on a nonsectarian basis, but we are a church organization."

Some intimidation can come from government funding sources. One archbishop was asked to sign a statement that his religious faith had nothing to do with the social services provided by the archdiocese. He was also asked to change the name of the St. Vincent de Paul Society to Mr. Vincent de Paul. He refused.

Some programs can remain very professional but lose their Catholic character when the religious staff is replaced by a lay personnel, as occurred in the children's institutions in St. Louis. "There are no religious in them, and they have forgotten about teaching religion," complains the director of Catholic Charities, who recently got the school office to set up a religious education program for these institutions.

Some Catholic social service programs have large numbers of non-Catholic employees (for example, one third of the Catholic Charities employees in Chicago). Questions are being raised about hiring personnel solely on their professional competence without considering their religion and values. For example, in Mobile, when the Catholic Charities board was considering candidates for a counseling position, the Episcopalian chairman of the board asked if they were Christians. Some professionals "would never dream of asking that question of an employee," complains Archbishop Lipscomb. "They tell you, 'That's unprofessional.' Well, it is also un-Catholic to do it the other way, and we are first *Catholic* social services."

Most archbishops support running social service programs under Catholic auspices because they believe that helping people in need is required by the gospel. They also recognize that social programs can present a good image of the church to the community. When Archbishop Hurley arrived in Anchorage, Catholic social services was a one-nun operation. "We were asked to take over the state care of the handicapped because that had failed twice," he recalls. "I was very eager because the church needs to be out in the public as part of the community serving the community. Having shown that we could do it, we were the targets for 'Could you do more if you had the money?' I kept saying yes."

But some talk of only doing programs that are "Catholic," although this is never clearly defined. For some it appears to mean programs that flow from the pro-life concerns of the bishops, while for others it means programs that respond to the preferential option for the poor. Sometimes it means programs that are aimed at the parishes. But it rarely would mean that the beneficiaries are only Catholic. In Chicago, for example, Catholic Charities estimates that 65 to 75 percent of its caseload is non-Catholic.

For many involved in social services, their Catholic character comes more from motivation and spirituality than from the mechanics of the programs. As a result, indoctrination and formation of new employees becomes important, as do opportunities to articulate and celebrate shared Christian values. This becomes particularly important when staffs become predominantly lay and when there are large turnovers in personnel.

At the same time they are concerned about the Catholic character of these programs, many archbishops also see social services as an area of ecumenical cooperation. It is not unusual for non-Catholics to be involved with Catholic Charities. The chairman of the board in Mobile is an Episcopalian, as is the director of Catholic Charities in San Francisco. Cooperation also occurs with Protestant and Jewish social service agencies. In Los Angeles, one shelter for the homeless operates as a partnership of twelve different organizations. "The county provided two wings of a hospital; the state and United Way provided some money," explains the director of Catholic Charities. "The southern California ecumenical council provides volunteers, the Disciples of Christ provides transportation, Travelers Aid and Lutheran Social Services provide intake, Jewish Family Services provides job development, and we provide fiscal management and staffing."

Serving the Parishes

Many Catholic social services programs are run independently without any relation to other archdiocesan programs, including the parishes. This is especially true of agencies and institutions run by professionals who get most of their money from fees, contracts, and grants so that they have little financial dependence on the archdiocese. In many archdioceses, these agencies are being challenged and asked what they do for the parishes, especially when they seek archdiocesan money.

Pastors often complain that although millions of dollars are being spent on social services, the programs never help them. "We don't need institutional programs," pastors told the director of Catholic Charities in New Orleans. "We don't know what to do with women and children when they appear at the rectory at night with no place to go." The director responded by installing a 24-hour hotline to meet their needs. "We take the person off the hands of the priest that night and work out some solution the next day."

Many Charities directors are responding to complaints from pastors by stressing parish outreach in their programs. In Newark, a parish outreach coordinator, whom pastors could call for information and referrals, was hired for each county. In addition, social concerns coordinators were hired who "spend 90 percent of their time out in the parishes talking to social concerns groups, talking to deaneries, and the like."

The National Conference of Catholic Charities also developed a parish-outreach program.[22] "It does an assessment of the parish, what the strengths and weaknesses are, what are their resources, and what can you do to match these things," explains the St. Paul director who was the president of the National Conference of Catholic Charities. "It works wonderfully well, then they change the pastor. You get some top-down SOB in there who throws it all out. It is frustrating as hell."

Parish outreach involves the education and training of volunteers in parish social concerns committees, St. Vincent de Paul societies, or other groups attempting to help people in need. Outreach coordinators connect these parish groups with archdiocesan agencies that can help them or whom they can help. In New York, for example, the department of aging in Catholic Charities is "working with over 140 parishes in their senior citizens program," says the director. "It is a whole range of programs—nutritional, recreational, transport services."

In addition, many archdioceses, rather than having all of their staffs "downtown," have opened offices in parishes. In Philadelphia, Catholic Social Services pays the salaries of social workers in inner-city parishes. Baltimore has a counseling program based in about sixty parishes that operates mostly in the evening for family counseling.

Archbishop

The archbishop is ultimately responsible for archdiocesan social services, but he usually has no expertise in the area. One Catholic Charities director recalls a conversation he had with an archbishop on the relation between bishops and Catholic Charities. The archbishop said,

The trouble is, a bishop is supposed to be a [expletive deleted] know-it-all. We all went to Catholic schools, we understand that. We all went to Catholic seminaries, and we all understand that. Most of us have worked in tribunals, and we understand that.

Most of us have never been inside Catholic Charities. We do not know anything about that, so we are suspicious of it, we are afraid of it, we want to leave it alone, we are benign. If we are not benign, we want to take it over and control it.

Few archbishops (Cooke, Mahony, Stafford) have experience in Catholic social services. A few archbishops, like Archbishop Hannan of New Orleans, are very active in promoting social services. But in most archdioceses, the archbishop pays little attention to the social service programs except when they want money or when they get into controversy. If the archbishop has a secretary for social services or a director of Catholic Charities whom he trusts and a board that does its work responsibly, he will usually let them do what they think best.

The St. Paul director of Catholic Charities, who has the confidence of his archbishop, explains the kinds of things he would take to the archbishop:

Anything that is controversial, we check with him, like the service to gays and lesbians. Or where we need his clout for financial backing. We remodeled the children's home for $3 million. He gave a token $75,000, then we said to the foundations that the diocese is doing what it can.

The day-to-day operation, he doesn't get involved in. He doesn't want to, and he doesn't need to. We alert him to potential PR problems. Some of the stuff we get into can be very controversial in the diocese, just so he is aware of it.

In most archdioceses, if social services wants to start a major new program, it will have to get the archbishop's approval. Frequently he will ask if anyone else is doing it. "We don't want to duplicate services," explains Archbishop Flores of San Antonio. "The first thing we ask is, 'Is anyone else doing it? Do we need to get involved? Can we afford to get involved because we are involved in other things?' " The archbishop's permission will also be needed for borrowing money.

Some archbishops, like Archbishop Hannan, are real activists in pushing and developing social service programs. Because the mayor of New Orleans told him that the city was going to do nothing about low-income housing, Archbishop Hannan put the archdiocese heavily into housing, including 6,000 apartments for elderly. In addition, the archdiocese was asked to take over six low-income housing projects that were being poorly run by the local housing authority. On the other hand, Cardinal Krol in Philadelphia opposed involvement in low-income housing lest the church end up looking like a slum landlord.

Other archbishops, after taking office, have changed the directions of social service programs in their archdioceses. For example, Cardinal Hickey found that Catholic Charities was doing little for the blacks in Washington, DC. Its adoption service had not even sponsored any black babies. In addition, the professionals running the agency were more interested in counseling services than in soup kitchens and shelters. He, on the other hand, felt the program should serve the poorest of the poor.

Some archbishops are also important spokesmen on social issues. When American Motors announced the closing of a Milwaukee plant with 6,000 workers, the archdiocesan social concerns delegate came to the archbishop. "He asked, 'Would you be willing to make a statement with the governor asking American Motors to sit down with the employees?' " recalls Archbishop Weakland. "I said, 'Great idea.' Then he does the rest of the work and I get in front of the cameras and get all the praise." Similarly, in New York, Cardinal O'Connor called for a moratorium on the conversion of single-occupancy hotels to condominiums.

Conclusion

Catholic education and Catholic social services are two of the largest programs in an archdiocese. As large complex organizations, they require sophisticated management of their finances and programs. In simpler days, the archbishop might have gotten involved in the direct supervision of programs, but today he is usually forced to act through a superintendent of schools, a director of religious education, or a director of Catholic Charities who is more knowledgeable and experienced than he is. As a result, if these people do not have his trust, they will soon be replaced.

Nevertheless, the archbishop would become involved in approving any major change in policy affecting these programs, especially programs that would require archdiocesan funds or directly impact on pastors or other important constituencies. Anything that would cause a major controversy, the archbishop wants to know about ahead of time. No archbishop wants to learn about something for the first time from the newspaper.

The control mechanism most frequently used by the archbishop in overseeing archdiocesan programs is the budgetary process. At budget time, agency directors must report on their programs and answer questions. Here the archbishop can set priorities by favoring one program with funds rather than another. But in the normal course of events, the changes are incremental rather than drastic.

Many of the factors examined in this chapter when discussing education and social services are also important when examining other archdiocesan programs. The issues of governance, finances, and Catholicity are important for every program. In addition, the role of middle managers at the cabinet level is becoming common for other areas besides education and Catholic social services. Finally, in all areas of church governance, consultation and conflict avoidance are important.

Not surprisingly, the Catholicity of archdiocesan programs is a major concern of archbishops and their top staff. A secular social service or educational program, while good in itself, is not enough. The programs must be in keeping with the teachings of the church and reflect gospel values. The concern for orthodoxy has been reinforced by Rome in its dealings with the American hierarchy, as will be seen in the next chapter.

8. Beyond the Archdiocese

> The hardest part of my job is to be sandwiched between Roman orders and my people and priests' hopes and ideals.
>
> ————ARCHBISHOP WEAKLAND

> I say no to altar girls. Oh God, what troubles I get into by saying no to altar girls.
>
> ————ARCHBISHOP LIPSCOMB

A bishop's primary concern is the internal governance of his local church, but what happens in his local church can be affected by church institutions outside his diocese. Decisions made by church organs, especially the Vatican and the National Conference of Catholic Bishops, can sometimes be binding on the bishop.

Bishops, as successors of the apostles, are also responsible for the welfare of the whole church, not just their dioceses. By their participation in various church organs (ecumenical councils, Roman synods, national conferences, Vatican congregations), bishops help in the governance of the entire church.[1] Cardinals and archbishops exercise this responsibility to a greater extent than other bishops. As a result, archbishops are both governors and governed.

Province Metropolitan

What makes an archbishop different from a bishop is that he is a metropolitan, the head of an ecclesiastical province that contains his archdiocese and one or more dioceses. More than half of the thirty-one provinces in the United States have boundaries coextensive with those of a single state (Alaska, Florida, Illinois, Indiana, Iowa, Kansas, Louisiana, Michigan, Missouri, Nebraska, New Jersey, New York, Ohio, Pennsylvania, Texas, Washington, and Wisconsin). Only California has more than one province (part of Maryland is in the province of Washington, DC). The remaining provinces contain more than one state.

The metropolitan has practically no power over the diocesan bishops in his province who are called suffragans. He is involved primarily in ceremonial functions such as attending the celebration of anniversaries or the installations and burials of bishops in his province. "You go over and show the archbishop's flag on those occasions when they have special events and ceremonies," explains Archbishop Lipscomb of Mobile whose province includes Alabama and Mississippi.

If a problem arises in a diocese in his province, the archbishop may get involved. Priests of the diocese might complain to him, or he might be approached by the pro-nuncio for information. He might also take the initiative and bring things to the attention of the pro-nuncio. "It is up to me to inform the pro-nuncio if a bishop is getting ill," says Archbishop Hannan of New Orleans. "I always talk to the bishop first and tell him what I am going to do because you have to get his cooperation." But if the bishop does not want to resign or take the archbishop's advice, there is nothing the metropolitan can do about it.

Archbishop Hannan as metropolitan of Louisiana was very active behind the scenes in Lafayette, LA, where a priest admitted to sexually abusing thirty-five children and was sentenced to twenty years in jail. Fourteen families sued the diocese, whose insurance companies eventually paid them an undisclosed sum that was estimated to be as high as $5 or $10 million. It became impossible for the local bishop to deal with this crisis, because he had transferred the priest to his current parish after knowing of his involvement in an earlier incident. The bishop, who had sent the priest to a psychiatrist, admitted making a mistake in not recognizing the depth of the priest's illness.

Archbishop Hannan became involved because the Vatican

wanted to avoid the publicity that would surround a criminal trial. "My job was to see that the right steps were taken to make sure that there wasn't any trial," says Archbishop Hannan. He visited the priest in jail and convinced him to accept a plea bargain.

In addition, after the diocese settled with the parents, the insurance companies began arguing about who should pay what. The crimes occurred over a number of years when different companies were insuring the diocese. Each company wanted someone else to pay. One source says that Archbishop Hannan brought representatives of the insurance companies together in his office and told them they were not leaving until they agreed on a settlement. They settled.

A metropolitan can also come to the defense of his suffragan bishops. Archbishop Borders of Baltimore, whose province includes Virginia, objected to Rome's proposal for a visitation or investigation of the diocese of Richmond by a Vatican official. He argued that if a visitation was necessary, it should be done by an American bishop. Ultimately it was done by Archbishop May of St. Louis.

The bishops of a province meet under the chairmanship of the archbishop to draw up the provincial list of episcopal candidates (see chapter 1). The provinces also set up provincial tribunals to review annulments as was called for by the new code of canon law. Some provinces also work on other common projects. But bishops usually work under the auspices of state Catholic conferences, which are composed of all the bishops of one state.

State Catholic Conference

Bishops gather one or more times a year as a state conference usually chaired by the archbishop.[2] As a state conference, they can develop common policies and programs aimed at both religious and public concerns. Normally decisions are made by consensus rather than by vote. The state conference may have a small staff (one to fifteen employees) including a lobbyist who works in the state capital. Additional staff work is often done by committees made up of officials (chancellors, superintendents of schools, directors of Catholic Charities) from the various dioceses in the state. They might also invite outside experts and observers to attend their meetings. As a regular practice, some include representatives from priests' councils at their meetings.

In the religious sphere, a conference might develop common programs and policies on sacramental preparation, faculties, the implementation of canon law, etc. Less confusion and problems exist when these policies are the same for the entire state. For example, if one diocese requires attendance at an extensive marriage preparation program, while its neighbor does not, problems can arise. Some conferences have agreed on a common policy for dealing with holy days that fall on Saturdays or Mondays.

Joint pastoral letters have also been issued by state conferences. The California conference wrote one on AIDS; the Texas conference did one on pastoral care of Hispanic immigrants and another on the sacrament of reconciliation; the Louisiana conference published one on social ministry and another on creationism. After the NCCB pastoral letter on the economy, the Kentucky, Maryland, and West Virginia conferences issued their own pastoral letters on the economies in their states.

Other conferences, such as California and Michigan, developed common services like health and liability insurance or retirement plans. The dioceses of Louisiana join together in running a three-day conference for their new principals each year.

State conferences also focus on public policy concerns. State conference lobbyists represent the bishops before the legislature in twenty-seven state capitals. State laws governing zoning, building codes, bingo, tax exemptions, private education, churches, hospitals, and social agencies can have a direct impact on activities of church organizations. The state of Nebraska, for example, requires every high school to have a vocational program. Catholic college preparatory schools must get a waiver every year from this requirement. State money for Catholic schools (textbooks, busing) or programs run by Catholic social service agencies would also be high on the agenda.

State conferences of bishops have also taken positions on numerous public policy issues that do not directly impinge on church institutions. Often the conferences are applying to the state level positions that have been taken by the National Conference of Catholic Bishops. For example, numerous state conferences have opposed capital punishment and public funding of abortions in their states. Frequently, a conference will make a statement on citizen responsibility prior to an election. Conferences have also taken positions on state legislation dealing with brain death, living wills, surrogate mothers, homosexual bill of rights, public school health clinics, sex education, welfare reform, shelters for the homeless, public housing, the farm crisis, migrant workers, prostitution, criminal justice system, pornography, etc.

Finally, meeting either as a province or a conference allows the bishops to discuss various concerns in an informal way. Some conferences also sponsor spiritual retreats for bishops or even time to relax together. In all of this, the archbishop can play a leadership role in developing consensus among the other bishops. If he prefers to act alone, the state conference will do little. If he opposes an action, the province or state conference is unlikely to act.

NCCB/USCC

All the American bishops meet once or twice a year as the National Conference of Catholic Bishops and the U.S. Catholic Conference (NCCB/USCC) to deal with religious and public issues of common concern. Retired bishops cannot vote, but all other prelates have an equal vote except on financial issues, where only diocesan bishops (and not auxiliaries) can vote. The bishops elect a president and vice-president, who act as conference spokesmen on national and international issues during their three-year terms. These officers are almost always arch-bishops.

When writing its pastoral letters on peace and on economic justice, the NCCB received wide attention in the news media. The bishops have also made public statements on Central America, South Africa, the Middle East, Northern Ireland, the church in Communist countries, racism, capital punishment, health care, abortion, the Equal Rights Amendment, care for the terminally ill, food stamps, Medicaid, education, home-lessness, international debt, immigration, tax reform, labor re-lations, etc.

A great deal of their time, however, is devoted to church issues, like ecumenism, Catholic education, evangelization, family ministry, Hispanic ministry, catechetics, women in the church, liturgy, and sacramental practice. The NCCB, with the approval of the Vatican, can set policy that is binding on all the bishops. Matters that are binding on the bishops require a two-thirds vote.

Before an item is voted on by the bishops, it is normally considered in committee. Sometimes the committees them-selves issue statements rather than bringing the question to the entire body of bishops. The NCCB and USCC have standing committees and ad hoc committees to deal with various con-cerns: budget, liturgy, doctrine, pastoral practice, canon law, farm labor, Hispanics, missions, ecumenism, laity, pro-life, priestly life, priestly formation, vocations, Latin America, per-manent diaconate, women, education, communications, social development, and world peace. Also, an administrative com-mittee draws up the agenda for the conference meetings and makes policy when the conference is not in session. Committee work can be very time consuming when a major document is being prepared, especially for the chairmen.

The committees and leadership of the conference are helped by the bishops' staff based in Washington, DC. The staff is headed by a general secretary and has experts on issues of concern to the bishops: public relations, liturgy, doctrine, church finances, education, priestly life and formation, civil and canon law, domestic and international affairs, etc.

Some archbishops play a larger role in the bishops' conference than others. Officers of the conference, like archbishops May (president) and Pilarczyk (vice-president), play a very active role, as do former presidents of the conference: cardinals Krol and Bernardin and archbishops Quinn and Roach. Archbishop Kelly, as a former general secretary of the conference, is also influential. Others, like Archbishop Weakland and Cardinal O'Connor, have been chairmen of major committees.

On the other hand, some who would have liked to play a larger role in the conference have not been supported by the other bishops. In the past, Cardinal Spellman of New York was kept from having much influence in the conference although he was very influential in Rome under Pius XII. More recently, Cardinal Law of Boston and Archbishop Mahony of Los Angeles were defeated in 1986 when their names were put on the ballot for positions in the conference. Both men were seen as challenging the current direction of the conference. Some also feared that they would be more interested in the views of Vatican officials than in the views of their fellow bishops. The following year, however, Archbishop Mahony was elected chairman of the committee on international affairs.

International Responsibilities

American bishops are involved with issues that affect the Catholic church throughout the world. Individually and through their national conference, they have been supportive of local churches experiencing difficulties in Latin America, Asia, and Eastern Europe. They normally avoid saying anything on a topic affecting these churches without checking with them. For example, they wanted to know what the bishops of South Africa thought about divestiture before they made a statement. They also give financial assistance to poor churches around the world individually or through agencies such as the Catholic Relief Services and the Propagation of the Faith. Bishops have also sent their priests to mission lands.

The American hierarchy frequently interacts with the Holy See, which is responsible for central governance in the church. Those who were bishops during the Second Vatican Council acted, with the pope, as the supreme governing body of the Catholic church. They played an important role at the Council in pushing through the decree on religious liberty. For most of the American bishops, the Council was an educational and spiritual experience that influenced the rest of their years as bishops.

Although councils are extremely rare, the synod of bishops, which advises the pope, meets every three years or when called to Rome by the pope. Four American bishops are usually elected by their peers to attend the synod. In addition, the pope usually appoints two or more Americans. Attending the 1987 Synod on the Laity as elected representatives were Cardinal Bernardin, archbishops Weakland and May, and Bishop Stanley J. Ott. Appointed to the synod were Archbishop Mahony and then-Bishop Bevilacqua.

In the past, other archbishops elected to synods have included Carberry, Dearden, Flores, Krol, Quinn, Roach, Sanchez, Stafford, Whealon, and Wright. Papal appointees have included cardinals Baum, Cooke, Krol, Law, Manning, Szoka, Wright, and archbishops Martin O'Connor, Quinn, and Weakland (when he was an abbot). Cardinal Bernardin has attended almost every synod since 1974 and has been elected by those at the synod to plan future synods as a member of the council on the synod.

Although the synodal meetings are closed, press briefings and leaks reveal some of what goes on. In 1980 at the synod on the family, American bishops were especially concerned about defending their tribunals, which were under attack for granting large numbers of annulments. Archbishop Quinn also came under attack when he gave a speech that was interpreted as calling for a rethinking of the church's prohibition against artificial birth control.[3] At the 1987 synod on the laity, American bishops were joined by bishops from around the world in urging a greater role for women in the church, but their views did not make it into the final document.

American cardinals and a few archbishops serve on Vatican congregations that help govern the whole church.[4] Cardinal William Baum, prefect of the Congregation for Seminaries and Institutes for Study, is the only American cardinal working full time in Rome. He is a member of a number of Vatican congregations, councils, and agencies. In addition, Archbishop Paul C. Marcinkus is involved in administering the Vatican bank and the Vatican state. Archbishop Justin Rigali is president of the Pontifical Ecclesiastical Academy, and Archbishop John P. Foley is president of the Pontifical Council for Social Communications.

Despite the Vatican bank scandal, Archbishop Marcinkus is still one of the most influential Americans in Rome. Cardinal Baum and Archbishop Rigali are also important Americans in Rome. Archbishop Rigali worked closely with the pope on the speeches he gave while visiting the United States in 1987.

Cardinals residing in the United States also serve on Vatican congregations and councils, but their involvement is less than those who work full time in Rome. As mentioned in chapter 1, Cardinal O'Connor of New York is on the Congregation for Bishops and the Council for Social Communications. Cardinal Bernardin of Chicago is on the congregations dealing with liturgy and evangelization and the Council for Christian unity. Cardinal Krol of Philadelphia is on the congregations for clergy and the Oriental churches. He also advises the office of economic affairs. Cardinal Law of Boston and Cardinal Manning of Los Angeles served on the Congregation for Institutes of Consecrated Life. Cardinal Law is also on the Congregation for Evangelization of Peoples. Cardinal Hickey of Washington is on the Congregation for Seminaries and Institutes of Study and the one for canonization of saints.

A few archbishops also serve on congregations: Archbishop O'Meara of Indianapolis is on the Congregation for Evangelization of Peoples; Archbishop Mahony of Los Angeles, on the pontifical councils for justice and peace and for migrants.

The actual work of non-Roman members of the congregations is not great. "They have periodic meetings and you have to prepare for those meetings, but there isn't a lot of ongoing work," says Cardinal Bernardin. Members not residing in Rome usually attend only about one meeting a year. "The one that really requires more," says the cardinal, "is the Council of the Synod, because you have to meet two or three times a year, and you have to prepare for it."

In fact, the American archbishops have devoted more time to ad hoc work for the Holy See than working on permanent Vatican congregations. For example, while an archbishop, Hickey conducted the visitation of the Seattle archdiocese for the Vatican. And as chancellor of the Catholic University of America, he has been prominent in dealing with Rev. Charles Curran, the moral theologian. Cardinal Bernardin, Cardinal O'Connor, and Archbishop Quinn of San Francisco spent countless hours resolving the Seattle controversy, discussed on page 337. Archbishop Quinn also worked tirelessly as chairman of the papal commission on religious life in the United States, of which Archbishop Kelly of Louisville was also a member.

Other bishops spent months visiting seminaries and reporting on their condition. Cardinal Krol has been an advisor to the pope on Vatican finances and has worked raising money for Poland. Cardinal Law is on the papal commission responsible for writing an international catechism. Archbishop Kelly chaired the committee that planned the pope's 1987 visit.

Relations with Rome

But most archbishops' experience with the Vatican is as the governed rather than as participants. When appointed, all bishops take an oath of loyalty to the pope. "I take that very seriously," says Archbishop Kelly. "I also take seriously my responsibilities to the pastoral needs of my people. I am the bishop here. I am not an animated instrument of someone else. But I look to him for example, and he gives forceful example to me by the way he preaches and by his personal holiness. I wish I could be as good as he is."

Some archbishops stress that they are responsible to the pope and not to Vatican officials. "One of the secrets of the Catholic church is how independent the bishop is," says Archbishop Whealon of Hartford. "And he should be, he is a successor of the apostles. He really isn't under Peter's advisors, or Peter's helpers, he is under Peter." In fact, however, when Peter's helpers say they are speaking for the pope, an archbishop has little recourse.

There is a natural and inevitable tension between those concerned about the universal church and those concerned about their local churches. Bishops rarely speak on the record about problems in their relationship with Rome. In his final address as president of the bishops' conference in November 1983, Archbishop Roach of St. Paul spoke of the problem of communications between the United States and Rome. Three years later, in his final address as president, Bishop James Malone of Youngstown spoke of "a growing and dangerous disaffection of elements of the church in the United States from the Holy See." How do Rome and the church in the United States communicate and what issues have been controversial?

Ad Limina Visit

Every five years, the American diocesan bishops make an ad limina visit to Rome where they meet with the pope and various Vatican officials.[5] It is called an ad limina visit from the Latin *ad limina apostolorum* by which the church refers to the tombs of Saints Peter and Paul in Rome that the bishops visit. While this book is being written, the bishops are making their 1988 visit.

Before the visit, each bishop prepares for the Congregation for Bishops a quinquennial report describing in detail the state of his diocese. This report is divided into thirteen sections asking for information on (1) the pastoral and administrative organization of the diocese, (2) the general religious situation, (3) the economic situation of the diocese, (4) liturgical and sacramental practice, (5) the clergy, (6) religious and secular institutes, (7) cooperation with the missions, (8) seminaries and universities, (9) Catholic education, (10) the life and apostolic action of the laity, (11) ecumenism, (12) social assistance, (13) other pastoral questions. In addition, the report asks for statistical data on advisory councils, the tribunal, publications, the clergy, and educational institutions. After being received by the Congregation for Bishops, the various parts of the report are distributed to the Vatican congregations specializing in the particular concerns.

Although they get a written response some months later, some archbishops expressed disappointment that, when they reached Rome, they found no one who had read their reports. One archbishop describes his experience in 1983:

> I really worked hard on it. I made up my mind this was going to be my chance to put down on paper where I think my diocese really is. I put down some tough stuff. What I thought was really true about it. Well, I didn't hear from anybody.
>
> And although the document is in Rome before you go for your ad limina, you know that nobody looked at it. So there's no input, and there's no feedback. You kinda wonder, is it worth all that effort of trying to get through somewhere?

Since there are so many American bishops, they come to Rome in groups, usually by geographic region, for the ad limina visit. The bishops meet with Vatican officials in groups and, in the past, were mostly lectured to. One bishop complained that when a bishop questioned an official at one such meeting, the official noted down the bishop's name, which killed any further questioning.

Recently there has been more dialogue as bishops have expressed their views on church issues and tried to explain themselves to Rome. The bishops have also used their visits as an opportunity to question Vatican officials about their actions. For example, in 1983 Cardinal Oddi, prefect of the Congregation for the Clergy, while visiting the United States, was interviewed in *The Wanderer* and spoke before a conference sponsored by Catholics United for the Faith (CUF),[6] two conservative organizations that have been critical of the bishops. According to an archbishop who was present,

> some of the bishops were pretty indignant about some of the things he had to say about American bishops and the American church. They asked Cardinal Oddi whether he read *The Wanderer*. Did he know the kind of newspaper it is and how it makes people neurotic and maybe psychotic about some of the things in the church today? Well, he said he didn't know anything about *The Wanderer*.

The bishops also met with cardinals Baum and Ratzinger, prefect of the Congregation for the Doctrine of the Faith. One of the items the bishops brought up with Cardinal Ratzinger and the pope was the "very, very slow" rate of dispensations from celibacy for priests who have left the ministry. "You can talk to Cardinal Ratzinger and you can talk to the Holy Father about things that concern you," says one archbishop.

Each bishop also meets individually with the pope for about fifteen minutes. The first thing the bishop does is give the pope an envelope containing a donation from the diocese. Although the bishops look forward to these meetings, they are not very productive. "The pope has no resume of your quinquennial report," one archbishop explains. "He asks you all the questions over again that were on it. Silly questions—how many people in your diocese, how many priests, and so on—which is pure fact."

Archbishop Hurley of Anchorage, however, reports, "You were free to say what you wanted." In 1983 he wanted to speak to the pope about ecumenism and about the positive things religious were doing in his archdiocese. He felt parish priests needed encouragement for ecumenical work, and he felt that religious women were being unfairly criticized.

When I went in he started the usual thing about your diocese, size, all that type of thing. I cut in on him to bring up what I wanted to bring up. Which turned out to be the way it had to be done. The pope doesn't know me, doesn't know anything about Alaska really. What kinds of questions can he really ask? So you really have to take the lead.

Women religious also came up when Archbishop O'Meara of Indianapolis met the pope, who asked him how he got along with the religious in his archdiocese. "I think I get along with them pretty well, Holy Father," Archbishop O'Meara responded. "Better you should ask them that question, because their view of it is more meaningful." Some bishops felt that the Vatican was surprised by the generally positive view of religious women expressed by the bishops.

Sometimes the pope may have something very specific to say to an archbishop. For example, Pope Paul VI told Archbishop James Casey of Denver during his ad limina to tell his auxiliary, Bishop George Evans, to stop publicly supporting the ordination of women.

After meeting with the pope individually, the bishops in groups of about twelve have lunch with the pope, where various topics are discussed. "There were no topics barred," says one archbishop. "We didn't get organized to have prepared topics, they just came up casually. The Holy Father is open to discussing any topic."

The pope is the center of attention, but "he made sure that every man spoke," says Archbishop Hurley who describes the lunch he attended in 1983. As they sat down, the pope identified every bishop by the name of his diocese, not necessarily by the bishop's own name. Then the archbishop recalls,

we went through an unstructured conversation.

The pope said, "I have learned two new words: undocumented and unchurched." So we talked about that and pointed out that unchurched in the U.S. does not mean atheistic. We were able to point out to him that atheism is not a major force in the U.S. in a formal way. Mark [Hurley of Santa Rosa] said to him that there was no place in the U.S. where any avowed Communist has won a political campaign.

We talked about the poor, what do we do about the poor. I said, "One of the things is to work cooperatively with government, because we do not have the funds ourselves." I gave a quick reference to my own experience. He wanted to know about working with the government, is that a problem? Not in the United States. There are lots of examples of it as they help us to do our work.

We went on for an hour and a half, two hours. That part was very good.

In the last part of the visit, the bishops as a group meet with the pope. The senior bishop, usually a cardinal, briefly addresses the pope on their behalf, and then the pope addresses the visiting bishops. The speeches of the pope appear to be written before the bishops gather in Rome. As a result, one archbishop complained, "He did not seem to reflect, in what he said, what he had heard from the American bishops."

The Issues

The pope's ad limina addresses are one of the few public indications of what the pope thinks about the American church and its hierarchy. When one bishop asked the pope what he thought of the American church, the pope responded, "Read my ad limina talks." These speeches are therefore worth examining to see what he says to the American bishops.

Three popes addressed the American bishops during their 1978 ad limina visit.

Paul VI spoke to the New York bishops on the importance of the sacrament of penance.[7] He explicitly asked for "faithful observance of the norms" limiting general absolution to extraordinary situations of grave necessity. "General absolution is not to be used as a normal pastoral option, or as a means of confronting any difficult pastoral situation." He also insisted on the practice of First Confession before First Communion. He repeated a statement he had made to other bishops: "The faithful would be rightly shocked that obvious abuses are tolerated by those who have received the charge of the 'episcopate,' which stands for, since the earliest days of the church, vigilance and unity."

In a very positive address to the bishops of Ohio, Michigan, and Minnesota, Paul VI spoke of his closeness to them in "the splendid efforts, the sustained efforts, the united efforts that you have made on behalf of life. . . ."[8] He supported them in "protecting life in its multiple facets" including "efforts directed to the eradication of hunger, the elimination of subhuman living conditions, and the promotion of programs on behalf of the poor, the elderly, and minorities" and human rights and their struggle against abortion.[9] He also noted initiatives sponsored in the United States to explain natural family planning.

In his last address to the American bishops, Paul VI spoke on the Eucharist as the summit of Christian life and noted that extraordinary ministers of communion should be used only where there is a genuine lack of priests.[10]

In his only address to the American bishops, John Paul I talked about the Christian family with many references to Vatican II but without mentioning *Humanae Vitae*.[11] He reiterated the indissolubility of marriage but said that people with difficulties "must always know that we love them."

In his first address to the American hierarchy, Pope John Paul II articulated the two issues that have continued to mark his pontificate: fidelity to doctrine and church discipline.[12] Quoting from John XXIII, he said that the great concern of Vatican II and "my own deepest hope" was "that the sacred deposit of Christian doctrine should be more effectively guarded and taught." His second hope was "for the preservation of the great discipline of the church." He went on to say that it was his "ardent desire today that a new emphasis on the importance of doctrine and discipline will be the postconciliar contribution of your seminaries."

In 1983, John Paul II returned to these themes and made them more explicit. Speaking to the New York bishops, he repeated Paul VI's warnings on general absolution. Citing canon law, he said, "General absolution is not envisioned solely because of large numbers of penitents assembled for a great celebration or pilgrimage." He asked for their zealous pastoral solicitude "to help ensure that these norms, as well as *the norms regulating the First Confession of children*, are understood and properly applied."[13]

To the second group of American bishops he said that they must be holy and a sign of Christ's love, but "there can be *no dichotomy* between the bishop as *a sign of Christ's compassion* and as *a sign of Christ's truth*."[14] As part of that truth, the pope wanted the bishops to proclaim "the indissolubility of marriage . . . , the incompatibility of premarital sex and homosexual activity with God's plan . . . , the unpopular truth that artificial birth control is against God's law . . . ," and "the rights of the unborn, the weak, the handicapped, the poor and the aged. . . ."

The bishop must also explain the church's teaching on the exclusion of women from priestly ordination and "give proof of his pastoral ability and leadership by withdrawing all support from individuals or groups who in the name of progress or compassion, or for other alleged reason, promote the ordination of women to the priesthood."

In a later address to a third group of American bishops, the pope spoke on the priesthood whose identity is found in the ministry of the sacraments of the Eucharist and reconciliation. He also confirmed the "*general exclusion of priests from secular and political activity*."[15]

To the next group of bishops, he referred to his June 1983 letter asking the American bishops to exercise special pastoral service to the religious.[16] This letter announced the formation of a papal commission on religious life headed by Archbishop Quinn of San Francisco. The pope explained his action as an example of collegiality and asked the bishops to give to religious "a call to holiness, a call to renewal, and a call to penance and conversion." In his address, he stressed the importance of prayer and union with the magisterium as essential aspects of religious life.

Finally, to the last group of American bishops, he spoke of the church's "mission of proclaiming Christ's good news about Christian married love, the identity and worth of the family, and the importance of understanding its mission in the church and the world."[17] As bishops, they are "called upon to help couples know and understand the reasons for the church's teaching on human sexuality," including the church's teaching on natural family planning. He commended the bishops for the concern shown for needy families through their social service agencies.

Papal Visits 1979 and 1987

During these ad limina addresses, the pope speaks to groups of bishops from various parts of the United States. He addresses all of the bishops together only when he comes to this country. In 1979 he spoke to the U.S. bishops in Chicago, who were kept waiting for over an hour because he was running late. Although the press received copies of his talk in advance, the bishops did not. Complaints were also heard because the bishops had no real opportunity to dialogue with the pope.

In his speech, he noted the "long tradition of fidelity to the Apostolic See on the part of the American hierarchy."[18] He urged them to lives of personal holiness. He repeated his favorite quotation from John XXIII about guarding and keeping the deposit of doctrine. Then in a long section he commended them for doing this in their pastoral letter "To Live in Christ Jesus." He also referred to a pastoral letter on racism and one on homosexuality by individual bishops.

He encouraged the bishops to work for Christian unity but noted that "intercommunion between divided Christians is not the answer." He asked them to safeguard the sacrament of reconciliation, referring to the limits of general absolution. He also spoke of the Eucharist and of the communion of the local church with the universal church.

On his 1987 visit, his meeting with the American bishops in Los Angeles began in the morning so that the bishops would not be kept waiting, but once again the press and not the bishops received advance copies of his talk. The meeting was structured as a dialogue. He was addressed by four archbishops whose speeches had been given to the Vatican in advance so that the pope could prepare a response.[19] Cardinal Bernardin of Chicago spoke of the church as "a *communio*: a communion of particular churches in which and from which exists the one and unique Catholic Church; a communion which is not fully the church unless united with the Bishop of Rome."

The church in the United States, he said, is situated in American culture "where everyone prizes the freedom to speak his or her mind . . . , to question things," and to "want to know the reasons why certain decisions are made, and they feel free to criticize if they do not agree or are not satisfied with the explanation." Since the church "values both its unity and diversity, there are bound to be misunderstandings and tensions at times." The ministry of the bishops is "to provide for the unity of the particular churches, and the Petrine ministry to promote and protect the unity of the universal church."

The practical question is "how to maintain our unity while affirming the diversity in the local realization of the church; how to discern a proper balance between freedom and order." He made some suggestions, including the following: "We must be able to speak with one another in complete candor, without fear. This applies to our exchanges with the Holy See as well as among ourselves as bishops. Even if our exchange is characterized by some as confrontational, we must remain calm and not become the captives of those who would use us to accomplish their own ends." Also, "we must affirm and continue to grow in our appreciation of the conciliar vision of collegiality as both a principle and style of leadership in the Church," and he pointed to the NCCB as a visible expression of collegiality.

In his response, John Paul II did not directly react to the cardinal's comments on American culture or on the need for candor between bishops and Rome. He picked up on the description of the church as a communio but stressed the "vertical dimension" of communion—communion with God and communion of the local churches with the pope. Without explicitly disagreeing with the cardinal, the pope made clear that the tension between unity and diversity should be resolved in favor of unity.

Next Archbishop Quinn of San Francisco spoke on the state of moral theology in an address that is not easily summarized. He defined moral theology as "human wisdom struggling to understand God's revelation about how we live." He said, "the revolutionary changes which have occurred in personal and societal life in the twentieth century are not grounds for dismissing church teaching as outmoded. . . ."

But as pastors, the bishops must address new realities: the military role of the United States in the world, divorce and family instability, the high standard of living, new medical technologies, the insights of psychology and sociology into the nature of human sexuality, the sexually permissive climate, the changing social status of women, and the higher level of education among American Catholics. Archbishop Quinn said, "We cannot fulfill our task simply by an uncritical application of solutions designed in past ages for problems which have qualitatively changed or which did not exist in the past."

He cited the American bishops' pastoral letters on peace and on economics as examples of a moral pedagogy that distinguishes universally binding moral principles from specific applications and recommendations that allow for a diversity of opinion. He supported dialogue and discussion as an effective method of understanding moral questions and developing responses.

The pope picked up on Archbishop Quinn's statement that the church wishes to remain faithful to the moral teaching of Jesus. He said that claiming "that dissent from the magisterium is totally compatible with being a 'good Catholic' and poses no obstacle to the reception of the sacraments . . . is a grave error that challenges the teaching office of the bishops of the United States and elsewhere." He did not comment on the new realities moral theology must deal with. He ignored the distinction between principles and applications. The impression given was that the magisterium has clear and definitive answers to the issues raised by Archbishop Quinn, and these answers must be proclaimed more forcefully and courageously by the bishops.

Archbishop Weakland of Milwaukee spoke on the role of the laity in society and the church. He noted their increased education and increased participation in American society. They look at the intrinsic worth of an argument rather than accept it on the authority of church teachers. As a result, "an authoritarian style is counterproductive, and such authority for the most part then becomes ignored." The faithful look for a spirituality that integrates their lives, and they want to contribute their skills and knowledge to the life and growth of the church. Women want to be equal partners in the church's mission.

John Paul II acknowledged the growing role and education of American Catholics, but he asked what has been their impact on American culture. The bishops should provide the laity with a comprehensive and solid program of catechesis so that they can bring the gospel's purifying influence to the world of culture. He spoke of the need for pastoral care to families and of natural family planning. He quoted Paul VI's 1978 ad limina address commending the bishops on their work for peace and justice. He spoke of the "equal human dignity of women and their true feminine humanity."

Finally, Archbishop Pilarczyk of Cincinnati spoke on lay, religious, and clerical vocations in the United States. He noted the decline in religious and priestly vocations and the rise of lay ministry. Mandatory priestly celibacy is questioned as is the church's teaching on the ordination of women. As positive points, he noted the broadening concept of church ministry and the increasing appreciation of prayer, Scripture, and liturgy. While admitting to plenty of problems and loose ends to deal with, he felt that the Holy Spirit was hard at work in the dioceses and parishes of our country. What is happening "is not the turmoil and crisis of death and decay, but of development and of life."

In responding, John Paul avoided the term *lay ministry* but spoke of the "active participation of the laity in the mission of the church." He stressed the vocation of the laity in the world rather than in the church.

Finally, he mentioned some things not brought up by the bishops. He asked the bishops "to be vigilant that the dogmatic and moral teaching of the Church is faithfully and clearly presented to the seminarians, and fully accepted and understood by them." Once again he returned to his favorite quotation from John XXIII that the greatest concern of Vatican II is that "Christian doctrine should be more effectively guarded and taught."

He also asked the bishops to make every effort to ensure that the norms for the use of general absolution are observed. He encouraged pastoral care to homosexuals that included a clear explanation of the church's teaching, "which by its nature is unpopular." He referred in a positive way to the California bishops' pastoral letter, "A Call to Compassion," which spoke of the need of the recovery of the virtue of chastity.

But as opposed to his address in 1979, what was striking in Los Angeles was the lack of any reference to the American bishops' pastoral letters on peace and the economy, although they were cited by Archbishops Quinn and Weakland. He never mentioned the peace pastoral during his visit and referred to the economic pastoral only twice in passing. Many believed that he disagreed less with the substance of the letters than with the widely consultative public process that was involved in their writing.

Ad Limina 1988

While this book is being written, the American bishops are making trips to Rome for their 1988 ad limina visits. By the end of September, seven groups of bishops had visited Rome. Four more groups will visit before the end of the year. Early in 1989, there will be an additional meeting of a representative group of American bishops with the pope. The Brazilian bishops had a similar meeting at the end of their ad limina visit in 1986. At this meeting, the Brazilians discussed liberation theology with the pope and Vatican officials. The Brazilians were pleased with the meeting and felt that the Vatican had a better understanding of them after this visit.

The pope's talks to the American bishops during their 1988 ad limina visits had a more positive tone than those given previously. Bishop Michael Pfeifer of San Angelo, TX, reports that after his 1983 trip to the United States the pope "had a different view of the American Catholic" than he had previously "because he was given some rather negative publicity before he came that he didn't find true."[20] The pope noted that the demonstrations against him predicted in the press did not happen.

In March 1988, the pope spoke to the first group of visiting bishops about his 1983 trip to the United States. He noted that "One of the great riches of the church in the United States is the way in which she herself incarnates universality and catholicity in her ethnic makeup, taken as she is 'from every nation and race, people and tongue' (Rv. 7:9)."[21] He said he was "convinced of the openness of the church in the United States to challenge, of her good will and, above all, of Christ's grace active within her." He noted the church's response to the farm crisis and "the panorama of charitable works and health care that was presented to me" during the visit. He challenged the bishops not to forget the missions and cited their 1986 pastoral statement on world missions.

In his address to the second group of American bishops, which included the Texas bishops, the pope recalled "my recent visit to San Antonio, the wonderful welcome given me and the impressive faith of the people."[22] He also cited the Texas bishops' pastoral statement on human sexuality as "a much appreciated pastoral effort to present the church's teaching on chastity without fear or reticence." The rest of the address spoke of the pastoral vision needed for the third millennium, a topic relevant to the entire church. But he did ask "in a special way" that the bishops of the United States promote "the centuries-old practice of individual confession." He expanded on this theme with the third group of bishops whom he also asked to enforce the church law limiting general absolution to cases of grave necessity.[23]

In June, the pope spoke on the importance of prayer to the fourth group of bishops. As in 1983, he noted the "superb history of eucharistic participation by the people"[24] of the United States which has a higher rate of church attendance than most other countries. To a group of bishops in July he spoke about catechetics. He complimented the bishops for calling "your people to a sense of solidarity with those in need," for standing "by all those who are struggling to live in a way consonant with their human dignity," especially migrants and immigrants, and for "sustained dialogue and fraternal collaboration in projects of service to humanity."[25]

In September, John Paul surprised everyone by speaking positively of the draft of the bishops' pastoral letter on women. First he spoke of human rights in general and thanked the bishops for their persevering efforts in "defense and support of human life."[26] Then in speaking of women's rights, he said that the draft letter showed a "sensitivity" in dealing with women's issues. "You are rightly striving to eliminate discrimination based on sex," he said.

A week later, for the first time, he spoke favorably of the bishops' pastoral letters on peace and economic justice. He cited them for their support of solidarity and development in the face of global interdependence. He noted that "great openness to others has been characteristic of the church in the United States."[27] He commended the solidarity of men and women in the United States "pledged to the defense and service of human life." And he cited Catholic Relief Services as "one extraordinary example of the creative solidarity of American Catholics."

A number of bishops noted the change to a more positive tone in the pope's speeches to the American bishops. Some explained this resulted from the favorable impression he received while visiting the church in the United States. Some also felt that the pope had changed speech writers because he recognized that his U.S. speeches, especially his response to the American bishops, did not go over well. The pope appears to be relying less on Archbishop Justin Rigali, the American prelate who is president of the Pontifical Ecclesiastical Academy. In addition, informed observers pointed to the replacement of Archbishop Eduardo Martinez Somalo with Archbishop Edward Cassidy as asssistant secretary of state. Some believe Somalo, who was promoted to cardinal, has a negative view of the church in the United States. The Australian Cassidy appears to be more open to the American situation.

At their lunches with the pope, the American bishops discussed a number of current concerns: women's ordination, peace and unity in the world, the alleged Marian apparitions at Medjugorje (Yugoslavia) and the case of French conservative Archbishop Marcel Lefebvre who was excommunicated for ordaining bishops. The bishops also discussed various issues with the Vatican curia, including a statement on AIDS by the NCCB Administrative Committee.

Letters from Rome

In between ad limina visits and papal visits, communications between Rome and the bishops is usually by letter. Most archbishops say that they are rarely bothered by Rome.[28] The communications from Rome they receive are mostly of a general nature distributed through the NCCB. "There would be very, very little addressed specifically to this diocese," said Archbishop Donnellan of Atlanta. Archbishop Gerety of Newark said that he got letters from the Vatican "fairly frequently, and sometimes they don't amount to a hill of beans." Most of the letters were responses on marriage cases that he just forwarded to the tribunal.

"I don't get a lot [of inquiries from Rome]," reports Archbishop Roach of St. Paul.

I don't feel that the Holy See is bugging me. Over a period of years I have gotten some letters that irritated me and have responded to them. It was dropped, and so we let it go at that.

Considering the climate of critics which we've got here [St. Paul is the headquarters of a number of conservative Catholic organizations], apparently the Holy See has been pretty good, because I don't get a lot of it back. They don't make me defend positions. Periodically things come, but it is not a major problem.

The impact of negative letters on Rome is a much debated issue. "I get many letters from the United States," reports Cardinal Ratzinger, prefect of the Vatican Congregation for Doctrine of the Faith. Most of the letters are from those in "deep loyalty" to the Holy See, he said, adding that they deal frequently with controversial issues in the news. He mentioned as an example the case of Father Charles Curran who has been criticized for his views on moral theology. "I think that the letters provide us with a reflection of typical Catholics," he said. "They are people who are preoccupied with the thought that the Catholic Church should remain the Catholic Church."[29]

But many people fear that letters from right-wing Catholics have tarnished the Vatican's view of the American church and its bishops. The vicar general of Denver reports that Cardinal Baggio, prefect of the Congregation for Bishops, told Archbishop Casey in 1983,

Would you please get across to your people that if things are going right we would like to hear about them, because all we get is "hate mail." If we get a lot of this negative mail, then we think the diocese is in trouble, and we have to check up on it. So if you can get the word around, let us know both sides.

When an archbishop receives a letter from a Vatican official inquiring about a controversy or problem, frequently the Vatican learned about the problem through letters from America. These complaints usually come from disaffected conservatives complaining about something in the archdiocese, especially alleged liturgical abuses by priests.

Archbishop Gerety of Newark explains:

> The Vatican gets all sorts of people writing in. There are more writing in than there used to be because of the changes. It's gotten to be the fashion these days to go over the head of the local bishop and appeal to the nuncio and send a copy to the pope and this office and this cardinal and all the rest.
>
> So they write back and say, "We have this letter from so and so; give it the pastoral attention you think it deserves."

When I interviewed Archbishop Gerety, he had on his desk a letter from Cardinal Mayer, prefect of the Congregation for Worship. A man in the archdiocese had written Rome complaining that the only way of receiving the precious blood in the archdiocese was by the cup, while he preferred intinction where the host is dipped into the chalice before it is given to the communicant. "Cardinal Mayer is just saying that he replied and [is] bringing it to my attention," explains Archbishop Gerety.

> Mayer just says, from the cup "is the most desirable form, but it is not the only way" and "expressing the hope that this matter does not cause your Excellency any inconvenience, I remain. . . ." That means Mayer can now say that he has replied.

Archbishop Pilarczyk of Cincinnati agrees that often the Vatican official will simply forward the letter to the bishop saying, "We received this letter, will you please give it the attention that it deserves."

> And we do, we always give it the attention that it deserves. Sometimes it deserves very little attention.

Occasionally I will get letters from the Holy See saying, "So and so said that Father so and so said such and such. Would you please look into that." Or, "This article was published in your diocese, and we would like for you to explain what this is all about." I have found that by and large it's not unreasonable.

Archbishop Quinn of San Francisco says that he rarely receives letters forwarded from Rome. "The experience I have had," he says, "has to do with a parishioner writing Rome about something the parishioner regards as liturgically abusive. Then Rome may write back directly to that parishioner or may write to me and inquire about it. But that is very rare."

When a Vatican official answers the writer directly without notifying his bishop, the results can be embarrassing to the local bishop. One archbishop reports,

There has been a real problem when an individual writes the Holy See and gets a letter back from the Holy See and then goes running to the bishop and says, "See you are wrong."

"What are you talking about?"

"I got this letter from Cardinal so and so." Sure enough, there is a letter from the cardinal or the congregation with no notice whatsoever to the bishop. Several bishops raised hell over that. Really blasted them.

An example of such an embarrassing incident occurred in 1986 when Cardinal Edouard Gagnon wrote a Milwaukee member of CUF (Catholics United for the Faith) describing "New Creation," a sex education series used in about eighty dioceses, as "a travesty of sex education." His problem appears to have been with explicit pictures of the human anatomy. In a subsequent letter, he wrote that he had consulted the pope and "expressed the judgment of the Holy Father."

When the letters became public, Archbishop Kucera of Dubuque, who (together with his predecessor) had given the series an imprimatur, stated, "At no time had Cardinal Gagnon contacted me about the material contained in his letters." He first learned of the letters when they were sent to him by someone other than the cardinal. Nor had the publisher been contacted by the Vatican about the series. The archbishop noted that catechetical books were under the jurisdiction of the Congregation of Clergy, not the Pontifical Council for the Family, which Cardinal Gagnon heads. More than a year after the letters were made public, the archbishop had still not heard from anyone in the Vatican about the series, which still has his imprimatur.

Liturgy is another area where the bishops have been repeatedly embarrassed by Rome. In many dioceses, the Pre-Vatican II Tridentine Mass had been offered by dissident priests associated with Archbishop Lefebvre or other priests not in union with Rome. After fighting conservatives over the Tridentine Mass, the American bishops were caught off guard when Rome decided to permit it. Many bishops felt betrayed by this action. Under the new Vatican norms, the local bishop would determine when the Tridentine Mass could be offered. But one archbishop, who would not allow the Tridentine Mass on Sundays, complained that someone from his archdiocese called Cardinal Mayer, who told the man that they could have the Tridentine Mass on Sunday. The archbishop was even given a transcript of the telephone call. More recently, Cardinal Mayer has objected to the faculties or powers given by the bishops of Michigan to their priests.

On the other hand, Archbishop Virgilio Noè, who works in the Congregation for Divine Worship, sent Archbishop Hurley a copy of a letter he had received complaining about a priest in Anchorage. He also sent his reply to the complainant. "If you think it is proper to forward my letter, feel free to do so," Archbishop Noè wrote. "So I did," reports Archbishop Hurley who was pleased with this approach. "I got the pastor, the pastor went to see the couple. We took care of it. Everyone lived happily ever after."

Another area of Roman concern has been the American tribunals, which grant more annulments than all the other tribunals in the world put together. When visiting Roman congregations, Archbishop May, president of the NCCB was asked about the tribunals.

They get all these complaints that the tribunals are nothing but divorce mills; constant letters going over there from people here. A lot of it is organized mail, mostly right wing.

Most of the countries of the world, very frankly, don't even have functioning tribunals. If they exist, they might have half a dozen cases a year. And in this diocese [St. Louis] there might be 1,000, and this is just one diocese.

Well, we go over there, and they look upon us as having caved in on the divorce mentality. They don't understand that we are simply trying to serve these people with their needs, which are not the same as those in other countries.

The American bishops have defended their tribunals against Roman attack. They argue that their tribunals produce more annulments because they are better staffed with canon lawyers and secretaries, better equipped with computers and other office equipment, and because they work longer hours. "We are open 8:30 A.M. to 5:00 P.M.," explains one archbishop. "In Rome they don't open until 10:00 or 10:30, and we work without a long lunch and a siesta."

More recently, the bishops have been having trouble getting indults (dispensations) for people without canon law degrees to work in the tribunals. One archbishop tried to get an indult renewed for a sister.

They wrote back and said no. I wrote back and said, "You said no, but didn't say why." They wrote back and said no and still didn't say why. I wrote back and said, "You said no, but still didn't say why." Then they wrote back and told me why, and still didn't say why.

Archbishop Hurley had better luck getting an indult for a lay woman by visiting the Signatura, the office in Rome responsible for such indults. "The first thing I learned was nobody speaks English in the Signatura," recalls the archbishop, who finally found a part-time person to translate. He found that, although sympathetic, they were not persuaded by the great need and lack of priests in Alaska. What the Signatura wanted to know was how much theological training she had. Luckily, she had gone through the same training program as her husband who is a deacon. After sending the Signatura a description of the courses she had taken, her indult was extended for five years.

Hunthausen Case

The most extreme intervention in a U.S. archdiocese by the Vatican was in Seattle, where an auxiliary was appointed who was supposed to have final authority over important areas of diocesan life including the tribunal, liturgy, former priests, priestly formation, medical ethics, and ministry to homosexuals.

Such interventions are rare, but in a few other dioceses, auxiliaries or coadjutors have been appointed with special powers. Bishop Francis J. Furey had full powers when he came as coadjutor to the bankrupt diocese of San Diego in 1963. Likewise, Bishop Norman F. McFarland had special faculties when he went to the bankrupt diocese of Reno–Las Vegas in 1974. In 1983, a coadjutor was appointed to Lafayette, LA, with powers over the clergy after a scandal involving child abuse. Finally in 1986, Bishop David Foley was appointed auxiliary in Richmond, VA, although the extent of his powers was never revealed.

The Hunthausen case is worth examining because it shows what concerns Rome has about the American church. In addition, it shows how Roman procedures and American concepts of due process come into conflict.

It all began in May 1983 when Archbishop Laghi approached Archbishop Hunthausen at a meeting of the American bishops in Chicago and told him that the Vatican wanted to have a visitation of Seattle. Hunthausen agreed, not having the slightest idea what a visitation was. Archbishop Hickey of Washington, DC, was appointed visitor.

Later, Hunthausen began to question the visitation when it

became clear that its purpose was to evaluate criticisms about his ministry as archbishop. He objected that he was never given any specifics about what was to be investigated so that he could defend himself. In addition, the Vatican wanted the visitation to be secret, but he argued that was impossible. When the fact of the visitation became known, Seattle officials insisted that the leak occurred in Washington, DC.

In November 1983, Archbishop Hickey spent a week in Seattle conferring with the archbishop and over seventy priests, religious, and laypersons, many of whom were suggested by the archbishop. He also examined documents issued by the archbishop or the archdiocese. Hunthausen was never given a copy of the report sent by Archbishop Hickey to the Vatican. The Vatican argued that those interviewed were promised anonymity, and therefore he could not see it.

In September 1985, the archbishop received a letter from Cardinal Ratzinger concluding the visitation and outlining its findings.[30] The letter is important because it shows what things worry the Vatican, not only in Seattle, but in other dioceses in the United States.

The six-page letter begins by complimenting Hunthausen: "You have striven with heart and mind to be a good bishop of the church, eager to implement the renewal called for in the decrees of the Vatican Council II." It also commends him for bringing into existence consultative bodies, for his efforts to involve the laity in the work of the church, and for his concern for justice and peace. "You have given clear evidence of your loyalty to the church and your devotion and obedience to the Holy Father." The letter notes that he has "suffered from exaggerated criticisms and routine misunderstandings" and disassociates itself from "extremist groups."

The letter then goes on to list the abuses that Ratzinger said exist in Seattle.

First, the letter deals with marriage and divorce, citing the "rather widespread practice of admitting divorced persons to a subsequent church marriage" without an annulment. "Catholics have been advised that after divorce and civil remarriage, they may in conscience return to the sacraments." "A clear presentation of the sacramentality and indissolubility of Christian marriage should be made to all your people." And the tribunal should conform to the prescriptions of canon law.

Second, some doctrinal problems are listed. Concern is expressed about those "who seem reluctant to accept the magisterium as capable of giving definitive direction in matters of faith and morals." The church should be portrayed not simply as a sociological entity "in opposition to its divine origin, mission, and authority." Faulty Christologies lead to these misunderstandings. Stress should be put on Christ's divinity, humanity, salvific mission, and union with and lordship over the church. A correct appreciation of the priesthood and role of the laity should be inculcated in the seminary program. Policies and programs of the archdiocese should reflect a vision of the human person based on the gospel and not just on human sciences. The authoritative teaching of the church has a valid claim on the Catholic conscience. "No bishop should hesitate to overrule advisors who propose opinions at variance with the authentic teaching of the Holy See."

Third, the letter states that Archbishop Hunthausen has taken steps to correct the practice of contraceptive sterilization in local Catholic hospitals.

Fourth, "first confession should precede first communion."

Fifth, "the use of general absolution must be strictly limited." Large crowds of penitents at Christmas and Easter do not constitute the necessary condition required by canon law.

Sixth, "Routine intercommunion [non-Catholics receiving communion at Mass] on the occasion of weddings or funerals . . . should be recognized as clearly abusive and an impediment to genuine ecumenism."

Seventh, practices not in accord with liturgical directives should be eliminated.

Eighth, priests who have left the ministry and not been laicized by Rome cannot be employed by the church. When a priest is laicized, that is, returned to the lay state, he is often prohibited from doing certain things by his rescript of laicization, the Vatican document by which he is laicized. This frequently means they may not teach in Catholic schools or act as lectors or extraordinary ministers of communion. Cardinal Ratzinger complained that these prohibitions were not being observed.

Ninth, in 1976 and 1979 the archdiocese distributed a questionnaire that revealed deficient doctrinal understandings and led some to believe it "to be a kind of voting process on doctrinal or moral teachings."

Tenth, the exclusion of women from the priesthood should be explained unambiguously.

Eleventh, "The archdiocese should withdraw all support from any group that does not unequivocally accept the teaching of the magisterium concerning the intrinsic evil of homosexual activity. . . . A compassionate ministry to homosexual persons must be developed that has as its clear goal the promotion of a chaste life-style."

It is noteworthy that five of the issues listed in the letter (general absolution, first confession, women priests, intercommunion, homosexuality) were mentioned by the pope in talks to American bishops. The Vatican also emphasized privately that the visitation had nothing to do with Archbishop Hunthausen's vocal opposition to nuclear weapons or his refusal to pay some of his taxes as a protest. His authority on social justice and peace issues in his archdiocese was never challenged.

The Vatican did not want this letter made public, but Archbishop Hunthausen insisted that some public report was necessary lest he be accused of misrepresenting its findings. In November 1985, a letter to the archbishop from Archbishop Laghi was published that summarized the contents of the Ratzinger letter. Archbishop Hunthausen said that he was firmly committed to dealing with the areas of concern listed in the letters. But he and others in Seattle asked for specific instances of when and where these abuses had taken place. Many of the abuses, he said, never occurred or had been dealt with.

In December 1985, Donald W. Wuerl was appointed auxiliary bishop in Seattle. Seattle sources insist that from the very beginning the Vatican wanted to appoint an auxiliary or coadjutor with special powers but that Archbishop Hunthausen had refused to accept this. Bishop Wuerl was seen by Seattle as a compromise—an auxiliary without special powers but one not nominated by the archbishop. Vatican officials saw the compromise differently. Bishop Wuerl did not have special powers from the Vatican, but Archbishop Hunthausen was supposed to give him these powers himself.

By Easter of 1986 it became clear that Bishop Wuerl and Archbishop Hunthausen had different understandings of the bishop's powers. When Rome was questioned, Archbishop Hunthausen was told that he was supposed to delegate to Bishop Wuerl final authority over the tribunal, liturgy, priestly formation, former priests, medical ethics, and ministry to homosexuals. Again the Vatican did not want this made public, but the archbishop said that he could not pretend he had full power when he did not.

When it was made public in September 1986, most of the priests and religious of the archdiocese were outraged.[31] Some canonists argued that it was against canon law for a diocesan bishop to delegate final decision-making authority to anyone, even an auxiliary bishop. Meetings were held, petitions were signed, protests were made. It soon became clear that no matter what his legal authority, Bishop Wuerl was, in fact, isolated, with the archbishop being one of his few defenders in Seattle.

Meanwhile, shortly before the November 1986 meeting of the American bishops, Archbishop Laghi issued a chronology of the case giving the Vatican's side.[32] It said that at least since 1978, "the Holy See sought the assistance of the archbishop of Seattle in responding to the high volume of complaints that were sent to Rome by priests, religious, and faithful in the archdiocese." After hearing a preliminary report on the visitation, "the Holy See considered him [Hunthausen] lacking the firmness necessary to govern the archdiocese." It also said that Archbishop Hunthausen had agreed to the delegation of powers when Bishop Wuerl was first appointed. In a closed session at the meeting of bishops, Archbishop Hunthausen gave his version of the events, which differed significantly from Archbishop Laghi's.[33]

Up until this point, most bishops had given Rome the benefit of the doubt, since they did not know the facts. Once the chronology gave the Vatican's side of the story, the bishops were asked to judge the case on the facts rather than on faith. The administrative committee of the NCCB recommended that the bishops support the Vatican action in Seattle as "fair and just." But after studying the chronology and listening to Archbishop Hunthausen, the bishops were confused and divided. They were asked to support the Vatican's actions in Seattle but refused. Rather they simply acknowledged the right of the Vatican to do what it did and offered their services to bring about a resolution to the conflict.

As it became clear that the Vatican solution was not working in Seattle and, in fact, was causing controversy across the country, the American bishops worked to settle the question before the pope's visit in September 1987. The pope agreed in February 1987 to appoint a three-man papal commission "to assess the current situation in the archdiocese of Seattle."

In May, the commission, consisting of cardinals Bernardin of Chicago and O'Connor of New York and Archbishop Quinn of San Francisco, agreed with the Vatican's assessment of the situation in Seattle but recommended the restoring of Archbishop Hunthausen to full power. The commission reported, "No matter how personally firm in his teachings and practices the archbishop himself may be, without intending it, he is perceived as generating, or at least accepting, a climate of permissiveness within which some feel themselves free to design their own policies and practices."[34] They also recommended the appointment of a coadjutor, Bishop Thomas J. Murphy, who would not have special powers. Bishop Wuerl was to receive another assignment (ultimately he became bishop of Pittsburgh), and the commission was to continue in existence to help Archbishop Hunthausen deal with the problems identified by the Vatican. The pope accepted their recommendations.

Several significant lessons can be learned from this case. First, the Vatican could do to Archbishop Hunthausen only what he allowed it to do. If he had refused to accept the visitation, if he had refused to accept Bishop Wuerl, if he had refused to delegate to Wuerl any powers, there was little the Vatican could do. It could not send in the Swiss Guard to restore order. The power of the Vatican is based on its moral authority and the willingness of Catholics to agree and obey. All of the Vatican's efforts to deal with Cardinal Cody in Chicago or to deal with Archbishop Lefebvre failed because they simply ignored it. Ultimately Archbishop Lefebvre was excommunicated for ordaining bishops without papal approval.

Second, misunderstandings occur when Roman procedures clash with American conceptions of fairness and due process. Roman procedures presume a benign, wise, and paternal authority that does what is best for the local and universal church. American concepts of due process institutionalize a fear that authority is not always wise and sometimes abuses its power. The desire for a bill of particulars giving specific and concrete charges, the right of the accused to face and cross-examine his accusers, the desire for an open process—all of these come from a tradition where power is suspect. Vatican officials argue that such procedures are not necessary and are counterproductive—they are no more needed in the church than they are in a family. In addition, differences in language and style can lead to misunderstandings, as appears to have happened in the appointment of Bishop Wuerl.

A third lesson from the case is the growing reliance by the Vatican on local church officials to deal with problems. First, Archbishop Hickey conducted the original investigation rather than a Vatican official. It is impossible to evaluate his role in the affair since his report was never made public. Second, the Vatican tried to get the National Conference of Catholic Bishops to endorse its actions in Seattle. This failed. Later, the three American prelates on the papal commission worked out the compromise that settled the controversy. The recent studies of seminaries and religious life were also conducted by American bishops. Rome refers to this as collegiality.

A final lesson of the case is the recognition that the Vatican is capable of changing its mind; its decisions are not always set in concrete, as many believe. The Vatican appears to have been convinced by right-wing letter writers that the people of Seattle were scandalized and upset by the actions of their archbishop. Wholesale repudiation of the Vatican's actions by the Seattle priests and religious showed that Vatican intervention was not welcome and was, in fact, counterproductive.

The commission constructed a compromise that withdrew Bishop Wuerl and restored Archbishop Hunthausen while at the same time supporting the Vatican's view that there were problems in Seattle—the diagnosis was correct, the cure was not working. The Vatican reversal was portrayed as tactical, not substantive. But even this compromise required intensive negotiations that would not have succeeded if the three American prelates had not been solidly united behind their recommendations when facing both Seattle and Rome. When finally presented with their recommendations, the pope responded, "If that is what you want, fine." In addition, he was undoubtedly pleased that this matter was settled before his trip to the United States.

Gerety Case

Another archbishop who came under fire in Rome was Archbishop Gerety of Newark. CUF (Catholics United for the Faith) attacked him because Renew began and is based in his archdiocese. CUF disapproved of its emphasis on community and claimed that it was doctrinally unsound. In addition, Rome forced him to withdraw the imprimatur of *Christ Among Us*, a very popular book used in adult catechesis. Archbishop Gerety's resignation was accepted two years early, shortly before the NCCB committee on doctrine gave a generally favorable report on Renew while also calling for more doctrinal and catechetical content to its materials.

After claiming victory in Seattle and Newark, conservative Catholic organizations like CUF targeted Archbishop Weakland as their next victim. He was especially vulnerable in Rome because, in what he thought was an off-the-record talk to the Milwaukee press, he had described the newly elected pope.

I had watched him once in Czestochowa with 200,000 people in the crowd. I said, he works that crowd better than any ham actor could. And I said, he's very bright, catches on fast, but he is stubborn. The press the next day had, "Archbishop says 'Pope ham actor who is stubborn.' "

Despite CUF and the press, Rome has not moved against Archbishop Weakland. Having worked in Rome as abbot primate of the Benedictines, he knows Roman ways and has Roman friends. In addition, he is widely respected by the other American bishops who elected him one of their delegates to the 1987 synod. Many observers consider him the brightest member of the American hierarchy. If Rome tried to discipline him, the Seattle controversy would look, in contrast, like a tempest in a teapot.

The Man in the Middle

A number of archbishops described themselves as being in the middle between Rome and their archdioceses. "The hardest part of my job is to be sandwiched between Roman orders and my people and priests' hopes and ideals," reports Archbishop Weakland. "I live that struggle day in and day out. I feel frustrated with no channels of communication and just kind of caught."

Archbishop Roach of St. Paul describes it in similar terms:

There is conflict between what is perceived as local need and universal teaching. A classic example would be the question of the order of penance and first Eucharist.

I feel a very strong responsibility to recognize what is the order in the universal church. I also feel a very strong responsibility to be sensitive to the pedagogical, psychological, catechetical needs as perceived by the people who are responsible for the preparation of youngsters. And that is always a stress, that's always a strain.

Another case where the bishops were caught in the middle between Rome and their flock was over the issue of altar girls. "I say no to altar girls," recounts Archbishop Lipscomb of Mobile. "Oh God, what troubles I get into by saying no to altar girls." Cardinal Bernardin of Chicago also wrote his pastors telling them not to have altar girls, but press reports indicated he did not discipline pastors who did not follow the directive.

Some archbishops feel that it is difficult for Rome to understand the American church. "The Vatican is predominantly European. It's Italian. It's Roman," says Archbishop Flores of San Antonio. "Very often they do not understand the realities out here. But I think they are making an effort, and we've been trying to dialogue individually and collectively." As an example, he cited Rome's desire that religious in his archdiocese live in community.

In the city, most of the nuns live in communities. But we have [poor rural] areas where sisters are living alone, and they're sixty or eighty miles from the nearest community. Well, we had to argue that point—that it's just not possible, and yet we need the service of a qualified sister way out there in the middle of nowhere.

Rome also wanted the sisters to wear habits. But many of the nuns were from Mexico where they had never worn habits because the government forbids it. In addition, as opposed to Europe, "here it is so hot that you just can't stand it," he says. "For the nuns to be modestly dressed is enough. The people respect them. Everybody knows they are nuns."

Another archbishop caught in the middle was Archbishop Sanchez of Santa Fe, who was asked by the Vatican to take over the University of Albuquerque when it was going broke. "We did so reluctantly because we knew that it was in tough financial condition," says Archbishop Sanchez, "but we hoped for the best." Two years later the school closed, and the archdiocese was stuck with its $8 million debt.

Conclusion

Besides governing their archdioceses, archbishops are also involved in their provinces, their state conferences and the National Conference of Catholic Bishops. A few play a role in the international church. All of this work involves travel and meetings outside the archdiocese, to say nothing of the time spent in the archdiocese preparing for these meetings. Archbishops who are prominent in national and international church affairs estimate that 20 to 30 percent of their time is devoted to work outside their archdioceses.

Chancery officials have mixed feelings about this work by their archbishops. They are usually proud that their archbishop is playing an important role in the larger church, but they also complain that the work makes him less available in the archdiocese. Many of the archbishops also complain that they have to spend so much time on matters outside of their archdioceses, but it rarely stops them from being involved in something they consider important.

Not only do archbishops have an impact on the church outside their archdioceses, that same church also has an impact on them. They cannot govern their archdioceses in a vacuum independent of what happens in other parts of the church. Decisions made by the National Conference of Catholic Bishops can sometimes bind the local bishop. Even what happens in neighboring dioceses can influence opinions and actions in their archdioceses.

But it is the Vatican that can have the most significant impact on the local archdiocese. The appointment of the archbishop and the parameters of his authority are mostly determined in Rome. While Rome is not a constant concern of the archbishops, it is ever present as a source of normative policies and procedures. After examining the ad limina and U.S. speeches of the pope (and the correspondence with Seattle), it is obvious that he wants the American bishops to deal with a number of issues.

The limits to general absolution were mentioned most consistently by Paul VI in 1978, by John Paul II in 1979, 1983, 1987, 1988, and in Seattle. First confession before first communion has also come up repeatedly, as have the indissolubility of marriage and prohibitions on intercommunion. While acknowledging the need for compassion, John Paul stresses that this is not incompatible with preaching the truth. All of this was summed up in his very first ad limina address to the American bishops when he called for fidelity to church teaching and discipline.

On the other hand, Paul VI and John Paul II both praised the American church for its concern for the poor at home and abroad. Both commended the bishops for programs like Catholic Charities and Catholic Relief Services. The bishops have also been praised for their concern for human rights, including the right to life.

The bishops give careful attention to the pope when he speaks, and when making decisions, the views of the pope are very influential. In the Conclusion we will examine how archbishops make decisions.

Conclusion: Episcopal Decision Making

No one seems to worry about who ministers to the bishops.

——————ARCHBISHOP WEAKLAND

My mistakes have always happened in the cases where I did not really consult.

——————ARCHBISHOP QUINN

Episcopal governance is the product of a number of factors: the personality and style of the archbishop, the makeup and needs of his archdiocese, and the governing structures of the church. Who is appointed archbishop makes a tremendous difference. His talents, values, style, and preferences have an impact on his archdiocese. But he does not write on a clean slate with complete freedom. Canon law gives him power but also restricts him. The demographic and financial condition of his archdiocese as well as its history provides him with opportunities and restraints. And it is through the structures of governance that he must interact with other actors in the archdiocese and attempt to influence its direction.

Chapters 4, 5, 6, and 7 examined how archbishops govern their parishes, deal with finances and personnel, and oversee the operations of their education and social service programs. A number of themes were common to all of these situations, which give us a picture of the episcopal decision-making process.

Reactive and Crisis Management

A characteristic of episcopal governance is that it is primarily reactive and not proactive. Like other leaders of organizations, archbishops respond to problems by searching for solutions.[1] An archbishop's time and attention is predominantly controlled by what hits him in the mail and on his schedule. Thus the mail brings in information, requests, and complaints. People desiring to see him do the same. His confirmation schedule forces him out among the people. His regularly scheduled meetings with various boards and councils force him to go over agenda material and to listen to the advice and opinions of others. The annual budgetary cycle forces him to review expenditures and budgetary projections.

Crises, especially those that might reach the press, also focus the archbishop's attention. A potential scandal, demonstration, or protest will consume his energy. A labor dispute or the closing of a school will always be controversial and require the archbishop's attention. Archbishops do not like surprises, but, in fact, they must spend a good amount of time responding to crises.

Being in a reactive mode is not necessarily a negative pattern. By reacting to crises and stimuli, an archbishop responds to the needs and the desires of the people in his local church. In fact, this reactive management style helps him to be pastoral in orientation. On the other hand, these concrete events can easily consume his time so that he does not have time to update himself theologically or to deal with broader issues. He fails to scan the environment for opportunities.

But while responding to immediate concerns is necessary and good, many archdiocesan officials, including archbishops, complain of the lack of long-range planning. Programs and policies are made in response to requests and perceived needs, but when limited resources demand selectivity, there is no sense of priorities to guide choices. Where some long-range planning is taking place, it is usually in response to a perceived crisis such as the decline in the number of priests.

Incrementalism vs. Comprehensive Planning

Some archdioceses have developed mission statements and pastoral plans. A few even have an office of planning and research. These offices are concerned with goal setting and the planning process within the diocesan structure. They also act as consultants.[2] But often the planners complain that their advice is not taken or they are ignored by the real decision makers. Their critics reply that the planners have biases and that their opinions are no more weighty than those of other participants.

Despite attempts at planning, setting priorities, and mission statements, most episcopal decision making is incremental.[3] Archdioceses have tried management by objectives, PPBS (program, planning, budgeting system), zero-based budgeting, and other management techniques. But when the final decisions are made, they are almost always only incrementally different from what was done in the past. This should not be surprising, since these management techniques have proven less than perfect when applied to government programs. In archdioceses, when money is tight, choices are rarely made among programs. Rather budgets are frozen or across-the-board cuts are made. When money is available, most budgets are expanded incrementally. Recognizing that programs are rarely closed down and that employees are rarely let go, archbishops place high thresholds in front of new programs or hirings.

Incremental change since the Vatican Council has meant mostly expansion—more programs, more offices, more lay personnel, more money. These many incremental changes have added up to substantial expansion on the part of archdioceses. This expansion together with a more rapidly changing environment has made the job of the archbishop more difficult. The creation of secretariat structures and budgetary systems have been attempts by archbishops to find means of governing these new programs and agencies.

One difficulty archbishops face in governing is that there are few empirical ways of measuring whether a program is successful or not. In a business, there are a number of indices: profit, market share, efficiency, growth. Like any nonprofit organization, the church lacks a bottom-line criteria of success. The Catholic church has for many years counted baptisms, Mass attendance, communions, collections, etc. All of these can be used as measurable criteria. But theologically, the church is interested not only in quantity but quality. Measuring quality of a liturgy or a sacramental experience is much more difficult.

In addition, the archbishops' lack of sophistication in social sciences makes it difficult for them to think in these terms. Those, like Andrew Greeley, who have been involved in empirical research on Catholic questions, complain that the bishops do not pay attention to their work. While no one argues that empirical research will answer every question, the church funds far less research than any other complex organization of comparable size. Nor do many Catholic foundations fund research.

Finances

One empirical measure most archbishops do understand is money. Some people are shocked and disappointed at the amount of time that bishops must devote to finances. Archbishops, however, recognize that they can do little without money. Their agencies and programs are bottomless pits that can always use more money. If an archbishop gives them all they want, the archdiocesan budget will be permanently in the red. Every archbishop knows of dioceses that overspent and were heavily in debt. They have heard from their friends how difficult and painful it was to turn those dioceses around and pay off the debts. None of them wants that problem. Nor do many enjoy raising money. As a result, most insist that the archdiocesan budget be balanced.

Finances are also important to some archbishops because they recognize the power of the purse. He who controls the funds, controls the organization. When my father presented the articles of incorporation for the Los Angeles Catholic Big Brothers to Cardinal James McIntyre, the cardinal said, "I only want to know one thing: How do I control the funds in this organization?" He was very angry when told he did not control the funds.

The power of the purse is seen at budget time. Funding determines what new programs are started. And the budgetary process is usually the only mechanism for reviewing existing archdiocesan programs. It is a time when questions are asked and programs must be defended. It is a time when an archbishop is guaranteed an agency's undivided attention.

On the other hand, extensive involvement in financial administration is also a temptation for bishops. Organizational theorists call this displacement of goals thorough overcommitment to means.[4] This danger, however, is not simply present in financial administration but in all kinds of administrative procedures: planning, meetings, newsletters, rules, and procedures.

Catholicity

Archbishops are also concerned about the Catholicity of archdiocesan programs, especially the Catholic character of their schools and social programs. Having programs that are professional and efficient is not enough; archbishops want something distinctively Catholic about these programs. This can be controversial if there is disagreement over what is "Catholic." While a certain amount of legitimate pluralism is acknowledged by most bishops, they also recognize their responsibility for the Catholic character of their agencies and programs. It is within the role of bishops as institutional leaders (rather than simply managers or technocrats) to be concerned about "meaning," legitimation, and higher level support, which makes the achievement of goals possible.[5] The difficulty comes when

"Catholic" is defined in a legalistic way that eliminates creativity in responding to a changing environment.

Consultation

Because they are dealing with so many uncertainties, few archbishops are willing to make decisions without consulting others. Archbishop Quinn of San Francisco admits that his "mistakes have always happened in the case where I did not really consult, where I just made my own decision without discussing or consulting with anybody. I don't usually do that. I usually do consult with wise people. But when I haven't, then I see that it has very often been the wrong decision."

Archbishops consult many people, including other bishops. Many archbishops find out what other bishops are doing before making a decision. Smart diocesan administrators know that if they can show that a program or policy has been adopted in a number of other dioceses, especially by bishops whom their archbishop respects, they will have an easier time selling their proposal. At a cabinet meeting discussing when and how often to allow Tridentine Masses, one archbishop reported calling Archbishop Kelly in Louisville to find out what he was doing.

Consulting other dioceses often gains valuable information and advice by profiting from their experience. Such a strategy helps an archbishop avoid making mistakes or at least avoid being alone in the mistake. One of the reasons Renew was adopted by so many dioceses was the high marks it received from bishops who had tried it. Likewise, when Archbishop Roach of St. Paul wanted to reorganize his diocesan agencies, he sent his moderator of the curia to Chicago to learn about their reorganization.

Most archbishops are not afraid to make decisions, but they realize that they need the advice of others. Whom they consult is important. Some consult widely; others tend to consult those they consider expert on the issue in question.

Cardinal Krol of Philadelphia explains:

In arriving at decisions, an archbishop must be well informed, must consult with people who know and have something to offer. It is a popular tendency today to have so-called grass-roots input, which is valid if the grass roots know what the issues are, what the problems are, what the goals are.

[Government officials in a democracy] do not go to grass roots every time they have to make a decision. They have to consult, they call the experts and the people who are in the know, and they do have hearings. But that town hall kind of a syndrome, which was valid with very small communities, is not applicable when you have a country such as ours or a diocese which exceeds 1.3 million Catholics.

Limiting consultation to experts is efficient, but it sometimes prevents the archbishop from getting advice from people who will be affected by the decision. In addition, if their support is necessary to carry out the policy, consultation is a method of fostering ownership over the decision. For example, while an archbishop might think RCIA or Renew would be good for the parishes, he should recognize that adopting them without consulting the priests would be a disaster. Bishops who follow a consultative style realize their dependence on others and the necessity of cooperative strategies to reduce uncertainty, gain commitments, and make goals more easily achievable.[6]

Sometimes the consultation process is in form only because those consulted know the archbishop has already made up his mind. For example, the priests' council in New York voted to have an archdiocesan synod because they knew Cardinal O'Connor wanted one, but there was little enthusiasm among the priests for the idea. On the other hand, in some situations the archbishop can be embarrassed when a consultative body flatly turns down his recommendation. The St. Paul council of priests in 1985 told Archbishop Roach that they did not support his plan to renovate the seminary. He postponed the project until he could win over their support.

When working with consultative bodies, archbishops look not only for advice, they are also attempting to form consensus. A majority vote in favor of a proposal is rarely sufficient. If 49 percent of the council opposes the proposal, the archbishop will rarely proceed. Rather he will call for more discussion and perhaps modifications to take into consideration the views of those opposed. This frequently means that the final decision is postponed.

The archbishop also wants consensus among his consultative groups. He would not want his priests' council and pastoral council in conflict like an upper and lower house.[7] If the pastoral council has one view and the priests' council has another, he is in trouble.[8] He or his staff will have to broker a compromise and work for consensus. The desire for consensus is one example of the high priority archbishops place on unity.

Some archbishops (for example, Cardinal Bernardin) go through wide consultations in an attempt to reach a consensus before making a decision. They are reluctant to do anything without wide support. Here, frequently the complaint is that decisions take too long to make. Similarly, while Archbishop Quinn wanted some kind of renewal program for his archdiocese, he wanted the priests' council to recommend which program should be adopted. They, on the other hand, wanted him to make a recommendation. The result was no program.

Other archbishops are accused of giving the appearance of consultation while really manipulating the group to agree with their preordained decision. Some priests believe their archbishop does not take their council seriously. One member of an executive committee described a meeting where liturgy and personnel were chosen as priority topics for the year.

The archbishop was invited to discuss these with the executive committee. This was his chance to influence the proceedings. He saw *Liturgy* and *Personnel* on the blackboard, and he said, "They just want a gripe session. They want more money for the liturgy committee. Personnel? Gripe session! Priests are never happy with personnel decisions."

Later when the archbishop addressed the entire council, he told them their choice of issues was wonderful. "Liturgy and personnel, these are my concerns, too." As soon as there was a coffee break, everyone learned what he had said to the executive committee.

Few archbishops are comfortable with group decision making in large consultative councils, such as a pastoral council or priests' council. These bodies tend to be uninformed and slow in coming to a consensus on a course of action. The archbishops find these councils most useful as feedback mechanisms where they can hear the reactions of people about what is happening in the archdiocese. Smaller specialized boards whose members are familiar with particular agencies are more successful.

Despite these problems, few archbishops will move on a major decision until after wide consultation leads to a consensus. While recognizing that they always have the last word, the archbishops also recognize that forcing a program on the archdiocese, and especially on the diocesan priests, can be counterproductive. Without enthusiastic support of the priests and archdiocesan lay leaders, most archdiocesan programs will not work anyway.

Primacy of Charity

In the decision-making process, archbishops place a priority on unity and charity, which take precedence over efficiency and effectiveness. This can be seen not only in the consultative process, but in other decision-making situations. For example, almost all archbishops pointed to personnel as their most difficult area. Most archbishops want to be loving fathers; they do not like to confront or fire people. As a result, people are not challenged, they are not dealt with honestly, and personnel problems are unresolved. For example, computerizing the business office will wait for the retirement of an elderly bookkeeper. Reductions in personnel can only be made through not replacing retiring personnel. The resulting inefficiencies can cause staff morale problems and ineffectiveness in archdiocesan programs.

The primacy of charity over efficiency can also be seen in the desire of archbishops to keep open inner-city parishes with declining congregations. While retailers and services flee to the suburbs, Catholic churches remain open and staffed. Inner-city schools for blacks are another example of charity outweighing efficiency. Although black children are helped tremendously by these schools, few are Catholic and few become Catholics.

The primacy of unity and charity encourages archbishops to avoid conflict whenever possible. Few archbishops are combative by nature or enjoy a fight. Planning has been ineffective in most archdioceses because planning means making choices, and choices bring conflict with those who prefer the status quo. Plans are invariably postponed until a consensus supports them or until lack of resources (either money or personnel) forces a decision.

Archbishops also avoid conflict by delegating decisions. Department budgets might be cut and then the department heads told to make the necessary cuts among their offices.

The biggest problems for archbishops come when the interests of one group conflict with another. For example, most archbishops would like to raise teachers' salaries, but this would require raising tuitions. Or on an individual basis, there can be a conflict when two priests want the same pastorate. Or conflict can occur between the needs of a pastor and the needs of a parish.

In secular society, such conflicts would be resolved in favor of the strongest; in the church, they are just as apt to be resolved in favor of the weaker party. Priests in Chicago joke that priests who do well in a difficult assignment are rewarded with an even more difficult job, whereas those who fail are given a soft job. Charity takes priority over merit.

Keeping the Pastors Happy

When making decisions, the most important constituency for the archbishop is his priests, especially the pastors. Keeping his priests happy is a high priority. Because of their permanent commitment to the archdiocese, they are like members of a family in a family business. This "clerical club" is based on extended relationships that have grown over time, beginning in the seminary. The large exodus of priests also made bishops sensitive to priestly needs. With the decline in the number of priests, each diocesan priest becomes an irreplaceable employee.

All of this means that keeping the priests happy is good for the archdiocese and the archbishop. Practically every archbishop, for example, tells his secretary that he is available for any priest who wants to see him at any time. Even cardinals and archbishops involved in national or international work will come under criticism if they become unavailable to their priests.

Keeping the priests happy has important ramifications on archdiocesan governance. For example, one favorite pastime of the clerical club is complaining about the chancery, especially that it is wasting money. Whether or not this is true, their attitude puts pressure on the archdiocesan budget because of an unwillingness of archbishops to raise parish assessments or diocesan appeal goals. The archbishops would usually rather cut or freeze budgets than face the wrath of pastors by proposing a tax increase.

Priests also complain that the chancery and archdiocesan agencies are not doing anything to serve the parishes. Archbishops have responded by asking agencies at budget time what they are doing for the parishes. Agencies, like Catholic Charities, that for many years operated independently from the parishes, are now developing programs aimed at fulfilling parish needs. Agencies that the pastors think are wasteful tend to be the ones that get cut at budget time because they have lost the support of this important constituency.

Another example of this attitude toward pastors is the reluctance of archbishops to mandate any policies or programs. Most archbishops want to respect the autonomy of the local pastor as much as possible. In addition, they do not want to place additional burdens on pastors who are already overworked. As long as there are not too many complaints from the parishioners, pastors can pretty much get away with almost anything.

The priests' personnel board and priests' personnel directors can be understood in this light also. By using a board and following its recommendations, the archbishop can distance himself from possible conflict with his priests. Rather than telling a priest that he is not fit to be a pastor, he can say, "The personnel board does not think you are ready to be a pastor. This is the way they see you. . . ." He can even have the personnel director convey the bad news. In one archdiocese, the archbishop notifies the priest who gets a parish, while the clergy personnel director notifies those who were passed over.

Coping with Uncertainty

One of the most important functions of an organization's leadership is to deal with the constraints and contingencies imposed by its environment and its technology. For a pencil factory, this means organizing the capital, raw materials, workers, and equipment as well as marketing the output. The simpler the technology, the more benign and stable the environment, the easier the job. The more complex the technology, the more unstable the environment, the more difficult the leader's task. Complexity and instability introduce uncertainty into the decision-making process.

Especially since Vatican II, bishops have had to face a more complex and constantly changing environment. Old ministries (technologies) have not produced the desired effects (e.g., Mass attendance and vocations have gone down). New ministries have been developed, but the effectiveness of these ministries has been uncertain. In addition, lack of agreement has existed over the desirable outcomes of various ministries. Lacking consensus on goals and lacking certainty on effectiveness, bishops have found themselves in the worst possible position to make what has been traditionally considered a "rational" decision: choosing the most efficient and effective means to obtain a goal.

Bishops have followed strategies that would be expected in such a situation.

1. They have created new units (liturgy office, social ministries, Renew, ecumenical commission, personnel office, family life office) within the organization that employ people trained in the new ministries (technologies). Sometimes the units (like minority offices, personnel offices) will be buffers or communication channels between the environment and the rest of the organization. The danger here is creating a multitude of uncoordinated units.
2. Rationality has been imposed on those parts of the system where it is possible both technically and politically. Thus, computers and modern business methods are making headway in financial administration but only where inertia is overcome by political means. Personnel procedures have been professionalized. The danger here is attempting to impose rules and standardization where it is not appropriate.
3. Where there is lack of consensus on goals or where the effectiveness of new technologies (ministries) is uncertain, social or political or ideological (theological) criteria are used in decision making. And decision making is incremental.

Church leaders in the face of uncertainty use social and political criteria in decision making: peer group evaluation, wide consultation, consensus decision making, appeals to higher authority, appeals to experts, and limiting the number of variables examined because of ideological reasons. Thus, while a bishop may not understand what his Catholic Charities is doing, he will be satisfied if (1) it is accredited through peer evaluation, (2) government and private agencies have enough confidence in it to give it money, (3) those it serves are pleased, (4) the board of directors approves the programs, and (5) little negative feedback comes from important constituencies, like the pastors.

Ideological (theological) premises that ignore or deny the validity of environmental signals also ease decision making. Altars are turned around despite complaints of some parishioners. The requirement of priestly celibacy is retained despite the decline in vocations. Or uncertainty can also be resolved by appeals to higher authority or by eliminating any experimentation until it is mandated from above. Fear of exercising discretion is especially high when the consequences of error are considered great. What is started as an experiment is sometimes difficult to stop. And no bishop wants to be accused by the Vatican of being unorthodox.

The primacy given to unity and charity reflect the use of social and political criteria in decision making. Concern for unity and charity give a special orientation to ecclesial decision making. Keeping important constituencies happy, especially priests and chancery employees, encourages delegation, consultation, and consensus decision making. Extensive consultation has become an accepted part of contemporary American ecclesial life. It is a time-consuming process, but few archbishops would try to govern their archdioceses without it. Consultation is not simply a means of gaining information; it is also a method of developing support and consensus for a program or policy.

But an archbishop cannot simply respond to local constituencies. While their desires and opinions are important, he also is constrained by finances, church law, and the views of Roman officials, as was seen in the last chapter. He must see to it that programs are solvent and truly Catholic.

There is no such thing as an ideal archdiocesan organization. The organizational structure must be tailored to meet the personality and desires of the archbishop and the needs of the archdiocese within the constraints imposed by the environment. In large archdioceses, secretariat-level administrators have become necessary because of the proliferation and growth of archdiocesan agencies. The archbishop needs help if agencies and offices are going to be supervised and coordinated. Regional vicars also make the archbishop's presence felt in the parishes, especially if the archdiocese is large and he is busy with administration.

The danger of these new structures is that they will become bureaucratic and unresponsive either to the archbishop or to his people. Thomas F. O'Dea explained this well in looking at the pre-Vatican II church, but the dilemmas of institutionalization also exist for the post-Vatican church:

> It is characteristic of bureaucratic structure to elaborate new offices and new networks of communications and command in the face of new problems. Precedents are established which lead to the precipitation of new rules and procedures. One result may indeed be that the structure tends to complicate itself. This state of affairs evolves in order to cope with new situations and new problems effectively. Yet such self-complication can overextend itself and produce an unwieldy organization with blocks and breakdowns in communication, overlapping of spheres of competence, and ambiguous definitions of authority and related functions. In short, developments to meet functional needs can become dysfunctional in later situations. . . . The tendency of organization to complicate itself to meet new situations often transforms it into an awkward and confusing mechanism within whose context it is difficult to accomplish anything.[9]

Although structures are important, the key to successful governance is not so much an ideal structure as the ability of the archbishop to find people who can do the things he cannot do and give them the resources they need. Thus, an archbishop who has difficulties relating to his priests would be wise to seek out a vicar for priests who is well liked and trusted by the priests. An archbishop who dislikes administration needs to look for a competent vicar general to take care of as much administration as possible. Archbishops who spend much time on administration need their auxiliaries to be an episcopal, pastoral presence in the parishes. Rather than trying to turn themselves into something they are not, wise archbishops lead with their strengths and find others to cover their weaknesses. But he must be willing to give them real authority and not just a title.

But there are some things that the archbishop simply cannot delegate to others: dealing with the Vatican, with the NCCB, with other bishops (including his auxiliaries), with priest personnel problems, with budget deficits, with the closing (or opening) of parishes and schools, with problems that will make the front page of the local newspaper, and with the appointment of pastors and cabinet-level administrators. He can get help from others on these matters, but they are too important for him to ignore. In addition, he must be sensitive to the long-range good of the archdiocese and the church as a whole since others in the diocese will be focused only on parts.

Finally, the archbishop must take care of himself. He is responsible for ministering to his priests, but there is no one to minister to him. There are few with whom he can share his problems. If he has close friends among the diocesan clergy, he will be accused of preferring them over others. Even these priest friends are under him in authority, which is why many bishops seek out religious priests as spiritual directors. One archbishop reported that he had a hard time finding any priest who was willing to be his spiritual director.

Bishops can become isolated with no one supporting them, as Archbishop Weakland of Milwaukee explains:

I'm finding that more and more bishops are isolated. We religious had our own support groups, and we had superiors who were interested in us. I find that more and more bishops somehow don't get any support groups and they get isolated. They come to the bishops' meetings, they smile and greet people, and they go home, and no one seems to worry about who ministers to the bishops.

As a church leader, the archbishop must also nourish his spiritual life. Archbishop Kelly of Louisville speaks of the need of a bishop to be "sustained and nurtured by prayer." He says,

All of this stuff, the programmatic stuff, the financial, the management, none of it can hold a candle to my responsibility to preach and therefore to pray.

I am to be the best preacher in the diocese. I am to be the best celebrant, and that means a deep spirituality. I haven't got it there yet, but I want to be there. That is very, very important to me.

This book has been about the archbishop's role in the governance of his archdiocese. As a result, I have not been able to devote much space to his role as liturgist, teacher, or spiritual leader. Nor have I been able to examine the theological views or spiritual lives of archbishops. All these aspects of episcopal life are very important, but they are less susceptible to analysis by social scientists.

What this book has shown is the way archbishops respond to their environment, organize their archdioceses, and make decisions dealing with such important matters as personnel, finances, parish life, social services, and education. These are all vital to the life of the local church that is his archdiocese. The archbishops have a tremendous impact on the lives of their local churches. The decisions they make today will determine the shape of the church in the United States in the next century.

Notes

Introduction

1. Chester I. Barnard, *The Functions of the Executive* (Cambridge, MA: Harvard University Press, 1938), 5.
2. Eugene C. Kennedy, M.M., and Victor J. Heckler, *The Catholic Priest in the United States: Psychological Investigations* (Washington, DC: U.S. Catholic Conference, 1972), 216.
3. For a cybernetic analysis of the church, see Patrick Granfield, *Ecclesial Cybernetics: A Study of Democracy in the Church* (New York: Macmillan, 1973).
4. James D. Thompson, *Organizations in Action* (New York: McGraw-Hill, 1967).
5. All quotations that are not footnoted are from these interviews.
6. *The Official Catholic Directory 1988* (Wilmette, IL: P. J. Kenedy & Sons, 1988). Estimates of the percentage of Catholic population in the United States by Gallup are higher than estimates in the directory. See Dean Hoge, *Future of Catholic Leadership* (Kansas City, KS: Sheed & Ward, 1987), 228.
7. Thomas J. Reese, S.J., "A Survey of the American Bishops," *America* 149 (November 12, 1983): 287.

Chapter 1. The Selection of Bishops

1. This is a revised and expanded version of Thomas J. Reese, S.J., "The Selection of Bishops," *America* 151 (August 18, 1984): 65–72.
2. See Giuseppe Alberigo and Anton Weiler, *Election and Consensus in the Church*, *Concilium* 77 (1972); William W. Bassett, ed., *The Choosing of Bishops* (Hartford, CT: Canon Law Society of America, 1971); Peter Huizing and Knut Walf, eds., *Electing Our Own Bishops*, *Concilium* 137 (1980); Raymond Kottje, "The Selection of Church Officials: Some Historical Facts and Experiences," *Concilium* 63 (1971): 117–26; Joseph O'Donoghue, *Elections in the Church* (Baltimore, MD: Helicon Press, 1967); G. Sweeney, " 'The Wound in the Right Foot': Unhealed," *Clergy Review* 9 (1975): 574–93; also in *Bishops and Writers: Aspects of the Evolution of Modern English Catholicism*, ed. Adrian Hastings (Wheathampstead, England: Anthony Clarke, 1977), 207–34; L. John Topel, "Ways the Church Selected Its Bishops," *America* 127 (September 2, 1972): 119–21; Edward Schillebeeckx, *The Church with a Human Face* (New York: Crossroads, 1985), 124–48.
3. John Tracy Ellis, "On Selecting American Bishops," *Commonweal* 85 (March

10, 1967): 643–49; John Tracy Ellis, "On Selecting Catholic Bishops for the United States," *The Critic* 26 (June–July 1969): 42–48; John Tracy Ellis, "The Selection of Bishops," *American Benedictine Review* 35 (June 1984): 111–27; James Hennesey, " 'To Chuse a Bishop': An American Way," *America* 127 (September 2, 1972): 115–18; Robert Trisco, "Democratic Influence on the Election of Bishops and Pastors and on the Administration of Dioceses and Parishes in the U.S.A.," *Concilium* 77 (1972): 132–38.

4. *Code of Canon Law, Latin-English Edition* (Washington, DC: Canon Law Society of America, 1983), Canon 378 §1.

5. Cover letter (1984) from apostolic delegate requesting information on candidate for the office of bishop. All caps and bold in original. See also "Instruction on the Pontifical Secret," February 4, 1974, *Origins* 4 (May 30, 1974): 9–11.

6. Canon 377 §2.

7. Council for the Public Affairs of the Church, "Norms for the Selection of Candidates for the Episcopacy in the Latin Church," March 25, 1972 (Washington, DC: U.S. Catholic Conference, 1974) [also in *Origins* 2 (May 25, 1972): 1–9], article 6.2, p. 5.

8. Ibid.

9. Ibid., article 1.2, p. 3.

10. Ibid.

11. "Delegation Official Explains Bishop Selection Process," NC [National Catholic] News Service, August 4, 1983.

12. *Priests' Forum* 1 (March/April 1969): 26–28.

13. James H. Provost, "Selection of Bishops—Does Anybody Care?" *Chicago Studies* 18 (Summer 1979): 215.

14. For a general discussion of professional advancement in the church, see Robert W. Peterson and Richard A. Schoenherr, "Organizational Status Attainment of Religious Professionals," *Social Forces* 56 (March 1978): 794–822.

15. "A Statement by the Ten Black Catholic Bishops of the United States," presented by Most Rev. Joseph L. Howze (Washington, DC: National Conference of Catholic Bishops, November 1985, Mimeographed), 8.

16. A nuncio is a papal ambassador accredited by the government of the country in which he resides. He is also dean of the diplomatic corps in that country. A pro-nuncio is accredited but is not the dean.

17. See Gerald P. Fogarty, S.J., *The Vatican and the American Hierarchy from 1870 to 1965* (Stuttgart, Germany: Anton Hiersemann, 1982) and (Wilmington, DE: Michael Glazier, 1985); Robert A. Graham, *Vatican Diplomacy* (Princeton, NJ: Princeton University Press, 1959); Thomas J. Reese, S.J., "Diplomatic Relations with Holy See," *America* 152 (March 16, 1985): 215–16, and "Three Years Later: U.S. Relations with the Holy See," *America* 156 (January 17, 1987): 29–35; Robert J. Wister, "The Establishment of the Apostolic Delegation in Washington: The Pastoral and Political Motivation," *U.S. Catholic Historian* 3 (Spring-Summer 1983): 115–29.

18. Arthur Jones, "Jean Jadot: Pope's Man in U.S.," *National Catholic Reporter*, March 25, 1977, 7.

19. Thomas J. Reese, S.J., "Diplomatic Relations with the Holy See," *America* 152 (March 16, 1985): 215.

20. Harold L. Ickes, *The Secret Diary of Harold L. Ickes*, vol. 3 (New York: Simon

& Schuster, 1955), 55. For more on Sheil, see pp. 36, 45, 55–56, 63–65, 110, 114, 159, 382–83, 403–4.

21. Fogarty, *The Vatican and the American Hierarchy*, 264.
22. Ickes, *Secret Diary*, 65.
23. Thomas J. Reese, S.J., "Three Years Later: U.S. Relations with the Holy See," *America* 156 (January 17, 1987): 29–35.
24. James Hennesey, S.J., *American Catholics: A History of the Roman Catholic Community in the United States* (New York: Oxford University Press, 1981), 72.
25. Graham, *Vatican Diplomacy*, 84.
26. For several years, the appointment of an auxiliary was done in two stages: the bishop would make the request, submit his reasons to the pro-nuncio, who would send it to the Congregation for Bishops and the pope. If the response from Rome was positive, then the second stage would begin with proposing names, questionnaires, and a ternus. Around 1982, the congregation returned to the older practice of the request and the ternus being submitted simultaneously as it is being described here. Such changes do occur occasionally, but they are not announced or generally made known.
27. *The Official Catholic Directory 1987* (Wilmette, IL: P. J. Kenedy & Sons, 1987). At the time of this study, Santa Fe (with 272,338 Catholics) and Indianapolis (with 201,883 Catholics) were the only archdioceses with more than 200,000 Catholics that did not have auxiliaries.
28 Canon 377 §3. *Terna* is the Italian word in common use by the participants, but *ternus* is the English term used in *Code of Canon Law, Latin-English Edition* (Washington, DC: Canon Law Society of America, 1983).
29. Canon 377 §4.
30. Thomas J. Reese, S.J., "The Seattle Way of the Cross," *America* 155 (September 20, 1986): 111–12 and "Hunthausen forced by Vatican to yield powers to auxiliary bishop," Religious News Service, September 5, 1986.
31. John Tracy Ellis, *Catholic Bishops: A Memoir* (Wilmington, DE: Michael Glazier, 1983), 59.
32. Canon Law Society of America, *Procedure for the Selection of Bishops in the United States* (Hartford, CT: Canon Law Society of America, 1973), 20. Also see Norman P. Bolduc, "Report of Committee on Selection of Bishops," *Reports Prepared for 50th Annual Convention, Oct. 10–13, 1988* (Washington, DC: Canon Law Society of America, 1988), 27–33.
33. "Material Used in the Archdiocese of Baltimore," in *Selection of Bishops Process*, comp. NFPC's Committee on Ministry and Priestly Life Task Force on the Selection of Bishops Process (Chicago: National Federation of Priests' Councils, October 1974).
34. Ibid.
35. "Material Used in the Archdiocese of Santa Fe," *Selection of Bishops Process*.
36. Thomas P. Doyle, O.P., "The Selection of Bishops in the United States," (Washington, DC: Apostolic Delegation Press Release, Undated [1983?], Mimeographed), 4.
37. Mary Ann Walsh, "Wide Consultation Called Key in Picking New York, Boston Archbishops," NC News Service, December 22, 1983.
38. Canon 377 §3.

39. John Thavis, "The Pope's Bishops: Consulting on the Selections," NC News Service, January 13, 1988.
40. Fogarty, *The Vatican and the American Hierarchy*, 314.
41. Ellis, *Catholic Bishops*, 19, and Fogarty, *The Vatican and the American Hierarchy*, 315.
42. John Thavis, "The Pope's Bishops: Shaping the World's Hierarchy in His Image," NC News Service, January 13, 1987.
43. Ibid.
44. Andrew M. Greeley, *The Catholic Priest in the United States: Sociological Investigations* (Washington, DC: U.S. Catholic Conference, 1972), 126.
45. If the appointment involves a priest who is to be made a bishop, his candidacy must be considered by the congregation. If the appointment involves a bishop who is being promoted, the episcopal members of the congregation usually review the promotion, but it can be handled by the cardinal prefect and the staff. In this case, the staff would prepare a three- to five-page memo (*Foglio d'Udienza*) summarizing the documents, which the prefect would then take with his recommendation to the pope in a private audience. Cardinal Gantin, the current prefect of the congregation, takes most appointments to a meeting of the congregation before he takes them to the pope. His predecessor, Cardinal Baggio, would more frequently bypass the congregation, but even under him, appointments to large dioceses would go through the congregation.
   On rare occasions only one, two, or three members of the congregation may be consulted by the prefect before taking the name of the candidate to the pope. If, for example, an urgent appointment comes in during the summer when the congregation does not meet, the prefect could ask one, two, or three members of the congregation to study the dossier and give their opinions. But appointments in the United States can usually wait until October when the congregation begins meeting again.
46. Sometimes the *ponente* is referred to as the *relator* (summarizer).
47. Up to the mid 1970s, former papal representatives were often put on the Congregation for Bishops. A former representative would often then be the relator or ponente for the country where he had served. From 1976 on, the trend has been against putting former representatives on the congregation, and therefore other cardinals have been the ponentes.
48. Muriel Bowen, "The Appointment of Bishops in Britain since Vatican II," in *Concilium* 137 (1980): 87. Upper Volta was not a very good example since its episcopal candidates would go through the Congregation for the Evangelization of Peoples.
49. Statistics updated from Thomas J. Reese, S.J., "A Survey of the American Bishops," *America* 149 (November 12, 1983): 286.
50. Fogarty, *The Vatican and the American Hierarchy*, 26.
51. Peterson and Schoenherr, "Organizational Status Attainment," 813. See also John D. Donovan, "The American Catholic Hierarchy: A Social Profile," *The American Catholic Sociological Review* 19 (June 1958): 109.
52. Bowen, "Appointment of Bishops in Britain," 87.
53. John Thavis, "The Pope's Bishops: Consulting on the Selections," NC News Service, January 13, 1988.

54. John Thavis, "The Pope's Bishops: Shaping the World's Hierarchy in His Image," NC News Service, January 13, 1988.
55. John Thavis, "The Pope's Bishops: Consulting on the Selections."
56. John Thavis, "The Pope's Bishops: Shaping the World's Hierarchy in His Image."
57. "Ad quosdam episcopos e Statibus Foederatis Americae Septemtrionalis occassione oblata 'ad Limina' visitationis coram admissos" (September 5, 1983), Acta Apostolicae Sedis 76:103–4, italics in original.
58. Peter Hebblethwaite, Synod Extraordinary (Garden City, NY: Doubleday, 1986), 44. (The two sentences in parenthesis were in the written text but omitted by the pope in his delivery.) For other controversial European appointments, see Peter Hebblethwaite, "Rome's Choices Spark Uproar in Austria," National Catholic Reporter, May 15, 1987, and "Bishops Against the Tide in Their Sees," National Catholic Reporter, May 22, 1987. See also Dirk Visser, "Vatican Angers Dutch Catholics in Death of Bishop of Haarlem," Religious News Service, October 25, 1983; Agostino Bono, "Austrian Hierarchy Told to Resolve Conflict over Bishop Choices," NC News Service, June 25, 1987; John Thavis, "The Pope's Bishops: A Trend in Appointments" and "The Pope's Bishops: Consulting on the Selection," NC News Service, January 13, 1988; Olivia O'Leary, "The Battle for the Diocese of Dublin," Magill, June 1984; Louis McRedmond, "Archbishop Needed," The Tablet, August 18, 1984, and "Dublin's New Archbishop," The Tablet, January 30, 1988. Also for Latin America, see José Pedro S. Martins, "Brazil: Church Uneasy Over Recent Papal Appointments," Latinamerica Press, May 12, 1988, 6.
59. John Thavis, "The Pope's Bishops: A Trend in Appointments."
60. Ellis, Catholic Bishops, 105.
61. The Report of the Bishops' Ad Hoc Committee for Priestly Life and Ministry (Washington, DC: U.S. Catholic Conference, 1974), 10.
62. John F. Fahey, "Sorry, These Norms Won't Do," America 127 (September 2, 1972): 113–14; Ladislas Orsy, "What the New Norms Say and Don't Say," America 127 (September 2, 1972): 111–13; Canon Law Society of America, Procedure for the Selection of Bishops (Hartford, CT: Canon Law Society of America, 1973); "Theologians React," Origins 2 (May 25, 1972): 4 and 18; "National Federation of Priests' Councils Statement," Origins 2 (May 25, 1972): 3–4.
63. Canon Law Society of America, Procedure for the Selection of Bishops (Hartford, CT: Canon Law Society of America, 1973), ii.
64. Orsy, "What the New Norms Say," 112.
65. Ibid., 113.
66. Canon Law Society of America, Procedure for the Selection of Bishops, 9–20; see also Canon Law Society of America's Selection of Bishops Committee, "The Plan for Choosing Bishops," Origins 2 (May 25, 1972): 3–4.
67. Fahey, "Sorry," 114.
68. John Jay Hughes, "Selecting Your Bishops," America 126 (March 25, 1972): 310–12.
69. Greeley, Catholic Priest, 146. Using a slightly different question, a 1985 survey found 49 percent of the diocesan priests agreed it would be a good idea if the priests in a diocese were to choose their own bishop. See Dean

R. Hoge, Joseph J. Shields, and Mary Jeanne Verdieck, "Attitudes of American Priests in 1970 and 1985 on the Church and Priesthood," Study of Future Church Leadership, Report No. 4 (Washington, DC: Catholic University of America, March 1986, Mimeographed), table 2, p. 2.

70. NFPC's [National Federation of Priests' Councils'] Committee on Ministry and Priestly Life Task Force on the Selection of Bishops Process, *Materials for Priests' Council Use on the Selection of Bishops Process* (Chicago: National Federation of Priests' Councils, October 1974).

Chapter 2. The Ecclesial Environment

1. For a discussion of the impact of environment on organizations, see James D. Thompson, *Organizations in Action* (New York: McGraw-Hill, 1967), 25–38.
2. "There is an abundance of organizational forms in European dioceses, responding to various sociological and pastoral conditions. The diocesan curia in European dioceses is also affected by the Church-State relations in individual nations, particularly on the level of trusteeship which is governed by specific legislation in the different countries." Roland-Bernhard Trauffer, O.P., "Diocesan Governance in European Dioceses Following the 1983 Code: An Initial Inquiry," in *The Ministry of Governance*, ed. James K. Mallet (Washington, DC: Canon Law Society of America, 1986), 195.
3. Joseph H. Fichter, S.J., *Religion as an Occupation: A Study in the Sociology of Professions* (Notre Dame, IN: University of Notre Dame, 1961), 268.
4. Robert F. Szafran, "The Distribution of Influence in Religious Organizations," *Journal for the Scientific Study of Religion* 15 (1976), 348. See also Thomas Ference, Fred Goldner, and R. Ritti, "Priests and Church: The Professionalization of an Organization," *American Behavioral Scientist* 14:507–22.
5. Andrew M. Greeley, *The Catholic Priest in the United States: Sociological Investigations* (Washington, DC: U.S. Catholic Conference, 1972), 143.
6. For a discussion of domain consensus, see Thompson, *Organizations in Action*, 29.
7. Avery Dulles, S.J., *Models of the Church* (Garden City, NY: Doubleday, 1974). This book was spontaneously mentioned by more interviewees than any other book.
8. George Gallup, Jr., and Jim Castelli, *The American Catholic People* (Garden City, NY: Doubleday, 1987), 43.
9. Gallup and Castelli, *American Catholic People*, 56. See also Dean R. Hoge, Joseph J. Shields, and Mary Jeanne Verdieck, "Attitudes of Priests, Adults and College Students on Catholic Parish Life and Leadership," Study of Future Church Leadership, Report No. 3 (Washington, DC: Catholic University of America, January 1986, Mimeographed), table 5.
10. Greeley, *Catholic Priest*, 86.
11. Ibid., 136.
12. Ibid., 147.

13. For a discussion of a "zone of acceptance of authority," see Herbert A. Simon, *Administrative Behavior* (New York: Free Press, 1957).
14. Greeley, *Catholic Priest*, 206.
15. Ibid., 147.
16. Dean R. Hoge, Joseph J. Shields, and Mary Jeanne Verdieck, "Attitudes of American Priests in 1970 and 1985 on the Church and Priesthood," Study of Future Church Leadership, Report No. 4 (Washington, DC: Catholic University of America, March 1986, Mimeographed), table 9, p. 1.
17. For a summary of the canon laws affecting bishops, see Thomas J. Green, *A Manual for Bishops: Rights and Responsibilities of Diocesan Bishops in the Revised Code of Canon Law* (Washington, DC: U.S. Catholic Conference, 1983). See also Sacred Congregation for Bishops, *Directory on the Pastoral Ministry of Bishops* (Ottawa: Canadian Catholic Conference, 1974); Thomas J. Green, "The Diocesan Bishop in the Revised Code: Some Introductory Reflection," *Jurist* 42 (1982): 320–47; Thomas J. Green, "Rights and Duties of Diocesan Bishops," *CLSA [Canon Law Society of America] Proceedings* 45 (1983): 18–36; James A. Coriden, Thomas J. Green, and Donald E. Heintschel, eds., *The Code of Canon Law: A Text and Commentary* (New York: Paulist Press, 1985); Rembert G. Weakland, O.S.B., "Local Implementation—Ecclesial Life Under the 1983 Code," *CLSA Proceedings* 46 (1984): 12–23; Michael A. Fahey, S.J., "Diocesan Governance in Modern Catholic Theology and in the 1983 Code of Canon Law," and James H. Provost, "Canonical Reflection on Selected Issues in Diocesan Governance," in *The Ministry of Governance*, ed. James K. Mallet (Washington, DC: Canon Law Society of America, 1986), 121–39, 209–51. For the historical view, see John E. Lynch, C.S.P., "The Changing Role of the Bishop: A Historical Survey," *Jurist* 39 (1979): 289–312.
18. Since canon law makes few distinctions between the authority of a diocesan bishop and an archbishop in his diocese, I will refer to bishops in general in this section except where archbishops are specifically meant.
19. *Code of Canon Law, Latin-English Edition* (Washington, DC: Canon Law Society of America, 1983), Canon 375 §1.
20. Canon 375 §1–2.
21. Canon 381 §1. Some canonists argue that it is not the bishop's power that is restricted but only his discretion to exercise it. As a result, he could validly but not licitly exercise his power in areas where its exercise is restricted. See Provost, "Canonical Reflection," 218–19.
22. Thomas J. Green, "Title I: Particular Churches and the Authority Established in Them," in *The Code of Canon Law: A Text and Commentary*, ed. Coriden, Green, and Heintschel, 325.
23. Canon 391 §1–2.
24. Canons 495–501.
25. Canons 511–14.
26. Canon 502.
27. Canon 492.
28. Canon 1277.
29. Canon 473 §1.
30. Canon 475.
31. Canon 479.

32. Canon 476.
33. Canon 482.
34. Canon 473 §2.
35. Canon 494. See John J. Myers, "The Diocesan Fiscal Officer and the Diocesan Finance Council," *CLSA Proceedings* 44 (1982): 181–88.
36. Statistics updated from Thomas J. Reese, S.J., "A Survey of the American Bishops," *America* 149 (November 12, 1983): 287.
37. For statistics on U.S. dioceses, see "General Summary," *The Official Catholic Directory 1988* (Wilmette, IL: J. P. Kenedy & Sons, 1988).
38. Thompson, *Organizations in Action*, 68.
39. Mary P. Burke and Eugene F. Hemrick, *Building the Local Church: Shared Responsibility in Diocesan Pastoral Councils* (Washington, DC: U.S. Catholic Conference, 1984), 18.
40. John Seidler, "Priest-Protest in the Human Catholic Church," *National Catholic Reporter*, May 3, 1974, 14.
41. Joseph H. Fichter, S.J., *Priest and People* (New York: Sheed & Ward, 1965), 177.
42. Ibid., 166–67.
43. Seidler, "Priest-Protest," 14.
44. Thompson, *Organizations in Action*, 45.
45. Seidler, "Priest-Protest," 14.
46. Burke and Hemrick, *Building the Local Church*, 12.
47. On the effect of a hostile environment on the diocesan structures in early American history, see Thomas Curry, "The Emergence and Development of a Style of American Diocesan Governance in Response to External Factors," in *The Ministry of Governance*, ed. Mallet, 1–20.
48. Thompson, *Organizations in Action*, 68–70.
49. Seidler, "Priest-Protest," 14.
50. Thompson, *Organizations in Action*, 70–71.
51. Ibid., 73–79.

Chapter 3. Style and Structure

1. Andrew M. Greeley, *The Catholic Priest in the United States: Sociological Investigations* (Washington, DC: U.S. Catholic Conference, 1972), 27–28. Greeley found that bishops come from higher socioeconomic families than do priests, as measured on the occupational scores of their fathers, but that a smaller percentage of bishops' fathers graduated from high school. This is quite different from the Church of England, where bishops have higher social origins than the local clergy. See Kenneth Thompson, "Church of England Bishops as an Elite," in *Elites and Power in British Society*, ed. Philip Stanworth and Anthony Giddens (Cambridge: Cambridge University Press, 1974), 198–207. See also John D. Donovan, "The American Catholic Hierarchy: A Social Profile," *The American Sociological Review* 19 (June 1958): 98–112; Robert W. Peterson and Richard A. Schoenherr, "Organizational Status Attainment of Religious Professionals," *Social Forces* 56 (March 1978): 794–822.

2. Statistics are updated from Thomas J. Reese, S.J., "A Survey of the American Bishops," *America* 149 (November 12, 1983): 287.

3. Greeley, *Catholic Priest*, 126.

4. For a description of the styles of early American bishops, see John Tracy Ellis, "American Catholic Bishops: Changing Leadership Styles," *Church* 1 (1985): 21–30. He notes John Carroll was "devoid of flamboyance" but of "sound judgment, prudence and tact." John England was forceful, imaginative, eloquent, and a civic leader who felt the church should adapt to its American environment. His French-born colleagues opposed him in this. John Hughes was a "fighter," while Francis Kenrick was "mild." Midwestern bishops were initiators, especially in pushing for a plenary council in 1884; easterners were "more conservative." At the council, John J. Williams was taciturn, while Richard Gilmour, John Ireland, and Spalding "were heard frequently and forcefully." Archbishop James Gibbons was "unoriginal" but acted "with consummate tact and prudence." From 1916 to 1965, archbishops from Chicago "let things happen," permitting numerous initiatives for the promotion of family life, youth, liturgical reform, etc.

5. Avery Dulles, S.J., *Models of the Church* (Garden City, NY: Doubleday, 1974). See also James H. Provost, "Structuring the Church as a Communio," *Jurist* 36 (1976): 191–262; James H. Provost, "Structuring the Church as Missio," *Jurist* 39 (1979): 220–88.

6. *Code of Canon Law, Latin-English Edition* (Washington, DC: Canon Law Society of America, 1983), Canon 375 §1.

7. "Bishops Who Write Newspaper Columns," *The Catholic Journalist* 39 (December 1987): 6. Cardinals Bernardin, Law, O'Connor, and Szoka and archbishops Flores, Hannan, Levada, Lipscomb, Mahony, May, McCarrick, McCarthy, Stafford, Strecker, Weakland, and Whealon.

8. Andrew M. Greeley, *The Catholic Priest in the United States: Sociological Investigations* (Washington, DC: U.S. Catholic Conference, 1972), p. 185.

9. Issues examined were for *Origins* volumes 7–17 (May 1977 to May 1988). Bernardin was cited as an author 62 times, Roach 44, Quinn 43, Mahony 20, O'Connor 17, Weakland 16, May 16, Hickey 14, Pilarczyk 14, Stafford 12, Borders 11, Bevilacqua 11, Law 11, Krol 10, McCarthy 10. All the rest were cited less than 10 times. As recent appointees, Bevilacqua's, Mahony's, and Stafford's numbers will certainly increase in the future.

10. Gerald P. Fogarty, *The Vatican and the American Hierarchy from 1870 to 1965* (Stuttgart, Germany: Anton Hiersemann, 1982; Wilmington, DE: Michael Glazier, 1985), 17–18.

11. Roland-Bernhard Trauffer, O.P., "Diocesan Governance in European Dioceses Following the 1983 Code: An Initial Inquiry," in *The Ministry of Governance*, ed. James K. Mallet (Washington, DC: Canon Law Society of America, 1986), 204.

12. Francis Kelly Scheets, O.S.C., "A Sketch of American Diocesan Organization 1900–1978," *The Priest* 37 (January 1981): 30–38.

13. James D. Thompson, *Organizations in Action* (New York: McGraw-Hill, 1967), 51.

14. Ibid., 54.

15. George Sarauskas, "Diocesan Reorganization: Part One: Organizational

Principles and Diocesan Reorganization," [National Pastoral Life Center] *Center Papers* 2 (Winter 1985): 2–8; C. Reid, "Some Applications of Principles of Management Theory to Diocesan Structures," *Jurist* 44 (1984): 448–56; R. Howes, "Reflections of a Pastoral Planner on the New Code of Canon Law," *The Priest* 38 (April 1982): 15–19; James H. Provost, "Diocesan Administration: Reflections on Recent Developments," *Jurist* 41 (1981): 81–104; James K. Mallet, "Diocesan Structure and Governance," *CLSA Proceedings* 42 (1980): 151–60; Charles Torpey, "Offices of the Diocesan Curia: Interrelationships and Creative Possibilities," *CLSA Proceedings* 45 (1983): 112–25.

16. William L. Murphy, "A Case Study of the Detroit Archdiocese: Developing a Responsive Organizational Structure," in *CARA Church Management Program Proceedings Diocesan Workshop*, ed. Francis K. Scheets, O.S.C. (Washington, DC: Center for Applied Research in the Apostolate, January 1980), 116–21; James H. Provost, "Diocesan Administration: Reflections on Recent Developments," *Jurist* 41 (1981): 87–89. For similar concerns in businesses, see Alfred D. Chandler, Jr., *Strategy and Structure* (Cambridge, MA: M.I.T. Press, 1962).

17. For statistics on the appointment of women to cabinet-level positions, see Catholics for a Free Choice, "All Work and No Say," (November 1988).

18. Philip Murnion and Harry Fagan, "Diocesan Reorganization Part Two: Current Trends in Diocesan Reorganization," [National Pastoral Life Center] *Center Papers* 2 (Winter 1985): 9–10.

19. Thompson, *Organizations in Action*, 57.

20. Canon 473 §1.

21. Canon 473 §2. Robert G. Howes, "Moderator of the Curia: New Boy in Town," *Jurist* 42 (1982): 517–23.

22. Canon 479 §1.

23. Colin Campbell, S.J., *Managing the Presidency* (Pittsburgh, PA: University of Pittsburgh Press, 1986).

24. For a perceptive description of the Denver archdiocese under Archbishop Casey, see Martin H. Work, "A Case Study of the Denver Archdiocese: Developing a Decision-Making Process," in *CARA Church Management Program Proceedings Diocesan Workshop*, ed. Francis K. Scheets, O.S.C., (Washington, DC: Center for Applied Research in the Apostolate, January 1980), 89–99.

25. The 1983 code speaks of an optional "episcopal council consisting of the vicars general and the episcopal vicars," but since lay people cannot be "vicars," archbishops have instead consulted with their cabinets. See canon 473 §4.

26. Richard A. Schoenherr and Eleanor P. Simpson, "The Political Economy of Diocesan Advisory Councils," Respondent Report 3 (Madison, WI: Comparative Religious Organization Studies, University of Wisconsin, 1978), 45.

27. Canon 502. See John Hannon, "Diocesan Consultors," *Studia Canonica* 20 (1985): 147–79.

28. Canon 421.

29. Canons 494, 1277, and 1292.

30. Schoenherr and Simpson, "Political Economy," 11.

31. Second Vatican Council, "Decree on the Ministry and Life of Priests," no. 7, in *The Documents of Vatican II*, ed. Walter M. Abbott, S.J., and trans. Joseph Gallagher (New York: America Press, 1966).
32. Second Vatican Council, "Decree on the Bishops' Pastoral Office in the Church," no. 27, in *The Documents of Vatican II*.
33. John Seidler, "Priest-Protest in the Human Catholic Church," *National Catholic Reporter*, May 3, 1974, 14.
34. Francis F. Brown, *Priests in Council: A History of the National Federation of Priests' Councils* (New York: Andrews & McMeel, 1979), 3. By 1974, 98 percent of the dioceses had priests' councils, see Schoenherr and Simpson, "Political Economy," 10. See also Thomas P. Sweetser, *Council Effectiveness Study* (Chicago: National Federation of Priests' Councils, 1977); Joseph W. Purcell, "The Institute of the Senate of Priests," *Jurist* 36 (1976): 191–262; Sidney J. Marceaux, "Presbyteral Councils," *CLSA Proceedings* 44 (1982): 198–206; J. Francis Stafford, "The Presbyteral Council," *Origins* 15 (1986): 503–4.
35. In 1966, 67 percent of the priests said they did not have a senate but approved of the idea. Another 27 percent had senates and favored them. See Joseph H. Fichter, S.J., *America's Forgotten Priests* (New York: Harper & Row, 1968), 63.
36. Canon 497.
37. Canon 500 §2.
38. Sacred Congregation for Bishops, *Directory on the Pastoral Ministry of Bishops* (Ottawa: Canadian Catholic Conference, 1974), no. 203 b, p. 104.
39. John A. Alesandro, "Title III: The Internal Ordering of Particular Churches (cc. 460–572)," in *The Code of Canon Law: A Text and Commentary*, ed. James A. Coriden, Thomas J. Green, and Donald E. Heintschel (New York: Paulist Press, 1985), 405.
40. Canon 500, §1.
41. Schoenherr and Simpson, "Political Economy," 29 and 93.
42. Second Vatican Council, "Decree on the Bishops' Pastoral Office in the Church," no. 27, in *The Documents of Vatican II*.
43. Mary P. Burke and Eugene F. Hemrick, *Building the Local Church: Shared Responsibility in Diocesan Pastoral Councils* (Washington, DC: U.S. Catholic Conference, 1984). Another study reports that half the dioceses had pastoral councils in 1974, see Schoenherr and Simpson, "Political Economy," 10.
44. Canon 511.
45. Burke and Hemrick, *Building the Local Church*, 18–21.
46. Canon 512 §2.
47. Burke and Hemrick, *Building the Local Church*, 20.
48. George Wilson, S.J., "Structures for Sharing Responsibility," in *Journeying Together*, ed. Dolores R. Leckey (Washington, DC: U.S. Catholic Conference, 1985), 22.
49. Alesandro, "Title III," 411.
50. Canon 511.
51. In Europe, the experience is similar: "these councils have not been formed everywhere, and where they have been established they do not function very well in practice." Roland-Bernhard Trauffer, O.P., "Diocesan Gover-

nance in European Dioceses Following the 1983 Code: An Initial Inquiry," in *The Ministry of Governance*, ed. Mallet, 196.
52. Canon 460.
53. Canon 463.
54. Canons 463 and 464.
55. Canon 466.
56. James Provost, "Diocesan Synods," [National Pastoral Life Center] *Center Papers* 1 (September 1984): 2.
57. James Provost, "Diocesan Synods," 1–2.
58. Seidler, "Priest-Protest," 14.
59. Ibid., 14.

Chapter 4. Parish and Regional Governance

1. A series of reports on Catholic parishes has been done by the Notre Dame Study of Catholic Parish Life, University of Notre Dame, 1201 Memorial Library, Notre Dame, IN 46556. These are summarized in Joseph Gremillion and Jim Castelli, *The Emerging Parish* (New York: Harper & Row, 1987). Also see David Byers, ed., *The Parish in Transition: Proceedings of a Conference on the American Catholic Parish* (Washington, DC: U.S. Catholic Conference, 1985). Also see *New Catholic World* 228 (November-December 1985).
2. James D. Thompson, *Organizations in Action* (New York: McGraw-Hill, 1976), 56.
3. Ibid., 56.
4. George Gallup, Jr., and Jim Castelli, *The American Catholic People* (Garden City, NY: Doubleday, 1987), 44. Also, Dean R. Hoge, "Trends in Catholic Lay Attitudes Since Vatican II on Church Life and Leadership," Study of Future Church Leadership, Report No. 5 (Washington, DC: Catholic University of America, May 1986, Mimeographed), 12. No demographic category had less than 80 percent approving the priests. See appendix, p. 4.
5. William Bassett, "The Office of Episcopal Vicar," *Jurist* 30 (1970): 285–313; Robert Howes, "The Episcopal Vicar—Comments of a Pastoral Planner," *Jurist* 31 (1971): 506–14; Thomas P. Swift, S.J., "The Pastoral Office of Episcopal Vicars: Changing Roles and Powers," *Jurist* 40 (1980): 225–56.
6. Sacred Congregation for Bishops, *Directory on the Pastoral Ministry of Bishops* (Ottawa: Canadian Catholic Conference, 1974), 85–87.
7. For more on planning in Baltimore, see Dean Hoge, *Future of Catholic Leadership: Responses to the Priest Shortage* (New York: Sheed & Ward, 1987), 89–93.
8. For more about Cincinnati, see Hoge, *Future of Catholic Leadership*, 93–96.
9. Surprisingly, a Gallup survey done for Dean Hoge found that merging parishes was more acceptable to Catholics than other ways of dealing with the priest shortage, such as cutting back on services. One out of four said that, as a solution to the clergy shortage, a "merger of [their] parish and another parish" was "very acceptable" and another 51 percent said it was "somewhat acceptable." This could indicate that closing and merging of parishes must be clearly seen as resulting from the clergy shortage if they

are to be accepted by the people. On the other hand, Professor Hoge is suspicious of this data since many respondents might assume that "merger of [their] parish . . ." means the respondent's parish will survive and the other will disappear. See Gallup and Castelli, *American Catholic People*, 55, and Dean R. Hoge, "Attitudes of Catholic Adults and College Students about the Priest Shortage and Parish Life," Study of Future Church Leadership, Report No. 2 (Washington, DC: Catholic University of America, September 1985, Mimeographed), table 3.

10. "70 Dioceses Have Priestless Parishes; 51 Report Priestless Sundays," NC News Service, September 16, 1988. See also *NCCB Committee on the Liturgy Newsletter*, July-August 1988.

11. For more about Portland, see Hoge, *Future of Catholic Leadership*, 97–99.

Chapter 5. Financial Administration

1. Andrew Greeley and William E. McManus, *Catholic Contributions, Sociology and Policy* (Chicago: Thomas More Press, 1987), 2. Protestants give 2.2 percent of their income or $580 a year. See also Andrew Greeley, "Where Have All the Contributions Gone? And Why?" *National Catholic Reporter*, November 11, 1988, 17–19.

2. Richard A. Schoenherr and Eleanor P. Simpson, *The Political Economy of Diocesan Advisory Councils*, Respondent Report No. 3 (Madison: Comparative Religious Organization Studies, University of Wisconsin, July 14, 1978), 5.

3. James Gollin, *Worldly Goods* (New York: Random House, 1971). John Cooney, *The American Pope: The Life and Times of Francis Cardinal Spellman* (New York: Times Books, 1984), 79, 95–97.

4. See Donald J. Frugé, "Taxes in the Proposed Law," *CLSA [Canon Law Society of America] Proceedings* 44 (1982), 274–88. Donald J. Frugé, *The Taxation Practices of United States Bishops in Relation to the Authority of Bishops to Tax According to the Code of Canon Law and Proposed Revisions*, Canon Law Studies No. 506 (Washington, DC: Catholic University of America, 1982), 100–133.

5. Greeley and McManus, *Catholic Contributions*, 117–18.

6. Ibid., 2.

7. Ibid., 112.

8. Canons 492–94, 1254–1310.

9. John J. Myers, "Book V: The Temporal Goods of the Church (cc. 1254–1310)" in *The Code of Canon Law: A Text and Commentary*, ed. James A. Coriden, Thomas J. Green, and Donald E. Heintschel (New York: Paulist Press, 1985), 879. See also Jordan Hite, T.O.R., "Church Law on Property and Contracts," *Jurist* 44 (1984): 117–33; Austin Bennett, "The Practical Effect on the Fiscal Administration of Church Finances of Book Five: The Law Regarding Church Possessions," *CLSA Proceedings* 42 (1980): 93–104; John J. Myers, "The Diocesan Fiscal Officer and the Diocesan Finance Council," *CLSA Proceedings* 44 (1982): 181–88.

10. Myers, "Book V," 874.

11. Thomas M. Rowe and Gary A. Giroux, "Diocesan Financial Disclosure: A Quality Assessment," *Journal of Accounting and Public Policy* 5 (1986): 66.
12. National Conference of Catholic Bishops, *Diocesan Accounting and Financial Reporting* (Washington, DC: NCCB, 1971) and *Accounting Principles and Reporting Practices for Churches and Church-Related Organizations* (Washington, DC: NCCB, 1983). American Institute of Certified Public Accountants, *Accounting Principles and Reporting Practices for Certain Nonprofit Organizations, Statement of Position 78-10* (New York: AICPA, 1978) and *Audits of Certain Nonprofit Organizations* (New York: AICPA, 1981).
13. Rowe and Giroux, "Diocesan Financial Disclosure," 64.
14. Ibid., 66.
15. Canon 1287 §2.

Chapter 6. Personnel

1. Jackson W. Carroll, Dean R. Hoge, and Francis K. Scheets, O.S.C., "Costs of Professional Parish Leadership: A Cross-Denominational Study," (Washington, DC: Catholic University, January 13, 1988, Mimeographed), to be published in upcoming annual volume of the *Yearbook of American and Canadian Churches* (New York: National Council of Churches). In 1983, total pay (including benefits but not room and board) for priests ranged from $4,512+ to $14,179 for newly ordained priests to $4,512+ to $16,040 for a priest ordained forty years. Also see ". . . the Laborer is Worthy of His Hire" (Chicago: National Federation of Priests' Councils, 1984).
2. John Kinsella, *In Service to Church Ministers: A Brief Introduction to the Ministry of Church Personnel Administration* (Cincinnati, OH: National Association of Church Personnel Administrators, 1983), 35.
3. Helen Morrison, O.P., *The Third Age: Retirement Concepts for Clergy and Religious* (Cincinnati, OH: National Association of Church Personnel Administrators, 1986).
4. Kinsella, *In Service*, 23.
5. In 1966, 86 percent of the priests supported a personnel office to work out clergy assignments. Joseph H. Fichter, S.J., *America's Forgotten Priests: What They Are Saying* (New York: Harper & Row, 1968), 142.
6. Kinsella, *In Service*, 26.
7. Thomas J. Reese, S.J., "Fewer Priests for Better or Worse?" *America* 149 (September 24, 1983): 149–50.
8. George Gallup, Jr., and Jim Castelli, *The American Catholic People* (Garden City, NY: Doubleday, 1987), 53.
9. See Dean Hoge, *Future of Catholic Leadership: Responses to the Priest Shortage* (New York: Sheed & Ward, 1987); Richard A. Schoenherr and Annemette Sorensen, "From the Second Vatican to the Second Millennium: Decline and Change in the U.S. Catholic Church," Respondent Report 5 (Madison, WI: Comparative Religious Organization Studies, University of Wisconsin, 1981).
10. For description of today's seminarians, see Eugene F. Hemrick, "The Evolving Church and Church Governance," in *The Ministry of Governance*, ed.

James K. Mallet (Washington, DC: Canon Law Society of America, 1986), 142, especially footnotes 7–9.

11. Bishops' Committee on Priestly Life and Ministry, *Recommendations and an Enquiry about Alcoholism among Catholic Clergy* (Washington, DC: U.S. Catholic Conference, 1978) and Joseph H. Fichter, S.J., *Rehabilitation of Clergy Alcoholics* (New York: Human Science Press, 1982).

12. Andrew M. Greeley, *The Catholic Priest in the United States: Sociological Investigations* (Washington, DC: U.S. Catholic Conference, 1972), 216.

13. See Fichter, *Forgotten Priests*, 115–80; Greeley, *Catholic Priest*, 199–266. See also *The Report of the Bishops' Ad Hoc Committee for Priestly Life and Ministry* (Washington, DC: U.S. Catholic Conference, 1974) and *Reflections on the Morale of Priests* (Washington, D.C., U.S. Catholic Conference, 1988).

14. On conflicts between bishops and priests in the late 1960s, see John Seidler, "Priest-Protest in the Human Catholic Church," *National Catholic Reporter*, May 3, 1974, 7ff.

15. Dean R. Hoge, Joseph J. Shields, and Mary Jeanne Verdieck, "Attitudes of American Priests in 1970 and 1985 on Church and Priesthood," Study of Future Church Leadership, Report No. 4 (Washington, DC: Catholic University of America, March 1986, Mimeographed), table 9, p. 1.

16. Hoge, *Future of Catholic Leadership*, 20. See also Hoge, Shields, and Verdieck, "Attitudes of American Priests."

17. On priest resignations, see John Seidler, "Priest Resignations in a Lazy Monopoly," *American Sociological Review* 44 (1979): 763–83; John Seidler, "Priest Resignations, Relocation and Passivity," *National Catholic Reporter*, May 10, 1974, 7ff; and Greeley, *Catholic Priest*, 275–310.

18. Hoge, Shields, and Verdieck, "Attitudes of American Priests," table 9, p. 1.

19. Paul M. Dudziak, "The Marginalization of Associate Pastors: Some Implications for Seminaries," *Jurist* 43 (1983): 199–213.

20. Hoge, Shields, and Verdieck, "Attitudes of American Priests," table 9, p. 2.

21. Bishops' Committee on Priestly Life and Ministry, National Conference of Catholic Bishops, *The Priest and Stress* (Washington, DC: U.S. Catholic Conference, 1982). On other health problems, see Bishops' Committee on Priestly Life and Ministry, *The Health of American Catholic Priests: A Report and Study* (Washington, DC: U.S. Catholic Conference, 1985).

22. In 1960, 44 percent of the priests surveyed reported the degree of their bishop's personal interest in them at "hardly at all" or "not at all." In 1966, the percentage was 61. See Fichter, *Forgotten Priests*, 54–55.

23. John F. Whealon, "Homily—Closing of Emmaus Convocation," St. Joseph's College, Archdiocese of Hartford, June 15, 1983.

24. Bishops' Committee on Priestly Life and Ministry, *The Continuing Formation of Priests: Growing in Wisdom, Age and Grace* (Washington, DC: U.S. Catholic Conference, 1984).

25. Between 1967 and 1972, the number of U.S. dioceses with personnel boards increased from 2 percent to 80 percent. See Robert F. Szafran, "The Effect of Executive and Professional Organizations: Accounting for Organizational Patterns and Individual Perceptions," *Sociology of Work and Occupation* 7 (May 1980): 188–209, and "Preliminary Conclusions about the Creation of

Clergy Personnel Boards in Roman Catholic Dioceses," Respondent Report 2 (Madison, WI: Comparative Religious Organization Studies, University of Wisconsin, 1976). Also see Richard A. Schoenherr and Robert F. Szafran, "Growth and Decline Rates, 1966–1973, and Personnel Operations in the United States Catholic Dioceses," Respondent Report 1 (Madison, WI: Comparative Religious Organization Studies, University of Wisconsin, 1976).
26. In 1966, 89 percent of the priests surveyed said they did not have a personnel board but wanted one. Another 7 percent had boards and approved the idea. Fichter, *Forgotten Priests*, 64.
27. Ibid., 139.
28. Robert W. Peterson and Richard A. Schoenherr, "Organizational Status Attainment of Religious Professionals," *Social Forces* 56 (March 1978): 805–7, 818.
29. Fichter, *Forgotten Priests*, 144–46.
30. At the time of this study, Baltimore, Indianapolis, New Orleans, Omaha, San Francisco, and Washington did not have limited terms. Chicago had terms but was not enforcing them. For canonical issues, see J. Stanley Teixeira, "Clergy Personnel: Policy and Canonical Issues," *Jurist* 45 (1986): 502–20; Daniel F. Hoye, "The Implementation of the 1983 Code of Canon Law on the National Level: Progress and Problems," *CLSA Proceedings* 46 (1984): 7–9.
31. Hoge, Shields, and Verdieck, "Attitudes of American Priests," table 2, p. 2.
32. Hoge, *Future of Catholic Leadership*, 235. Gallup and Castelli, *American Catholic People*, 57.
33. Greeley, *Catholic Priest*, 146.
34. Barbara Garland, SC, *Personnel Policy Manuals* (Cincinnati, OH: National Association of Church Personnel Administrators, 1986), 5.

Chapter 7. Catholic Schools and Social Services

1. "General Summary: Complete Statistics for Archdioceses and Dioceses of the United States," *The Official Catholic Directory 1988* (New York: P. J. Kenedy & Son, 1988).
2. J. Stephen O'Brien, *Mixed Messages: What Bishops and Priests Say about Catholic Schools* (Washington, DC: National Catholic Educational Association, 1987), 59–75.
3. Thomas P. Walters, *National Profile of Professional Religious Education Coordinators/Directors* (Washington, DC: National Conference of Diocesan Directors of Religious Education, 1983), 56.
4. The Third Plenary Council of Baltimore (1884) legislated that a school commission should be established in each diocese, but prior to the 1960s few dioceses had active boards. For a history of diocesan school boards, see M. Lourdes Sheehan, R.S.M., "A Study of the Functions of School Boards in the Educational System of the Roman Catholic Church in the United States," (Dissertation at Virginia Polytechnic Institute and State University, 1981), 52ff.

5. Walters, *National Profile*, 10–11.
6. M. Lourdes Sheehan, R.S.M., "Policies and Practices of Governance and Accountability," in *Personnel Issues and the Catholic Administrator*, ed. J. Stephen O'Brien and Margaret McBrien, R.S.M. (Washington, DC: National Catholic Educational Association, 1986), 1.
7. Theodore Drahmann, FSC, *Governance and Administration in the Catholic School*, NCEA Keynote Series No. 5 (Washington, DC: National Catholic Educational Association, 1985), 15.
8. Robert J. Kealey, FSC, *Curriculum in the Catholic School*, NCEA Keynote Series No. 9 (Washington, DC: National Catholic Educational Association, 1985).
9. Medard Shea, C.F.X., "Personnel Selection," in *Personnel Issues and the Catholic School Administrator*, ed. O'Brien and McBrien, 13–33. Also, Francis Raftery, SC, *The Teacher in the Catholic School*, NCEA Keynote Series No. 8 (Washington, DC: National Catholic Educational Association, 1985).
10. Edwin J. McDermott, S.J., *Distinctive Qualities of the Catholic School*, NCEA Keynote Series No. 1 (Washington, DC: National Educational Association, 1985).
11. Muriel Young, C.D.P., "New Wine in New Wineskins: Challenge to Administrators," in *Personnel Issues and the Catholic School Administrator*, ed. O'Brien and McBrien, 65–70.
12. Terence McLaughlin, *Catholic School Finance and Church-State Relations*, NCEA Keynote Series 5 (Washington, DC: National Catholic Education Association, 1985).
13. O'Brien, *Mixed Messages*, 77.
14. John J. Augenstein and Mary O'Leary, O.S.U., "Just Salaries and Benefits," in *Personnel Issues and the Catholic School Administrator*, ed. O'Brien and McBrien, 35–64.
15. O'Brien, *Mixed Messages*, 77.
16. Ibid., 78.
17. *The Official Catholic Directory 1988*.
18. "1986 Social Services and Social Action Summary, Catholic Charities USA" and *1986 Annual Survey Catholic Charities USA* (Washington, DC: Catholic Charities USA, undated).
19. *1986 Annual Survey Catholic Charities USA*, 2–3.
20. James D. Thompson, *Organizations in Action* (New York: McGraw-Hill, 1967), 46–48.
21. *1986 Annual Survey Catholic Charities USA*, 6–7.
22. Alexandra Peeler, *Parish Social Ministry: A Vision and Resource* (Washington, DC: National Conference of Catholic Charities, 1985).

Chapter 8. Beyond the Archdiocese

1. Michael J. Sheehan, "Is There Life in the Church Beyond Diocese? Supra-Diocesan Structures and Church Governance in Book II, the People of God," *CLSA Proceedings* 42 (1980): 132–50.
2. Michael J. Sheehan, "State Catholic Conferences," *Jurist* 30 (1970): 285–313,

and Ian Jones, "Down Home, Bishops' Groups Ply Politics," *National Catholic Reporter*, Sept. 16, 1988, 1.

3. "Report from the Synod," Thomas J. Reese, S.J., *America* 143 (October 11, 1980): 199.

4. See Peter Hebblethwaite, *In the Vatican* (Bethesda, MD: Adler & Adler, 1986).

5. *Code of Canon Law, Latin-English Edition* (Washington, DC: Canon Law Society of America, 1983), Canons 399 and 400. Also see Congregation for Bishops, *Directory for the "Ad Limina" Visit* (Vatican City: Typis Polyglottis Vaticanis, 1988); Congregation for Bishops, "Quinquennial Report by Residential Bishops," *The Canon Law Digest* 9 (June 6, 1975): 214–39; and Congregation for Bishops, *Formula Relationis Quinquennalis* (Vatican City: Typis Polyglottis Vaticanis, 1982).

6. *The Wanderer*, July 28, 1983, 5.

7. Paul VI, "Address to Bishops of New York," *Origins* 7 (April 20, 1978): 721ff. Also *Acta Apostolicae Sedis* 70:328ff.

8. Paul VI, "Pope Praises U.S. Bishops for Pro-Life Efforts," *Origins* 8 (May 26, 1978): 41ff. Also *Acta Apostolicae Sedis* 70:412ff.

9. In 1983 Cardinal Bernardin spoke of a "consistent ethic of life" in terms similar to those used by Paul VI. See *Origins* 13 (December 29, 1983): 491ff.

10. Paul VI, "The Eucharist: Summit of Christian Life," *Origins* 8 (June 15, 1978): 89ff. Also *Acta Apostolicae Sedis* 70:419ff.

11. John Paul I, "Address During Ad Limina Visit of U.S. Bishops of the Pacific Northwest," *Origins* 8 (September 21, 1978): 254ff. Also *Acta Apostolicae Sedis* 70:765ff.

12. John Paul II, "Address During Ad Limina Visit of U.S. Midwestern and Southern Bishops," *Origins* 8 (November 9, 1978): 353ff. Also *Acta Apostolicae Sedis* 71:23ff.

13. John Paul II, "Address to the Bishops of New York," *Origins* 12 (April 15, 1983): 759ff. Also *Acta Apostolicae Sedis* 75:566ff. Emphasis in original. For Vatican view of this visit, see Pio Laghi, "The Central Significance of 'Ad Limina' Visits," *Origins* 13 (1983): 405–7.

14. John Paul II, "Address to U.S. Bishops on Women Priests, Marriage, Birth Control and Homosexuality," *Origins* 13 (September 5, 1983): 238ff. Also *Acta Apostolicae Sedis* 76:99ff. Emphasis in original.

15. John Paul II, "Address to U.S. Bishops on the Priesthood and the Eucharist," *Origins* 13 (September 9, 1983): 257ff. Also *Acta Apostolicae Sedis* 76:106ff. Emphasis in original.

16. John Paul II, "The Support Asked of Bishops for Religious," *Origins* 13 (September 19, 1983): 318–20.

17. John Paul II, "The Family, Marriage and Sexuality," *Origins* 13 (September 24, 1983): 316–18.

18. John Paul II, "An Address to the U.S. Bishops," *Origins* 9 (October 5, 1979): 287–91.

19. The speeches, given on September 16, were published in *Origins* 17 (October 1, 1987): 224–67.

20. "Texas Bishops Tell Human, Spiritual Sides of Ad Limina Visit," NC News Service, May 13, 1988.

21. John Paul II, "Pope Cites Church Strengths in United States," *Origins* 17 (March 25, 1988): 705.
22. John Paul II, "Developing a Pastoral Vision for the Year 2000," *Origins* 17 (April 28, 1988): 801.
23. John Paul II, "Pastoral Action Asked on Penance," *Origins* 17 (June 23, 1988): 85–88.
24. John Paul II, "Prayer as the Context for Christian Living," *Origins* 17 (June 23, 1988): 90.
25. John Paul II, "What is a Christocentric Catechesis?" *Origins* 17 (August 4, 1988): 161–62.
26. John Paul II, "The Rights of Women," *Origins* 18 (September 22, 1988): 243.
27. John Paul II, "Solidarity and Interdependence," *Origins* 18 (September 22, 1988): 241.
28. A survey covering 78 percent of the dioceses found only thirty-six formal cases appealing a decision of a diocesan bishop to an office of the Apostolic See over a fifteen-year period. Twenty-five of these dealt with clergy personnel issues (appeals from retirement, reassignment, or removal of pastors). James H. Provost, "Recent Experience of Administrative Recourse to the Apostolic See," *Jurist* 46 (1986): 142–63.
29. Gerald M. Costello, "U.S. Catholics Loyal to Church, Cardinal Ratzinger Says," NC News Service, February 1, 1988.
30. Joseph Ratzinger, "Cardinal Ratzinger's Letter, Sept. 30, 1985," *Origins* 17 (June 4, 1987): 41–43.
31. Thomas J. Reese, S.J., "The Seattle Way of the Cross," *America* 155 (September 20, 1986): 111–12.
32. "Vatican Releases Chronology of Events in Seattle," *Origins* 16 (November 6, 1986): 361–64.
33. Raymond Hunthausen, "Archbishop Hunthausen to the U.S. Bishops," *Origins* 16 (November 20, 1986): 401–8.
34. Joseph Bernardin, John O'Connor, and John Quinn, "A Resolution of the Situation in Seattle," *Origins* 17 (June 4, 1987): 37–41.

Conclusion: Episcopal Decision Making

1. James D. Thompson, *Organizations in Action* (New York: McGraw-Hill, 1967), 151.
2. Ruth N. Doyle, Eugene F. Hemrick, and Patrick Hughes, *National Pastoral Planning in the 1980s* (Newark, NJ: National Pastoral Planners Conference, 1983). See also Eugene F. Hemrick, "The Evolving Church and Church Governance," in *The Ministry of Governance*, ed. James K. Mallet (Washington, DC: Canon Law Society of America, 1986), 140–59.
3. On incrementalism, see Charles E. Lindblom, *The Policy-Making Process* (Englewood Cliffs, NJ: Prentice-Hall, 1986); Charles E. Lindblom, "The Science of Muddling Through," *Public Administration Review* 19 (Spring 1958): 79–88; Thomas J. Reese, S.J., and Paul J. Roy, S.J., "Discernment as Muddling Through," *Jurist* 38 (1978): 82–117.
4. Thompson, *Organizations in Action*, 79.

5. Ibid., 11.
6. For a discussion of cooperative strategies, see Thompson, *Organizations in Action*, 34–36.
7. Rembert G. Weakland, "Local Implementation—Ecclesial Life Under the 1983 Code," *CLSA Proceedings* 46 (1985): 19.
8. James H. Provost, "The Working Together of Consultative Bodies—Great Expectations?" *Jurist* 40 (1980): 257–81; Robert Kennedy, "Shared Responsibility in Ecclesial Decision Making," *Studia Canonica* 14 (1980): 5–23.
9. Thomas F. O'Dea, "Five Dilemmas in the Institutionalization of Religion," *Journal for the Scientific Study of Religion* 1 (1961): 35–36.

Index

Arias, David, O.A.R. (auxiliary
bishop of Newark), 81
Assessments, archdiocesan, 153,
173–78, 359, 379n.4; consultation
on, 58, 117; past due, 187. *See also*
Finances
Atlanta, archdiocese of, xii, 26, 30,
60, 89; demographics of, 21, 66,
67; education in, 262, 283; finances
of, 59, 152, 164, 165, 170;
personnel in, 130, 216–18, 221,
222, 224. *See also* Donnellan,
Thomas A.; Marino, Eugene
Auxiliary bishops, xi, xii, 68, 86,
115–16, 184, 364; appointment of,
1–17, 24–28, 46, 47, 369n.26,
369n.27; power of, 56, 59–60, 123,
311, 337, 341; promotion of, 24–
28, 47, 61, 77, 96; in personnel
work, 194, 211, 218–21, 251–52; as
regional vicars, 59, 65, 66, 72, 103,
112, 133–38, 140, 218–19, 364. *See
also* Coadjutor; Vicars, regional

Baggio, Cardinal Sebastiano, 34–38,
44, 332, 370n.45
Baltimore, archdiocese of, xii, 19, 26,
28; demographics of, 66, 67;
education in, 261–64, 276, 279;
finances of, 157, 164, 169, 180,
184, 378n.7; governance structures
in, 104, 110; parish and regional
governance in, 103, 133, 135, 141–
143; personnel in, 146, 216, 228,
243, 255, 382n.30; social services
in, 285, 293, 296, 302. *See also*
Borders, William D.; Shehan,
Cardinal Lawrence
Bank, archdiocesan, 163–68. *See also*
Debt, archdiocesan; Finances;
Parishes
Banks, Robert (auxiliary bishop of
Boston), 185
Baum, Cardinal William W., 30, 38,
48, 314, 315, 319
Bernardin, Cardinal Joseph
(archbishop of Chicago), xv, 282;
appointment of bishops, 15, 22,
23, 39, 45, 73; background of, 96;
and NCCB, 88, 96, 313, 325; and
personnel, x, 208; style of, 91–92,
97, 98, 102, 104, 110, 113, 356; as

teacher, 90, 375n.7, 375n.9; and
Vatican, 39, 87, 88, 314–16, 342,
346, 384n.9
Bevilacqua, Anthony J. (archbishop
of Philadelphia), 73, 88, 96, 314;
appointment of, 30, 45, 77; style
of, 91, 375n.9
Birth control. *See Humanae Vitae*
Black bishops, 5, 9, 16, 21, 28
Black Catholics, 9, 85, 121; office of,
68, 69, 105, 107, 287, 295; in
parishes, 141, 205, 228, 239; in
schools, 273, 276, 278, 358; social
services for, 304, 358
Board of education. *See* Education,
archdiocesan board of; Education,
parish board of
Borders, William D. (archbishop of
Baltimore), xv; appointment of
bishops, 19, 22; background of,
77–78, 96; and regional vicars,
135; style of, 79, 91, 98, 102, 110,
113, 375n.9; and Vatican, 309
Boston, archdiocese of, xii, 30;
demographics of, 64–67; finances
of, 73, 169, 176, 185, 186;
governance structures in, 59, 103–
8, 133, 135; personnel in, 198, 208,
224, 228, 229, 233, 234, 243, 245.
See also Banks, Robert; Cushing,
Cardinal Richard; Law, Cardinal
Bernard F.; Medeiros, Cardinal
Humberto
Brust, Leo J., (auxiliary bishop of
Milwaukee), 131, 194
Budget, archdiocesan, 95, 150, 201,
359; and archbishop, 76, 122, 358,
359, 364; process, 112, 130, 150,
176–86, 190, 289, 290, 305, 350–53;
and schools, 263, 269, 273, 276;
and social services, 288–91. *See
also* Finances
Budget, parish, 130, 136, 153–63,
275–76. *See also* Parishes
Burke, Mary P., 374n.39, 377n.43
Byrne, James J. (archbishop of
Dubuque), 73, 77, 334
Byrne, Leo (archbishop of St. Paul),
69

Cabinet, xii, 108, 110–12, 354; and
finances, 180, 181; membership of,